Philosophical Health

Re-inventing Philosophy as a Way of Life

Series editors: Keith Ansell-Pearson, Matthew Sharpe, and Michael Ure

For the most part, academic philosophy is considered a purely theoretical discipline that aims at systematic knowledge; contemporary philosophers do not, as a rule, think that they or their audience will lead better lives by doing philosophy. Recently, however, we have seen a powerful resurgence of interest in the countervailing ancient view that philosophy facilitates human flourishing. Philosophy, Seneca famously stated, teaches us doing, not saying. It aims to transform how we live. This ancient ideal has continually been reinvented from the Renaissance through to late modernity and is now central to contemporary debates about philosophy's role and future.

This series is the first synoptic study of the re-inventions of the idea of philosophy as an ethical pursuit or 'way of life'. Collectively and individually, the books in this series will answer the following questions:

1. How have philosophers re-animated the ancient model of philosophy? How have they revised ancient assumptions, concepts and practices in the light of wider cultural shifts in the modern world? What new ideas of the good life and new arts, exercises, disciplines and consolations have they formulated?
2. Do these re-inventions successfully re-establish the idea that philosophy can transform our lives? What are the standard criticisms of this philosophical ambition and how have they been addressed?
3. What are the implications for these new versions of philosophy as a way of life for contemporary issues that concern the nature of philosophy, its procedures, limits, ends, and its relationship to wider society?

Other titles in the series include:

The Selected Writings of Pierre Hadot, trans. Matthew Sharpe and Federico Testa
Effort and Grace, Simone Kotva
The Late Foucault, ed. Marta Faustino and Gianfranco Ferraro
Philosophy as a Way of Life, Matthew Sharpe and Michael Ure

Philosophical Health

Thinking as a Way of Healing

Edited by
Luis de Miranda

BLOOMSBURY ACADEMIC
LONDON • NEW YORK • OXFORD • NEW DELHI • SYDNEY

BLOOMSBURY ACADEMIC
Bloomsbury Publishing Plc
50 Bedford Square, London, WC1B 3DP, UK
1385 Broadway, New York, NY 10018, USA
29 Earlsfort Terrace, Dublin 2, Ireland

BLOOMSBURY, BLOOMSBURY ACADEMIC and the Diana logo are trademarks
of Bloomsbury Publishing Plc

First published in Great Britain 2024

For legal purposes the Acknowledgements on p. xv constitute an extension of this
copyright page.

Series design by Charlotte Daniels
Cover images: Vector illustration of caduceus © saemilee / Getty Images);
Vector Flying Owl stock illustration (© Magnilion / iStock)

A catalogue record for this book is available from the British Library.

A catalog record for this book is available from the Library of Congress.

ISBN: HB: 978-1-3503-5304-6
ePDF: 978-1-3503-5305-3
eBook: 978-1-3503-5306-0

Series: Re-inventing Philosophy as a Way of Life

Typeset by Deanta Global Publishing Services, Chennai, India

To find out more about our authors and books visit www.bloomsbury.com and
sign up for our newsletters.

This book is dedicated to Theo, born during the early stages of its conception; to Svea, who discovered philosophy when the manuscript was completed; and to the incomparable Maria, whose support was 'creally' inspiring all along.

Contents

Part III The World

Tables

Contributors

Lehel Balogh, PhD, is a Hungarian philosopher and scholar of religious studies working at the Center for Applied Ethics and Philosophy of Hokkaido University, Sapporo, Japan. In 2012 he moved to South Korea, where he taught philosophy and ethics until 2017 at Kyungsung and Gyeongju universities. In 2018 he won the JSPS postdoctoral fellowship of Hokkaido University and moved to Sapporo, Japan, to conduct research on the practical utilization of the philosophical concepts of emptiness and nothingness in Japanese psychotherapies. His main research interests include comparative and cross-cultural studies in philosophy and ethics, the philosophy of psychiatry and psychotherapy, as well as East Asian religions and ethics. He is a regular contributor to the *Religious Studies Review* of Rice University, where he is also the sub-editor for Japan.

Abdullah Başaran, PhD, is Assistant Professor of Philosophy at Hitit University, Turkey, and Adjunct Lecturer of Philosophy at Ibn Haldun University, Turkey. He received his BA from Ankara University in Divinity (2006–10) and his MA from Stony Brook University in Philosophy and the Arts (2013–15). He is the author of the book *Postmodern: Felsefe, Edebiyat, Nekahet* (The Postmodern: Philosophy, Literature, Convalescence), published in 2018. He earned his doctoral degree in 2020 from the Philosophy Department at Stony Brook University, with a dissertation entitled *Touching the Text, the Touching Text: The Carnal Hermeneutics of Reading*. Currently, he primarily focuses on literary and philosophical hermeneutics, reading theories, and phenomenology of body and place.

Elliot D. Cohen, PhD, is Executive Director of the National Philosophical Counseling Association (NPCA) and President of the Logic-Based Therapy & Consultation Institute in the United States. He was originally trained by Albert Ellis, the founder of Cognitive-Behavioural Therapy, and later developed his own approach, Logic-Based Therapy. He is Editor-in-Chief and Founder of *International Journal of Applied Philosophy* and *International Journal of Philosophical Practice* and is presently Ethics and Patient Rights Coordinator at Baptist Health South Florida. He is the author of thirty published books, among which are *What Would Aristotle Do? Self-Control Through the Power of Reason* (2003), *Making Peace with Imperfection* (2019), and *Cognitive Behaviour Therapy for Those Who Say They Can't: A Workbook for Overcoming Your Self-Defeating Thoughts* (2022).

Balaganapathi Devarakonda, PhD, is Professor of Philosophy at the University of Delhi in India. He is presently with the University of West Indies, Jamaica, as ICCR Chair for Indology and Gandhian Studies. In addition to teaching and researching

Indian philosophy, philosophy of religion and philosophical practice, he is Certified Philosophical Counsellor of APPA (American Philosophical Practitioners Association). Some of his publications include *Youth Participation in Democratic Politics* (2022), *Historiography of Indian Philosophy* (2022) and *Shifts in the Classical Indian Conception of Philosophical Practice* (2021). He is presently working on the project 'Yoga Consciousness in the Mahabharata: The Ethical Value for Societal/Political Well-being'. Associated with the editorial boards of journals such as the *Journal of Foundational Research* and the *Journal of Indian Council of Philosophical Research*, he is serving the Council for Research in Values and Philosophy, Washington DC as Regional Coordinator (India).

Eugenia I. Gorlin, PhD, is Clinical Associate Professor in the psychology department of the University of Texas at Austin, and was previously a faculty member in the Ferkauf Graduate School of Psychology at Yeshiva University. Her published research spans empirical, theoretical and philosophical psychology, with a common underlying focus on understanding how cognition and motivation jointly fuel or undermine ambitious self-creation. She is also a licensed psychologist with over ten years of experience practising and supervising psychotherapy, and she has built an international reputation for her work coaching ambitious creators and entrepreneurs towards a 'builder's mindset'. In addition to her scholarly and clinical work, she writes a popular Substack newsletter titled "Building the Builders."

Eli Kramer, PhD, is Associate Professor at the Department of Ethics of the Institute of Philosophy, University Wrocław, Poland. His work traverses philosophy as a way of life (PWL) and metaphilosophy, philosophy of culture, American and European idealism, classical American philosophy and process philosophy. Alongside Matthew Sharpe and Michael Chase, he co-edits the Brill book series 'Philosophy as a Way of Life: Text and Studies'. His first single-authored monograph is *Intercultural Modes of Philosophy, Volume One: Principles to Guide Philosophical Community* (2021). He has also co-edited and contributed to collections such as *Philosophy of Culture as Theory, Method, and Way of Life: Contemporary Reflections and Applications* (2022), *Rorty and Beyond* (2020) and *Contemporary Philosophical Proposals for the University: Toward a Philosophy of Higher Education* (2018).

Michael Loughlin, PhD, is Professor in Applied Philosophy at the University of West London (UWL) in the School of Biomedical Sciences, and Director of UWL's European Institute for Person-Centred Health and Social Care. He is Academic Visitor at the Nuffield Department of Surgical Sciences, University of Oxford Medical School, and Project Director at the Collaborating Centre for Values-Based Practice, St Catherine's College, Oxford. He has written extensively on the relationship between knowledge, science and value in clinical practice, on the relationship between epistemology and ethics, and analyses of the nature and role of rationality, evidence, judgement and intuition in medicine and health care. As Associate Editor of the *Journal of Evaluation in Clinical Practice*, he has edited numerous special issues on philosophy and health. He is the author of *Ethics, Management and Mythology* (2002), editor of *Debates in*

Values-Based Practice (2014) and co-author of *The Philosophy of Person-Centred Healthcare* (2023).

Laura McMahon, PhD, is Associate Professor in the Departments of History & Philosophy and Women's & Gender Studies at Eastern Michigan University, where she teaches courses in continental philosophy, social and political philosophy, and feminist philosophy. Her research is devoted to the phenomenological interpretation of liberatory personal and political transformation. Her work has appeared in *The Journal of Speculative Philosophy, Chiasmi International, The Southern Journal of Philosophy, Human Studies* and *Sartre Studies International.* She also has chapters published in the edited volumes *Phenomenology and the Arts* (2016), *Perception and Its Development in Merleau-Ponty's Phenomenology* (2017), *Transforming Politics with Merleau-Ponty* (2021) and *Hannah Arendt and the History of Thought* (2022).

Luis de Miranda, PhD, is a Senior Research Fellow at the Philosophy Department of the University of Turku, Finland, and a Fellow of the Turku Institute for Advanced Studies (TIAS). He is also an Affiliated Research Fellow at the Stockholm School of Economics, Sweden, and the founder of the Philosophical Health International network. Since 2018, he has also worked as a philosophical counsellor for individuals, care institutions and corporations. Until 2014, he was an independent author and publisher. He is the author of philosophical essays and novels based on his philosophy of crealectics, some translated into various languages: *Who Killed the Poet?* (2017), *Being and Neonness* (2019), *Ensemblance: The Transnational Genealogy of Esprit de Corps* (2020) and *Paridaiza* (2020). His work has appeared in academic journals such as *International Journal of Philosophical Practice, Deleuze Studies, Human Affairs, Eidos: A Journal for Philosophy of Culture, Games and Culture, Qualitative Inquiry, Acta Academica* and *Global Intellectual History.*

Brendan Moran, PhD, is Professor of Philosophy at the University of Calgary, Canada. He has published *Politics of Benjamin's Kafka: Philosophy as Renegade* (2018) and, under an anagrammatic 'pseudonym', *Wild, Unforgettable Philosophy in Early Works of Walter Benjamin* (2005). His articles often focus on philosophy and literature and on political philosophy, and discuss works by Benjamin, Agamben, Laruelle, Heidegger, Levinas, Kafka, Salomo Friedlaender and others. They have appeared in *Philosophy Today, Boundary 2, Philosophy and Social Criticism, Journal of Speculative Philosophy* and elsewhere. His co-edited books with Carlo Salzani are *Towards the Critique of Violence: Walter Benjamin and Giorgio Agamben (2015)* and *Philosophy and Kafka (2013); with Paula Schwebel, Benjamin and Political Theology* is in preparation.

Raja Rosenhagen, PhD, is Assistant Professor of Philosophy at Ashoka University in Sonipat, Haryana, India. He graduated in 2018 from the University of Pittsburgh with a thesis in philosophy in which he examined the conceptual leeway afforded, on different contemporary conceptions of experience, for beliefs to affect experience. Apart from philosophy of mind, his interests include epistemology, philosophy of science, philosophy of love, Iris Murdoch, logic, philosophical counselling and Jaina philosophy. He co-edited the volume *Love, Justice and Autonomy: Philosophical Perspectives* (2021). Recently, he became an APPA-certified philosophical counsellor (American Philosophical Practitioners Association).

Dennis Schutijser is Associate Professor in Practical Philosophy at the Pontifical Catholic University in Quito, Ecuador (PUCE). He holds a Master's degree in philosophy (Bordeaux, France), and a Master's degree in humanistic sciences (Utrecht, Netherlands), and is currently pursuing a Doctorate research with the University of Toulouse (France), dedicated to narrativity as a foundation for care practice. He has previously worked in international consultancy, as well as in journalism and translation. He has published academic and non-academic articles in different journals, such as *The Journal of Pastoral Care and Counseling* and *Akropolis*. His research mainly focuses on ethics, in particular virtue ethics and philosophy as a way of life (PWL), and applied philosophy. He is responsible for the philosophical counselling service of the PUCE Department of Philosophy.

Matthew Sharpe, PhD, teaches philosophy at Deakin University, Australia. His PhD work was on psychoanalytic theory and he has since worked on political theory and the history of ideas, including a focus on the idea of philosophy as a way of life (PWL). He is co-author with Michael Ure of *Philosophy as a Way of Life: History, Dimensions, Directions* (2021), with Federico Testa of the *Selected Essays: Philosophy as Practice* by Pierre Hadot (2021) and with Joanne Faulkner of *Understanding Psychoanalysis* (2014). He is author of *Camus, Philosophe: To Return to Our Beginnings* (2015) and *The Other Enlightenment: Self-Estrangement, Race, and Gender* (2022).

Andrei Simionescu-Panait, PhD, is Senior Lecturer at the Polytechnic University of Bucharest. He teaches philosophy of technology, ethics and communication. As a member of Romania's Philosophical Counsellors Association (APCFE), he is part of the first wave of philosophical counselling in Romania, a practice through which he blends phenomenology and Socratic dialogue to facilitate thinking and reflection for his students and counselees. He is the author of *The Reconciled Body. An Essay on the Phenomenology of Elegance* (2021). He has published in academic journals such as *Europe's Journal of Psychology* and *International Journal of Education and Psychology in the Community*. His research currently focuses on the philosophical counselling process.

Richard Sivil, PhD, is Senior Lecturer in the School of Religion, Philosophy and Classics at the University of KwaZulu-Natal, South Africa. His teaching repertoire includes modules on death, environmental ethics and philosophy, existentialism, moral psychology, propositional logic and Spinoza. His primary research interest is in philosophical counselling. He has authored several articles on the topic, including: 'Towards a Taxonomy of Philosophical Counselling' (with Julia Clare, *South African Journal of Philosophy*), 'Philosophical Counselling, Professionalization and Professionalism: A South African Perspective' (with Julia Clare, *International Journal* *of Applied Philosophy*) and 'Epimeleia Heautou as Philosophical Counselling' (*South African Journal of Philosophy*).

Jacob Vangeest is Doctoral Candidate at the Centre for the Study of Theory and Criticism at Western University, specializing in twentieth-century French philosophy, critical theory and political thought. His doctoral research focuses on the political ramifications of the ontological commitment to processes of entanglement, singularity and individuation as positioned in discourses of critical posthumanism and philosophies of becoming. He has authored several academic articles, including 'Forest Semiosis: Plant Noesis as Negantropic Potential' (*Footprint*) and 'Deleuzian Problematics: On the Determination of Thought' (*La Deleuziana*).

Acknowledgements

Luis de Miranda wishes to thank the Kjell och Märta Beijers Foundation and the Åke Wibergs Foundation, who funded him, thus helping him to conceive and produce this volume. The publisher De Gruyter and its journal Human Affairs are to be thanked for allowing the reprint of the article 'Artificial intelligence and philosophical creativity: From analytics to crealectics' (de Miranda, 2020, vol. 30, no. 4, 597-607), slightly edited to become chapter 11 in this anthology.

Introducing philosophical health

The healing dimension of making sense

Luis de Miranda

Am I philosophically healthy? Are you living your highest destiny? Do her actions reflect her thoughts? Do his words mirror his soul? What is our purpose in life? Do we live in shadowy contradiction with – or ignorance of – our deepest thoughts, values, beliefs, ideals? Did we develop a robust philosophical sense or are we, like Macbeth, the spectators or the regretful players of a global tale full of sound and fury, signifying nothing?

Imagine a book written in the early nineteenth century on the following topic: *physical health for all.* This book would have appeared as a novelty, because the practice of systematic exercise or diet for the sole sake of physical health was back then the privilege of an aristocratic minority. Today, physical health has become a concern for all.

Imagine now a book on *psychological health for all,* published at the beginning of the twentieth century: psychology (and psychotherapy) was then a new field, and the practice of psychological care was a privilege for the (un)happy few. Nowadays psychological health is indeed a global concern.

I and most of the authors of this book believe in *philosophical health for all.* A blooming field of practice, research and a diverse movement, philosophical health may one day be recognized as a universal necessity if we are to give sense to our – now more complex than ever – earthly existence. It's happening as we write: the number of philosophical counsellors is growing steadily year after year worldwide, in India or the United States, in Sweden, Romania or South America. People of all ages and various origins are deciding to use philosophical tools to guide their life. Sometimes, for matters of personal or collective meaning and coherent sense-making, they talk regularly to a philosophical practitioner such as myself or some of the authors of this book.

The present authors also come from various cultures and parts of the world, as well as diverse disciplinary focuses. Some might not fully agree on the particulars of philosophical health as I have previously sketched them (de Miranda, 2019; 2021a; 2021b; 2022); nevertheless, they are committed to its importance and general intention: thinking is a way of healing the self and the others.

As you read these lines, you are probably sensing your body in some way: perhaps you are standing in front of a digital screen or sunk in an armchair, with a book in your hands. Perhaps you are paralysed in a bed or blissfully seated on a bench by the sea as the wind stirs the pages of the book, echoing the sails of the passing boats. You take a deep breath: as a being pertaining to the realm of biology, you have a bodily sense. You sense your body and your body senses the world. Sometimes it speaks true to you via your intuition.

And there is *you* as a self-perspective: a person who might perceive yourself as more or less attuned with your body, everyday goals, tactics, fears or aspirations. You, the inner voice that evaluates, judges and wonders. You often say: My name is [*here insert your name*]: you have a sense of self. Sometimes you even manage to be consistently honest with yourself.

Now, you also know or hope that you are not alone. Perhaps you love and are loved, or perhaps you have felt estranged from your environment like an alien forgotten in this world by a crew of fellow others. You may or may not share deep bonds with your community or your surroundings; you have, strong or depleted, a sense of belonging. Sometimes you meet yourself in the face of the other and experience friendship and joy.

You may have lived for a few decades now, just enough to know that some evenings you felt heavy or empty as if the doors of the future were closed and the windows of the past darkened by black curtains. And yet some mornings you jump out of bed with a strong existential drive, boosted by a conquering élan towards a yet undefined horizon: you have, high or low, a sense of the possible. You sense it more or less acutely: sometimes you sense a living creative flux behind our routine protocols; you feel the pulse of ultimate possibility that is perhaps the creating source of the Real, or '*Creal*' (de Miranda, 2021c).

Bodily sense, sense of self, sense of belonging, sense of the possible: these ways of making sense of the world – universal in form and yet so diverse in practice – are to a certain extent shared with non-human creatures: an octopus has a bodily sense, a gibbon possesses some sense of self, fish manifest a sense of belonging and ants are equipped with a sense of the possible such that we can say that a common definition of health for all living beings is, simply put, *a good sense of the possible*. Etymologically speaking, this may be called *eudynamia* – from *eu-*, good and *dynamis*, potential, force, possibility (de Miranda, 2021b).

Now, there are two subsequent senses that most philosophers assume are specifically human. We can follow values, ideals or meaningful visions that give us a deep orientation in the longer run, beyond the present of our immediate perceptions: they constitute our sense of purpose. Through it, we may unveil and unfold our destiny in the form of a transpersonal project, supported by a creative dialectic between ideal, group and world. It manifests our freedom to thrive towards an imparadizing collective horizon. Few of us have a strong sense of purpose, which demands maturity, wisdom, and courage.

Moreover, we may explain the world and make sense of it via myths, cosmologies, structured narratives, conceptual edifications or systematic networks of ideas that guide and justify our purpose: that is our worldview, our philosophical sense. Ultimately, the property of our philosophical worldview is that once made explicit, it may generate wholesome benefits in the intercreative dynamics of the five previous senses. Bodily sense, sense of self, sense of belonging, sense of the possible, sense of purpose and philosophical sense are elements of philosophical health that, when harmonized rather than lacking, hurting or conflicting, contribute to creating wholesome persons, healthy groups or institutions. Our way of thinking and our way of doing may thus be attuned such that we may experience a deep integrity, and in the world.

Wholesome care and philosophical health

'Wholesome' is an interesting word; it carries the old German etymology of the word 'health' (*heil*), suggesting ideas of oneness, of totality. The German language still speaks of the deep relief of being *heilfroh*, completely appeased or relieved. 'The True is the whole', writes Hegel in the *Phenomenology of Spirit* (1977: 11): philosophy is the discipline that cares about the whole of reality and beyond, while other mainstream disciplines tend to care about specific parts or domains of the Real, the atmosphere (meteorology), machinery (engineering) or butterflies (lepidopterology). Philosophy is usually ignored, mocked or considered vain because it is very difficult, if not asymptotically possible, to know or intuit the whole, and easier to focus on only one aspect of the world as do biology, physics, palaeontology, economy, linguistics and all sorts of human affairs.

Medicine, for instance, is focused on eradicating disease here and there rather than on understanding what health is, holistically. Yet consider the widespread definition of health offered by the World Health Organization (WHO) in its Constitution (1948): 'Health is a state of complete physical, mental and social wellbeing and not merely the absence of disease or infirmity.' The adjective *complete* here again echoes the etymology of health as a whole, pointing to the all-encompassing unity, understanding or harmony that is the purpose of philosophy. What is then a healthy whole if not a mere juxtaposition of parts? What is a healthy person if not just a functioning biological body? What is a healthy action if not mere autopilot behaviour? What is a healthy institution if not a form of organized crime? What is a healthy society if more than a stochastic market?

This book is the first to propose a multifaceted and international reflection on the notion of *philosophical health* taken seriously as a theoretical and practical field. It is an idea that has emerged out of a historically novel practice: in the last decades, a few independent individuals across the world have started to take care of other fellow humans in terms of what they call 'philosophical counselling' or 'philosophy as therapy' (Banicki, 2014; Marinoff, 2013). There are today dozens of active practising philosophical counsellors on most continents, and as I mentioned earlier some of them, including myself, are among the authors of the present anthology. Philosophical counsellors are often practising their wholesome way of caring as a hobby because their activity is not yet a profession that is recognized by healthcare systems, or in some cases because they would not want to be fully professionalized or dogmatically institutionalized. Philosophical counsellors hold individual or group dialogues when they are not teaching, doing academic research, writing books or trying to make sense of unphilosophical job offers. They might be fully independent or organized in various associations, such as, among others, the APPA (American Philosophical Practitioners Organisation), the SSFP (Swedish Society for Philosophical Practice) and the PPAI (Philosophical Practitioners Association of India).

But why speak of *philosophical health* rather than, for instance, *mental well-being*? Because not everything that is just is mental and not everything that is right makes us feel comfortable. Health is not only one of humanity's foremost preoccupations, it is now a globalized concern dealing with our destiny on earth (Walraven, 2010; Frumkin, 2016). In the last century, physical health and psychological health have been systematized into a social imperative (Bell, Taylor and Marmot, 2010). Tangible positive results have been produced in terms of life expectancy or the cure of pathologies previously thought to be incurable, but a certain version of health care has also become a capitalist industry and a form of normative social governance (O'Byrne, 2019). In occidental societies, in the early twentieth century, gymnastics, diet and psychotherapy were a luxury for the few, but they became a necessity for the many by the end of the same century. National states finance and administer programmes for statistically governed psychological and physical health, in line with what Foucault (1975) called biopolitics or the control of populations. Institutions, the power of which is now reinforced by massive digital data, often promote a medicated way towards health based on a mechanical or chemical conception of the mind and body (Fee, 1999; Tyreman, 2020).

Physical health and psychological health are today well-accepted categories of health: they are considered necessary conditions for 'well-being', but they are not sufficient to account for the good life and sense of purpose of individuals and collectives. In 2019, the *Philosophical Health International* movement (PHI) was launched to initiate a global conversation on the theory and practice of philosophical health and care, including – but also beyond – the specific practice of philosophical counselling. This book is the first collective publication emerging from the blooming PHI network. It considers 'philosophical health' as a transdisciplinary concept and practice, shedding light on the idea that thinking can be a way of caring for individuals, groups or even worldviews, not in a normative manner but rather in a way that opens our sense of the possible in various forms and directions, exemplified in the present book by the diversity of perspectives on the idea of philosophical health: psychological, logical, person-care centred, mythological, hermeneutic, bibliotherapeutic, intersubjective, institutional, phenomenological, decolonial, Asian, African and so on.

In English, the phrase 'philosophical health' started to appear in a few publications at the end of the twentieth century: for instance, *Life & Health* suggested that philosophical health is a form of 'spiritual health and an essential element of wellness', in which our behaviour is 'in rhythm' with our values (Levy, Dignan and Shirreffs, 1984: 7). A decade later, in a monograph on Wittgenstein titled *Philosophical Health*, Richard A. Gilmore compared Wittgenstein to Socrates and wrote: 'The concept of philosophical or psychological "health" that I propose they both shared was one in which a person's ways of speaking and thinking is consistent with their ways of acting' (Gilmore, 1999: 134). While 'philosophical health' is a relatively new phrase, it is not a new idea, but rather a collective rediscovery: its essence has been embodied or defended more or less implicitly by a few notable figures in the history of philosophy, including Socrates, Epicurus, the Stoics or more recently Nietzsche, Bergson or indeed Wittgenstein. For them, philosophical health was about trying to live up to the highest possible version of one's destiny in accordance with – and constant wondering about – the meaning of being.

The current revival of the Greek and Roman forms of *care-full* philosophy seems to be part of a reinvention of philosophy as a form of existential therapy without diagnoses, and of the philosopher as an enhancer of lived harmony. Some have criticized the pertinence of this approach (Knapp and Tjeltveit, 2005; Louw, 2013), but whether one is sympathetic or not to the current movement of philosophical health, including philosophy as care, way of life and philosophical counselling, most concede that the approach needs more theoretical grounding and exploration – hence the present book.

The idea of philosophical health has a long genealogy, which is not the main focus of the following chapters; they are more interested in contemporary perspectives. Much has been written about the intellectual history of philosophy as therapy. In *The Hermeneutics of the Subject* (Foucault, 2005), the European source of the idea of philosophical health is located in the Platonic and Socratic conception of ἐπίμέλεία ἑαυτο (*epimeleia heautou*), the care for the soul or self. In Plato's *First Alcibiades*, philosophical care is a necessary condition not only for the virtue of the individual person but also to become a good governing actor or political agent of the city via some form of care ethics and self-sacrifice (Cawston and Archer, 2018). There was, for the Greeks, a connection between the collective idea of justice and the individual idea of balance. The philosophical mind was ultimately not only individual or logically rational, it was an inspirational reconnection with the divine or the sublime in us, an idea often illustrated by Socrates' daemon. The *daimon* was the intuitive spirit, the tutelary genius, the inner voice whispering words of wisdom (Silverman, 2010). The Greek concept of philosophical health articulated personal growth with a shared cosmology, a cosmo-political narrative.

Historically minded authors, such as Martha Nussbaum (1994), Pierre Hadot (1995) and again Michel Foucault (2005), have thus significantly contributed to a recognition that the philosophy of the Ancient Greeks and Romans was linked to a concern for health – for authors like Plutarch, philosophy and medicine were a single area, a common domain. According to Nussbaum (1994), the philosophical practice was characterized by arguments, precise reasoning, logical rigour and a search for definitional acuity. Building an art of living via philosophy had to be an art committed to rational truth and to a praxis of argumentation and interaction aimed at personal and societal transformation: ancient philosophers wanted to distinguish themselves from magicians, shamanic healers or sophists. This shifted the philosopher's interest towards the existential effectiveness of discourse and arguments (rhetorical, narrative, imaginary, mnemonic).

According to Hadot and Foucault, a philosophically therapeutic argument is also 'spiritual' and cannot be understood without its subjective context. Antique philosophy was not restricted to an intellectual activity of rationalizing; it was a *way of life* (Sharpe and Ure, 2021). Logical discourse was only *a part* of the philosophical way of life precisely because the acquired knowledge had to be implemented in messy practical life and flesh-and-blood comportment. Philosophy, in the words of Seneca, 'teaches us to act, not to speak' (Inwood, 2005). One could not claim to possess genuine philosophical knowledge unless one produced a whole form of life which was authentically philosophical, a biographical and effectual exercise of fusion between truth and subjective embodiment (Foucault, 2005). Translating theoretical understanding into practical and embodied intuition – and vice versa – required persistent training and remembering of our sense of purpose and philosophical sense. This form of intellectual care was critical of a practice of culture and civilization consumed as a varnish, a superficial façade that fails to hide our ego-centredness, irrational fears, immature nihilism or hubris.

Closer to us, Nietzsche considered philosophy as the foundation of mental and physical health. He believed that so-called universal – philosophical or moral – arguments are often biased by some esprit de corps and cannot be discussed without reference to their recipients and authors, who embody the values. Our contemporary recreation of the idea of philosophical health originates at least partly in Nietzsche's notion of 'great health', seen as a life- and value-affirming ethos and creative embodiment, ideally capable of resisting all sorts of social viruses and groupthink (Glenn, 2001; Nietzsche, 1979, 1982). With Nietzsche's tentatively non-dualist approach to health, philosophy began to aspire anew to an embodied practice and concrete attitude, a deeply honest and committed way of thriving purposefully in the world: health as actualization of one's highest destiny (*Bestimmung*) (Nietzsche, 2004: 67). Less differently than one would perhaps imagine, Ludwig Wittgenstein, in his late *Philosophical Investigations*, promoted a therapeutic understanding of philosophy as articulated to a 'form-of-life': 'The work in philosophy is really more a working on oneself' (Gilmore, 1999: 19).

Where are we today? The analytic and abstract foundations of 'ivory-tower philosophy' (Vossen, 2015) are shaken, not only by so-called 'continental philosophy' or 'global philosophy' but also by a surprising outsider: the international movement of philosophical counselling and philosophical practice, growing steadily, as said, in countries like Germany, the US, the UK, The Netherlands, Austria, Switzerland, Norway, Italy, Spain, Canada, Israel, Turkey, South Africa, India or Sweden (Louw, 2013). As to now, this movement has been widely ignored in academic research and teaching. The majority of university philosophers are not aware of it or according to the *New York Times*, even suspicious or hostile: 'Among serious academic philosophers – even those who address the so-called human-condition questions – there is an almost visceral revulsion at the very idea of philosophical counselling' (Duane, 2004). Many philosophy departments or universities are still doing active efforts to close their doors to versions of philosophy that are immersed in society and active in practical change. But philosophical health is, we believe, effectual research and praxis, and it should be embraced by academia.

Most psychologists, psychoanalysts and psychiatrists are also hostile regarding an activity that sometimes seems to claim therapeutic benefits without a well-defined or scientist protocol: 'Psychologists are increasingly encountering philosophers in independent practice who use philosophy to help individuals or groups work through practical problems. [. . .] Philosophical counselling is not currently a viable alternative to mental health treatment' (Knapp and Tjeltveit, 2005: 1). Is it not, really? Should we then continue to surrender the ecology of our minds and mental health to a psychiatric industry that seems to have abandoned the concern for the singularity of the person and our need for meaning, while its response to distress relies all too often on chemical pills, corseted questionnaires, pettifogging statistics, ephemeral behavioural tricks and a circumvoluted nomenclature of diagnoses? Plato is not Prozac (Marinoff, 1999) and philosophical pills are not chemical but rather dynamic ideas such as: thinking independently and yet engagingly with life, listening deeply and yet making sense of the world creatively, and being aware that health is only attained when mind and body are deeply attuned to a non-dogmatic and generous quest for truth, justice and honesty.

The *creative* aspect in the previous sentence is important if philosophical health is to be prevented from becoming yet another monochromatic normative discourse, a new dogma proclaiming what is meta-healthy or what should be done absolutely in order to avoid intellectual or moral sickness. As Nietzsche maintained, the 'concept of a normal health, along with those of a normal diet and normal course of an illness, must be abandoned' (Nietzsche, 2001 [1882]: 117).

The self, the others and the world

Philosophical sense-making and the corpus of philosophy are now increasingly used in practical contexts along with the belief that there can be a symbiosis between a healthy mind, a healthy embodiment and healthy environments (Banicki, 2014). According to philosopher Yolanda Angulo Parra, who is particularly interested in using philosophical counselling to help Mexican women, for example in prisons, 'the philosophical counsellor reinforces the individual's autonomy, upgrading people's reasoning capabilities, introducing them to philosophical research with the sole purpose of achieving an introspection process that will lead to a better understanding of the inner self [and] to become a better person' (Omelchenko, 2012: 78). Are these ambitious personal autonomies and self-development the core characteristics of a philosophically healthy person? Partly, but philosophical health is also, more humbly, deep-listening care for others and care for the earth, all these aspects being intertwined and intercreative. The present book is therefore divided into three parts – the Self, the Others and the World – even if such a sequential segmentation, necessary for analytic purposes, does not do justice to the fact that, in reality, we cannot fully isolate the self from the others nor the world.

Part I opens with Eugenia Gorlin's insightful proposition that 'self-honesty' is the foundation of philosophical health. Given the human propensity for self-deception, honesty cannot be taken for granted but needs, she argues, to be a principled commitment if one is to become philosophically healthy. Gorlin suggests the self-honesty framework can provide a unifying front for philosophers and psychologists interested in advancing human flourishing. We must, she says, learn to be honest about what we think, feel, believe, envision and want, such that we may choose our actions and build our life accordingly: 'The pursuit of philosophical health depends upon this willingness to follow one's reflections where they lead, no matter what truths or possibilities this may bring to light.' The author concludes with some techniques and practices for promoting self-honesty.

In Chapter 2, Lehel Balogh provides a much-needed and inspiring piece of recent intellectual history by examining how, in the existential-phenomenological tradition of the twentieth century, the ideal of authenticity as a token of mental health compares with the ideal of philosophical health. The chapter surveys various approaches inspired by the philosophical thoughts of such seminal thinkers as Kierkegaard, Nietzsche, Heidegger and Sartre: Ludwig Binswanger's and Medard Boss's *Daseinsanalysis*, along with Viktor Frankl's existential analysis and logotherapy, as well as Rollo May's and Irvin Yalom's American school of existential psychotherapy. Balogh writes that 'winning back the self from the hazy middle zone between authenticity and inauthenticity proves to be the key curative insight that guarantees not only the mental and physical sanity of the individual but one's philosophical health as well'.

Chapter 3 is an authoritative reflection by Michael Loughlin on person-centred care – and related terminology including shared decision-making, values-based practice, patient empowerment and patient expertise – which is now a core component of debates about the future of health service provision and practice. In it, the author argues that the most plausible forms of person-centred care need to incorporate, explicitly, the idea of philosophical health: in clinical settings, the discussion of philosophical health represents an exciting opportunity to expand our understanding of what it means to treat patients as persons. Just as importantly, writes Loughlin, the philosophical health approach helps us 'to appreciate the significance of recognizing the personhood of practitioners, and in the process clarifying the role of dialogue in diagnosis and care, the relational nature of personhood and the relationship between science and value in health and social care'.

In Chapter 4, Balaganapathi Devarakonda looks intriguingly into the Indian philosophical tradition, particularly the Bhagavad Gita, to defend his view that personal equanimity is a key component of philosophical health. By cultivating the perspective of *Samata drishti* or fair equipoise, an individual can achieve and maintain, explains Devarakonda, a form of holistic well-being that can be conceptualized as philosophical health. After reviewing several occidental problematic views on the meaning of health, the author details the benefits of defining philosophical health as 'a harmonious natural equipoised state contributing to a balanced perspective that helps individuals manage life by confronting various worldly objects, fellow beings, and subjective experiences'.

The last chapter of the part on the Self, Chapter 5, is written with experienced insight by Elliot D. Cohen, one of the pioneers of the practice of philosophical counselling in the United States and the founder of Logic-Based Therapy and Consultation. Cohen begins by reminding us that the ideal of philosophical health is at least as ancient as Plato, who in the *Republic* defined the health of the soul as a friendly harmony between the ruling principle of reason and the two subjected ones of spirit and desire. Cohen uses in his practice both formal logic (deduction) and informal logic (identification and avoidance of 'fallacies'). He believes that our irrational cogitations in general, and our perfectionism in particular, may lead to serious existential problems, and writes: 'I am inclined to think that philosophical health is the basic construct, and that mental health is a function of the latter. When philosophical health suffers to the point that a counselee is not able to function in everyday life, then he can be said to be mentally ill.'

Part II of this book – on The Others – opens (Chapter 6) with an empathetic phenomenological account by Laura McMahon on the importance of vulnerability to our philosophical health as existential selves living in families, groups and collectives. For McMahon, vulnerability is a virtue in the Aristotelian sense, the capacity to situate ourselves in connection with others by surrendering our illusion of egotistic omnipotence. A central insight here, inspired by Merleau-Ponty, is that personal identity is always already interpersonally accomplished, and therefore that psychological problems should not be sought 'in' the individual but rather in the interpersonal systems to which the individual belongs. McMahon writes that it is 'crucial to our existential health that we recognize our vulnerability as a positive capacity to be, at the hearts of our "own" identities, open to and shaped by our intertwining with things and others in the world.'

In Chapter 7, Raja Rosenhagen proposes a sharp analysis of some previous literature on the notion of 'philosophical health' (de Miranda, 2021a, 2021b, 2021c), in order to lay the foundations for his definition of philosophical health as 'trans-subjective good'. Rosenhagen then combines elements from the works of Iris Murdoch and Marshall Rosenberg to sketch a practice he dubs 'non-violent just communication', which he argues convincingly can help to connect philosophical health with notions of epistemic justice and collective good life. 'A philosophically healthy subject', writes the author, 'is at one with themselves in how they think, speak, act, and feel, and at one with others (humans and non-humans) in being oriented in thought and action towards the actualization of the common good of all.'

Chapter 8 is an inspiring attempt at a hermeneutic approach to philosophical health written by Dennis Schutijser under the influence of Paul Ricœur. What does it mean to consider that our life is meaningful? To answer this question, we need to comprehend that flourishing cannot be only subjective but must also be intersubjective: therefore, rather than attempting to answer the question of the meaning of life on our own, we should, argues Schutijser, investigate how that meaning tends to be constituted collectively and narratively. He writes: 'Philosophical health is hermeneutic because it constantly moves between one's own experiences and interpretations [...] and intersubjective frameworks of understanding.' The interplay between the particular and the universal, between text and context, is how philosophical health can unite personal perspectives and shared interpretations.

In Chapter 9, Richard Sivil thoroughly explores the contribution that the Afro-communitarian *Ubuntu* worldview could make to philosophical counselling and philosophical health. Viewed through a lens of individualism, one might understand philosophical health as a form of personal flourishing, but Ubuntu expands the notion of philosophical health from a notion of individual flourishing to communal flourishing in such way, argues Sivil, 'that the person is understood as socially embedded – an entanglement, necessarily interconnected with others'. This, adds the author, 'expands the notion of philosophical health beyond a narrow coherence of the individual's thought and action to something that arises in and through the coherence of the community.'

Chapter 10 looks at the relationship between the philosophical counsellor and the counselee from a phenomenological perspective. In it, Andrei Simionescu-Panait, one of Romania's notable philosophical counsellors, explains how the Husserlian notions of 'I can consciousness', *epoché* and reduction are tested gates into a good practice of deep listening and focusing. The counselee needs to be offered a form of attention that Simionescu-Panait calls 'observational empathy', and therefore philosophical health can better be nurtured via dialogue with a trained other. The author adds: 'The counselee finds deep orientation into oneself by separating and even discriminating between ideas.' In curating affects and concepts according to their relevance, writes Simionescu-Panait, 'one finds one's way through the jungle of one's thinking by cutting down paths through abundant and disorganized vegetation.'

The last chapter of the part about the Other considers the recent epistemological challenge of artificial intelligence from the perspective of philosophical health. In it, I distinguish three modes of intelligence: analytic, dialectic and crealectic. The world can to a certain extent be divided into concrete analytic parts for the sake of manipulation and possession; it can partly be divided into dialectic tensions of agonistic unfolding to mediate power struggles. Yet, neither of these two forms of understanding is sufficient to achieve philosophical health, argues this chapter, since reality as a mere set of things or bits does not exhaust our living need for sublimity. A healthy form of intelligence needs to collaborate with our sense of the possible, that is our relationship with the creative foundation of the Real, or 'Creal'.

Moving beyond the Self and the Other while including them, the third part of the book – The World – opens with an exhilarating chapter by Matthew Sharpe and Eli Kramer (Chapter 12). In it, the authors show how certain features of the current global professional environment for academics in general, but especially academic philosophers, are incompatible with the five principles of philosophical health (de Miranda, 2021a): mental heroism, deep orientation, critical creativity, deep listening and the Creal (the creative Real as ultimate possibility). Sharpe and Kramer diagnose a culture of 'philosophical ill-health' in academia, which, they write, 'has five counterpart "maladies": mental cowardice, shallowness, the cult of the commentator, dismissive listening, and fatalistic dogmatism'. Moving beyond critique alone, the chapter concludes by advocating for ways that can foster philosophical health in academia and beyond.

In Chapter 13, Abdullah Başaran looks remarkably at the therapeutic and transformative function of storytelling from the perspective of philosophical health. Literary stories and philosophical texts that include transformational narratives can be used, he argues, as a practice of philosophical treatment not only for the counsellors but also for those who wish to take care of themselves via reading. The author convinces us that storytelling, with its 'what if' quality, is a fruitful way to constantly redefine our place in reality. He writes: 'The pedagogy of storytelling for philosophical health is that personal, biographical or fictional stories of transformation have a distinctive attribute to formulate the essential concepts that bond us together.'

Chapter 14 is a provocative take on decolonization as philosophical health, inspired by the writings of Franco-Algerian philosopher Seloua Luste Boulbina. Brendan Moran claims that decolonization and philosophical health are complementary and require the dismantling of various sorts of colonial attitudes that cannot be healthily deconstructed without a deep philosophical impetus via first-person reflection and voice. The purpose of this practice of philosophical care and listening is that neither individuals nor societies may be devoid of possibilities for questioning constraints and beginning anew. 'Philosophical health', writes Moran, 'is simply the capacity to revisit and engage life conditions without the stultification that those conditions might otherwise entail.' The author brings the priority of the first person into debate with Gilles Deleuze and Roberto Esposito and their claim that philosophical health is enhanced by a third-person rapport with ourselves.

In Chapter 15, Jacob Vangeest dives into a thought-provoking journey of planetary thinking, bringing together cosmopolitan posthumanism (Rosi Braidotti), entanglement (Karen Barad) and philosophical health, to think our possibilities for flourishing. The chapter outlines a framework of cosmopolitan posthumanism grounded in a theory of intersubjective obligation while also bringing this concept of obligation towards the other into the realm of planetary philosophical care. Vangeest writes: 'Caring-for within entangled interdependence serves as the condition for cosmopolitan posthumanism, insofar as this concept stresses the intersubjective dimensions of philosophical health.'

Chapter 16 by Lehel Balogh introduces with enlightening clarity the ways in which traditional East Asian philosophies envisage the connections between the individual and its larger milieu and how such philosophical thinking can foster an enlightened awareness of reality. Buddhism, Confucianism and Daoism in their many forms all share the fundamental conviction that the normal, everyday state of the human person is not its ideal state. The chapter scrutinizes in particular the idea of *ki-energy* as a universal and creative source of life and how its nurturing and controlling may enable a person to build up a balanced character, in harmony with society and the cosmos. Balogh argues that East Asian schools of thought put us into a better position to 'see more clearly how philosophical health could facilitate establishing a social order that could contribute to the improvement of general health, mental balance, and an altruistic, ethical, socially responsible lifestyle that allows one to engage in peaceful cohabitation with others and with one's environment.'

In Chapter 17, I look at how the notion of philosophical health can help us resolve apparent dichotomies between the self, the others and the world, as well as between humans and non-human beings. Under the notion of crealectic health, I present what I believe is an ontologically secure yet creative middle way between methodological individualism in philosophical practice – the focus on the self – and the focus on intercreative compossibility, a term inspired by G. W. Leibniz to suggest a harmonious compatibility of diverse forms of life. All beings, humans and non-humans, share a sense of the possible which can be more or less expanded (*eudynamia*) or depleted (*adynamia*). Philosophical health cannot be merely about building a strong sense of human self or private ontological security: we also need a strong sense of compossibility between humans and non-human realities or potentials.

An epilogue concludes the book, providing a method to help philosophical counsellors conduct semi-structured dialogues with their counselees, along the six senses I alluded to in the first paragraphs of this introduction: bodily sense, sense of self, sense of belonging, sense of the possible, sense of purpose, and philosophical sense.

The future of philosophical health

It is a matter of constant astonishment to see so many of us delay indefinitely a confrontation with the higher meaning we ought to give to (our) life or postpone the instauration of a deep and meaningful orientation in the conduct of our biography. If a philosophical sense or a sense of purpose is what distinguishes us from our fellows of fauna and flora, how is it that, in a century of global challenges, most of us go about in everyday life without a(n) – individual or common – sense of purpose, a – personal or shared – minimal cosmology of care? The usual argument that we refrain from cultivating philosophical health because we prefer to adopt a *don't-worry-be-happy* attitude does not hold water, since most of humanity is in fact often worrying – about the present and future, domestic affairs, narcissistic fears, stereotyped problems or exaggerated mediatic threats.

Philosophical health is not an academic privilege. Who are we, us academics, to criticize the average citizen for neglecting their philosophical health if we ourselves are – despite our title of 'PhD', which often means *philosophical* doctorate only superficially – anxiously swallowed by the career game or the groupthink of tribalistic disciplines, while avoiding the duty of grounding our endeavours in psychically and socially embodied philosophical care? Not only all disciplines but most occupations are concerned – questioned – by the philosophical health perspective in one way or another, and therefore professionals from all fields, in an outside academia, should today reclaim more *slow time*, time to think and reflect.

In the year of my birth, 1971, the French comic strip magazine *Charlie Hebdo*, now globally known because of the 2015 terrorist attack that killed several of its staff, began to publish *L'An 01* ('Year 01') by cartoonist Gébé, a fable in which the entire population of France decides to pause working and producing commodities in order to think about life and the world. Half a century later, we still need to pause and think about what we are doing. This book is meant to suggest and create a space for deep listening and a calm requestioning of our ways of life and their compossibility. Shall we have a conversation about the necessity, in our disparate practices, of, not just physical health or psychological health but also philosophical healing?

References

Banicki, Konrad (2014), 'Philosophy as Therapy – Towards a Conceptual Model'. *Philosophical Papers*, 43 (1): 7–31.

Bell, Ruth, Sebastian Taylor and Michael Marmot (2010), 'Global Health Governance: Commission on Social Determinants of Health and the Imperative for Change'. *The Journal of Law, Medicine & Ethics*, 38 (3): 470–85.

Cawston, Amanda and Alfred Archer (2018), 'Rehabilitating Self-Sacrifice: Care Ethics and the Politics of Resistance'. *International Journal of Philosophical Studies*, 26 (3): 456–77.

Duane, Daniel (2004), 'The Socratic Shrink'. *The New York Times*, 21 March. https://www.nytimes.com/2004/03/21/magazine/the-socratic-shrink.html (accessed 15 August 2022).

Fee, Dwight (1999), *Pathology and the Postmodern: Mental Illness as Discourse and Experience*. Thousand Oaks: SAGE Publications.

Foucault, Michel (1975), *Discipline and Punish: The Birth of the Prison*. New York: Vintage.

Foucault, Michel (2005), *The Hermeneutics of the Subject*, trans. Graham Burchell. New York: Palgrave Macmillan.

Frumkin, Howard (2016), *Environmental Heath: From Global to Local*. Hoboken: Wiley.

Gilmore, Richard A. (1999), *Philosophical Health: Wittgenstein's Method in 'Philosophical Investigations'*. Lanham: Lexington Books.

Glenn, Paul F. (2001), 'The Great Health: Spiritual Disease and the Task of the Higher Man'. *Philosophy & Social Criticism*, 27 (2): 100–17.

Hadot, Pierre (1995), *Philosophy as a Way of Life*. Oxford: Blackwell.

Hegel, G. W. F. (1977), *Phenomenology of Spirit*, trans. A. V. Miller. Oxford: Oxford University Press.

Inwood, Brad (2005), *Reading Seneca: Stoic Philosophy at Rome*. Oxford: Oxford University Press.

Knapp, Samuel and Alan Tjeltveit (2005), 'A Review and Critical Analysis of Philosophical Counseling'. *Professional Psychology: Research and Practice*, 36 (5): 558–65.

Levy, Marvin, Mark Dignan and Janet Shirreffs (1984), *Life & Health*. New York: Random House.

Louw, Dirk (2013), 'Defining Philosophical Counselling: An Overview'. *South African Journal of Philosophy*, 32 (1): 60–70.

Marinoff, Lou (1999), *Plato Not Prozac!* New York: MJF Books.

Marinoff, Lou (2013), *Therapy for the Sane: 10th Anniversary Edition*. New York: Argo-Navis, Perseus Books.

de Miranda, Luis (2019), *Philosophical Health International*. https://philosophical.health

de Miranda, Luis (2021a), 'Five Principles of Philosophical Health: From Hadot to Crealectics'. *Eidos: A Journal for Philosophy of Culture*, 5 (1): 70–89.

de Miranda, Luis (2021b), 'Think into the Place of the Other: The Crealectic Approach to Philosophical Health and Care'. *International Journal of Philosophical Practice*, 7 (1): 89–103.

de Miranda, Luis (2021c), 'Crealectic Intelligence'. In V. Gläveanu (ed.), *The Palgrave Encyclopaedia of the Possible*, 250–7. Cham: Palgrave Macmillan.

de Miranda, Luis (2022), 'Philosophical Health'. In V. Gläveanu (ed.), *The Palgrave Encyclopaedia of the Possible*, 1003–8. Cham: Palgrave Macmillan.

Nietzsche, Friedrich W. (1979), *Ecce Homo*, trans. R. J. Hollingdale. New York: Penguin.

Nietzsche, Friedrich W. (1982), *The Antichrist*. In *The Portable Nietzsche*, trans. Walter Kaufmann. New York: Viking Penguin.

Nietzsche, Friedrich W. (2001), *The Gay Science*, trans. Josefine Nauckhoff. Cambridge: Cambridge University Press.

Nietzsche, Friderich W. (2004), *On the Future of Our Educational Institutions*, trans. M. W. Grenke. Indiana: St. Augustine's Press.

Nussbaum, Martha (1994), *The Therapy of Desire: Theory and Practice in Hellenistic Ethics*. Princeton: Princeton University Press.

O'Byrne, Patrick (2019), 'Population Health and Social Governance: A Review, an Update, Some Clarifications, and a Response'. *Qualitative Health Research*, 29 (5): 731–8.

Omelchenko, Nikolay (2012), 'Philosophy as Therapy'. *Diogenes*, 57 (4): 73–81.

Sharpe, Matthew and Michael Ure (2021), *Philosophy as a Way of Life. History, Dimensions and Directions*. London: Bloomsbury.

Silverman, Sam (2010), 'The Death of Socrates: A Holistic Re-Examination'. *OMEGA - Journal of Death and Dying*, 61 (1): 71–84.

Tyreman, Stephen (2020), 'Person-Centred Care: Putting the Organic Horse Back in Front of the Mechanical Cart'. *European Journal for Person Centered Healthcare*, 8 (1): 86–93.

van der Vossen, Bas (2015), 'In Defense of the Ivory Tower: Why Philosophers should Stay Out of Politics'. *Philosophical Psychology*, 28 (7): 1045–63.

Walraven, Gijs (2010), *Health and Poverty: Global Health Problems and Solutions*. Abingdon, Oxon and New York: Routledge.

Part I

The Self

1

Living for real, not counterfeit

'Self-honesty' as a foundation for philosophical health

Eugenia I. Gorlin

A key insight of the philosophical health movement is that we need to think about what we are doing in order to do it well – and that this applies not only to discrete endeavours (like driving a car or writing a novel) but to our lives as a whole. What are the beliefs and values on which we are basing our actions? How do we conceive of virtue and the good life, and what other conceptions might be available to us upon further study and reflection? What kind of future are we striving to create for ourselves, and what unexamined fears or self-imposed limitations might constrain our ambitions? These are the kinds of questions that philosophical counselling aims to guide counselees in asking and answering for themselves, so that they may gain the wisdom and agency to live their own fullest, most flourishing lives (e.g. Taylor, 2002).

To reap the benefit of such questions, however, one must engage with them in good faith: that is, with the honest intent to discover and act upon the answers. For instance, she must actually be interested in learning what values are motivating her actions, even if it turns out that those values run counter to those of her family or society. She must actually be interested in learning what fears or self-imposed limitations have been holding her back, even if this knowledge fills her with regret at not having identified and cast off these limitations sooner. In sum, she must actually be interested in living her best, most flourishing life, rather than merely avoiding or rationalizing away her awareness of the ways in which she is failing to do so. She must be honest with herself about what she thinks, feels, believes, envisions and wants, so that she may choose her actions and build her life accordingly. The pursuit of philosophical health depends upon this willingness to follow one's reflections where they lead, no matter what truths or possibilities this may bring to light.

In this light, eliciting a counselee's commitment to *self-honesty* (akin to what has been described elsewhere as *cognitive integrity*; Gorlin and Schuur, 2019) is arguably one of the first and most important tasks of a philosophical counsellor. The rest of this chapter synthesizes insights, findings and techniques from the philosophical and psychological literatures in order to provide a coherent framework for doing so effectively. Drawing on neo-Aristotelian accounts of virtuous habit formation (e.g.

Kraut, 2012), I posit that the repeated, self-conscious exercise of self-honesty fosters its habituation as a stable virtue with which a person can come to identify as a core part of themselves, thus providing one's present and future selves with a source of continuity through change. By consistently engaging in actively self-honest mental activity, one lays the groundwork for more informed and efficacious action, which in turn provides new experiential data that get integrated into one's growing model of oneself, one's world and the future one is acting to create.

Defining and philosophically situating 'self-honesty'

The many varieties of human self-deception, from the overt lies by which addicts try to convince themselves they are not addicted (Pickard, 2016), to the subtler forms of bullshit wherein we posture at making truth claims without any actual concern for their truth or falsehood (Frankfurt, 2005), to the inauthentic 'play-acting' by which we attempt to escape awareness of our own agency (Sartre, 1993: 167), have received ample scholarly attention among philosophers and psychologists alike (see also Mele, 1990; Chance and Norton, 2015). Yet there is not so much as an established term for the opposite practice: that of *self-honesty* – that is, intentionally refraining from self-deception to build and maintain a credible conceptual foundation for living one's best life. The closest term to self-honesty in the philosophical literature is 'intellectual honesty', which is often mentioned but less often explored in work on virtue epistemology and the ethics of belief (e.g. Adler, 2002; Zagzebsaki, 2018). Whereas some people may hear the term 'intellectual honesty' as pertaining primarily to abstract, theoretical matters, the term 'self-honesty' is meant to capture an insight at the heart of the philosophical health paradigm: that the way we think has direct and far-reaching practical consequences for how we live. From this perspective, such practical matters as how to earn one's living, or whether to ask someone out on a date, require every bit as much grappling with ideas as any 'purely theoretical' matter: ideas about what kind of work is noble and fulfilling, for example, or on the nature and meaning of courage. Indeed, self-honesty becomes more mission-critical – and often more difficult – the more concretely personal the question at hand.

Self-honesty is importantly distinct from, though intimately related to, the virtue of honesty as traditionally understood in the Western philosophical canon. Moral philosophers ranging from Aristotle (Curzer, 2012) to Kant (Kant and Friedrich, 1977) to Fried (1989) to Cabot (1938) have conceptualized honesty as a primarily social virtue involving the non-deception of others. Three common classes of philosophical arguments have been given in defence of this outward-facing virtue (as summarized by Smith, 2003): (1) that dishonesty is bad for those being deceived, as it tricks them into acting on false information and thus places them at an unjust disadvantage; (2) that it is bad for those doing the deceiving, who not only put themselves in the complicated position of having to maintain the lie (contra the witticism widely attributed to Mark Twain, 'if you tell the truth, you don't have to remember anything') but also erode others' credibility and trust in them over time; and (3) that it is bad for society as a whole, given that it disintegrates the fabric of social trust on which our communities and institutions depend. As Cabot (1938: 6) compellingly argues this third point, 'Dishonesty cuts the arteries by which social life is nourished. Mutual deceit is social murder'. This rings particularly true in our current 'post-truth' era of 'fake news', widespread vaccine hesitancy and conspiracy theories run amok. When members of a society cannot trust each other even on basic facts about the number of votes cast in an election or the authenticity of a global pandemic, the very foundations of social cooperation and communal progress start to wear thin.

While these arguments, in favour of traditional, other-facing honesty, have their merits, they are also vulnerable to tough critiques that call into question its status as a virtue, if by virtue we mean what neo-Aristotelian virtue ethicists like Hursthouse have in mind (and what I have in mind in this chapter): an 'excellence of character' that consistently 'makes its possessor good', manifesting in right attitudes and right actions across the numerous particular circumstances in which it can be applied (Hursthouse, 1999: 12). It is not hard to imagine various circumstances in which deceiving others may be the right course of action: not only in blatant cases like Kant's infamous 'not lying to the murderer at the door' example (which has been widely criticized as an unintended indictment of his own case for honesty as a categorical imperative; e.g. Varden, 2010) but also in more mundane cases, such as when the 'truth' is a private matter, or would ruin what is meant to be a playful and fun surprise or would risk being misconstrued or misapplied without the right background knowledge.

By contrast, Smith (2003, 2006: 75–105) proposes conceiving of honesty as a deeper, meta-level commitment to keeping one's own mind anchored to reality, rather than as the relatively narrow injunction against deceiving others (Smith here is elaborating on ideas from Rand [1957, 1019] and Peikoff [1990: 267–76]). My proposed virtue of self-honesty extends this re-conceptualization. Rather than prescribe the particular actions we should or should not take in any given circumstance, the virtue of self-honesty prescribes only that we base our judgements – including even our judgements about whether or not to lie in a given circumstance, or whether or not to adopt a given conception of the virtue of honesty – on an authentic rather than a counterfeit thought process. It is only by basing our choices on our own authentic thought process, I contend, that we can fully realize our potential for human agency and flourishing (Gorlin and Schuur, 2019).

Along these lines, several philosophers have stressed the respects in which we can exercise agency over how we think, and the manner in which we form our judgements and beliefs, even if we do not directly choose the content of our judgements and beliefs as such (Audi, 2001; Steup, 2011; Paul, 2015). Some philosophers have even argued that this freedom over our thought processes is the source and prerequisite of our moral agency (e.g. Binswanger, 1992; Clifford, 1877/1999; Ghate, 2016; Rand, 1957; 1961; Salmieri and Bayer, 2014).

Building on this literature, I propose that most human adults, barring severe brain damage or disability, have the metacognitive capacity to choose between engaging in any given mental process authentically or merely engaging in its counterfeit. This alternative applies to the whole vast range of mental processes in which we could volitionally choose to engage: inquiring about ourselves, other people or the world; imagining possible futures; deliberating about what goals to pursue; monitoring our progress; exercising our creativity through fantasy or games; savouring the fruits of our goal-striving; and so on. Counterfeit cognition occurs when we, in effect, 'spin the wheels' of a given mental process to fake ourselves out into *feeling as if* we are engaging in it, without actually putting forth the effort or mustering the courage that genuine engagement might entail, given our needs, values and circumstances at the time. For instance, we might tell ourselves we are engaging in a process of inquiry when we are actually just seeking to reaffirm our own biases; we might tell ourselves we are formulating a plan of action when we are actually just indulging in idle fantasy with no serious intent to ever act on it; and so on.

The choice of whether to engage in an authentic or a counterfeit thought process does not always consciously present itself: at times we may simply be on mental auto-pilot without the guidance of any particular metacognitive intention, as when our minds wander without awareness of having done so. But whenever we do become even momentarily aware that we have been on autopilot, we face a metacognitive choice of how to proceed: Do we chastise ourselves for having mind-wandered and reassert whatever intention we had most recently set for ourselves (e.g. 'read this chapter' or 'pay attention to this TV episode')? Do we intentionally keep daydreaming about whatever it was our minds had wandered off to because we find it is actually a more interesting and rejuvenating topic than whatever we were focused on before? Or do we intentionally pause to deliberate about what makes sense to do next, since it's not immediately obvious what would actually serve us best? Each of these is a genuine intention we might choose to pursue, depending on the circumstances. But each of them implies a good-faith effort to take responsibility for what we do with our minds; for every such good-faith effort, there are self-deceptive shortcuts we can take if we want to dodge that responsibility. Perhaps we chastise ourselves for lacking the discipline to stay focused on the book we were reading, when in fact we just don't want to admit to ourselves that we see no real value in the book (and thus might need to let down the friend who recommended it to us). Or perhaps we tell ourselves our daydreams are more interesting and rejuvenating than the book we were reading, when in fact we suspect we could be getting a lot more out of the book if we approached it a bit differently (and we don't want to face the embarrassing possibility that we've been approaching it wrong).

Another common impetus for the choice to exercise either self-honesty or self-deception is when we become momentarily aware of a potential problem in our lives. For instance, when we have the sudden thought, 'Did I forget to pay my heating bill last month?', we can make a real plan to check our account later that evening, or we can tell ourselves, 'I'll check my account later tonight' with no real intention of doing so – merely so we can *feel as if* the problem is resolved. Likewise, when we become aware of a painful failure or setback (e.g. oversleeping an important interview), we can either try to minimize the damage for real (e.g. by apologizing and asking to reschedule) or we can rationalize to ourselves that 'I would never have gotten that job anyway', so we can *feel as if* there is no damage to minimize. Of course, it is also possible that, upon some self-honest introspection, we would discover that we did not really want the job and that perhaps this was even our implicit motivation for letting ourselves oversleep. If so, we would face the further question of whether our implicit distaste for the job stems from a genuine understanding of what we want from our lives and what the job would actually entail, or whether it is based on a knee-jerk fear of defying convention (say, by leaving the safety and stagnation of our current nine-to-five job for something more adventurous and intellectually stimulating). By blocking ourselves from such self-honest introspection, we rob ourselves of the opportunity to discover what is really motivating our decisions, much less whether those motivations hold up to our own considered judgement of what is best for us. Absent the opportunity to weigh these questions in the light of day and bring our own independent scrutiny to bear on them, we are left at the mercy of whatever culturally inculcated assumptions or unchecked biases might be pushing us around. Put another way, we deny ourselves the chance to provide or withhold our own informed consent over the factors influencing our actions, thus robbing ourselves of at least some crucial portion of our agency (see Gorlin and Schuur, 2019).

Self-honesty, by contrast, amounts to the deliberate commitment not to do this to ourselves: a refusal to fake ourselves out through counterfeit cognition a moment longer than necessary. At first blush, this may sound like a mere negation, but what it manifests and affirms, I will argue, is a deep, abiding love of life and existence: a choice to really, fully live, rather than merely go through the motions of living (*à la* Sartre's bad-faith café waiter; 2022 [1943]).

Making the case for self-honesty

The case for the value of practising and habituating the virtue of self-honesty is twofold. First, on a prudential level, shielding oneself from uncomfortable aspects of one's mind or world does not make them go away, but only hamstrings one's ability to deal with them (e.g. Chance et al., 2011). While counterfeit cognition may achieve its unacknowledged goal of making us feel (or not feel) a certain way in the moment, it tends to perpetuate our distress and dissatisfaction in the longer term, given that the cause of those feelings remains unidentified and unresolved. Thus, for instance, we will no longer derive emotional relief from our avoidance of the heating bill once we discover that our heat has been shut off; nor will we be spared feeling guilty about the missed job interview once we hear that someone less qualified has just accepted the job.

Multiple philosophers within the Evidentialist tradition have gestured at the practical necessity of self-honesty, at least as narrowly applied to the considerations on which we base our beliefs. For instance, Locke (2017 [1690]: 3064) asserted that 'to love truth for truth's sake is the principal part of human perfection in this world, and the seed-plot of all other virtues'. The best test of whether one loves the truth in earnest, according to Locke, is 'The not entertaining any Proposition with greater assurance than the Proofs it is built upon will warrant'. By contrast, he criticized the practice of succumbing to what he termed 'enthusiasm', akin to what modern psychologists refer to as 'motivated reasoning', that is, letting non-epistemic considerations, such as what one hopes or wishes to be true, sway one's beliefs about what is actually true. When we skew our own judgement of the truth in this manner, he argues, we misuse the 'Discerning faculties' we have been given to 'keep [us] out of Mistake and Error.' Clifford (1999 [1877]) further extends this argument in an essay introducing his famous Clifford Principle: 'It is wrong always, everywhere, and for anyone to believe anything on insufficient evidence.' He illustrates this principle with the story of a shipowner who strongly suspects his ship needs repairs and is not seaworthy but rationalizes away these concerns:

> These doubts preyed upon his mind, and made him unhappy; he thought that perhaps he ought to have her thoroughly overhauled and refitted, even though this should put him to great expense. Before the ship sailed, however, he succeeded in overcoming these melancholy reflections. He said to himself that she had gone safely through so many voyages and weathered so many storms that it was idle to suppose she would not come safely home from this trip also. He would put his trust in Providence, which could hardly fail to protect all these unhappy families that were leaving their fatherland to seek for better times elsewhere. He would dismiss from his mind all ungenerous suspicions about the honesty of builders and contractors. In such ways he acquired a sincere and comfortable conviction that his vessel was thoroughly safe and seaworthy; he watched her departure with a light heart, and benevolent wishes for the success of the exiles in their strange new home that was to be; and he got his insurance-money when she went down in mid-ocean and told no tales. (Clifford, 1877/1999: 1)

Clifford goes on to argue that the shipowner is morally culpable for the deaths of the ship's passengers because he formed his belief in the ship's safety – which informed his subsequent decision to let the ship sail – 'not by honestly earning it in patient investigation, but by stifling his doubts. And although in the end he may have felt so sure about it that he could not think otherwise, yet inasmuch as he had knowingly and willingly worked himself into that frame of mind, he must be held responsible for it'.

Put simply, the trouble with counterfeit cognition, as the sort Clifford's shipowner engages in, is that faking does not make it so. In practical terms, the choice of whether to pursue *real* or counterfeit intentions (e.g. the intention of actually ascertaining the ship's seaworthiness versus the intention to convince oneself of its seaworthiness) amounts to the choice of whether to invest energy in actually striving towards one's valued goals or in semi-consciously manipulating one's emotions so that one can temporarily *feel as if* one is striving towards them (or, alternatively, as if one has no means of doing so, and thus is absolved of the responsibility). This distinction can apply to virtually any goal pursuit in which we can either honestly engage or just go through the motions of engaging: for instance, we might spend hours studying for an exam because it is genuinely important to us to master the material and earn the credential; or we might tell ourselves this is our reason, when in fact we are just using our studies to procrastinate on asking out someone we like, or take a leap and apply for that intimidating but intriguing creative arts internship. We might spend two hours watching the news every night because we find genuine value in staying informed of current affairs – perhaps because it serves us in our writing or aids our investment decisions – or we might tell ourselves these are our reasons, when in fact we are merely chasing a temporary illusion of control (which only depresses us and detracts from our actually valued goal pursuits in the long run). Notably, the two kinds of pursuits can look virtually identical to the naive observer; it is only by examining our underlying motivations, in the context of our current needs, values and circumstances, that we can parse out the real from the counterfeit. But every time we let ourselves get away with a counterfeit pursuit, it is our actual valued goal pursuits that suffer – our effectiveness and credibility as shipowners, or our chance at finding love, or our dream of an artistic career, for example.

Yet the short-term relief offered by counterfeit cognition makes it a particularly powerful temptation in distressing or complicated times – all the more so if we believe that our world is fundamentally incomprehensible and unmanageable or that we are incapable or unworthy of engaging with it. Thus a vicious cycle ensues: the less comprehensible and manageable we believe our world to be, the more tempted we are to self-deceive (Lauria, Preismann and Clément, 2016); and the more we self-deceive, the less comprehensible and manageable our world seems to become. Unsurprisingly, philosophers who defend self-deception and 'as-if' thinking (e.g. Vaihinger, 1925) as necessities of healthy human functioning tend to hold relatively pessimistic views about the human capacity to comprehend and deal with the world. By contrast, my defence of self-honesty rests on the more optimistic tradition of Bacon, who marvelled, as I do, at the power of human reason to understand and master nature in all of its complexity. My clinical experience with individuals reaching new heights of authentic insight and agency in the face of even the most difficult, complex circumstances consistently bears this out, as does the history of human growth, resilience and progress in the face of all manner of calamity.

By the same token, I agree with Bacon that 'Human knowledge and human power meet in one; for where the cause is not known the effect cannot be produced. Nature to be commanded must be obeyed' (1650): that is, we cannot hope to shape nature (including the nature of our own character!) except by understanding how it works and what it will take to change it in reality. Knowledge is power: the more accurate and integrated our model of ourselves and the world around us, the greater our agency in changing and improving both (see Gorlin and Bekes, 2021). This does not mean we should consume information indiscriminately or purposelessly – in fact, self-honest goal pursuit requires that we make authentic judgements about what knowledge we put our limited time and mental energy into pursuing, based on an ongoing assessment of what our needs and valued goals require. In the case of our love-shy student and our compulsory news watcher above, the more self-honest move would be to set deliberate limits on the information they are consuming. But it is by actively seeking out and bringing to bear the knowledge relevant to a given decision – such as knowledge about the range of valued goals we could be pursuing at a given time, and their relative upsides and downsides – that we are best equipped to make an effective decision in each case.

Of course, being self-honest does not guarantee that we will not still make errors of judgement or fail to achieve our valued goals. Even with the best of metacognitive intentions, we will sometimes miscalculate our ship's seaworthiness, so to speak, or misjudge the value of an opportunity. But by consistently engaging in real rather than counterfeit cognition, we commit to correcting errors and learning from setbacks whenever we become aware of them. The benefits of this kind of psychological transparency for psychological health and thriving are akin to what Rogers (1961) described as 'congruence' – that is, the state of being 'fully open to experience' and thus having 'access to all of the available [and relevant] data in the situation'. By opening oneself to all the relevant aspects of one's experience, Rogers argued, the person gains the ability to 'consider each stimulus, need, and demand, its relative intensity and importance, and out of this complex weighing and balancing, discover that course of action which would come closest to satisfying all his needs in the situation' (Rogers, 1961: 190). The real-time psychological experience resulting from this kind of characteristic openness to one's experiences, Rogers observed, is often one of almost effortless insight into what one wants and needs to do at a given point in time, so that the best decision just 'feels right' – without always needing to rehash at a conscious level all the accumulated experiential data and logical connections informing one's decision, because one can trust in the process by which one has integrated that knowledge into one's mental model over time.

This brings me to the second reason why we need self-honesty: on a characterological level, we earn or erode our trust in our own ability to live and thrive in the world by how honestly or evasively we communicate with ourselves (Zeigler-Hill, Chadha and Osterman, 2008). If we routinely set intentions that part of us knows we will not keep, we eventually struggle to take any of our own intentions seriously. If we routinely talk ourselves into accepting judgements that part of us knows are bullshit, we start doubting our judgement even when it is sound. *What if there is some lurking disaster I'm hiding from myself?* we wonder, whether in words or the form of vague anxiety. We do not trust ourselves to operate in the world, because we know our vision is compromised. As a result, we either stall out or defer to other people's judgement of what is best for us – including their judgement of what an 'honest' person would do, as conventionally defined rather than independently derived from our own experience and reasoning. Either way, we give up more and more of our agency.

This, in turn, does have a parallel in the effects of (dis)honesty in a social context. The more we characteristically bullshit other people, the less they trust and respect us over time. But whereas we can always find other friends or associates or minimize our dealings with those who distrust us, we ultimately have no choice but to deal with our selves. The choice we *do* have, however, is over the character traits we cultivate over time. By deliberately choosing real over counterfeit cognition at every opportunity, we give ourselves practice in identifying and exploiting these opportunities across an ever-widening range of contexts and circumstances, seeing our judgement and decisions incrementally improve as a result; and we gain trust and credibility with ourselves over time, leading to a virtuous cycle of ever-greater courage and confidence in the bets we are willing to take and the bold ventures we are willing to pursue.

Once understood in these terms, the cultivation of self-honesty becomes a non-negotiable goal for anyone with other, more particular valued goals: it is one's internal protection against the risk of defrauding or sabotaging one's own long-term joy and fulfilment for the sake of a temporary illusion.

Forming a united front: Self-deception as a common challenge for psychology and philosophical health

Anytime we enter into a dialogue about philosophical health – be it about the meaning and significance of the concept itself, about whether it is an end worth pursuing, about the best means to pursuing it, or about whether these are even the right questions to ask – we must assume, at minimum, a shared commitment to dialoguing in good faith. That is, we must be able to trust that each conversant sincerely strives to understand or enact whatever questions or aims they purport to be striving to understand or enact. Whatever the differences in our value systems and conceptions of philosophical health – and indeed, there is room for ample differences, as the diverse perspectives represented in this book will attest – there is at least one fundamental value on which we must agree if we are to engage in a constructive idea exchange and synthesis: we must share a commitment to being honest with ourselves about whether this is what we are actually trying to do. Are we actually trying to better our understanding of someone else's perspective, or are we just telling ourselves that this is what we are doing (when in fact we are just trying to get them to reassure us of our view)? Are we actually trying to promote greater flourishing in ourselves or others, or are we just telling ourselves that this is what we're doing (when in fact we are just going through the motions so we can get the corresponding ego boost)? Are we actually trying to exercise virtue, or are we just virtue-signalling? To be able to answer these questions credibly, either to ourselves or to those in our counsel, we need a firm distinction between self-deception and self-honesty, and a shared normative commitment to the latter.

Psychologists face the same need for a shared normative commitment to self-honesty when working to effect mental health changes in their patients. Most schools of psychotherapy implicitly rely on patients to engage in some form of active, honest thinking – to challenge their existing assumptions about themselves and others, to consider new perspectives and ways of engaging with the world, to take responsibility for symptoms and problem behaviours they previously felt helpless to effect – as essential ingredients in the therapeutic change process (Gorlin and Bekes, 2021). For instance, psychodynamic therapy aims to bring a patient's unconscious motives and emotions into conscious awareness, thus presumably freeing her to make more informed choices instead of being compelled by her unconscious drives. Similarly, cognitive behaviour therapy (CBT) helps a patient identify and challenge the distorted beliefs and thinking errors that underlie her moods and behaviour urges, thus gaining greater awareness and agency over how she responds. Mindfulness-based therapies (Kabat-Zinn, 1990) guide patients to practice disengaging from their autopilot thought stream and instead intentionally directing their awareness to some aspect of the present moment. Likewise, various metacognitive interventions have been developed to exercise and strengthen people's awareness and management of their own minds. For instance, Wells' (2011) metacognitive therapy helps patients identify and reappraise the metacognitive beliefs (such as 'rumination helps me understand myself' or 'worry helps me problem-solve') that motivate them to engage in various unconstructive thought processes. Research on the efficacy of cognitive-behavioural and recovery-oriented therapies for patients with severe mental illness suggests that even highly impaired individuals can learn to reflect on and intentionally modify their mental processes. Indeed, I have directly observed how several patients with paranoid psychotic delusions – like 'that man in sunglasses who followed me out of the grocery store was a CIA agent tracking my movements' – were able to generate their own 'alternative explanations' for the same occurrence (e.g. 'The man was wearing sunglasses because his eyes are sensitive'; 'The man was following me because he saw me drop something at the store'; 'the man was following me because he needed help finding his car'; etc.) after some initial guidance and modelling by the therapist. Even more strikingly, I've seen these patients loosen up on the rigidity of their delusions, holding them more as working hypotheses than as unquestionable certainties, as a result of this simple cognitive flexibility exercise. In Aaron Beck and colleagues' reflections (2021) on his late-life work developing recovery-oriented CBT for severely mentally ill patients, he likewise describes multiple instances in which patients with chronic, seemingly intractable schizophrenia showed a dramatic improvement in functioning once they shifted their focus from dwelling on their psychoses and symptoms to identifying and engaging with meaningful, personally valued real-world activities, such as preparing and serving food at a beloved restaurant or learning to play their favourite songs on guitar. Consistent with Beck's own explanation, I suspect that such activities activated a more reality-oriented mental 'mode' in which patients could implicitly experience themselves, not as helpless refugees seeking some form of counterfeit relief from an incomprehensible, threat-filled world, but as efficacious agents authentically engaged with a navigable, value-filled world (Beck, Finkel and Beck, 2021).

Across these various therapeutic schools and approaches, the best psychologists implicitly share at least one of the overarching goals of philosophical counsellors: to help patients form a more credible conceptual map of themselves, the world they are living in, and the life they are working toward – as well as the action paths that might plausibly get them there. They help patients gain insight into their own motivations and moods, discover that they can tolerate situations or emotions they previously thought intolerable, recognize the negative toll of their behaviour and explore the more positive futures that might lie within their reach, as well as the steps they may need to enact to get there. But to form and appropriately update such a complex conceptual model can itself be some of the hardest and, at times, most painful work of therapy, as it often requires questioning one's long-held assumptions, confronting one's fears in action, recognizing the negative consequences associated with one's problem behaviours and grappling with aspects of one's life and experience that one has previously avoided thinking about. By contrast, self-deception is often the more accessible and immediately gratifying alternative. Thus it is no wonder that patients often use self-deceptive defence mechanisms during therapy (Babl et al., 2019). For instance, patients may tell themselves and their therapist that they intend to make a change they do not in fact intend to make so that they can temporarily *feel as if* they will make it (Oettingen, 2012). Conversely, they may tell themselves they are incapable of change, not because this is their sincere, all-things-considered judgement, but so that they may shield themselves from the potential disappointment of trying and failing (e.g. Elliot and Church, 2003). Or they may ruminate on past or future problems in a manner that helps them 'avoid the direct experience of sadness [or anxiety], whilst simultaneously giving the mistaken impression (smokescreen) that they are actually, in some way, processing their emotional experiences and dealing with their problems' (Thomas, Raynor and Ribott, 2015: 59; see also Nolen-Hoeksema, Morrow and Fredrickson, 1993). To make matters more complicated, even a therapeutic strategy intended to promote awareness and engagement can be deployed in service of a counterfeit metacognitive goal: for instance, a patient might engage in a mindfulness exercise on the pretence that they are getting connected to the present moment when on some unadmitted level they are just using it as a distraction tactic to avoid dealing with an important but difficult problem in their lives.

Unfortunately, the short-term relief associated with these strategies often comes at the cost of informed and effective therapeutic change. Indeed, research suggests that patients routinely misrepresent their symptoms in therapy, and that this presents an obstacle to successful treatment (VanDyke and Pollard, 2005), as it prevents both patient and therapist from arriving at an appropriate treatment plan. More generally, people who rely more on defence mechanisms to shield themselves from uncomfortable truths demonstrate greater instability in self-esteem and mood, compared to those who cope in more realistic ways (Zeigler-Hill, Chadha and Osterman, 2008; Koenigsberg et al., 2001; 2002). Likewise, those who hold less realistic views about their social competence tend to struggle more with adjusting and adapting to changes in their environment and navigating challenges in their social life (Colvin, 1993; John and Robins, 1994) – and they tend to score higher on both narcissism and depression measures. Contrary to popular wisdom on the benefits of maintaining positive illusions about ourselves, there is now a lion's share of research showing that distorted self-appraisals – both positive *and* negative – go hand in hand with more depression, not less (Joiner et al., 2006; see also Kim and Chiu, 2011). Aristotle could have anticipated this finding when he described the truly virtuous person as naturally motivated to present themselves accurately, rather than being either too boastful or self-deprecating (Curzer, 2012).

Given that self-deception is both so common and so apt to undermine effective mental health treatment, it is perhaps unsurprising that 40–60 per cent of patients drop out or do not benefit from even the most allegedly rigorous therapies (Hofmann et al., 2012). While these 'evidence-based' therapies offer reliable change strategies for the patient who self-honestly engages with them, they lack any philosophically-informed vision of the good life – leaving psychologists ill-equipped to motivate such self-honesty, to begin with. The advent of philosophical counselling is a much-needed corrective to this failure (e.g. de Miranda, 2021), and is well-positioned to champion a positive vision of the self-honest life for those who want the freedom and inspiration to flourish on their own terms. Yet the philosophical health literature and the clinical psychology literature are still largely siloed and not benefiting from each other's progress and insights. In the concluding section of this chapter (below), I offer my preliminary effort to bridge these literatures and foster a constructive dialogue between them, by integrating a philosophical account of self-honesty with findings and techniques from clinical psychology in a novel synthesis of vision and strategy.

Conclusion: Techniques and practices for promoting self-honesty

The following elements may be incorporated or flexibly adapted as and when appropriate, given the particular therapeutic or counselling services being offered and the particular needs and circumstances of the person receiving them. None of these techniques will be universally applicable to every practitioner's work with every client, of course, but my hope is that this sampling of techniques can inspire other self-honesty-oriented modifications that serve to deepen and expand the practitioner's repertoire.

The philosophical texts and citations cited throughout this chapter can serve as valuable resources for sensitizing clients (and practitioners!) to the 'what', 'why' and 'how' of self-honesty. This is where philosophers who have championed related values like love of truth or authenticity can be great sources of inspiration. For instance, a person may both take solace from and find renewed resolve in Locke's admonishment that 'here are very few lovers of Truth for Truth's sake, even amongst those, who persuade themselves that they are so' (Locke, 1690/2017). Locke's subsequent reflection on 'enthusiasm', quoted earlier, provides a valuable heuristic by which to self-assess one's progress in cultivating a love of truth – a disposition closely aligned with the virtue of self-honesty.

To connect this philosophically informed conception of the virtue of self-honesty with a client's own understanding and experience, the practitioner might guide her to reflect on what does or does not resonate about this philosophical account, including any instances in which she herself has either exemplified this virtue or particularly struggled with it. This reflection might be accompanied by an experiential exercise of revisiting particularly salient moments of self-honesty (e.g. when she acknowledged a difficult or painful truth to herself for the first time), and recalling as vividly as possible how these moments played out, as in contrast to moments when she 'took the shipowner's approach' (e.g. in reference to Clifford's evocative anecdote of the ship in need of repair). When possible, the practitioner can draw upon observed instances when the client has embodied this virtue in the therapy room – as often occurs when clients first 'let their guard down' and start grappling with their problems in an active and non-defensive way. Throughout this process, the practitioner can elicit and validate the client's affective experience, normalizing and empathizing with any distressing aspects ('some very smart philosophers, like Vaihinger, wouldn't even think it possible to face what you are doing now!'), as well as highlighting any positive affective states (e.g. authenticity, serenity, an increased sense of agency) uniquely associated with the self-conscious exercise of virtue (Nussbaum, 1999).

In order to sensitize a person to the diverse contexts in which she may stand to benefit from practising self-honesty, the practitioner may first need to raise her awareness of instances in which she tends to self-deceive, as well as the prudential and characterological consequences of this self-deception. Thus, for instance, if a client has provided an unconvincing excuse for passing up a promising social opportunity (e.g. 'I was just too busy'), the practitioner, after listening closely and asking many Socratic questions to facilitate a mutual understanding of the person's internal experience and context, might venture a guess as to the counterfeit metacognitive motivation at play: for example, 'I wonder if saying you were "too busy" is a bit of a front for you, when what you actually mean is that you were too afraid?' Once the person has consciously acknowledged a given instance of self-deception, the practitioner can (1) genuinely celebrate her virtuous exercise of self-honesty in doing so, and (2) reflect with her on the prudential and/or characterological consequences of the self-deception, both short- and long term (e.g. reduced risk of rejection in the short term; little to no chance of finding the intimacy and connection she seeks, nor gaining greater confidence and credibility with herself, in the long term).

In addition to noting instances of self-deception when they arise, the practitioner can also target a client's self-deceptive processes more directly by guiding her to keep a written log of her most common self-deceptions. If necessary, the practitioner may prompt the client by suggesting some common self-deceptive strategies that tend to come up for individuals in similar circumstances to her's (e.g. minimizing the consequences of her current behaviour, pretending greater certainty than she has about a highly desired but not-fully-predictable outcome, worrying or self-sabotaging to avoid the emotional risk of unanticipated failure, berating herself for past failures to avoid dealing with the problem at hand etc.). For each type of self-deception the client identifies, the practitioner can further guide the client to identify the 'suspected truth' underlying it (e.g. 'I've messed up my life beyond repair', 'I don't really love my children' etc.).

For each 'suspected truth' the client identifies, the practitioner can then help her process the item rationally and constructively so that she can ultimately benefit from the increased awareness and action guidance it provides. This will often mean using Socratic techniques to arrive at an informed view of whatever aspects of reality the client was previously avoiding or distorting, as well as encouraging her to take action in order to gather further experiential data. In some cases, this may lead to the discovery that the client's 'suspected truth' (e.g. 'I've messed up my life beyond repair') is based on a false or oversimplified inference, whereas the more nuanced, reality-based conclusion is less threatening and more readily solvable (e.g. 'I'm still young, and plenty of things in my life are actually going well despite this drinking problem'). In other cases, the 'suspected truth' will correspond to a more painful or complex aspect of reality: for example, that the client has truly damaged important relationships in potentially irreparable ways with her drinking, or was truly helpless to prevent the traumatic experiences she has undergone. In these instances, the practitioner might connect the client to an Existentialist perspective like Sartre's, helping her lean into the authenticity and increased freedom of confront all aspects of her situation, even the profoundly distressing ones: 'Authenticity, it is almost needless to say, consists in having a true and lucid consciousness of the situation, in assuming the responsibilities and risks it involves, in accepting it . . . sometimes in horror and hate' (Sartre, 1948: 90). To aid her in tolerating this 'horror and hate' without retreating back into self-deception, the practitioner might incorporate certain psychological techniques for tolerating acute emotional distress (such as sensory grounding and radical acceptance strategies from Dialectical Behaviour Therapy; Linehan, 2015), while also calling attention to the ways in which even these profoundly painful 'truths' become more manageable once engaged with openly and honestly.

To help the client internalize and habituate to the virtue of self-honesty over time, the practitioner can guide her to create a routine of regular self-honesty logging, reappraisal, action and review, whether at scheduled intervals or anytime she feels blocked or conflicted with respect to a goal. Client and practitioner may also develop a repertoire of shorthand labels or philosophical references, ideally selected by or with the client, that allow for quick detection and tracking of her most common self-honest and self-deceptive modes: for example, 'am I loving the truth right now' (channelling Locke), 'is this a belief or is this bullshit' (channelling Frankfurt) and so on. Likewise, shorthand phrases like 'act on what you know' (instead of the common adage 'fake it till you make it') can help keep this perspective salient and accessible.

In sum, the self-honesty framework has the potential to strengthen existing philosophical and psychological health paradigms alike by providing a philosophically informed virtuous alternative to self-deception, along with technical tools for its habituation. This framework offers a promising new pathway for inspiring and empowering wide-ranging individuals across wide-ranging contexts to achieve real, authentic philosophical health, rather than merely chasing after its counterfeit.

References

Adler, Jonathan (2002), *Belief's Own Ethics*. Cambridge, MA: The MIT Press.

Audi, Robert (2001), 'Doxastic Voluntarism and the Ethics of Belief'. In M. Steup (ed.), *Knowledge, Truth and Duty*, 93–114. Oxford: Oxford University Press.

Babl, Anna, Martin Holtforth, John Perry, Noemi Schneider, Eliane Dommann, Sara Heer, Annabarbara Stähli, Nadine Aeschbacher, Michaela Eggel, Jelena Eggenberg, Meret Sonntag, Thomas Berger and Franz Caspar (2019), 'Comparison and Change of Defense Mechanisms over the Course of Psychotherapy in Patients with Depression or Anxiety Disorder: Evidence from a Randomized Controlled Trial'. *Journal of Affective Disorders*, 252: 212–20.

Bacon, Francis (1650), *Novum organum scientiarum*. Lvgd. Batav: Ex officina A. Wyngaerden. Aphorism 3, Book 1.

Beck, Aaron, Molly Finkel and Judith Beck (2021), 'The Theory of Modes: Applications to Schizophrenia and Other Psychological Conditions'. *Cognitive Therapy and Research*, 45: 391–400.

Binswanger, Harry (1992), 'Volition as Cognitive Self-regulation'. *Organizational Behavior and Human Decision Processes*, 50 (2): 165–78.

Cabot, Richard (1938), *Honesty*, 6. New York: MacMillan.

Chance, Zoe and Michael Norton (2015), 'The What and Why of Self-deception'. *Current Opinion in Psychology*, 6: 104–7.

Chance, Zoe, Michael Norton, Francesca Gino and Dan Ariely (2011), 'Temporal View of the Costs and Benefits of Self-deception'. *Proceedings of the National Academy of Sciences of the United States of America*, 108 (Supplement 3): 15655–9.

Clifford, William (1877/1999), 'The Ethics of Belief'. In T. Madigan (ed.), *The Ethics of Belief and Other Essays*, 70–9. Buffalo: Prometheus Books.

Colvin, Randall (1993), 'Childhood Antecedents of Young Adult Judgability'. *Journal of Personality*, 61 (4): 611–35.

Curzer, J. H. (2012), 'Truthfulness and Integrity (NE IV.7)'. In *Aristotle and the Virtues*, 195–220. Oxford: Oxford University Press.

Elliot, Andrew and Marcy Church (2003), 'A Motivational Analysis of Defensive Pessimism and Self-handicapping: A Motivational Analysis'. *Journal of Personality*, 71 (3): 369–96.

Frankfurt, Harry (2005), *On Bullshit*. Princeton: Princeton University Press.

Fried, Charles (1989), 'The Evil of Lying'. In Christina Sommers and Fred Sommers (eds), *Vice and Virtue in Everyday Life*, 371, 380. New York: Harcourt Brace Jovanovich.

Ghate, Onkar (2016), 'A Being of Self-made Soul'. In Allan Gotthelf and Gregory Salmieri (eds), *A Companion to Ayn Rand*, 105–29. Chichester: John Wiley & Sons Ltd.

Gorlin, Eugenia and Vera Bekes (2021), 'Agency via Awareness: A Unifying Meta-process in Psychotherapy'. *Frontiers in Psychology*, 12: Article 698655.

Gorlin, Eugenia and Reinier Schuur (2019), 'Nurturing Our Better Nature: A Proposal for Cognitive Integrity as a Foundation for Autonomous Living'. *Behavior Genetics*, 49 (2): 154–67.

Hofmann, Stefan, Anu Asnaani, Imke Vonk, Alice Sawyer and Angela Fang (2012), 'The Efficacy of Cognitive Behavioral Therapy: A Review of Meta-analyses'. *Cognitive Therapy and Research*, 36 (5): 427–40.

Hursthouse, Rosalind (1999), *On Virtue Ethics*. Oxford: Oxford University Press.

John, Oliver and Richard Robins (1994), 'Accuracy and Bias in Self-perception: Individual Differences in Self-enhancement and the Role of Narcissism'. *Journal of Personality and Social Psychology*, 66 (1): 206–19.

Joiner Jr., Thomas, Janet Kistner, Nadia Stellrecht and Katherine Merrill (2006), 'On Seeing Clearly and Thriving: Interpersonal Perspicacity as Adaptive (not Depressive) Realism (or Where Three Theories Meet)'. *Journal of Social and Clinical Psychology*, 25 (5): 542–64.

Kabat-Zinn, Jon (1990), *Full Catastrophe Living: Using the Wisdom of Your Body and Mind to Face Stress, Pain and Illness*. New York: Delacorte.

Kant, Immanuel and Carl Friedrich (1977), *The Philosophy of Kant: Immanuel Kant's Moral and Political Writings*. New York: Modern Library.

Kim, Young-Hoon and Chi-Yue Chiu (2011), 'Emotional Costs of Inaccurate Self-assessments: Both Self-effacement and Self-enhancement can Lead to Dejection'. *Emotion*, 11 (5): 1096–104.

Koenigsberg, Harold, Philip Harvey, Vivian Mitropoulou, Antonia New, Marianne Goodman, Jeremy Silverman, Michael Serby, Frances Schopick and Larry Siever (2001), 'Are the Interpersonal and Identity Disturbances in the Borderline Personality Disorder Criteria Linked to the Traits of Affective Instability and Impulsivity?' *Journal of Personality Disorders*, 15 (4): 358–70.

Koenigsberg, Harold, Philip Harvey, Vivian Mitropoulou, James Schmeidler, Antonia New, Marianne Goodman, Jeremy Silverman, Michael Serby, Frances Schopick and Larry Siever (2002), 'Characterizing Affective Instability in Borderline Personality Disorder'. *The American Journal of Psychiatry*, 159 (5): 784–8.

Kraut, Richard (2012), 'Aristotle on Becoming Good: Habituation, Reflection, and Perception'. In C. Shields (ed.), *Oxford Handbook on Aristotle*, 529–57. Oxford: Oxford University Press.

Lauria, Federico, Delphine Preismann and Fabrice Clément (2016), 'Self-deception as Affective Coping: An Empirical Perspective on Philosophical Issues'. *Consciousness and Cognition*, 41: 119–34.

Linehan, Marsha (2015), *DBT® Skills Training Manual*, 2nd edn. New York: Guilford Press.

Locke, John (1690/2017), *Complete Works of John Locke (Illustrated)*. Delphi Classics.

Mele, A. (1990), 'Irresistible Desires'. *Nous*, 24 (3): 455–72.

de Miranda, Luis (2021), 'Five Principles of Philosophical Health for Critical Times: From Hadot to Crealectics'. *Eidos. A Journal for Philosophy of Culture*, 5 (1): 70–89.

Nolen-Hoeksema, Susan, Jannay Morrow and Barbara Fredrickson (1993), 'Response Styles and the Duration of Episodes of Depressed Mood'. *Journal of Abnormal Psychology*, 102 (1): 20–8.

Nussbaum, Martha (1999), 'Virtue Ethics: A Misleading Category?' *The Journal of Ethics*, 3: 163–201.

Oettingen, Gabriele (2012), 'Future thought and Behaviour Change'. *European Review of Social Psychology*, 23 (1): 1–63.

Paul, Sarah (2015), 'Doxastic Self-control'. *American Philosophy Quarterly*, 52 (2): 145–58.

Peikoff, Leonard (1990), *Objectivism: The Philosophy of Ayn Rand*. London: Penguin.

Pickard, Hanna (2016), 'Denial in Addiction'. *Mind & Language*, 31 (3): 277–99.

Rand, Ayn (1957), *Atlas Shrugged*. Signet / NAL.

Rand, Ayn (1961), *The Objectivist Ethics*. Literary Licensing, LLC.

Rogers, Carl (1961), *On Becoming a Person: A Therapist's View of Psychotherapy*. London: Constable.

Salmieri, Gregory and Ben Bayer (2014), 'How We Choose Our Beliefs'. *Philosophia*, 42: 41–53.

Sartre, Jean-Paul (1943/2022), *Being and Nothingness: An Essay in Phenomenological Ontology*, trans. S. Richmond. Oxfordshire: Routledge.

Sartre, Jean-Paul (1948), *Anti-semite and Jew*. New York: Schocken Press.

Sartre, Jean-Paul (1993), *Essays in Existentialism*. New York: Citadel Press.

Smith, Tara (2003), 'The Metaphysical Case for Honesty'. *Journal of Value Inquiry*, 37: 517–31.

Smith, Tara (2006), *Ayn Rand's Normative Ethics: The Virtuous Egoist*. Cambridge: Cambridge University Press.

Steup, Matthias (2011), 'Belief, Voluntariness and Intentionality'. *Dialectica*, 65 (4): 537–59.

Taylor, James (2002), 'The Central Value of Philosophical Counseling'. *International Journal of Philosophical Practice*, 1 (2): 1–9.

Thomas, Justin, Monique Raynor and David Ribott (2015), 'Depressive Rumination and Experiential Avoidance: A Task Based Exploration'. *Personality and Mental Health*, 9: 58–65.

Vaihinger, Hans (1925), *The Philosophy of "As If": A System of the Theoretical, Practical and Religious Fictions of Mankind*, translation of Die Philosophie des Als Ob by C. K. Ogden. New York: Harcourt, Brace & Co.; reprinted, Petoskey: Random Shack, 2015.

VanDyke, Melanie and Alec Pollard (2005), 'Treatment of Refractory Obsessive-Compulsive Disorder: The St. Louis Model'. *Cognitive and Behavioral Practice*, 12: 30–9.

Varden, Helga (2010), 'Kant and Lying to the Murderer at the Door... One More Time: Kant's Legal Philosophy and Lies to Murderers and Nazis'. *Journal of Social Philosophy*, 41 (4): 403–4211.

Wells, Adrian (2011), *Metacognitive Therapy for Anxiety and Depression*. New York: Guilford Press.

Zagzebski, Linda (2018), 'Intellectual Virtues: Admirable Traits of Character'. In H. Battaly (ed.), *The Routledge Handbook of Virtue Epistemology*, 26–36. Oxfordshire: Routledge.

Zeigler-Hill, Virgil, Sumeer Chadha and Lindsey Osterman (2008), 'Psychological Defense and Self-esteem Instability: Is Defense Style Associated with Unstable Self-esteem?' *Journal of Research in Personality*, 42 (2): 348–64.

2

Existential-phenomenological approaches in psychiatry and psychotherapy to the idea of philosophical health

Lehel Balogh

Introduction: The ideal of authenticity as an indicator of philosophical health

Existential-phenomenological psychiatry and psychotherapy, notwithstanding its diversity of approaches to healing and health, lays down and defends the fundamental claim that health is equivalent to the actualized potential of an individual to live authentically. The idea of authenticity in psychiatry has its forerunners in existential philosophy, in particular in the thoughts of such authors as Søren Kierkegaard, Friedrich Nietzsche, Martin Heidegger and, perhaps most famously, Jean-Paul Sartre. Based on these thinkers' judgement, the counter-ideal of authenticity, that is, inauthenticity, describes a mode of being in which the individual has lost their pre-ontologically given intimate connection to the core of their own subjectivity (Carman, 2006). This loss also points to the loss of touch with one's inborn, nonconceptual understanding of being as well as one's inherent feeling of belongingness to the world. Restoring philosophical health, therefore, implies resetting one's deep connection to both the self and the world.

One can lead an inauthentic mode of life in all sorts of ways just as one can suffer from several – and multiple – mental disorders at the same time. According to the existential-phenomenological approach, we are mentally unwell and philosophically ill to the extent that we have built a distance between the core of our authentic selves and our current, inauthentic selves. The notion of authenticity is itself but an ideal, in a similar fashion to the concept of health which, rather than an attainable practical goal, displays the abstract concept of perfect well-being. As ideals, both of them are forever approachable, yet neither of them can be completely reached. They are not end goals, and they are not static conditions that could be attained once and for all. On the contrary, both authenticity and philosophical health designate a *direction* which can be followed indefinitely without actually accomplishing the goal of seizing them. Correct attitudes and the right modes of behaviour can always take one a step closer to these ideals, but they can never be entirely mastered or grasped. Their essence lies in their continual movement *away* from themselves and from all attempts that try to conceptualize them once and for all (Schneider, 2007).

Living authentically means to live with the determination to return to the truth of the self (Nietzsche), to the inwardness of the subjectivity (Kierkegaard), to accept the *originary disclosedness* and interconnectedness of the *Dasein* (Heidegger's human existence) and to act in good faith with the unbound freedom that one is condemned to possess (Sartre). In this sense, becoming authentic involves accepting one's self together with the self's unique possibilities and its delimiting facticity (the deterministic factors of one's personal existence). At the same time, taking responsibility for the choices that form one's life and living in accord with one's innermost calling as Heidegger puts it are of special importance, too. Hence, in light of the premises of existential-philosophical philosophy and psychiatry, to be philosophically healthy is to *dare* to be ourselves, without self-deceit, without deliberately distorting reality. Consequently, when a person does *not* dare to be themselves in terms of staying open to creatively actualizing their existential possibilities, or when they miss the opportunity to become their very own forms of becoming – either in the eyes of others or in their own eyes, or both – they step onto a dangerous and ultimately destructive path that can only lead to illness (Jacobsen, 2007).

It might be clear from the above that only those individuals can live more or less authentically that can live autonomously as well: those who are able to wilfully construct themselves against the opposing wills of the world. Those who are capable of expressing their very own personal tendencies when confronted with the views and values of their cultural traditions, societal norms and familial customs can be called authentic. Being existentially authentic – and thus being philosophically healthy – entails having the ability to create or discover in good faith one's moral laws, values and preferences (Sartre: see in Balogh, 2022) without becoming a reactionary agent that is the victim of waxing and waning trends in morality (Nietzsche, see in Wirth, 2019). The person that wants to live authentically must question the unasked questions and presuppositions of their sociocultural milieu and must find out, in the process, how the real, true, inner autonomous core of their self feels about the decisive questions of life. Then again, even this might not be quite sufficient: one must also take a concrete stance and commit publicly to one's discovered views and values (transparency and honesty). In this manner, the person that is seeking philosophical health can become morally autonomous and existentially authentic at the same time (Groth, 2008).

One of the implicit premises of the movement of existential-phenomenological psychiatry nowadays is that the aetiology of a sizable portion of the psychological disorders of the day cannot be accounted for and explained away by solely referring to the inadequate or maladaptive actions of the individuals. Rather, the geneses of such disorders as generalized anxiety disorder (GAD) and panic disorder (PD) are associated largely with the interplay of such varied factors as destructive human relations as well as the negative influences of those societal institutions that fundamentally misunderstand, misinterpret or neglect the basic needs of a human being. In short, the philosophically ill individual is unaware of those all-too-human limitations and potentials that could provide a framework within which one could exist – and not merely exist but *thrive* – joyfully and effectively. The therapist in existential therapy assists the clients in opening their eyes to the existence of this framework of potentialities: to the experiential fact that one must cope with life amid a permanently moving set of rules (Cooper, 2003). But the therapist also assures the client that one can, indeed, obtain a bodily felt wisdom that will guide one in making the right decisions in the middle of ever-changing circumstances. The existential-phenomenological approach does not provide fixed and reliable handrails to which the person seeking guidance could grip interminably. Instead, it teaches one how to live in a world where the handrails are constantly in movement. The crucial wisdom the therapy offers is that it is, in fact, possible to hold on to experiential truths that can be obtained from one's body, even while the world is in a dizzying flux (as it always is).

From *Logotherapy* to *Daseinsanalysis*: Psychiatrists on authentic existence and philosophical health on the Old Continent

It was famed existentialist philosopher Karl Jaspers's epochal work *General Psychopathology* in 1913 that introduced the phenomenological method into the domain of psychiatry and had, incidentally, also exerted a landmark influence on the development of psychiatry in the twentieth century (Bormuth, 2006). Before the publication of this work, it was the scientific method as well as such pioneering psychologists and psychiatrists as fellow Germans Wilhelm Wundt and his disciple Emil Kraepelin that dominated the scene of medical sciences. Owing principally to the impact of Jaspers's efforts on the field, the phenomenological approach had gradually achieved the rank of a viable alternative to the more widely accepted 'objective' methodology of the sciences. Even at the earlier stages of Jaspers's career, it was his professional conviction that, in the course of treating particular mental disorders, a patient-empowering educational method should be granted precedence over the manipulative and openly paternalizing practices that were prevalent of the time. The educational method was created to assist the ill in discovering their own capacity to develop insights into their diseases and to learn to take responsibility for their actions during their fight for recovery. In other words, Jaspers propagated an approach that re-humanized the mentally ill, giving back to them their moral agency, along with the hope to improve their condition (Jaspers, 1959: 1.ff). At the same time, he also encouraged the noting down of the patients' subjectively felt experiences, alongside the application of an empathetic interpretation of these inwardly experienced psychic phenomena by their therapists. As Nietzsche maintained, the 'concept of a normal health, along with those of a normal diet and normal course of an illness, must be abandoned' (Nietzsche, 1882/2001: 117.). Along the lines of these thoughts by Nietzsche, Jaspers also argued that health and illness are as diverse as people are. Therefore, if two patients receive identical diagnoses, this in itself will not guarantee that the same treatment will be effective for both of them (Jaspers, 1959). Individual differences cannot be levelled to the ground: singularly subjective traces in a person's personality will always distinguish them from other individuals. This, in turn, will be reflected in the differences in their individual needs for health: one's physical, philosophical or mental health will always differ according to their character, personality and inherited genetic traits. Jaspers maintained that the human being, conceived of as an object of knowledge for the sciences, will forever remain unknowable, for the individual cannot be reduced to its *genus*: no person can be abstracted from the general concept of humanity (Jaspers, 1955; Jaspers, 1971).

The founder of *logotherapy* and *existential analysis*, Austrian-born Viktor Frankl echoes in many ways Jaspers's sentiments in relation to the dignity of the individual and one's right to define the meaning of one's life. When not characterizing human existence as the victim of such fatalistic forces within the self as sexual drives and other biological instincts, Frankl's existential analysis goes against the Freudian deterministic conception of man (Askay and Farkuhar, 2006). Frankl saw man as a being that is defined by its ability to make decisions and to take responsibility for its decisions. He worked out with meticulous fine detail a philosophical anthropology that supported his therapeutic approach to the greatest problem of the age: the loss of meaning. For Frankl the adjective 'existential' means, above all, 'the striving to find a concrete meaning in personal existence, that is to say, the *will* to meaning' (Frankl, 1949). Logotherapy is frequently called a meaning-centred therapy, because it prioritizes the discovery of meanings and values for the clients, rather than directly attempting to do away with their pathological symptoms (Balogh et al., 2021). In Frankl's anthropology, the person is an *individuum*, that is, a unity that cannot be split into parts: an indivisible entity. Not only is the person an individuum, however, but, as Frankl put it, *insummabile*, as well: it is impossible to reduce a person to its constituents (Frankl, 1982: 108–9). To put it another way, the person is a unity and a totality. The individual arises at the intersection of three planes of existence: bodily, psychic and spiritual. For Frankl, the individual is not merely the unity of body and mind but body and mind *and* spirit. What truly makes one distinct and unique is the absolute novelty that the personal spiritual component adds to one's character. It is important to note here that the personal spiritual existence of an individual is both connected *and* beyond the other two planes of existence, the somatic and the mental. Only by conscious and persistent reflection can one get to know and experience one's spiritual core. This personal spiritual core is endowed, in turn, with absolute dignity, which, in the field of mental care, signifies that those who suffer from psychological disorders are equally human persons, similarly to those who are not deemed to be normal and healthy (Frankl, 2010). A person's pathology cannot take away their personhood and their unbreakable ties to their spiritual core and human dignity, for the simple reason that one's spirit simply cannot get sick: according to Frankl, it is always intact. Consequently, healing in logotherapy involves not only treating the body and the soul, both of which are exposed to illness, but also the re-establishment of meaning in one's life that will aid one to learn about one's individualizing and invigorating personal spiritual existence (Frankl, 2004).

Frankl maintained that the last word about the self is not that it is drastically vulnerable to the whims of the instincts and drives which determine the course of action that one will take. Quite the opposite: he claimed that the person is ultimately a meaning-oriented and meaning-giving, free creature. One can sustain a life with all sorts of deprivations; however, one cannot live without *meaning*. The role of the therapist in logotherapy is to channel the attention and the efforts of the client into thoughts and action that are conducive to exploring one's potentials and to remain radically open to the possibilities of life. In existential therapy the person must acquire the skill to existentially reset themselves – that is, so to speak, to wilfully go through an existential conversion. As Frankl explained, 'Logotherapy . . . attempts to bring about within the patient a transformation of attitude; in other words, it is really a conversion therapy' (Frankl, 2010: 88). Contrary to Freud, Frankl argued indefatigably that the ego is, indeed, the master in its own house. The notion of unconscious has an important role in logotherapy as well; nevertheless, it is provided with a different meaning: it comes to signify the unreflected contents of the self's consciousness. Bringing into focus these elusive contents is possible and often feasible, too, especially when doing so directly serves the chief aim of existential analysis: finding personal meaning. In fact, the creed of the approach could be succinctly summed up as the commitment to the idea that human existence has the inborn ability to transcend its circumstances and overcome whatever adverse situations one finds oneself in. As Frankl famously put it, 'For what then matters is to bear witness to the uniquely human potential at its best, which is to transform a personal tragedy into a triumph, to turn one's predicament into a human achievement' (Frankl, 1949). That is why the spirit's ability to rise above the facticity of the body-mind is crucial for him: only through this can a person give meaning, goals and direction to life. Logotherapy, in this regard, is nothing less than healing by way of eliciting meaning from the self.

Around the same time that Frankl experimented with and fine-tuned the methodology of logotherapy and existential analysis, two other eminent psychiatrists, both from Switzerland, established the branch of existential-phenomenological therapy that came to be known as *Daseinsanalysis*. Ludwig Binswanger and Medard Boss did not work together, yet they both based their theories and clinical practices on Martin Heidegger's analysis of human existence, which he explicated in his 1927 magnum opus, *Being and Time*. It was first Binswanger who elaborated a theory that rested firmly on Heidegger's ontological principles. It was Binswanger, too, who in effect coined the phrase *Daseinsanalysis* (Spiegelberg, 1972: 193). To avoid confusion, later on Boss distinguished his approach from Binswanger's by calling it *Daseinsanalytik* (van Deurzen et al., 2019). In any case, Binswanger himself built his theory around the Heideggerean notion that human existence as being-in-the-world grasps reality in a more accurate and phenomenologically precise manner than the ways in which the reductionist and positivistic sciences do. The primary target of both Heidegger's and Binswanger's epistemological critique was of course the Cartesian mind-body dualism which sharply contrasted the individual's somatic functions with the cognitive activities of the mental faculties, keeping them apart artificially and arbitrarily. Upon this view of human nature were erected the superstructures of sciences that depicted man as a part mind/part body form of existence, without at the same time satisfactorily explaining how these two were related and why, in the first place, they needed to be separated.

In Binswanger's understanding, the concept of *Daseinsanalysis* includes, above all, a phenomenological anthropology that he defines as an empirical science (Binswanger,

1958: 191 ff.). To avoid methodological misunderstanding, though, he quickly clarifies that by calling it 'empirical' he does not mean to indicate its affinity with the natural sciences that are, in fact, based on ἐμπειρία, that is, on experiences, but to signify that they do not go beyond what the phenomenon of the consciousness reveals. In other words, his understanding of 'empirical' has a great deal more to do with the Husserlian description of the phenomenological method than with, for instance, the approach of biomedical sciences. What Binswanger is really after is, in effect, the rehumanization of the patients of mental institutions, and along with them the sympathetic observation and analysis of their subjective, inwardly felt experiences regarding all the diverse facets of their existence (Craig, 2019: 33 ff.). Therefore, by keeping in mind at all times Heidegger's guidelines vis-à-vis the analysis of Dasein, Binswanger's *Daseinsanalysis* is designed to gather evidence to support the belief that those who suffer from mental illnesses are not so far removed from those others that society – as well as the mainstream of the early twentieth-century psychiatry – liked to call 'the normal ones'. That is to say, he set out to truly understand the experiences and observations of the people that were treated as less than human: the unsanes and the insanes. Via noting and collecting the events and developments of his patients' inner, psychic, worlds, down to the minutest details, Binswanger believed to be able to build his case to prove that even the seemingly most irrational symptoms and behaviours are completely warranted and reasonable if one considers the bigger picture (the being-in-the-world) that is most significant for the individual's personal existence. Looking at it from the individual's point of view, the bizarre symptoms of a mental disorder are nothing but practical as well as sensible reactions of the mental apparatus to perceived dangers. These responses from the self are intended to protect it from a major threat that the individual could not face up to in a direct fashion. If that threat had come out to the open, as it were, the self would have dreaded its own complete disintegration, which is the greatest threat there is: losing oneself eternally. That is why winning back the self from the hazy middle zone between authenticity and inauthenticity proves to be the key curative insight that guarantees not only the mental and physical sanity of the individual but one's philosophical health as well.

The first step to philosophical health in the *Daseinsanalytic* sense is, then, to map out the idiosyncratic being-in-the-world of the person which move will likely hold the key to discovering the special significances and values of the self: whatever is being dearly protected is usually surrounded by existential anxiety and feelings of irrational dread. In this way, Binswanger's theory is closely linked with Frankl's logotherapy, too: finding the central values by which the individual can securely lead their life can be brought forth by examining what things one most dreads (of losing). Binswanger maintained that those who suffer from psychological disorders can be characterized as human existences whose worlds have shrunken to an excessive degree: their potential field of action is being experienced as minimal (see de Miranda in this volume, Chapter 17, on the 'sense of the possible'). In other words, they are unable to see the forest (of infinite possibilities of thought and action) for the trees (of their very limited and severely limiting anxieties). Philosophical health would thus consist in having the patient see once again the forest (de Miranda, 2020), to help the sufferer to experience the incessantly forming flux of reality and not to permit one's need for self-protection to debilitate the self's need to act freely. Furthermore, the therapist is responsible, according to Binswanger, to plant deeply in the patient the seed of hope that even though one sees it improbable that one day healthy choices could be made again by the self, with gradual improvement the ideal of health can be brought within a hand's reach (Binswanger, 1958: 195). Incidentally, it was Binswanger's conviction – as well as a rare instance of his criticism on Heidegger – that, rather than *care* (*Sorge*), it was *love* (*Liebe*) that typified the most fundamental motivation of Dasein. Love for Binswanger pointed to the originary belongingness and togetherness (*Wirheit*) of mankind. This also explains why he supplemented the Heideggerean theory of Dasein with a crucial addendum of what he called being-beyond-the-world (über-die-Welt-hinaus-sein) (Spiegelberg, 1972: 224–5). By placing the superior category of being-beyond-the-world over and above the existential category of being-in-the-world, Binswanger managed to replace the Dasein's customary preoccupation with its own self by a heartfelt affection for the other. In contrast with *care* (which, for Heidegger connotes not only *caring for* but *worrying about* as well), *love* introduces the individual to the most precious, bona fide ontological structure of its own existence, which allows the person to take a huge step beyond the ego-centric finiteness that is eminently emblematic of the category of *care*. Only love has the potential to fling the self over its usual fixation with its own being-in-the-world and to gently shepherd it into the realm of genuine being-together (*Mitsein*) with other individual existences.

In the history of the existential-phenomenological tradition of psychiatry, it is a known fact that Heidegger himself did not think much of Binswanger's reinterpretation of his theory of being. Likewise, Freud was also rather unsupportive of Binswanger's efforts to 'improve' his – Freud's – psychoanalytic method and to wed it with existentialist philosophy. Nevertheless, both Heidegger and Freud respected Binswanger, were on friendly terms with him and seemed to have been keen to know about the developments that came out of his clinic in Kreuzlingen (Spiegelberg, 1958: 197 ff.; 204 ff). With Medard Boss, the other famous Swiss psychiatrist from the *Daseinsanalytic* school of thought, things were markedly different. His version of *Daseinsanalysis* has undoubtedly enjoyed Heidegger's trust, appreciation and support, so much so that Heidegger frequented as a lecturer Boss's own psychiatric clinic for a decade, elaborating for an audience of physicians on the relevance of his phenomenological theory of Dasein, especially in relation to mental health. The so-called *Zollikoner Seminare* (Zollikon Seminars) that took place between 1959 and 1969 led eventually to the development of Boss's own theory concerning the existential foundations of medicine and psychiatry (Boss, 2001). His theory, which closely followed Heidegger's own, was distinct from Binswanger's in that while the latter was only familiar with the earlier works of Heidegger, Boss richly drew from Heidegger's later musings as well, in particular from his conviction that the role of mankind is to become the 'Shepherd of Being' (Heidegger, 1993: 234). As to Freud, Boss did not reject psychoanalysis, as long as it was understood as a set of therapeutic techniques, not as a comprehensive and all-explaining theory. Similarly to his forerunners in the existential-phenomenological tradition, he was a staunch opponent of the Freudian image of instinct-driven humanity which he judged to be tragically inadequate. The *Daseinsanalytik* therapist in his view should not take a stance regarding the existence of an individual soul or psyche of the person. Rather, one should remain a discerning observer: a phenomenologist who begins the monitoring of whatever phenomena is given in the awareness with a wide-ranging Husserlian *epoché*, that is, with the suspension of judgements and unfounded speculations concerning the actual existence of phenomena. Hence, just because mental or psychic phenomena can be observed and assessed, this does not in itself permit the inference that such substantially construed entities as the mind or the psyche do, in fact, exist, as well. The therapist must remain as open and non-judgemental vis-à-vis the nature of reality as humanly possible, sticking strictly to the observable phenomena, and striving to see the actual reality of another human being in a complete immediacy of the unfolding of that reality.

In line with the early Heidegger's fundamental ontological analyses, the human Dasein *in general* for Boss is that being that has the exceptional ability to shed light on the meaning of being and to continuously interpret and reinterpret the significance of events. A *concrete*, individual Dasein, in contrast, is a radically singular existence that is never quite what it imagines itself to be: it is always someone or something else than what one thinks oneself to be. These ideas, which were made up as an amalgam from Heideggerean and Sartrean concepts of authenticity, explicate that the individual human Dasein must become an existence that takes responsibility for its own destiny (Balogh, 2022). Taking responsibility for one's destiny, in turn, embraces the notion that one acknowledges one's own form of existence as something that is necessarily always bound to remain open for ever newer possibilities. One is responsible for keeping this attitude of openness to being unharmed. On top of this, from a fully mature human individual, it is also expected that they undertake, as a personal life mission, the disclosure of existential possibilities for themselves and for others as well. This explains why the role of the therapist is exceptional in this regard: they are in the best position to assume responsibility for revealing the limitless palette of colours that human existence can offer. Consequently, humanity's freedom consists in progressively enabling the recognition of the existence of all the beings as they already are and to allow them to continue to exist in their own distinctive ways – in other words, to build an awareness of them without distortions and self-deception. Coming to terms with life by letting beings be as they are, while forgoing the desire to constantly manipulate the world, is what differentiates this approach from most other philosophical and psychiatric approaches in the West while connecting itself to the Eastern traditions of the Three Teachings: Buddhism, Confucianism and Daoism (see in this volume Balogh on 'East Asian Somatic Philosophies', Chapter 16). Whereas the majority of Western approaches to the self proliferate the idea that controlling other beings and the world *in toto* is the hallmark of normalcy, traditional East Asian teachings on the non-substantial, fleeting nature of the self as well as the mutual interdependence of beings commend living in a non-aggressive fashion, in harmony with nature and with other sentient beings. Just like with the late Heidegger's – as well as Boss's – concerns with the notion of *Gelassenheit* or 'letting-be' (Heidegger, 1960), the notion of letting other beings be as much as possible, without transgressing one's inalienable responsibility for one's own existence, is vital in traditional Eastern thought, too.

To recap, then, in Boss's psychiatric theory an existential demand is put upon the individual Dasein. This demand which arises from the depth of one's self – it is virtually identical to saying that it arises from the depth of being – insists that one is to *become* something else than one already is; to transform into a more authentic form of existence. The feeling of guilt, as in Heidegger, is the best indicator for Boss, too, that one has drifted away from one's ownmost potentialities for being. The experience of guilt can be traced back to the particular feeling one must face when the voice of conscience reminds us that there is an inherent existential debt to one's being that one ought to pay up. As Boss elaborates, 'All actual, concrete feelings of guilt and pangs of conscience are grounded in this existential "being-in-debt" [Schuldigsein] toward his whole existence, lasting all through life . . .' (Boss, 1982: 48). The extreme variants of guilt frequently manifest in neurotic symptoms when one's entire organism gives somatic signs that one is getting perilously far away from the person one is meant to become. The chief function of the therapy is, therefore, to examine the phenomenological experiences of the clients, paying particular attention to their dreams, for it is in their dreams that the connections and correspondences of one's unique being-in-the-world come to the fore most distinctly (Boss, 1982). The therapy is successful when it credibly demonstrates the causes and conditions that may be behind the individual's turning away from their potential for an authentic existence; moreover, the therapist must also advise the client on the ways in which realizing their very own life possibilities could become attainable. Realizing one's very own possibilities is what, after all, constitutes philosophical health in the Daseinsanalytic tradition.

Existential-phenomenological psychiatry in America: Rollo May and Irvin Yalom

Notwithstanding the indisputable merits of Central Europe in establishing the existential-phenomenological approach in psychiatry, it was in the United States that the movement grew to become a remarkably potent alternative and, oftentimes, a supplementary methodology as well as an underlying worldview to the widely popular humanistic therapies (Burston, 2003). It was in the 1960s when, in Britain, Ronald D. Laing also applied the theories of existential philosophy to psychiatry and psychotherapy (Laing, 1961; Laing, 1969) that the human potential movement, boasting such recognizable figureheads as Abraham Maslow and Carl Rogers, began to produce a lasting effect on the American landscape of mental health care. The publication of *Existence: A New Dimension in Psychiatry and Psychotherapy* in 1958 was a pioneering achievement that presented the European style of existential analysis of famed phenomenological psychiatrists like Eugene Minkowski and Ludwig Binswanger to the American audiences for the first time. The volume was co-edited by psychologist Rollo May, who, along with Irvin D. Yalom, came to be respected as the most accomplished American existential psychologist of the twentieth century (May and Schneider, 1995).

Both May and Yalom located the starting point of existential psychotherapy in the experience of existential anxiety, or, to paraphrase Tillich, in the fundamental ontological insecurity of modern man (Tillich, 1980). The philosophical genealogy of existential anxiety or dread can be traced back to Kierkegaard, but it also heavily featured in the writings of Heidegger, Jaspers and Sartre. In Heidegger, for instance, ontological anxiety is essentially an existential disposition (*Befindlichkeit*) of Dasein which overshadows one's life from its outset till the very end; it is an existential fact that constitutes, among others, one's facticity and that leads one to confront such 'limit situations', or *Grenzsituationen* (Jaspers, 1919), as suffering and death. Ignoring one's existential anxiety is, to some degree, possible, but this will bound to produce neurotic symptoms and, after a while, cause psychological disorders for the individual that will confine the person to a very limited set of life possibilities.

Anxiety has a goal and function, maintains May: it is a response to an approaching danger that is not clearly identifiable yet whose arrival is sensed to be imminent. The logic of anxiety demands that we pay heed not to a particular source of threat but to the total experience of being threatened. More often than not the threat lies in the inaction or the wrong actions of the self – an attitude that keeps the person from feeling whole and connected. In this interpretation, although existential anxiety is evidently a highly negative experience, it protects the self from an even more threatening and dangerous eventuality that might, like in Binswanger, disintegrate the self. Thus existential anxiety is an extreme reaction to an extreme situation; specifically, to the extreme situation of having been born human and having to deal with both our boundless freedom and our facticity that dictates our playing field. For May, anxiety is the acute awareness that we must somehow tackle the apparently unsolvable mystery of our personal finitude and mortality (May, 1977). As such, existential anxiety cannot be obliterated from our existence: hence, it is named *existential*. The measure of it, however, can be reduced to a normal level with which one can not only live well but can live *exceptionally* well if one learns to constructively exploit the energies that are resting inside it and transforms them into creativity and joy (May, 1983).

Yalom in his exhaustive seminal work titled *Existential Psychotherapy*, which appeared for the first time in 1980, endeavoured to corroborate other existentialist thinkers' prominent stress on the universality of ontological anxiety by giving empirical evidence from his own clinical engagement with people suffering from mental disorders. He named his approach *existential psychodynamics* which, when contrasted with the classical psychodynamic theory of Freudian psychoanalytic school, provides a number of novelties. For example, whereas in Freud it is the unresolved conflict among the subconscious drives that creates anxiety which the mental apparatus, in turn, tries to cope with by giving birth to various defence mechanisms, in Yalom's model, existential anxiety is seen as a normal response to the realization of the so-called *ultimate concerns* that are akin to the Jaspersian limit situations (Yalom, 1980). The personality theory of this psychiatric model portrays anxiety as a fundamentally general and natural human attribute which is by no means a negative or pathological psychic phenomenon. Being anxious for Yalom simply means being alive. To put it differently, having (to manage) a life comes inevitably with having to confront the anxiety that comes with it. The experience of anxiety is unsettling and characteristically unpleasant; however, one cannot but accept its existence since it is both an experimentally gathered factual reality and an unavoidable metaphysical fact that needs to be dealt with; neglecting, or worse, ignoring it could only lead to more trouble.

Yalom differentiates four basic 'existential givens' a human individual must cope with: freedom, isolation, death and meaninglessness (Yalom, 1980: 8–9). These four together effectively shape the horizon of meanings existential therapy undertakes to sort out. Like Sartre, Yalom also believes that we live in an unstructured universe that is devoid of inherent meaning and cosmological necessity. Our lives are inescapably contingent and this constitutes an existential fact. This contingency exposes us to our common human fate that lies in the circumstance that we must make our own choices by relying on ourselves: nobody else can make our choices for us. One cannot find comfort in the idea that the world and one's own self are indispensable parts of the fabric of being, and the awakening to this truth is invariably a rude one. We would all wish to hold dearly to the naïve belief that our existence is absolutely significant and necessary for the world's subsistence. This regressive tendency of the individual to look for solace in its own self by projecting exaggerated importance and magical omnipotence (as well as immortality) to itself is completely insufficient to deal with the existential givens of life in an effective manner, points out Yalom – not to mention that it prevents one from stepping on the path that leads to maturity. Having to bear the absolute freedom that one is doomed with is a task that surpasses most people's limitations in their ordinary everydayness. When noticing how one flees from one's freedom over and over again, one comes to realize one's existential anxiety. The same is true of the rest of the existential givens in Yalom's list: isolation, death, meaninglessness. These four are all intertwined, and together they all point to existential problematic that is irresolvable. One wants to belong and be profoundly connected to other human beings, yet there is an existential wall that keeps separating the self from the other which cannot be overcome. One wants to avoid death and preferably live forever, yet, as far as we know, this feat has never been attained by anyone to date (Yalom, 2008). Finally, one wants to discover the originally given meaning structure of the universe, for having a reliable structure would mean that one could rely on the securely established constitution of the world. Yet, where we prefer to see natural laws and universal truths, we most likely come face to face with our own projections. As a consequence, the existential givens of life can never be done away: only ignored or dealt with.

Dealing with the existential givens is what constitutes the philosophically healthy attitude for Yalom, for reflecting on these ultimate concerns of human existence and actively shaping one's life rationally is the only antidote to submitting oneself to desperation. The main hope and commitment of existential therapy is that it facilitates the reduction of the pathological (secondary) anxiety to the normal levels, thus allowing the client to find out what their existential (primary) anxiety is about. At the same time, the therapist also trains the clients in focusing on how the primary anxiety can be utilized constructively for life-affirming thoughts and deeds (Yalom, 2002). Owning up to one's habitual turning away from the responsibility for the unsuccessful and unhappy events in one's life, coupled with the deliberate disabling of the consistent blame game of our everyday stream of consciousness is a vital achievement in the course of seeking a philosophically healthier lifestyle. This lifestyle is *philosophically* healthier because it helps one to clarify one's goals as well as one's roles in not having been able to achieve one's goals previously; it assists one in designing better ways of dealing with problems in a rational manner. Setting free the energies that are imprisoned in our bodies due to the paralysing effects of anxiety has the power to radically transform one's perception of reality and of oneself. Philosophical health, in the existential-phenomenological tradition of psychiatry, is based on the premise that although one is not yet living an authentic life, finding the way back to one's authentic existence is not beyond anyone's means. Therefore, the liberation of the self from both its detrimental social conditioning and its self-inflicted negative patterns of thought and action can be rectified. To be philosophically healthy in this worldview is to consciously cultivate and cherish the core belief that one has the potential to become even healthier the next day. The praxis of philosophical health care is thus a never-ending project.

Conclusion: Focusing on the more positive and constructive aspects of life

The existential-phenomenological approach to psychiatry and psychotherapy has no doubt enriched the repertoire of therapists and counsellors of all creeds in combating pathological phenomena that restrict a person's freedom and health. On the other hand, the overwhelming emphasis on the more negative aspects of human existence – death, isolation, anxiety and so on – has been invoking heavy criticism from various sections of the psy-circles. A recent response to this enduring criticism within the existential analytical tradition has been the deliberate opening up to other approaches in psychology and psychiatry, most importantly, to positive psychology. Alexander Batthyany, who is the director of the Viktor Frankl Institute in Vienna, Austria, along with his colleagues put considerable effort over the last decade to blot out the darker undertones of the tradition by offering a more upbeat version of existential therapy (Batthyany and Russo-Netzer, 2014; Russo-Netzer, Schulenberg and Batthyany, 2016). At the same time, leading cross-cultural psychotherapists such as Manu Bazzano and his associates have been working tirelessly on the blending of the methodologies of the existential-phenomenological tradition with those of Zen Buddhism, while making the point that the new approach in cross-cultural psychotherapy should not be *more* but rather *less* optimistic (Bazzano, 2014; Bazzano and Webb, 2016; Bazzano, 2017). Between these two recent developments the emerging movement of philosophical health can offer a third alternative: an alternative that underlines the importance of moving away from the psychiatric model of health definitions altogether. Instead of repeatedly pointing out the worrisome aspects of human existence, a crealectic approach to philosophical health considers abundance and creative joy as the source of life (de Miranda, 2023). As such, it is inherently positive and constructive; it does not allow room for anxiety and depression to breed and flourish. As de Miranda puts it:

> We may think of the crealectic feeling as the opposite of depression. . . . In the crealectic experience of the world, we are not looking at reality as a static and scarce resource but as a compossible and moving manifestation and interpretation among many others of an invisible source of felt abundance, a co-creation in which we are dynamically engaged. Crealectics is a program of harmonisation of our collective capacity to feel, imagine, envision, realise, and co-actualise a world emerging from the cosmological source of the Real as a metaphysical and practical 'possibility of possibility'. (de Miranda, 2021: 95)

References

Askay, Richard and Jensen Farquhar (2006), *Apprehending the Inaccessible: Freudian Psychoanalysis and Existential Phenomenology*. Evanston: Northwestern University Press.

Balogh, Lehel (2022), 'The Evolution of Sartre's Concept of Authenticity. From a Non-Egological Theory of Consciousness to the Unrealized Practical Ethics of the Gift-giving (No-)Self'. *Journal of Applied Ethics and Philosophy*, 13: 1–10.

Balogh, Lehel, Masaru Tanaka, Nóra Török, László Vécsei and Shigeru Taguchi (2021), 'Crosstalk between Existential Phenomenological Psychotherapy and Neurological Sciences in Mood and Anxiety Disorders'. *Biomedicines*, 9 (340): 1–19.

Batthyany, Alexander and Pninit Russo-Netzer, eds (2014), *Meaning in Positive and Existential Psychology*. New York: Springer.

Bazzano, Manu, ed. (2014), *After Mindfulness: New Perspectives on Psychology and Meditation*. New York: Palgrave Macmillan.

Bazzano, Manu (2017), *Zen and Therapy: Heretical Perspectives*. London and New York: Routledge.

Bazzano, Manu and Julie Webb, eds (2016), *Therapy and the Counter-Tradition: The Edge of Philosophy*. London and New York: Routledge.

Binswanger, Ludwig (1958), 'The Existential Analysis School of Thought'. In Ernest Angel, Henri F. Ellenberger and Rollo May (eds), *Existence: A New Dimension in Psychiatry and Psychology*, 191–213. New York: Simon & Schuster.

Bormuth, Matthias (2006), *Life Conduct in Modern Times: Karl Jaspers and Psychoanalysis*. Dordrecht: Springer.

Boss, Medard (1982), *Psychoanalysis and Daseinsanalysis*. New York and London: Basic Books.

Boss, Medard (2001), *Zollikon Seminars. Protocols, Conversations, Letters*, trans. Franz Mayr and Richard Askay. Evanston: Northwestern University Press.

Burston, Daniel (2003), 'Existentialism, Humanism and Psychotherapy'. *Existential Analysis*, 14 (2): 309–19.

Carman, Taylor (2006), 'The Concept of Authenticity'. In Hubert L. Dreyfus and Mark A. Wrathall (eds), *A Companion to Phenomenology and Existentialism*, 229–39. Oxford: Blackwell.

Cooper, Mick (2003), *Existential Therapies*. London, Thousand Oaks and New Delhi: Sage.

Craig, Erik (2019), 'The History of Daseinsanalysis'. In Emmy van Deurzen, et al. (eds), *The Wiley World Handbook of Existential Therapy*, 33–54. Croydon: Wiley Blackwell.

van Deurzen, Emmy, et al., eds (2019), *The Wiley World Handbook of Existential Therapy*. Croydon: Wiley Blackwell.

Frankl, Viktor E. (1949), *Man's Search for Meaning*. Boston: Beacon Press.

Frankl, Viktor E. (1982), *Der Wille zum Sinn*. Bern: Hans Huber Verlag.

Frankl, Viktor E. (2004), *On the Theory and Therapy of Mental Disorders: An Introduction to Logotherapy and Existential Analysis*, trans. J. M. Dubois. Routledge: New York.

Frankl, Viktor E. (2010), *The Feeling of Meaninglessness: A Challenge to Psychotherapy and Philosophy*. Milwaukee: Marquette University Press.

Groth, Miles (2008), 'Authenticity in Existential Analysis'. *Existential Analysis*, 19 (1): 81–101.

Heidegger, Martin (1960), *Gelassenheit*. Tübingen: Günther Neske Verlag.

Heidegger, Martin (1993), 'Letter on Humanism', trans. Frank A. Capuzzi, J. Glenn Gray and David Farrell Krell. In David Farrell Krell (ed.), *Martin Heidegger: Basic Writings*, 213–66. San Francisco: Harper.

Jacobsen, Bo (2007), 'Authenticity and Our Basic Existential Dilemmas: Foundational Concepts of Existential Psychology and Therapy'. *Existential Analysis*, 18 (2): 288–96.

Jaspers, Karl (1919), *Psychologie der Weltanschauungen*. Berlin: Springer.

Jaspers, Karl (1955), *Reason and Existenz*, trans. William Earle. New York: The Noonday Press.

Jaspers, Karl (1959), *Allgemeine Psychopathologie*. Berlin, Göttingen and Heidelberg: Springer-Verlag.

Jaspers, Karl (1971), *Philosophy of Existence*, trans. Richard F. Grabau. Philadelphia: University of Pennsylvania Press.

Laing, Ronald D. (1961), *The Self and Others*. London: Tavistock Publication.

Laing, Ronald D. (1969), *The Divided Self*. New York: Pantheon Books.

May, Rollo (1977), *The Meaning of Anxiety*. New York: W. W. Norton.

May, Rollo (1983), *The Discovery of Being: Writings in Existential Psychology*. New York and London: Norton.

May, Rollo and Kirk Schneider, eds (1995), *The Psychology of Existence: An Integrative, Clinical Perspective*. New York, St. Louis and San Francisco: McGraw-Hill.

de Miranda, Luis (2020), 'Artificial Intelligence and Philosophical Creativity: From Analytics to Crealectics'. *Human Affairs*, 30 (4): 597–607.

de Miranda, Luis (2021), 'Think Into the Place of the Other: The Crealectic Approach to Philosophical Health and Care'. *International Journal of Philosophical Practice*, 7, no. 1 (Spring): 89–103.

de Miranda, Luis (2023), 'Philosophical Health, Crealectics and the Sense of the Possible'. In Luis de Miranda (ed.), *Philosophical Health: Thinking as a Way of Healing*, chap. 17. London and New York: Bloomsbury.

Nietzsche, Friedrich W. (1882/2001). *The Gay Science*, trans. Josefine Nauckhoff. Cambridge: Cambridge University Press

Russo-Netzer, Pninit, Stefan E. Schulenberg and Alexander Batthyany, eds (2016), *Clinical Perspectives on Meaning: Positive and Existential Psychotherapy*. Cham: Springer International.

Schneider, Kirk, ed. (2007), *Existential-Integrative Psychotherapy: Guideposts to the Core of Practice*. New York and London: Routledge.

Spiegelberg, Herbert (1958), 'Zur Ontologie des idealen Sollens'. *Philosophisches Jahrbuch*, 66: 243.

Spiegelberg, Herbert (1972), *Phenomenology in Psychology and Psychiatry: A Historical Introduction*. Evanston: Northwestern University Press.

Tillich, Paul (1980), *The Courage to Be*. New York: Yale University Press.

Wirth, Jason M. (2019), *Nietzsche and Other Buddhas: Philosophy after Comparative Philosophy*. Bloomington: Indiana University Press.

Yalom, Irvin D. (1980), *Existential Psychotherapy*. New York and London: Basic Books.

Yalom, Irvin D. (2002), *The Gift of Therapy: An Open Letter to a New Generation of Therapists and Their Patients*. New York and London: Harper Collins.

Yalom, Irvin D. (2008), *Staring at the Sun: Overcoming the Terror of Death*. San Francisco: Josey-Bass.

3

Mechanisms, organisms and persons

Philosophical health and person-centred care

Michael Loughlin

In his initial call for contributions to this volume and in the opening paragraph of the *Philosophical Health International* (*PHI*) website, the volume's editor, Luis de Miranda, characterized 'philosophical health' as 'an emerging concept' (https://philosophical .health/). While he offers his own account of its meaning (to be considered in what follows), he stresses that the concept is 'open' and that the whole purpose of the new PHI movement is to explore 'its full and multifarious potential'. Elsewhere, de Miranda states that, in contrast to 'physical health' and 'psychological health', 'the idea of "philosophical health" may still appear to be a curiosity' (de Miranda, 2021). However, he also points out that, far from being entirely new inventions, the notions of philosophical care and counselling represent a partial revival of Ancient Greek ideas regarding 'the holistic good of humans' (de Miranda, 2022: 1).

Ten years earlier, in one of the first editions of *The International Journal of Person Centered Medicine*, its editors characterized person-centred medicine in similar terms. Describing it as 'an emergent model of modern clinical practice' with the potential to revive the ancient conception of medicine as care for 'the whole person', they note its transformative potential and regard it as an attempt to restore 'the soul of the clinic' (Miles and Mezzich, 2011: 207). However, they also note the serious concern that 'the nomenclature of "person-centred medicine" risks the accusation that such a term represents a further rhetorical addition to the already rhetorically overburdened nature of health services' (Miles and Mezzich, 2011: 216).

In this chapter, I will argue that the movements for philosophical health and person-centred medicine (or as it is now more typically, and in my view far more appropriately called, person-centred care) are indeed related. It is fair to say that, at the moment, both concepts are 'up for grabs' (Loughlin, 2014: 20) in that there is no agreement on a standard definition to cover all legitimate uses of the terms. Since I made this comment regarding person-centred care in 2014, the debate in that area has moved on considerably, with different views emerging regarding what is needed for care to be 'genuinely' person-centred (Fulford, 2020: 66, Loughlin, 2020: 22). It is perhaps no longer appropriate to characterize the language of 'person-centredness' and 'personalized care' as 'emerging', given its incorporation into numerous widely read, influential policy documents, including the 2019 NHS long-term plan (Department of Health, 2019; PCTC Scoping Group, 2018; Health Foundation, 2016). Over a relatively short period, this language has shifted from being marginal in health discourse to being a core component of debates about the future of health service provision and practice (Loughlin et al., 2019). However, the significant differences regarding its proper interpretation and implementation are by no means resolved, with astute critics noting a radical disconnect between understandings of this terminology in the context of policy discourse and the progressive philosophical aspirations of many authors in the field (Arnold, Kerridge and Lipworth, 2020).

My argument here is that the emerging debate about philosophical health (exemplified by the arguments in the chapters of this volume) has an important contribution to make to the development of this ongoing dialogue. On the one hand, the most plausible forms of person-centred care need to incorporate, explicitly, the idea of philosophical health. While this idea can be argued to be implicit in the work of numerous authors in the field, it is typically not spelled out, even when the contributors have an impressive background in the discipline of philosophy and its application to debates about healthcare. On the other hand, philosophical health can best be understood as a logical development of the core insights of the movement for person-centred care (PCC).

I appreciate that exponents of PCC will initially have legitimate questions about the introduction of this latest 'rhetorical addition' to the discourse, just as health workers have raised legitimate concerns about the language of person-centredness in clinical contexts. We have seen that, by addressing such valid questions, we can generate fruitful exchange on underlying issues about the nature of health, science and value, as well as the relationship between health and our understanding of physical, psychological and social well-being (Loughlin et al., 2019). The conceptual borders between health and social care have effectively been challenged, with substantive implications for health education, policy and practice (Loughlin et al., 2015). The discussion of philosophical health represents a further opportunity to expand our understanding of what it means to treat patients 'as persons', as well as clarify and vindicate the significance of key components of the PCC lexicon, including 'patient expertise', 'patient empowerment', 'shared decision-making' and 'values-based practice'.

To make the case for these claims, I will begin by identifying a common starting point for PCC and the PHI movement considering, in the first instance, what it is that they both reject. I will then use de Miranda's statements on 'philosophical health' as indicative of the positive conception of health each view embodies. This sets the scene for a contrast between what I see as the two key alternative positions regarding the nature of person-centred care. Thus, when I set out my reading of de Miranda, I will do so with the specific goal of using it to inform the debate about PCC – ideally promoting further dialogue between participants in each debate.

Philosophical health and PCC: 'Pragmatically attuned' ideas

What, then, is de Miranda's conception of philosophical health, and why do I regard it as a logical extension of the arguments for person-centred care? The emergence of these academic movements represents a progressive development in our ongoing thinking about health and care: what they reflect is an important re-focusing on ideas that have never been entirely abandoned or forgotten in healthcare thinking and practice, but that have been somewhat sidelined in the modern era (Tyreman, 2020; Loughlin, 2020). Both movements can partially be defined with reference to what they reject. They represent a reaction against the dominance of 'reductionist accounts of the person and the sort of narrow scientism that threatens to reduce both professional judgement and patient care to forms of technocratic "know-how"' (Loughlin, 2014: 18). Scientism in medicine privileges causal, biomedical accounts of disease over accounts of health and illness based on human experience, regarding the latter as the phenomenal data to be fully and reductively explained with reference to the former. At the right point in history, this privileging represented real progress, as reductionist science delivered extraordinary advances in our understanding of bodily mechanisms. However, there are inherent dangers as methodological reductionism (entirely legitimate in certain areas of science) slips into philosophical reductionism – when focusing on the workings of 'the parts' leads one to believe that the whole does not exist, that the parts are all there 'really is'. As will be explained in more detail, in biological science this frequently involves a shift from understanding the mechanisms at work within an organism to treating the organism itself as a mechanism (Tyreman, 2020).

This is a philosophical position that often does not identify itself as such, because its most strident exponents regard philosophy as a discipline irrelevant to all truly pragmatic discourse, enabling them to systematically equate the questioning of scientism with an attack on science (Colquhoun, 2011). Despite their unwillingness to subject their own underpinning assumptions to scrutiny, or to recognize them as philosophical in nature, the worldview they presuppose can be articulated and subjected to appropriate intellectual interrogation (Loughlin, Bluhm and Gupta, 2017). As a consequence of doing so, defenders of PCC have argued convincingly that we have reached a point in intellectual history when we need to reintroduce more holistic understandings of organisms, persons and communities (Thornquist and Kirkengen, 2020; Parvan, 2020; Tyreman, 2020). Scientism now stands in the way of further progress. Indeed, prominent thinkers have argued that scientism's insistence on a reductionist account of thinking and value renders it ultimately incapable of explaining the nature of scientific reasoning and the value of science itself (Popper, 1989).

What is the type of understanding that has been ignored or sidelined in the modern era but which now needs to be re-established as a central focus in healthcare? De Miranda (2022: 1) characterizes philosophical health as 'a state of fruitful coherence between a person's ways of thinking and speaking and their ways of acting, such that the possibilities for a sublime life are increased and the needs for self- and intersubjective flourishing satisfied'.

While there is plenty to unpack in this quotation, it is worth noting its significance in the context of the debate about person-centred care. The notion of 'fruitful coherence' is an interesting one, suggesting a focus on the need for integration between the different aspects of our humanity, if we are to realize our full potential. The employment of the Aristotelian notion of 'flourishing', linked subsequently to the importance of a 'balance' between our physical, psychological and social aspects (de Miranda, 2021: 4), suggests that the realization of this human potential is being equated with living a healthy life. In the context of the debate about the nature of health, this is very much a 'positive' and holistic definition, a long way away from the traditional, negative biomedical definition of health as 'the absence of disease or infirmity' (Boorse, 1975: 60). The definition put forward by de Miranda takes the rejection of this approach as its starting point, building on the decades of debate that led to the development of person-centred approaches to health.

The emphasis on 'intersubjective flourishing' is also significant and reflects extensive arguments regarding relational and contextual accounts of personhood and their implications for the traditional distinctions between health and social care (Slagstad, 2020; Loughlin et al., 2015). De Miranda stresses that this notion of 'health' can be ascribed to a group as well as an individual, and in each case, it ensures that 'the goals and purposes of the whole are pragmatically attuned with its highest ideals while respecting the regenerative, plural, and possibilizing future of multiple forms of life' (de Miranda, 2022: 1).

As we will see, the most plausible accounts of a 'person-centred' approach to health and care stress the need for an explicit focus on the concept of flourishing and the corresponding need to construe human beings as subjects of a whole life, embodied agents negotiating their physical and social environments, attempting to preserve their identity and coherence in the context of an ever-changing world (Tyreman, 2020; Hamilton, 2020; Thornquist and Kirkengen, 2020). The methodology of breaking a subject down into its component parts fails when we are thinking about how to improve human health, as does the attempt to insist on any strict, ontological dichotomy between the social and the biological. As Richard Hamilton (2020: 101) notes, 'the whole human being is not a composite made up of biological and cultural bits' because 'culture goes all the way down, while biology goes all the way up'.

What is needed instead is what Ketil Slagstad (2020: 383) characterizes as 'a truly integrative approach where the social is biological and the biological social'. Slagstad's concern is that even the biopsychosocial model – designed initially to challenge the reductionist tendency in medicine – can function in health discourse to reinforce the conceptual dichotomies of the scientistic system, such as 'nature versus culture, brain versus mind, somatic versus mental or hard facts versus soft sciences' (Slagstad, 2020: 376). There is always the temptation (in the context of our modern intellectual heritage, shaped by often unexamined scientistic assumptions) to try to 'piece together' these components of our modern, fractured reality. Something more fundamental is required if progress is to be possible at this point in our intellectual history: the replacement of the dominant worldview with a conceptual framework that does not fracture our shared, lived reality in the first place.

When we consider the 'science plus' account of PCC in the next section, it will be clear that it, too, is an attempt to 'piece together' the 'objective' and 'subjective' sides of the scientistic world, rather than challenging its underlying dichotomies. The need to avoid the fragmentation of our lived reality, if we are to develop a proper understanding of health, is a key theme to be found in the contributions to the current volume by authors focusing on the debate about philosophical health. See, in particular, de Miranda's Chapter 17 in this volume discussing the need to get beyond the 'mind-earth divide', but also Laura McMahon's discussion of embodiment and engagement (Chapter 6). Her argument that 'our very identities are from the beginning and irrevocably intertwined with and shaped by others' in a world where 'things and others call out for our engagement' strikingly evokes the arguments of authors such as Thornquist and Kirkengen (2020), for the relational conception of personhood central to the more philosophically radical approach to PCC discussed in the ensuing section of this chapter.

Thus, de Miranda's holism, his emphasis on inter-subjectivity and the realization of diverse potentials are features of his account that resonate with the work of such thinkers as Tyreman, Hamilton and Slagstad. To any student of the philosophy of health over the last few decades, the most obvious point of comparison between de Miranda's definition and the work of these theorists is its unequivocally value-laden nature. The oft-quoted negative definition of health as 'the absence of disease or infirmity' is invariably accompanied in biomedical reductionist literature by an account of 'disease' as a value-neutral term. It is the assumption of such influential biomedical theorists as Christopher Boorse that, however we (patients, practitioners and members of the public) use the term in the course of our ordinary lives, endeavours and practices, any adequate theoretical account of 'health' must explain what it 'really is' without reference to such 'subjective' ideas as 'value'. Such work takes as its starting point a strict theory-practice divide, distinguishing carefully between the language of health and illness as used in the context of our subjective, human projects and a true, objective theoretical account of health and disease provided by science. For Boorse, it is the confusion between 'the theoretical and the practical senses of "health"' (Boorse, 1975: 49) that generates the conviction that health is a value-laden concept.

On his view, 'illness' is a value-laden term because it expresses the human experience of 'disease and dysfunction', objective processes whose true description is to be found in the 'theoretical corpus' of medicine: 'a body of doctrine that describes the functioning of a healthy body' and 'classifies various deviations from such functioning', identifying the causes of such deviations with reference to known forms of 'disease' (Boorse, 1975: 55–6). The underlying logic of this position treats 'objectivity' and 'engagement' as diametrically opposed, a stipulation that not only renders our understanding of other persons strictly impossible but which also ignores the fact that science is itself a practice, and that knowing, investigating and theorizing are definitively human (and social) activities (Loughlin, 2020: 27). As noted earlier, Karl Popper demonstrated that a framework based on such strict dichotomies cannot accommodate such things as 'theoretical systems', 'problems and problem situations' and 'critical arguments'. As such, it cannot accommodate the normative structures that make scientific thinking possible (Popper, 1989).

With specific reference to 'disease', Alexandra Pârvan (2020: 104) argues that the 'split between disease/body and person' is so enshrined in modern biomedical thinking that it has become an 'instinctive ontology', not only for biomedical theorists but also for practitioners and patients. The achievement of health is equated with the identification and removal of a separate entity, the disease, that is treated as the cause of dysfunction. However, this instinctive ontology must be replaced if we are to meet the challenges facing contemporary health services, including the rise of chronic conditions, co- and multi-morbidity and the pressing need to facilitate 'health-within-illness' – and 'being healthy-with-disease' – for persons living with a wide range of diagnosed medical conditions (Pârvan, 2020: 109). The alternative, person-centred ontology involves the revival of an idea dating back to antiquity, which can be found in the theological work of such thinkers as Augustine.

For Augustine, the term 'evil' does not refer to a real property of the world, a substance or entity existing in opposition to 'good'. Rather, evil is a privation – the diminishment of that which is real, a failure to exist to the full (Menn, 2002). Similarly, Pârvan notes that something is identified as a disease because it is harmful to the whole being, to a particular person or community. This irreducibly evaluative concept of harm is essential to our understanding of the broad range of diseases identified in clinical practice. Disease is not an independent being, substance or 'natural kind' but a diminishment of the person. To understand what it 'really is', we need to understand the person, her full potential and what it means to live well within the context of that specific and unique life. When treating real people, we have to abandon the idea that there is an ideal state of 'normal health' to which they need to return, focusing instead on enabling them to realize their possibilities given their actual capacities and situation. This requires attending to their ideas and goals, their understanding of themselves and the relationship between their ideals, lives and habits.

In other words, what Pârvan (2020: 103) characterizes as the person-centred 'method of working' seems to incorporate what de Miranda would characterize as 'philosophical counselling': understanding the relationship between their ways of thinking and acting, with not simply the goal of ensuring consistency but with the aim of enabling them to realize their potential and to flourish. The concept of philosophical health is both compatible with and a natural development of the best work in PCC. Arguably, its explicit articulation could help to move the debate about PCC forward, by facilitating a clearer expression of the distinction between two dominant accounts of PCC, explaining why one of these accounts must be fully embraced and defended if the full, transformative potential of PCC is to be realized.

Two concepts of PCC

While the work of the thinkers cited earlier represents what I consider to be the most convincing and valuable expressions of PCC, as indicated in my opening comments, not all uses of the terminology reflect those I have been emphasizing in the preceding section. In this section, I will identify two ways of understanding the meaning and practical significance of a 'person-centred' approach to medicine and healthcare. I will expand on the account of the important work of Stephen Tyreman, building on his exposition of two alternative conceptions of person-centred practice and bringing out the relevance of the concept of philosophical health to the debate – in particular, seeing the introduction of this concept as a logical implication of Tyreman's analysis.

On the one hand, PCC can be understood as 'a humanitarian addition to good medical practice – considering the person's personal needs and wishes on top of mending the body' (Tyreman, 2020: 86). In contrast to Pârvan's 'method of working', this view treats PCC as 'normal science plus' the consideration of additional human, social and context-specific factors. Influential policy guidelines such as the 'Grades of Recommendation, Assessment, Development and Evaluation (GRADE)' framework (Mercuri and Gafni, 2020) address the need to 'integrate' such 'subjective' factors as the personal 'values and preferences' of recipients of healthcare into a biomedical account of clinical reasoning. As Tyreman (2020: 87) notes, this approach presents person-centredness as a 'positive psychological adjunct' to sound scientific practice, making the experience of health services more 'bearable' and potentially improving clinical outcomes. It poses no challenge to the dominant conceptions of science or the 'instinctive ontology' Parvan identifies. As such, it renders PCC a 'merely desirable' feature of clinical practice, providing no 'theoretically compelling reasons' to make 'the person' central to healthcare decisions when 'the medical focus is primarily on the workings of the body' (Tyreman, 2020: 87).

On the other hand, Tyreman's preferred approach treats PCC as a 'fundamental essential of good practice', thus providing us with the 'theoretically compelling' reason to be person-centred that is missing from the 'science plus' account. This conception of PCC represents a call for a revision of the modern conceptual framework, including a philosophical reframing of the medical enterprise, raising underlying questions about nature, purpose, science and its relationship with value. As such, it represents an unapologetically philosophical account of PCC, grounded on the premise that 'the holistic person is primal to understanding human health and healthcare' (Tyreman, 2020: 86).

The attractions of the 'science plus' approach can perhaps best be explained by consideration of recent influential work on the topic of 'values-based practice', in particular the 'two feet principle' developed by authors such as Bill Fulford (2014) and Ed Peile (2014). I need to be careful in spelling out this point, though, so as not to mislead the reader unfamiliar with the work of Fulford and Peile. It is not my claim that they would endorse the 'science plus' position as characterized here. Given that its implications are strictly incompatible with their own account of shared decision-making, I'm actually certain that they would not. Rather, my discussion here serves as an illustration of a problem mentioned in the opening section of this chapter. Critics of PCC have focused on its interpretation and implementation in policy contexts, noting that the application of the terminology can be at odds with the progressive aspirations of its philosophical defenders – in particular lending support to consumerist arrangements and an ideology of 'preference-driven healthcare' (Arnold, Kerridge and Lipworth, 2020: 34).

As I have noted in response to such critics (Loughlin, 2020), this makes it imperative that we maintain a culture of inclusive critical reflection and dialogue, involving patients, practitioners and the broader public – with concerns about interpretation and application forming an important part of the ongoing dialogue. The understanding of 'philosophy' as something one does prior to practice, getting the theory accepted by policy makers and then instructing practitioners to 'get on with' its implementation represents a misconception of the theory-practice relationship (Loughlin, 2021). Thinking is not something we need to get 'over and done with' before launching into the 'real world' of practice; thinking (including philosophizing) is a practice. As de

Miranda (2022: 1) notes, philosophy – the reflection on our fundamental assumptions and conceptions that frame our every thought and action – is not something engaged in only by a small group of academics: 'any human being possesses philosophical beliefs, intellectual allegiances, and conceptual concerns, even if not yet fully explicit or compossible', and the role of philosophical dialogue is to render those underlying allegiances explicit. Failing to engage in this sort of critical reflection is to 'allow one's ideas and attitudes, and ultimately one's behaviour, to be shaped by forces which one fails even to perceive, let alone control' (Loughlin, 2002: 16).

Returning, then, to the influential 'two-feet' principle, while its defenders do not wish to challenge the traditional, Humean philosophical distinction between 'facts' and 'values', they are keen to stress that clinical decision-making stands on the 'two feet' of 'facts *and* values' (Fulford, 2014: 11). Fulford argues that the movements for evidence-based medicine and values-based practice are not 'in opposition' but rather they are 'partners'. Citing the work of one of the founders of the evidence-based medicine movement, David Sackett, he asserts 'the need for a "two feet" "evidence *plus* values" approach to health care decision making'. Peile (2014: 20) puts the point as follows: 'Whereas, arguably, any decision involves some, usually inexplicit, consideration of evidence and values, it is the professional obligation to explicitly consider both the relevant scientific evidence and the values of the individual patient that distinguishes clinical reasoning.'

The work by Sackett and colleagues that both authors cite characterizes 'patient values' as 'the unique preferences, concerns and expectations each patient brings to a clinical encounter and which must be integrated into clinical decisions if they are to serve the patient' (Sackett, Straus and Richardson, 2000). One natural reading of this principle, then, suggests that what the clinician supplies to the decision-making process is the 'objective' side of the equation – knowledge of 'the research evidence' plus 'clinical expertise' – while what the patient supplies is the 'subjective' side: the 'values' that Sackett equates with 'preferences'.

It is easy to see how this account of PCC or, as Fulford (2014: 8) prefers, 'person-*values*-centred-care' could be interpreted as providing the basis for a consumerist, 'preference-driven' approach to healthcare (Arnold, Kerridge and Lipworth, 2020). As Yves Aquino (2017) observes, in numerous countries, increasing numbers of Asian women have been requesting 'big-eye surgery' – surgical intervention to make the shape of the woman's face resemble more closely that of Caucasian women. If this is the individual's expressed preference, does it follow logically that the clinician is respecting her personhood and giving her proper, person-centred care by meeting this demand? If the clinician's role is simply to supply clinical knowledge and expertise, and it is the patient's role to supply 'the values', then the answer would appear to be a straightforward yes. In that case, what we have is a version of PCC that replaces a crude form of medical paternalism (where the clinician determines what is best and the patient complies) with a form of consumerism that reduces the clinician to the provider of the medical goods and services that the patient 'demands'.

This model is associated with simplistic readings of 'patient expertise' and 'patient empowerment': the evidence for what is best for the patient is whatever she says she wants, and the way to empower her is to provide what she requests. Yet cases such as this bring out the difficulty in drawing credible boundaries between psychological and social issues, between ethical and broader political concerns and between the health and well-being of individuals and groups. As Aquino argues, aesthetic judgements can reflect ingrained stereotypes reflecting prejudiced and oppressive attitudes. Real patient empowerment in this case might well require challenging the racist and misogynistic culture and campaigns driving the demand for this sort of intervention – the entrenched attitudes and social arrangements that make large numbers of women feel they are inherently inferior because they do not conform to a stereotype of the 'ideal' female appearance. In such a context, to agree to meet the demand is to risk further entrenching the aesthetic prejudices that damage the health of entire groups of people.

Does this mean we have to abandon the goal of empowering individuals, or indeed the very idea of patient expertise? Not at all. You do not respect or empower someone simply by asking them what they want and making a record of their answer. You treat them as an equal by *engaging* with them. This means entering into a dialogue: discovering their ideas and values, attempting to understand what matters to them, being prepared to question and challenge the claims they make. Mary-Clair Yelovich (2020) provides an impressively clear and detailed account of what this involves in the clinical context, and the sort of 'interactional expertise' the genuinely person-centred practitioner needs to develop. Understanding the broader context of the patient's life involves much more than simply inviting her to select between available interventions – a simplistic approach that of course reflects a consumerist framework. It requires a full, human conversation, learning from her expressions of her own needs and suffering and the meaning she ascribes to her experiences (Yelovich, 2020: 336). The recognition of her expertise requires the realization that, in addition to the clinical evidence available, this personal interaction with the patient is an indispensable source of evidence in the development of a treatment plan. The goal is to arrive at a shared decision that respects the personhood of both parties.

Yelovich's account of interactional expertise clearly resonates with de Miranda's explanation of the nature and goal of philosophical counselling. As noted earlier, the goal of 'fruitful coherence' is explained within the context of meeting the person's needs for 'self- and intersubjective flourishing', not simply as the quest to establish a consistency between their ways of speaking, thinking and acting. Suppose the person seeking 'big-eye surgery' explained that she really had internalized the philosophy that members of her racial group were inherently inferior, and this is why she is taking action to change her appearance, so that it can at least approximate more closely to that of the superior race. It is certainly my hope that the philosophical counsellor would consider that an important stage in the quest to identify the problem, not a satisfactory 'solution' and the conclusion of the dialogue ('Consistency achieved – next patient!'). Value neutrality is not an option for anyone seriously working to improve human health, any more than we can avoid having any particular underlying commitments regarding ontology and epistemology. The best we can do is to be as clear as possible about the values and underlying assumptions that inform our own practice (Loughlin, 2002; Loughlin and Miles, 2015). This is why some authors are advocating a training in philosophy as a crucial part of the education of health professionals (Milgrom, 2021).

What we need, then, is the more radical, philosophical reframing that Tyreman associates with the second, 'theoretically compelling' basis for PCC. He puts the point in a characteristically engaging way, arguing that the time has come for us to 'put the organic horse back in front of the mechanical cart'. The tendency to reduce the world to its 'building blocks' (Tyreman, 2020: 87) has indeed facilitated progress in our understanding of bodily mechanisms, but the machine metaphor has to be recognized as just that: a metaphor, not a philosophically sound reductive account of human nature. Organisms are essentially whole at all stages of their development. Machines, in contrast, are not whole until assembled from component parts. Referencing process philosophy (an influence also cited in de Miranda, 2022: 4), Tyreman notes that organisms are 'always in transition in response to the ever-changing environment'. Framing our understanding of humans in this way gives us the basis for an understanding of biological processes with reference to the broader ideas of purpose, meaning and narrative that define our personhood. Ultimately, our understanding of the role of the mechanism is dependent on an underlying understanding of its role in this whole process.

Persons are constituted by 'their unique set of experiences together with a narrative that interprets and gives meaning to them' (Tyreman, 2020: 86). Far from being a curious 'add-on' to our concepts of physical and psychological health, it would seem, then, that the idea of philosophical health is the logical implication of the only credible account of person-centred care. The work on 'engagement' and 'meaning-making' published in this volume can be understood as an important development of this ongoing project. It is only by understanding the nature and meaning of a specific person's unique narrative that we can assist them in realizing their human potentials, within the context of the complex and distinctive problems encountered on the specific journey that is that individual's life.

What is more, the focus on the individual's life does not require a form of 'individualism' associated with consumerism. Our concept of the person is relational. The dichotomy between understanding each person as unique and seeing each person as a member of a community (indeed, with an identity defined by her/his/their environment) is another conceptual divide that a philosophically informed conception of PCC should challenge. Just as we do not need to reject science to reject scientism, we do not need to abandon respect and concern for the individual to reject individualism. Indeed, a proper account of the good of the individual requires understanding her/his personhood as an ongoing interaction with the world, including communities, humans, non-humans and the natural environment. For the flourishing human being, to be is to be engaged.

References

Aquino, Yves (2017), '"Big Eye" Surgery: The Ethics of Medicalizing Asian Features'. *Theoretical Medicine and Bioethics*, 38 (3): 213–25.

Arnold, Mark, Ian Kerridge and Wendy Lipworth (2020). 'An Ethical Critique of Person-Centred Healthcare'. *European Journal for Person Centered Healthcare*, 8 (1): 34–44.

Boorse, Christopher (1975), 'On the Distinction between Disease and Illness'. *Philosophy & Public Affairs*, 5 (1): 49–68.

Colquhoun, David (2011), 'Why Philosophy Is Largely Ignored by Science'. http://www .dcscience.net/2011/10/28/why-philosophy-is-largely-ignored-by-science/ (accessed 20 January 2022).

Department of Health (2019), 'The NHS Long Term Plan'. https://www.longtermplan .nhs.uk/wp-content/uploads/2019/08/nhs-long-term-plan-version-1.2.pdf (accessed 15 June 2022).

Fulford, K. W. M. (Bill) (2014), 'Values-Based Practice: The Facts'. In M. Loughlin (ed.), *Debates in Values-based Practice: Arguments For and Against*, 3–19. Cambridge: Cambridge University Press.

Fulford, K. W. M. (Bill) (2020), 'Groundwork for a Metaphysic of Person-Centred Care: A Contribution from Ordinary Language Philosophy'. *European Journal for Person Centered Healthcare*, 8 (1): 58–69.

Hamilton, Richard (2020), 'The Person Is the Organism: Overcoming the Nature-Culture Dichotomy in Person-Centred Healthcare'. *European Journal for Person Centered Healthcare*, 8 (1): 94–102.

Health Foundation (2016), 'Person-care made Simple: What Everyone should know about Person-Centred Care'. London: Health Foundation.

Loughlin, Michael (2002), *Ethics, Management and Mythology*. Oxon: Radcliffe Medical Press.

Loughlin, Michael (2014), 'What Person-Centered Medicine is and isn't: Temptations for the "Soul" of PCM'. *European Journal for Person Centered Healthcare*, 2 (1): 16–21.

Loughlin, Michael (2020), 'Person Centred Care: Advanced Philosophical Perspectives'. *European Journal for Person Centered Healthcare*, 8 (1): 20–33.

Loughlin, Michael (2021), 'Forty-Seven Years Later: Further Studies in Disappointment?' *Bioethical Inquiry*, 19: 31–6.

Loughlin, Michael, Robyn Bluhm, Jonathan Fuller, Stephen Buetow, Kirstin Borgerson, Benjamin R. Lewis and Brent M. Kious (2015), 'Diseases, Patients and the Epistemology of Practice: Mapping the Borders of Health, Medicine and Care'. *Journal of Evaluation in Clinical Practice*, 21 (3): 357–64.

Loughlin, Michael, Robyn Bluhm and Mona Gupta (2017), 'Research Problems and Methods in the Philosophy of Medicine'. In J. Marcum (ed.), *The Bloomsbury Companion to Contemporary Philosophy of Medicine*, 29–62. London: Bloomsbury Publishing.

Loughlin, Michael, Stephen Buetow, Michael Cournoyea, Samantha Copeland, Benjamin Chin-Yee and K. W. M. Fulford (Bill) (2019), 'Interactions between Persons – Knowledge, Decision-Making and the Coproduction of Practice'. *Journal of Evaluation in Clinical Practice*, 25 (6): 911–20.

Loughlin, Michael and Andrew Miles (2015), 'Psychiatry, Objectivity and Realism about Value'. In P. Zachar and D. Stoyanov (eds), *Alternative Perspectives on Psychiatric Validation*, 146–63. Oxford: Oxford University Press.

Menn, Stephen (2002), *Descartes and Augustine*. Cambridge: Cambridge University Press.

Mercuri, Mathew and Amiram Gafni (2020), 'Defining the Meaning, Role, and Measurement of "Values and Preferences" in the Development of Practice Guidelines: The Case of GRADE'. *European Journal for Person Centered Healthcare*, 8 (1): 45–57.

Miles, Andrew and Juan E. Mezzich (2011), 'The Care of the Patient and the Soul of the Clinic: Person-Centred Medicine as an Emergent Model of Modern Clinical Practice'. *International Journal of Person Centered Medicine*, 1 (2): 207–22.

Milgrom, Lionel (2021), 'Against Scientism: Corrupted Science and the Fight for Medicine's Soul'. *Complementary Medicine Research*, 28: 56–63.

de Miranda, Luis (2021), 'Beyond Physical and Psychological Health: Philosophical Health'. https://blogs.bmj.com/medical-humanities/2021/04/15/beyond-physical-and -psychological-health-philosophical-health/ (accessed 18 January 2022).

de Miranda, Luis (2022), 'Philosophical Health'. In V. P. Glăveanu (ed.), *The Palgrave Encyclopedia of the Possible*. Cham: Palgrave MacMillan.

Pârvan, Alexandra (2020), 'What is this thing called "Health"?' *European Journal for Person Centered Healthcare*, 8 (1): 103–18.

Peile, Ed (2014), 'Values-Based Clinical Reasoning'. In M. Loughlin (ed.), *Debates in Values-based Practice: Arguments For and Against*, 20–36. Cambridge: Cambridge University Press.

Person-Centred Training and Curriculum (PCTC) Scoping Group (2018), 'Person-Centred Care: Implications for Training in Psychiatry'. College Report CR215. London: Royal College of Psychiatrists.

Popper, Karl (1989), *Objective Knowledge: An Evolutionary Approach*. Oxford: Clarendon Press

Sackett, David, Sharon E. Straus and Scott W. Richardson (2000), *Evidence-Based Medicine: How to Practice and Teach EBM*, 2nd edn. Edinburgh and London: Churchill Livingstone.

Slagstad, Ketil (2020), 'Meaning and Matter in Psychiatry: A Historical View and New Approach'. *European Journal for Person Centered Healthcare*, 8 (3): 376–84.

Thornquist, Eline and Anna Luise Kirkengen (2020), 'The Lived Body – A Historical Phenomenon'. *European Journal for Person Centered Healthcare*, 8 (2): 173–82.

Tyreman, Stephen (2020), 'Person-Centred Care: Putting the Organic Horse Back in Front of the Mechanical Cart'. *European Journal for Person Centered Healthcare*, 8 (1): 86–93.

Yelovich, Mary-Clair (2020), 'Acknowledging Patient Expertise and the Negotiation of Meanings in the Clinical Encounter'. *European Journal for Person Centered Healthcare*, 8 (3): 336–44.

4

State of equanimity (*Samata*) as philosophical health

A perspective from the Bhagavad-Gītā

Balaganapathi Devarakonda

The holistic conception of health cannot be reduced to either the physical or psychological components of human life. Endorsing this view, the chapter contests the biomedical reductionist approach to health. It proposes philosophical health as something that includes various other components of human life along with physical and psychological while transcending each. However, it doesn't presume philosophical health to be either superior to or a precondition of physical or psychological health. Rather it points out that these components alone do not encompass the individual's well-being. There are other aspects of individual life, both internal and external, subjective and objective, that influence human health and well-being.

This chapter points out the necessity of transcending the restrictive modern disciplinary divisions and boundaries of health that the Cartesian dualistic model largely enforces. It argues for philosophical health that includes contemporary specialized formulations of health while transcending each of them. It aims to explore the concept of philosophical health and further articulate *samata* as a self-balancing state to be philosophical health by drawing resources from the classical Indian philosophical text the Bhagavad-Gītā (hereafter the Gītā).

The first section of the chapter aims to delve into the concept of philosophical health in three ways: (1) by probing into the very epistemology of health, (2) by looking into the definition of the World Health Organization (WHO) in extending the conceptualization of health beyond 'absence of disease and infirmity' and (3) by analysing the understanding of philosophical counselling to infer whether the aim of this practice leads us to the formulation of philosophical health as presented by Luis de Miranda (2021a; 2021b; 2022).

While looking at the Gītā, the second section reaches out to the state of *samata* as a metaphysical concept and epistemological tool that contributes to the conceptualization of philosophical health. As a metaphysical state, *samata* is interpreted as a state of equipoise of peace and tranquillity. And as an epistemological tool, *samata drishti* is construed as a perspective of equanimity to deal with objects, beings and experiences that an individual confronts. While exploring chapter six of the Gītā titled *ātmasaṃyama yoga* (self-balancing), it is argued that by cultivating the perspective of *samata drishti*, or equanimity, an individual can achieve and maintain a form of holistic well-being that can be conceptualized as philosophical health. The Gītā considers health, peace and happiness to be states of equipoise. One who is at peace with himself and others can be happy and thus remain healthy. Identifying the states of equipoise in human life and attempting to reach and sustain such states contributes to the philosophical health of the individual. Strategies for achieving and maintaining such equilibrium as available in The Gītā are presented in this chapter.

I

Academic discussion on philosophical health is a relatively recent one initiated with the work of Luis de Miranda (2021a; 2021b and 2022). It requires deeper formulations, contestations and reconstructions that enlarge and deepen the discourse that de Miranda initiates. This section aims to arrive at a broader and deeper understanding of philosophical health different from the biomedical one by exploring the epistemology of health and analysing the definition of health by WHO. It further examines what was perceived to be the outcome of philosophical counselling and whether that can be related to philosophical health.

It is possible to conceptualize and determine physical and psychological health as per the prevalent medical protocols agreed upon by the global biomedical industry that controls the status of diagnosis, treatment and cure. Based on these established protocols, the question for discussion would be: Is it possible to conceptualize, determine, measure and provide an evidence-based explanation of philosophical health? However, such a biomedical understanding of health is reductive in approach and is based on two misapprehensions: one, it reduces all health to either physical or psychological states only, and two, it views health as quantifiable and measurable. Yet, it can often be noticed that even if a person is physically or/and psychologically healthy as per the standardized healthy biomedical protocols, s/he may not sometimes be well. Mere physical or psychological fitness doesn't always ensure an individual's well-being. There are other aspects of individual life, both internal and external to the individual, that contribute to human well-being. Internal aspects include epistemological, metaphysical and ontological, whereas external aspects include social, religious and environmental. These aspects together impact the well-being of the individual from a holistic perspective.

The foregoing misconceptions view health as an absence of disease, disorder or infirmity only. Health for them is a negative state of lack of ill-health rather than a positive state of well-being. To avoid such a narrow reductionist approach to health, one has to look for a deeper and broader positive perspective of health. Philosophical health is proposed to be such a positive concept in this chapter.

Epistemology of health

If health is viewed as a positive state, what does it comprise and how do we comprehend it? In the subsequent section, these two questions are addressed with the help of the concept of *samata* as available in the Gītā. In this section, let us discuss these two questions using the broader canvas of the epistemology of health – concerned with the knowledge of health and the means of knowing health. These concerns lead us to a deeper issue: How does one know one is healthy? To put it in a more philosophically relevant way: Does one have a first-person experience of being healthy? Is it that health is only an assumption, the exact knowledge of which is yet to be known? The significance of this concern is rooted in the fact that one can have a first-person experience of illness. McWhinney (1987: 3) observes illness as the subjective perception by a patient of an objectively defined disease. Despite the limitations of generalizing, such an observation stresses the place of first-person experience and an objectively defined state of disease in comprehending illness.

Further, it is worth noting that, at least in some instances, illness results in pain that is experienced instantly and directly, thus becoming a part of a first-person experience. Whether one experiences health similarly is hard to ascertain. Nevertheless, can one assume the state of health to be a fib if one cannot have a first-person experience? How important is a first-person experience to be aware of health – given that there are other means of knowledge such as perception (*pratyaksha*), inference (*anumāna*) and so on – requires proper attention.

Illness is known by various means of knowledge such as perception, inference and analogy (*upamāna*) that support biomedical research in its determination. Similarly, the same means of knowledge sometimes provide the understanding of health either in parts or in totality. Thus, by analysing the biomedical data, it is possible to assess, at least sometimes, the health or illness of the individual. However, one must note that this determination is possible by the physiological component alone. Therefore, determining health beyond the biomedical perspective emphasizes the place of first-person experience as an instrument of knowledge. This emphasis is rooted in the fact that one can feel unhealthy even if s/he is healthy as per the biomedical parameters and vice versa. In other words, first-person experience and biomedical determination can sometimes be different. It follows that ill health is available to first-person experience beyond biomedical determination. It also follows that biomedical determination of health and ill health is limited to physical and, to some extent, psychological components of human life. Thus, they cannot provide a comprehensive and holistic conception of healthy living. One can observe from the foregoing discussion that first-person experience helps us understand the limitations of biomedical determinations of health. However, it is essential to ask whether/how first-person experience helps us determine an individual's health, especially in the background of ill health. If one can have a first-person experience of illness, how can one not have such a first-person experience of health?

Various other internal and external aspects of human life play a significant role in healthy human life. The contemporary health industry has yet to identify and develop protocols for understanding the state and process of some of these aspects.

The interrelatedness, interdependence and harmony among these aspects may lead to a positive understanding of health beyond the reductionist perspective. Thus, an answer to the earlier query drives us to the supposition that health is a natural positive state of a being in harmony with the various aspects of human life. Though this natural state is continually present, one is unaware of it. It is consciously felt only when it is either disturbed or regained. When the natural state of harmony among various aspects of life is disturbed, the first-person experience of this disturbance is felt as illness, which is sometimes biomedical and sometimes beyond biomedical. One can only infer such a naturally balanced and equipoised state of health after overcoming a disturbed state of illness. In this way, health is taken for granted. Though health is always available in the first-person experience, one is hardly conscious of it. As a natural state of harmony among various aspects of human life, health equates with peace and tranquillity. Thus, it is essential to note that both illness and health are available to first-person experience. However, the first-person experience of illness is consciously felt as a state of disturbance of the natural harmonious state. The first-person experience of health is never consciously felt as a natural state of equipoise. Such an understanding of health facilitates a positive health perspective against the biomedical one, presenting a positive state of equanimity. Thus, the epistemological inquiry benefits us with a realistic metaphysical conception of health as a positive state of equilibrium.

Though the international global health industry primarily advocates a biomedical understanding of health, there were attempts to go beyond it globally. One such example is the definition of health provided by the World Health Organization (WHO). Let us briefly discuss how WHO's definition transcends the biomedical approach yet fails to provide a holistic explanation.

Unsettling the reductionist approach: Definition of WHO

The reductionist approach to health based on biomedical understanding was strongly unsettled by the World Health Organization's definition of health. Its definition upholds that 'Health is a state of complete physical, mental and social well-being and not merely the absence of disease or infirmity' (1948). This definition transcends the limitations of biomedical understanding by widening and deepening the scope and nature of health. It broadens the scope by including external and internal aspects of human life. Similarly, it deepens the understanding of health by prompting us to go for a positive conceptualization beyond its negative representations of the absence of disease. Though the definition mentions mental and social aspects along with the physical, it must be noted that other aspects of human life, such as emotional, spiritual, sexual, environmental and so on, play an appropriate role in determining the individual's health, and do not find their place in it. Stressing the importance of these varied factors while contesting the biomedical approach, the holistic approach argues for integrating biomedical, ecological and psychosocial aspects of life in determining the health of human life. Health is multidimensional, where varied aspects of human life function and interact with their uniqueness. Thus, though the definition of

WHO pushes the borders of the scope of health beyond the biomedical reductionist perspective, it prevents itself from reaching a holistic conception.

To sum up, the foregoing discussion presents the need for a positive holistic definition of health that transcends the limits to the definitions of both reductionists and WHO. Recognizing the due value of each component of human life as well as understanding their interrelatedness is necessary for a holistic conception of human life. Such a holistic conception presents the ontology of the 'being' in a harmonious way. The harmony among various aspects of human beings and human life is a natural state of equipoise that can be considered philosophically healthy. Such a state of equipoise contributes to a balanced perspective that helps individuals manage their life in confronting various worldly objects, fellow beings and subjective experiences.

Philosophical counselling leading to philosophical health

The previous two sub-sections delved into philosophical health with a comprehensive framework and broad epistemological, metaphysical and positive conceptualization. The following discussion sets the stage for focusing on the specificities of what constitutes philosophical health and how one reaches it. The particularities of philosophical health can be located in the discussions on a philosophical practice that developed in the form of philosophical counselling, which would be the concern of the present subsection.

Historically, the discovery of the 'means' (philosophical counselling) preceded the conceptualization of the 'end' (philosophical health). The modern formulation of philosophical counselling began with Gerd Achenbach's initiative in 1981, whereas the earliest programmatic conceptualization of philosophical health is available in Luis de Miranda's contemporary work (2021a). Since the practice of philosophy in counselling terms began at least forty years earlier than the current conceptualization of philosophical health, it would be profitable to explore what is specifically articulated as the result of philosophical counselling. This articulation can guide us to unveil the implicit meaning of philosophical health available in the discourse.

The discourse on philosophical counselling, though recent, is diverse and pervasive. Various scholars and practitioners have enriched the discourse with their contributions to concepts, methods, debates and practices. The goal of these contributions is to help the individuals (variedly termed as clients, counselees, visitors, participants etc.) address their immediate and long-term concerns in life. Immediate concerns can be moral dilemmas, cognitive biases or a lack of understanding of what is essential in a situation. Long-term concerns can be self-improvement, the meaning of life, worldview assessment and so on. However, both immediate and long-term perspectives focus on the participant's self-care and self-knowledge by using methods of reason and argument in a dialogue. Clarity of thought, avoidance of self-deception and development of a warrantable worldview are aimed at in the dialogue process. The result of philosophical counselling is conceptualized (Raabe, 2001; Schuster, 1999; Marinoff, 1999; Lahav, 1996) to be either one or all of the following: enhancing rational autonomy, attaining a greater degree of rational self-knowledge, pursuing authentic self-goals, achieving integrity and authenticity in self-knowledge and action and developing responsible self-control. These aspects are projected to be offshoots of resolving concrete life concerns while working on self-development. Resolving life concerns at both individual and societal levels and connecting an individual's life with that of life, in general, are specified to be an important part of the discourse on philosophical practice. It can be drawn from the foregoing that knowledge of the self as a rational, autonomous responsible individual is the goal of philosophical counselling. As knowledge must result in successful corroborative action, an individual needs to be philosophically healthy and should act according to this knowledge with integrity, authenticity and self-control.

Extending the earlier perspective of the outcome of philosophical counselling, Luis de Miranda articulated philosophical health aptly as

> a state of fruitful coherence between a person's ways of thinking and speaking and their ways of acting, such that the possibilities for a sublime life are increased and the need for self and intersubjective flourishing satisfied. A Philosophically healthy individual, group, system or protocol ensures that the goals and purposes of the whole are pragmatically aligned with its highest ideals while respecting the regenerative, plural and possibilising future of multiple forms of life. (2021b: 92)

This definition recognizes the importance of the individual and the community in conceptualizing philosophical health. At the individual level, coherence of thought with speech and action is emphasized, and at the community level, alignment of personal goals and ideals with the common good is underscored. Underlying significant aspects of this definition are the potentiality of possibilities and regeneration. Maintaining philosophical health depends on realizing the self as endowed with innumerable potentialities and acting by consciously exercising our choice to realize individual goals as per our potentialities. This process is not mechanical or uniform within an individual's life or in human life in general. Instead, it is regenerative in consciously creating and recreating itself. Knowledge of being endowed with innumerable potentialities and regenerative creative capacity is crucial to cultivating philosophical health. Such knowledge is possible only when one moves beyond physical or psychological health perspectives towards a holistic conception that includes other aspects of the individual in particular and human life in general. This is recognized by Luis de Miranda: 'One is engaging in philosophical health when one's behaviour is careful (and *care-full*) in considering not only the physical or psychological individual balance but also a certain idea of what the collective and holistic good of humans and all beings on earth might be, starting with one's own good' (2021b: 92).

It follows that individuals have to harmonize their lives with the larger community, nature, and spiritual and cosmic components of the universe through creative regenerative capabilities. In the process, one must align life's components with its potentialities. Though humans are not unique in being endowed with innumerable potentialities, they are unique in being aware of this fact and consciously working towards realizing the chosen goals of life. This is what makes humans capable of being endowed with philosophical health. In other words, philosophical health is constituted by being aware of oneself as a being with potentialities – consciously choosing goals with integrity and wilfully working towards achieving them responsibly. The crealectic framework developed by Luis de Miranda aptly summarizes the foregoing discussion. I quote (2022: 4): 'Crealectic philosophical health is a program of harmonisation of our collective capacity to feel, imagine, envision realise and co-actualise a world emerging from the cosmological source of the Real as a metaphysical and practical possibility of possibility.'

The earlier discussion shows that philosophical health has individual and universal dimensions that mutually contribute to each other. Philosophical health involves harmony between various aspects of human life and varied components of a human being without overemphasizing and prioritizing any. It is holistic in interrelating, integrating and aligning these components in a harmonious relation. As every human being is a combination of determinate natural laws and indeterminate free actions, balancing the combination in a creative and regenerative way is philosophical health. As humans comprise an objective world with various worldly objects (natural and artificial) and fellow beings and a subjective world with diverse experiences, retaining the harmony of the self in responding to both worlds is philosophical health.

Having developed a general discussion on the epistemology and definition of health in general and philosophical health in particular, let us now proceed to look at one of the perspectives of philosophical health that is available in the classical Indian philosophical tradition.

II

Assessing various cultural resources will provide us with broader and deeper perspectives on philosophical health. Diverse cultures may have their conceptualizations of health beyond biomedical ones. Exploring these cultural resources leads us to a pluralistic conceptualization of health. There are many such formulations of health within the Indian tradition. For instance, Patwardhan, Mutalik and Tillu (2015: 3), while recommending 'the integration of the best recourses and practices from biomedical sciences, Ayurveda and yoga as a smart strategy and practical approach', formulate Ayurveda and yoga to be experience-based, non-protocol-driven systems, of health beyond the reductionist biomedical systems. I attempt in what follows to assess another such formulation in the Indian tradition of the Gītā.

The Gītā is one of the principal philosophical texts of the Indian tradition, which is often considered a reservoir of knowledge, wisdom and praxis. The Gītā is an integral part of the epic *Mahābhārata*. Its context is the battleground where Arjuna, the prime warrior of the Pandava brothers, gets distressed by realizing that he has to fight and probably kill his own kin and teachers. Krishna (Arjuna's divine charioteer) counsels him to realize his duty. This conversation is developed in such a way that the insights that are provided in the text will be helpful in counselling practices aiming at self-balance (*samata*). I look at chapter six of the Gītā specifically, which presents *samata* as an equipoised state and equanimous epistemological perspective in dealing with objects, beings and experiences. It must be noted that the early Greek conception of *apatheia* proposed by the Stoics runs parallel to *Samata*. Though they conflate on a few aspects, they diverge in their metaphysical foundations.

The Gītā considers health, peace and tranquillity to be identical. One who is at peace with himself and others can be in a state of tranquillity and thus remain healthy. Similarly, one in a state of tranquillity can be at peace while maintaining health. These three cannot be reduced merely to either physical or psychological states, though they can sometimes be understood that way in a limited sense. While explaining their combination to be a state of equanimity (*Samata*), the Gītā names it 'yoga'. The term 'yoga' in this perspective goes beyond the popular understanding of 'cessation of mental modifications' as presented by Patañjali in his Yogasūtra (2008). The Gītā describes yoga as a state of equanimity of health, peace and tranquillity. Even if we conceptually accept such a perspective, addressing how one reaches and sustains will be a significant question to address. In its sixth chapter, named '*ātmasaṃyama yoga*' (yoga of self-balance), the Gītā articulates the process of self-balancing in dealing with both the internal and external world. Rejecting the internal and external binary, the text presents a symmetrical relationship between the two, where one affects the other. It is not just the internal or the external balance alone that is required; instead, a balance between them is enunciated.

The difference between a physical and philosophical understanding of life explains the distinction between pain and suffering. Being healthy is not limited to any one of them. Reducing pain and suffering is crucial in conceptualizing a philosophical understanding of health. Pain is presented to be rooted in the body, whereas suffering is in the self. The metaphysics of the Gītā posits the 'self' as that which transcends material existence and is eternal. Both body and the self mutually affect and limit each other until one realizes the fundamental nature of the self. The essence of self is explained in terms of '*sat-chit-ananda*' (existence-consciousness-bliss) and a state of *samata*, or equanimity, where peace and happiness are in equipoise. The realization of this real nature helps the individual overcome pain and suffering, thus leading to health beyond biomedical determination. It follows that 'self' is significant in understanding an individual's health.

Let us discuss the significance of 'self' in understanding philosophical health. The Gītā distinguishes between a universal 'Self', named *Brahman*, and an individual 'self', called *ātman*. In the following section, I refer to the self in the latter sense.

Why is the self so important?

The Gītā maintains that the self is central to human life because only the 'self' can uplift itself from life's predicaments (*uddhared ātmanātmānaṁ*. BG, chapter 6: verse 5). This statement has two implications. One is the importance of self-help. The locus of pain and suffering, happiness and peace is the self. Unless the self becomes aware of them (self-knowledge) and decides to help itself in overcoming/seeking them (self-will), upliftment is impossible. Two, no other thing can uplift the self, as everything other than the self is an object of knowledge of the self and thus can't intend to elevate the self (which is the subject). The object of knowledge can attract or repulse the subject but can't uplift the self.

The Gītā counsels not to denigrate the self (*nātmānam avasādayet!* BG, 6: 5). Belittling the self in terms of its possessions and relations with the other beings and objects results in experiencing an extension of suffering. This self-denigration happens in the form of a false understanding of itself. This false understanding is explained by distinguishing between the self as a friend and the self as an enemy.

The text indeed notes that the self can be a friend and an enemy (*ātmaiva hyātmano bandhur ātmaiva ripur ātmanaḥ.* BG, 6: 5). Now the question is, how can the same self be both a friend and an enemy? And how can this be central to human life? The Gītā addresses these questions by distinguishing between a false and correct understanding of the self. It maintains that the false understanding of the self is to be subjugated. The incorrect understanding is explained in terms of identifying body, mind and senses with the self. This identification leads to associating their limitations with the self, which is the cause of suffering. The Gītā argues for conquering such a false understanding of self. The self that prevails over the wrong understanding is presented as the friend, and the one that hasn't conquered the false identity with body, mind and senses is termed a foe of that self (*bandhur ātmātmanas tasya yenātmaivātmanā jitaḥ anātmanas tu śhatrutve vartetātmaiva śhatru-vat BG, 6: 6*). By overcoming the false understanding, one can get rid of the suffering attached to it and gain a state of equipoise.

Now, the troubling aspect of this discussion is: Who conquers whose false understanding? According to the Gītā, it is the self that has to conquer the false sense of itself. However, such an explanation appears troubling as to how the self, which has a false knowledge of itself, can even identify or reach out to its originality.

X understands itself to be B.
It has to apprehend that it is not B.
The awareness that it is not B leads to the realization that it is X.

Though the earlier presentation seems sensible, it is endowed with the logical fallacy of presupposing the epistemological capacity of transcending a self-conceptualization. Unless it has prior knowledge of what it is, can the self ever apprehend its understanding as false? If it already knows the real self, then false understanding itself is impossible. In both ways, this explanation fails.

However, when we look at our empirical pragmatic life, we encounter many situations where we understand ourselves wrongly and later realize it. For instance, a person may assume herself to be a coward until she acts courageously. It is not that the person has learnt to be courageous; rather, her courage is known by acting courageously. Similar is the case with intelligence. A person knows her intelligence by acting intelligently; even if until then, she believed herself to be unintelligent. The Gītā doesn't consider this to be a fallacy. It advocates self-inquiry to be the method to surpass the false notion of self. The false notion of self readily available to the individual must be investigated thoroughly to grasp its vainness and avoid suffering. The individual's health is connected with conquering the false notion of self that covers its real nature and projects suffering. Enquiry into the self leads to self-knowledge, a state of equipoise, of peace and happiness.

The self-inquiry – who am I? (*Ko aham*?) – has been the primary concern of classical Indian tradition, beginning with the Upanishads, which represent the philosophical knowledge part of the Vedas. The tradition prescribes various self-inquiry methods, such as *drik-drusya viveka* (discrimination between the seen and the seer) and meditation, proving the falsity of the wrong notions of self and helping realize the real nature of the self. Following the Upanishadic tradition, the Gītā presents a method of inquiry in which the objects of the world, the body, the senses and the mind with which humans incessantly identify are discovered to be non-self. The metaphysical presupposition of this enquiry is that the self is the subject, and whatever can become an object of knowledge cannot be the subject. In other words, the subject can never become the object of knowledge. Hence, one must exclude whatever can become an object of knowledge to be non-self or a false understanding of self. Wrong identification of the subject with the object as well as believing that the object is the subject is the root cause of all suffering. This systematic inquiry conquers the false notion of the self that is readily available for us to believe and helps to realize the first-person experience of the self as an equipoised state of peace and tranquillity. This exposition presents *samata* as a metaphysical reality.

Samata is presented in the Gītā both as a metaphysical reality and as an epistemological tool. Relating to the present theme, *samata* can be interpreted both as a state of philosophical health and the *pramana*, or instrument that ensures health. The Gītā advocates *samata* as an epistemological perspective to be cultivated to ensure the state of equipoise that can be considered philosophically healthy. Let us discuss the way this epistemological perspective ensures philosophical health.

Samata as a state and a perspective

The Gītā offers *samata drishti* (equanimous perspective) as a solution to the problems of human life. The text doesn't refer to human life in abstraction; instead, it addresses the concrete life of every human being. It follows the experience-based approach and focuses on the concrete problems of the everyday empirical life of individuals. Therefore, one can nurture the *samata drishti* to address life's issues with a balanced approach. Concrete human life is examined and analysed to indicate that every individual has to live with three essential components: objects, beings and experiences.

Throughout life, every individual has to deal with many objects – beautiful and ugly, expensive and economical, pleasurable and unpleasurable, desired and undesired, and so on. Similarly, one has to live with numerous fellow beings who may be good and bad, polite and rude, friends and foes, close and distant, and so on. Likewise, an individual has to live with varied experiences that s/he undergoes, such as pleasure and pain, hot and cold, honour and dishonour, and so on. Irrespective of age and social or economic or intellectual status, every individual (whether they belong to the past, present or future) has to live with these three components of life. If these three are wrongly handled, it disturbs happiness and further self-peace. This disturbed state is suffering, which results in a loss of philosophical health.

The Gītā recommends that by practising *samata drishti* one can eliminate the disturbance of the equipoised state of the self. It must be noted that *samata*, translated as equanimity, does not mean treating all similarly, as it is often understood. For instance, *samata drishti* does not prescribe the individual to treat all objects similarly – it doesn't, for example, ask to treat both gold and stone in the same way. Instead, it enunciates that every object has its due place in the world, and one must ensure its due place in one's life. This further implies that nothing should be given more or less value than what it merits. To continue the previous example, gold may not be able to do what a stone can do, and where gold is useful, a stone may be of no use. Similar is the case with wealth and food. Both have significance, and one can't be merited over the other. Understanding the place of each, giving its due place to them in one's life, is *samata drishti*, according to the Gītā. An individual possesses many objects, providing excessive value for a few and poor significance to a few others. This creates longingness and disorientation. Possession and loss of what one dislikes and longs for lead to happiness and suffering of the individual, respectively. As both craving and aversion result in suffering, the Gītā prescribes an equanimous perspective towards the objects so that the individual can give them due importance and, thus, balance oneself.

The human being is relational. Human life is endowed with various relations that one maintains with different individuals. Not all individuals are the same; instead, the difference establishes the uniqueness of each. Based on the possible relations that one can maintain, the Gītā classifies people into eight categories: the well-wisher friend (*suhrut mitra*), the enemy (*ari*), the indifferent (*udasina*), the middleman (*madhyastha*), the envious (*dvesha*), kin (*bandhu*), the righteous person (*sadhu*) and the unrighteous person (*papa*). This categorization is not claimed to be absolute – a person may be good to one and not good to the other; similarly, a person may be a friend now and become an enemy later on. Considering the asymmetricity of the relations, one has to nurture equanimity – *samata drishti* – towards fellow beings by giving them their due significance in one's life.

Since people are different and thus unique, an equanimous perspective suggests that one can't expect the other not to be someone else. Expecting one to be like the other results from comparisons we often resort to, based on our likes and dislikes. Comparison creates unwanted expectations and disappointments. That is why the Gītā prescribes acceptance of people as they are to any sort of comparison with each other. For instance, in a flower garden, one can't expect a rose to be a lily or criticize a lily for not being like a rose. Similarly, we don't blame fire for being hot and a stone for not being soft. We give them their due importance and value them. A similar equanimous perspective is advocated in maintaining human relations. For instance, we often help others with an expectation of equal reciprocation and get disappointed when the expectation is not met. Expecting reciprocation is natural on the part of the individual. However, if what is expected is more than what a person can deliver, it leads to disappointment. Even if the person can reciprocate similarly, many other factors may play their part in completing the act of reciprocation. Since even if we miss some of our own expectations, we should not insist on the fulfilment of the expectations wholly. By way of avoiding comparisons and limiting expectations, one would be able to maintain an equanimous perspective towards fellow beings.

Management of objects and individuals is less problematic than managing self-experiences, as both exist as a part of the objective world. But how one lives with one's experiences is a challenging task. Managing the experiences is complicated as they are part of the self. Most of the common health problems of individuals are rooted in the mismanagement of their experiences. The Gītā categorizes experiences into three: experiences of the body, experiences of the mind and experiences of the intellect. Experiences such as heat and cold belong to the body, whereas experiences of joy and sorrow are psychological states. In addition to these two, humans also experience honour and insult, which are intellectual judgements. Reactions to the experiences of the body fall under the realm of physical health, whereas responses to the experiences of the mind fall under the domain of psychological health. Reactions to the experiences of intellectual judgements fall under the sphere of philosophical health.

Dealing with these three kinds of binary experiences signifies maintaining an individual's health. It is often advocated that to be healthy, one of the pleasurable, favourable binaries such as joy and honour and so on must be maximized while minimizing the unpleasant and unfavourable. However, the Gītā points out that we can't escape the other among these binaries if we want one. If we accept one, we have to admit the other as well. This takes us to a tricky situation where we must accept or reject pleasant and unpleasant experiences. Accepting both presents a contradiction if one appears more inclined towards joy than sorrow. Similarly, rejecting both is impossible as they are invariably related to human life. Considering these possibilities, the Gītā advocates an equanimous perspective towards the binaries by *transcending* both. Freedom from binaries is possible only by nurturing an attitude of equanimity within the self. It is not by increasing one or decreasing the other of the binaries that an individual can be happy and peaceful; instead, it is by understanding the limitations of both and giving them their due value based on possible merit. This is the perspective of equanimity that the Gītā advocates for the philosophical health of the individual.

Samata sthiti does not limit the possibilities of being creatively engaging with the objects, peoples and experiences. Instead, it is a positive state reached by gaining discriminatory knowledge of what is determinate and indeterminate. Not all aspects of life are under one's control. There are certain aspects which cannot be changed; one has to learn to accept them, advocates the Gītā. A few aspects can be changed; one has to negotiate to alter them. *Samata dristhti* encourages to act as per this discriminatory knowledge and attempt to change only those that can be amended. It is interesting to note a parallel of similar encouragement for discriminative knowledge in Stoicism. Epictetus (*Discourses*, 2.5.4–5), a Stoic philosopher, states: 'The chief task in life is simply this: to identify and separate matters so that I can say clearly to myself which are externals not under my control, and which have to do with the choices I actually control.' Such a perspective that gives expected value to every aspect ordains people not to suffer in attempting to change something that cannot be modified.

Similarly, it encourages people to consciously and responsibly use their freedom creatively to change things that can be altered. The Gītā, thus, through *samata*, advocates a balance between determinate and indeterminate aspects of life: Living in consonance with natural, environmental, spiritual and cosmic laws that cannot be outrightly changed but can only be negotiated at a minimal level; and living with the exercise of individual freedom to contribute regeneratively to explore the 'possibility of possibility' (de Miranda, 2020) of the real. The previous section envisaged this process of harmonizing life with the creative regeneration of potentialities was envisaged as philosophical health in the previous section.

It must be noted that the Gītā's *samata* as equanimity comes closer to the *apatheia* of Stoicism. The method of self-inquiry in terms of self-reflection and discriminating what can or cannot be changed – discussed concerning *samata* above – is also at the core of stoicism. However, their presuppositions and the metaphysical background are varied. For both Gītā and stoics, self-reflection leads to self-knowledge, but that self-knowledge, unlike stoics, is indestructible eternal nature, according to Gītā: discriminatory knowledge extends to the distinctions between subject and object and matter and spirituality, unlike stoicism.

Broadly speaking, the metaphysical positions of Gītā and stoicism are varied in the sense that the former advocates spirituality of the soul, whereas the latter considers the Soul to be 'a certain kind of matter in a certain way' (Sellars, 2006: 35). Unlike the Gītā, which advocates ultimate spirituality, stoicism is based on naturalistic materialism. However, both conflate in advocating a similar perspective towards addressing the complexities of life. Both *Samata* and *apatheia* refer to a balanced state of mind undisturbed by the passions that allow individuals to deal with objects, people and experiences in a composed way.

Samata urges humans to reconnect with their creative source, the ultimate reality called *brahman*, by advocating the need to know the fundamental nature of self. It calls our attention to a false self-understanding regarding objects, fellow beings and experiences. Urging us to go beyond this false notion, *samata* advises us to explore the creative inner source, the self, which further connects to the universal creative source. The Gītā presents this creative source as a *brahman*, who is existence-consciousness-bliss (*sat-chit-ānanda*). This *brahman* is the pure consciousness and bliss within the actuality of what exists and the potentiality of what may exist.

Coda

The quest for knowledge in the recent past was driven towards specialization. Excessive stress on specialization has led the world to compartmentalize various aspects of human life. One such compartmentalization is the present reductionist understanding of human health from a biomedical perspective. If one de-compartmentalizes health knowledge by integrating the specializations to arrive at a holistic understanding, this will lead us to philosophical health. Without limiting oneself to or discrediting any aspect of human life, if one aspires to a harmonious and holistic conception of life, one arrives at philosophical health. Many of the world's classical traditions have conceptualized such a holistic and harmonious perspective on life. We discussed above one such perspective called *samata*, or equanimity, as available in the Gītā. Gītā advocates *samata* as a metaphysical state (*samata sthiti*) and an epistemological perspective (*samata drishti*). This state of philosophical health and epistemological tool can be useful for philosophical counselling. As a metaphysical state of philosophical health, it is a state of equipoise, of peace and tranquillity, that can be reached through self-enquiry and self-reflection. As an epistemological tool, it is described as a perspective of equanimity from which objects, beings and experiences are viewed in a balanced way.

References

Lahav, Ran (1996), 'What is Philosophical in Philosophical Counselling?' *Journal of Applied Philosophy*, 13 (3): 259–78.

Marinoff, Lou (1999), *Plato, not Prozac! Applying Eternal Wisdom to Everyday Problems.* New York: Harper Collins.

McWhinney, I. R. (1987), 'Health and Disease: Problems of the Definition'. *CMAJ*, 136 (8): 815.

de Miranda, Luis (2020), 'Artificial Intelligence and Philosophical Creativity: From Analytics to Crealectics'. *Human Affairs*, 30 (4): 597–607.

de Miranda, Luis (2021a), 'Five Principles of Philosophical Health: From Hadot to Crealectics'. *Eidos. A Journal for Philosophy of Culture*, 5: 70–89.

de Miranda, Luis (2021b), 'Thinking into the Place of the Other: The Crealectic Approach to Philosophical Health and Care'. *International Journal of Philosophical Practice*, 7 (1): 89–103.

de Miranda, Luis (2022), 'Philosophical Health'. In Vlad Glaveanu (ed.), *Palgrave Encyclopedia of the Possible*, 1003–8. Cham: Springer.

Patwardhan, Bhushan, Gururaj Mutalik and Girish Tillu (2015), *Integrative Approaches for Health.* Amsterdam: Academic Press.

Raabe, Peter (2001), *Philosophical Counseling: Theory and Practice.* Westport: Praeger.

Ranganathan, Shyam (2008), *Patañjali's Yogasūtra.* New Delhi: Penguin India.

Schuster, Shlomit C. (1999), *Philosophy Practice: An Alternative to Counseling and Psychotherapy.* Westport: Praeger.

Sellars, John (2006), *Stoicism.* Berkeley: University of California Press.

Srimad Bhagavad-Gītā with English Translation and Transliteration (2012), 13th edn. Gorakhpur: Gia Press.

5

Logical constructivism in philosophical health

Elliot D. Cohen

This chapter examines the concept of philosophical health from the viewpoint of philosophical counselling, specifically that of Logic-Based Therapy and Consultation (LBTC), an approach that I developed beginning in the mid-1980s based on the first cognitive-behavioural modality invented by psychologist Albert Ellis in the 1950s known as Rational-Emotive Behavior Therapy (REBT). The keynote of LBTC is that people upset themselves by deducing self-defeating conclusions from irrational premises, and it uses virtue theory and philosophy to overcome the latter 'fallacies', and aspire to virtuous living – cognitively, behaviourally and emotionally (Cohen, 2021a).

The latter approach is epistemically 'constructivist' in the sense that it tolerates a broad array of alternative philosophical conceptions that are conducive to philosophical health. This sense of constructivism is partly (although not entirely) captured by Richard Rorty's pragmatic view of philosophies as 'temporary resting-places constructed for specific utilitarian ends' (Rorty, 1982: xli). Thus, while an existential philosophical construct may be philosophically healthy for one person, it may not work for another who may be a diehard Platonist, for example. There are instead a diverse lot of philosophies from which to choose in following one's own philosophical predilections.

However, the focus here is on articulation of a form of constructivism that provides criteria for *delimiting* what constructs are, or tend to be, philosophically healthy. So, not just any philosophy can pass muster. For example, a person or group of persons who blindly embraced the 'philosophy' of a cult leader whose paranoid delusions and intoxicating charisma led his devout followers on a bloody rampage could not be said to have embraced a healthy philosophy, even if it worked for some (perverse) 'utilitarian purpose' (that of furthering the megalomaniacal interest of the cult leader). Inasmuch as the criteria proposed here to root out such counterfeit philosophical constructs use both formal logic (deduction) and informal logic (identification and avoidance of 'fallacies') to promote philosophical health, I here refer to this approach as *logical* constructivism. So logical constructivism arguably conduces to philosophical health – but what is philosophical health?

Philosophical health and rationality

The concept of 'philosophical health' is at least as ancient as Plato, who defined the health of the soul as a 'friendly harmony, in whom the one ruling principle of reason, and the two subject ones of spirit and desire are equally agreed that reason ought to rule, and do not rebel' (Plato, 1931: 65). For Plato, such 'friendly harmony' resulted in a Just soul wherein reason exemplified the virtue of Wisdom; the appetites exemplified Temperance; and spirit, Courage (Plato, 2016). It then took Plato's student Aristotle to expand these virtues to include a stock of other related virtues, chief among which included Phronesis (practical wisdom), which pertains to a settled habit or disposition to choose the situational mean between excess and deficiency, 'this being determined by a rational principle, and by that principle by which the man of practical wisdom would determine it' (Aristotle, 2009: bk. 2, ch. 6).

For Aristotle, Phronesis involved the practical syllogism, consisting of an 'opinion' and a 'rule', the former making an empirical judgement, the latter prescribing action, or forbidding it (Aristotle, 2009: bk. 7, ch. 3); for example, 'You should avoid unhealthy foods (the rule); this candy is unhealthy (the opinion)'; so you respond *behaviourally* by avoiding eating this candy (the conclusion in action). However, under the influence of a strong desire for sweets, one might instead reason, 'Sweet things should be eaten; this candy is sweet', and consequently gobble down the unhealthy candy!

In addition to behavioural responses, Aristotle held that such practical syllogisms could generate *emotional* incontinence:

> Outbursts of anger and sexual appetites and some other such passions, it is evident, actually alter our bodily condition, *and in some men even produce fits of madness. . . .*
> It turns out that a man behaves incontinently [has outbursts of emotion] under the influence (in a sense) of a rule and an opinion. (Aristotle, 2009: bk. 7, ch. 3)

It is in this Aristotelian sense that the 'friendly harmony' of the soul (philosophical health) addressed by Plato can be impaired by one's faulty behavioural and emotional reasoning in terms of the practical syllogisms one constructs to cope with the vicissitudes of everyday life. Such reasoning is largely enthymematic wherein the rule is often implicit, that is, assumed (Cohen, 2006). For example, in 'That crazy idiot just cut me off on the freeway going 100 miles per hour!' the rule that 'Anyone who would do such a thing is a crazy idiot' is assumed, not explicitly stated. It is also in these terms that healthy 'virtuous' constructions can be fashioned that situationally seek the mean between excess and deficiency. 'I should best maintain my composure else I defeat my concern for safety.'

Practical syllogisms and illocutionary acts

The idea that practical syllogisms (arguments involving conclusions about everyday life) can have as their conclusions acts as well as emotions raises technical questions. Inasmuch as the conclusion of a deductive argument is 'contained' in the premises

(Kant, 1999: A6–7), speaking of the conclusion as anything other than a linguistic construction raises some red flags.

Still, Aristotle seems right that there is at least a quasi-logical connection between the premises of a practical syllogism and actions and emotions. Thus, if I think sweet things should be tasted, and that this candy is sweet, then *ceteris paribus*, I will taste it. Of course, the *ceteris paribus* rider may not be satisfied in a particular case. I may be physically constrained from tasting the candy, or I may exercise willpower over tasting it because I entertain a syllogism bidding me to restrain myself ('I should avoid tasting unhealthy foods, and this candy is unhealthy'). This quasi-logical relationship is explicable in terms of the illocutionary act potential of the language used in practical syllogisms, for example, 'should' in the above example (Cohen, 2021a). Thus, in saying 'You *should* avoid unhealthy foods', one is not merely reporting or describing a state of affairs but instead *prescribing* an action, and it would be 'logically odd' although not contradictory to prescribe something yet not act on it when relevantly situated. Similarly, some language has emotive force such as 'bastard', 'loser' and 'worst thing ever' as in 'You are a bastard', 'I am a loser' and 'If I don't get into Harvard then it will be the worst thing ever'. The first *damns another*, the second *damns oneself*, and the third *catastrophizes*. Such linguistic acts are, in turn, associated with certain emotions: in particular, anger, despondency or depression, and anxiety.

The latter illocutionary acts are themselves deductions from a rule and a report premise in a practical syllogism, as in the below examples that track various (negative) emotions:

Anger:
If you lied to me then you are a bastard.
You lied to me.
So, you are a bastard.

Depression:
If my wife divorced me then I'm a loser.
My wife divorced me.
So, I am a loser.

Anxiety:
If I don't get into the school of my dreams, then it's the worst thing ever.
If I don't get into Harvard, then I don't get into the school of my dreams.
So, If I don't get into Harvard, then it's the worst thing ever.

Such syllogisms track streams of associated images and interoceptive feelings on a phenomenological level (Cohen, 2021a; 2021b). For example, I associate the negatively valent image of my being lied to with the damning rating of you being a 'bastard' wherein the latter pejorative term expresses a negatively valent somatosensory (visceral) feeling as well as amplifies such a feeling. Thus, it is false or oversimplified to maintain that the emotions in question are *caused* by their respective syllogisms and may be more accurate to say that their syllogisms *(interactively) express* them.

So understood, human beings construct their own behavioural and emotional reality by logically deducing conclusions with (prescriptive or emotive) illocutionary act potential from *irrational* premises in their practical syllogisms (Cohen, 2021a). However, they also have the capacity to 'deconstruct' (dismantle) and 'reconstruct' the latter reality constructions through philosophical interpretations of reality (Cohen, 2017). These irrational logical constructions consisting of such practical syllogisms are a choice, and human beings have the capacity to reject them and choose more life-affirming, productive syllogistic constructs. Unfortunately, many who embrace the former syllogisms live in 'bad faith', that is, lie to themselves, by denying their freedom and responsibility for their reality constructions (Sartre, 2007). Thus, they 'can'tstipate' themselves by holding on to them, telling themselves that reality cannot be constructed any other way – that the bleak reality they have painted is the only true reality (Cohen, 2022b). This in turn allows counselees to continue to uphold (ruminate about) and refuse to relinquish their self-defeating reality constructs. 'If you lied to me, you are a bastard and, *therefore*, I *can't* help feeling anger toward you.' In this manner, the counselee may sustain poor philosophical health.

The question of where poor philosophical health leaves off and mental illness begins is an interesting one. I am inclined to think that philosophical health is the basic construct and that mental health is a function of the latter. When philosophical health suffers to the point that a counselee is not able to function in everyday life, then he can be said to be mentally ill. According to American Psychiatric Association (2013), 'a mental disorder is a syndrome characterized by clinically significant disturbance in an individual's cognition, emotion regulation, or behaviour that reflects a dysfunction in the psychological, biological, or developmental processes underlying mental functioning' (p. 20), wherein 'clinical significance' is operationally defined in terms of distress or impairment in important areas of functioning such as socially and occupationally. This suggests that there are rational (or philosophical) limits beyond which one becomes mentally ill, that is, unable to function in everyday life.

Rational limits of reality construction: The Cardinal Fallacies

Thus, to say that counselees are free to accept and change their syllogistic constructions does not mean that there are no rational limits to what one can believe. Indeed, while there is more than one rational way of slicing reality, there are also limits to what can count as 'realistic' or 'reasonable'. The Aristotelian mean applies here insofar as irrational thinking tends to be extreme or absolutistic. For example, demanding perfection is irrational because it is all-or-nothing thinking; that is, things must be perfect, or they are awful or otherwise intolerable.

In LBTC, such rational limits are observed by avoiding eleven related forms of 'Cardinal Fallacies' in constructing behavioural and emotional reasoning. Hence, *ceteris paribus*, reality constructions that avoid these fallacies are considered realistic for practical purposes. That is, the reason for recognizing avoidance of these fallacies as the standard for acceptable reality constructions is purely pragmatic. In fact, I have defined a 'fallacy' operationally as 'a way of thinking or reasoning that has a proven track record of frustrating personal and/or interpersonal happiness' (Cohen, 2013a), and my counselling practice led me to identify eleven types of thinking that are especially dangerous to personal and/or interpersonal happiness – hence the term 'cardinal' (Cohen, 2013b).

Chief among these fallacies is Demanding Perfection, which arises from an absolutistic, unrealistic, anti-philosophical, perfectionistic view of reality. There are at least twelve different forms of this fallacy (Cohen, 2020; 2021a). Some of these are rooted in the Freudian id that seeks an 'excess of the satisfaction' which cannot realistically be obtained (Freud, 1922). This type of perfectionism appears to include perfectionism, such as the demand for control and the demand for immediate gratification. Other forms appear to be rooted in the Freudian superego (Freud, 1981), such as moral perfectionism (One must never do anything wrong) and existential perfectionism (Nothing bad must ever happen) (Cohen, 2020; 2019b).

Table 5.1 sums up some common forms of perfectionism.

Such diverse forms of perfectionism are at the root of different philosophical unhealth wherein there is disequilibrium between the Platonic (or Freudian) balance between reason/ego, the passions/id and the spirit/superego (Cohen, 2019a). Restoring philosophical health involves relinquishing such 'infected' premises and replacing them with empowering, homeostatic ones.

For example, the hedonic demand for immediate gratification leads to low frustration tolerance, which involves foregoing short-term pleasures for longer-lasting ones. This unhealthy reality construction might proceed syllogistically by deducing *can't*stipation from the latter demand:

1. I *must* not have to wait to get what I want.
2. But this will take a lot of time.
3. Therefore, I *couldn't stand* to wait.

Table 5.1 Perfectionism Types

Type of Perfectionism	Definition
Outcome Certainty	Demanding certainty about the outcomes of one's actions
Existential Certainty	Demanding certainty that bad things won't happen to oneself or one's loved ones
Control	Demanding control of actions or events to prevent unwanted consequences
Moral Certainty	Demanding certainty that one won't do (morally) bad things
Treatment	Demanding that others always treat one fairly
Expectation	Demanding that others always satisfy one's expectations
Existential	Demanding that the world not contain bad things
Performance	Demanding perfect or near-perfect performance at least in things one deems important
Hedonic	Demanding immediate (or fast) gratification
Epistemic	Demanding that reality be just what one says it is
Approval	Demanding the affection, confidence or approval of others as a condition of one's own self-worth
Neatness	Demanding that the world be neat and orderly

Here the counselee relinquishes his freedom and responsibility for his lack of motivation by deducing that he is incapable of waiting. That is, if he *can't* stand to wait, then it is not possible for him to wait. However, since it is not possible for him to wait, he is no longer responsible for not waiting, for he is not free to do what is not possible.

The illocutionary force of 'must' in the first premise is that of a demand for immediate gratification which is contradicted by the empirical report that the goal in question will not be achieved immediately. This contradiction is, in turn, destabilizing, which leads the counselee to *feel* threatened, thereby leading to the linguistic act of disavowing his freedom and responsibility in the conclusion of the syllogism. In this manner, unhealthy reality constructions are often products of destabilizing, threatening conflicts generated by a type of demand for perfection out of alignment with an empirical report in Table 5.1.

This is not to say that there are no healthy types of perfectionism. Indeed, many well-adjusted people have perfectionistic ideals towards which they strive. However, the difference lies in illocutionary force. Whereas healthy perfectionists *commend or approve* perfection *as an aspirational goal*, they do not *demand* that they attain it. Thus, the healthy virtuoso or seasoned athlete aspires to perform perfectly on the stage or in the field, but at the end of the day, he knows that there's always going to be room for improvement. So, he continues to practice improving his performance, realizing that mistakes are part of the process of growth, and thereby avoids the self-defeating anxiety of *demanding* perfection.

Table 5.2 Cardinal Fallacies and Their Respective Guiding Virtues in LBTC

Cardinal Fallacy	Guiding Virtue
1. Demanding Perfection	Metaphysical security (security about reality)
2. Jumping on the Bandwagon (blind conformity or parroting)	Authenticity (being your own person)
3. The World-Revolves-Around-Me (ego-centric thinking)	Empathy (connecting with others)
4. Awfulizing/Catastrophizing	Courage (in the face of perceived adversity)
5. Damnation (of self, one's life, others or the universe)	Respect (unconditional acceptance of self, one's life, others or the universe)
6. *Can't*stipation (disavowing freedom and responsibility by saying one can't):	Self-control:
Emotional	Temperance
Behavioural	Decisiveness
Volitional	Tolerance/Patience
7. Dutiful Worrying (perceived duty to worry)	Prudence (in addressing moral problems)
8. Manipulation (threats, well-poisoning, bullshitting, deception)	Empowerment (of others)
9. Oversimplifying Reality (overgeneralizing, bifurcating, dilemma thinking)	Objectivity (in making relatively unbiased discernments in practical affairs)
10. Distorting Probabilities	Foresightedness (in assessing probabilities)
11. Blind Conjecture (unsupported explanations, post hoc thinking, magical thinking, hypotheses contrary to fact)	Scientificity (in providing empirical explanations)

To facilitate such growth, the healthy perfectionist adopts and rationally applies a philosophical view that promotes virtues such as Patience and Tolerance (Cohen, 2021a). Each of the cardinal fallacies has at least one corresponding 'guiding virtue' that, following the Platonic-Aristotelian model, counteracts the fallacy in question (Cohen, 2007), which, in turn, helps to restore or improve philosophical health. Table 5.2 provides a list of each cardinal fallacy and its respective guiding virtue.

The Cardinal Fallacies and their respective guiding virtues

Fallacy sets 1 through 8 generally occur in the major premises of the syllogistic constructions of behavioural and emotional reasoning whereas sets 9 through 11 occur as empirical reports in the minor premises (Cohen, 2017). Collectively, in my counselling practice, I have found these eleven fallacies to be the most salient fallacies involved in counselees' behavioural and emotional problems (Cohen, 2013b). Cognitive-behavioural psychotherapies have identified many of them, but not all, as salient contributors to mental illness. Rational-Emotive Behavior Therapy (REBT) has tended to emphasize sets 1 through 9, particularly perfectionism, awfulizing, damnation and (volitional) *can't*stipation (Ellis, 1990), while Cognitive Therapy (Beck, 1979) has focused largely on fallacy sets 9 through 11, especially overgeneralizing and unsupported explanations.

Guiding virtues consist of habits or dispositions to think, feel, desire and act in ways that are conducive to mental and spiritual well-being. Therein lies the core meaning of philosophical health. Thus, the person who is metaphysically secure, authentic, empathetic, courageous, respectful, self-controlled, prudent, empowering, objective, foresighted and scientific is ipso facto philosophically healthy. Importantly, however, such habits are always in a process of development, and no one is entirely self-actualized. Thus, like the fine virtuoso, there is no limit to how philosophically healthy one can become. The more one *practices* these virtues in overcoming their corresponding fallacies, the more philosophically healthy one can become. I dare say that none of us ever reach perfection, and all of us, yes all of us, have fallacious tendencies. Thus, a recovery model (according to which we are always recovering and never cured and thus always subject to relapse) is a helpful approach (Cohen, 2019). We are all prone to commit fallacies; for example, based on a study I conducted of more than two thousand participants, about half tended to demand perfection of one sort or another (Cohen, 2019), and we are all subject to backsliding. So, the concept of 'recovery' rather than 'cure' makes sense in speaking about philosophical health.

Philosophical reality constructs

What makes philosophical health as defined here 'philosophical' is the intimate connection between being virtuous and being philosophical. More precisely, the guiding virtues of each of the eleven fallacies may be interpreted differentially according to one's philosophical worldviews. For example, to philosophically interpret Tolerance, a Stoic interpretation could be constructed by embracing the theory of human freedom according to which the physical world is wholly determined, whereas one's subjective life is wholly in one's power. Thus spoke Marcus Aurelius:

> Of things that are external, happen what will to that which can suffer by external accidents. Those things that suffer let them complain themselves, if they will; as for me, as long as I conceive no such thing, that that which is happened is evil, I have no hurt; and it is in my power not to conceive any such thing. (Aurelius, 2017: bk. 7, ch. 11)

The enthymematic conclusion yielded by such a philosophical construction of reality is clearly that it is in one's power not to suffer. As such, one's tolerance for emotional pain may largely if not entirely depend on one's conception of reality. Casting a perceived event as 'evil' – or 'awful' or 'horrible' – merely sets oneself up to suffer and to lose Tolerance or Patience. Thus, much depends on the language one uses to construct reality. The idea here is not merely to reframe a situation in less negatively valent language after the fact but to avoid use of such self-defeating language in the first place (Ellis, 2010).

Buddhism may provide an alternative construction of reality. On this view, the fixation on short-term gratification rather than long-term happiness, and the dysphoria it generates, is based on the illusion of a self – the 'I' or 'me' – that possesses pleasure and avoids pain (Shantideva, 1979). The Buddhist's answer is to reframe happiness and suffering as universal constructs, not individual possessions – that which is shared, not hoarded. To accomplish this, one needs to cultivate Patience – the 'stillness' of mind, to wait rather than to grasp and cling to the immediate feelings of gratification. Indeed, the pain arises because of such attachment and clinging, not in the loss of the gratifying feeling itself. When pleasure comes to the patient person, it is not in such a frantic way; it is thus enjoyable while it lasts without the dread of having to let go. 'It is the fault of the childish that they are hurt', admonishes Indian sage Shantideva (1979). 'For although they do not wish to suffer they are greatly attached to its causes'; that is, they defeat their own purposes by clinging to things that are by their nature impermanent.

Whether a counselee embraces Buddhism, Stoicism or some other philosophical antidote, it is not to be dictated by the philosophical practitioner, however. It is instead the counselee's worldview that is primary. One cannot force-feed philosophy. In the act of attempting to do so, the practitioner scuttles the prospect for philosophical health. Thus, while virtues such as Patience, Perseverance, Prudence and Temperance, among others are intersubjectively shared, the philosophical frames through which they are constructed or reconstructed are a function of the counselee's subjective view of reality.

Resonance of a philosophy for one counselee may be dissonance for another. A religious counselee may resonate with St Thomas. while an atheist may find the same thoughts abhorrent and resonate instead with the anti-religious (at least in the traditional sense) constructions of Nietzsche. This requires Tolerance and Patience of the practitioner, who models such virtues for counselees to emulate through their own philosophical lenses. Logical constructivism thus provides the form through which a diverse lot of philosophical perspectives are expressed. This form includes the form of the practical syllogism in terms of which behavioural and emotional reasoning is expressed; identification of Cardinal Fallacies such as Demanding Perfection, Catastrophizing and Damnation (of self, others, and the world) that can infect the premises of the latter syllogisms and destroy the prospect for philosophical health; the refutational process that exposes internal inconsistencies; and a corresponding set of guiding virtues for overcoming such fallacies, which are interpreted according to the diverse and sundry philosophical perspectives held by counselees (Cohen, 2007). Within this broad framework, counselees are free to construct their own philosophical worldviews.

Such philosophical constructs involve the *linguistic* construction of philosophical worldviews to build meanings that *empower* counselees to overcome self-defeating emotions and behaviour. As discussed in the section 'Phenomenology of Logical Constructivism', they also utilize *imagery* to key into felt meanings – the feelings of necessity expressed in deontic language such as 'ought', 'should' and 'must'; and the visceral feelings expressed, sustained and intensified by negative valences of language such as in 'awful', 'loser' and 'failure'. Such imagery helps counselees to key into the feelings expressed through such language in conflict with their reality judgements ('I *must* be in control at all times but I am *not* in control now!'). Indeed, as I discussed elsewhere applying neurological studies, it is such contradictory aspects of the logical construct that can lead to threatening and disempowering feelings (Cohen, 2021a).

Modal concepts and anxiety

Constructs such as 'possibility' and 'impossibility' are paramount in examining the latter conflicts – it is *impossible* to always be in control. It is always *possible* in the future to lose control even if one is presently in control. This gap between the present and the uncertainty of the future is indeed the basis of anxiety, which the philosophically healthy person comprehends on both intellectual and emotional levels.

Modal expressions of possibility, impossibility and necessity can figure in the practical syllogisms that track anxiety. In anxiety, the counselee commonly generates a rule perceived to be necessarily true and a report about a possible state of affairs or event. For example:

1. *Necessarily,* if I don't find a job teaching philosophy (after getting a PhD in it). then my life will not be worth living.
2. *It's possible that* (there's a possible world in which) I won't find a job teaching philosophy.
3. So, *it's possible that* my life will not be worth living.

In this case, it is thus the *possibility* as expressed in conclusion 3 that one's life will not be worth living which leaves one in a suspended state of anxiety. However, the refutation of such a reality construct may begin with the realization that premise 1 is false – that it is not necessarily true that not finding a job teaching philosophy implies a life not worth living. This is because one can also imagine a possible world in which one finds meaning in an alternative profession, for example, doing philosophical counselling. Since premise 1 is offered as a necessary truth, notice that all that is necessary to refute it is a thought experiment, that is, simply imagining a possible world in which it is false. This does not mean that the counselee must renounce his quest for a suitable teaching post. It simply means that he or she can still imagine a meaningful existence notwithstanding.

Once this necessity is thus refuted, the modal conclusion in 3 can be exposed as a non-sequitur. The possibility of not finding a job teaching philosophy does not entail a possible world in which one's life is not worth living. Still, it is the necessity of the rule and the possibility of the report that generate the possibility of a meaningless life ahead and hence the anxiety of not knowing whether this possibility will come to fruition. However, refutation of an irrational rule only sets the stage for more uplifting reality constructions.

Once the initial syllogism is rejected, a new more constructive reality can be built on its ashes:

Necessarily, if I can do something else like philosophical counselling, then I can still find meaning in the world.
It is possible that I can do something else like philosophical counselling.
So, it is possible that I can still find meaning in the world.

In the latter syllogism, the conclusion points to new yet unexplored possibilities for finding meaning in the world. This opens new avenues for reconstructing the way the future is itself perceived. Far from being a vast reservoir of woes waiting to besiege us as we make our way through time, the future becomes an infinite panoply of opportunities to explore new and exciting ways of fashioning a life. This is where the philosophical counsellor can help facilitate the counselee's identification and exploration of further possibilities and, ultimately, construction of a behavioural plan to bring about one of these possibilities (Cohen, 2021a).

Unfortunately, many counselees demand certainty about the future before they pursue such new avenues. This leaves them inertly tied to the status quo, afraid to take risks, clinging to the present, no matter how unfulfilling it may be.

I must be certain that I will succeed in whatever I do.
But it is possible that I won't succeed in doing something new and different.
Therefore, I *can't* take the risk!

Here, the counselee deduces 'can't' from 'must'. While the 'must' stipulates necessity, the 'can't' disavows the capacity to transcend this necessity. Thus, the perfectionistic demand utilizing modal terms such as 'must' ('need' or 'have to') set the logical stage for the deduction of incapacity to make constructive change.

The prime goal of philosophical therapy is thus to help such counselees to let go of their 'must' and accept possibility as an opportunity to find new meanings in the finitude of life. Aquinas once said that if a captain wanted to play it safe, he would keep his ship in port. But this would be to defeat the point of having a ship. By adopting a philosophical perspective that supports reconstructing possibility with a positive valence, the counselee can thus stop clinging to past as a way of coping with the future.

Existential philosophers have had much to say about how to think about the future in relation to the past. Thus, Sartre has proclaimed that 'existence precedes essence', meaning that we are free and responsible for who we are and who we become through the actions we take in confronting the future (Sartre, 2007: 20). This is a philosophy of courage wherein one can only define oneself (positively) through one's actions. Sartre admonishes,

> In life, a man commits himself and draws his own portrait, outside of which there is nothing. . . . What we mean to say is that a man is nothing but a series of enterprises, and that he is the sum, organization, and aggregate of the relations that constitute such enterprises.

Thus, philosophical health may involve overcoming the demand for certainty by adopting a philosophy of courage. For some, this may be facilitated by embracing an existential perspective such as:

Embrace possibility as an opportunity to define yourself through your actions. It is
    possible that I can find a new creative way to apply my philosophical training.
Therefore, I *can* define myself by pursuing such a creative possibility!

The term 'can' in the conclusion of the previous syllogism is the language of liberation from the modal prison erected using terms of necessity (and hence impossibility) to stifle one's own freedom. It is to accept rather than deny one's freedom and responsibility to make constructive change. To forestall any misunderstanding that this is simply a matter of language use, and therefore the remedy to overcoming one's *can't*stipation is simply to change one's language, it is important to emphasize that behind these modal terms are felt needs. So, a counselee who embraces the demand for certainty does not merely say that he must have certainty, he also *feels* this necessity. So, logical constructivism recognizes an introspective, affective, self-referential level of reality construction as well as a linguistic one. The felt need conditions the linguistic expression of the latter feeling as well as helps to amplify it. That is, saying 'I must' makes the feeling more compelling. Hence there emerges a vicious cycle.

Changing the language – saying 'I can' instead of 'I can't' or saying 'I prefer not' instead of 'I must not' – can mark a beginning to breaking the vicious cycle. However, much like the man who keeps repeating 'I am not afraid!' he may still be petrified because the feelings persist notwithstanding. Hence, working on the feeling phenomenologically as discussed in the following can be an important part of cultivating philosophical health.

The phenomenology of logical constructivism

In this regard, I have spoken of interoceptive imagery, which involves using a philosophical construction to reverse the somatosensory felt needs undergirding perfectionistic demands. So, the counselee may be asked to work herself into a state where she feels the necessity of being certain she will succeed at a new venture. Suppose she thinks of failing at a job for which she is considering applying. She then keys into the felt need to not fail and feels the threatening clash between this need and the possibility that she could fail at the new venture. She experiences a (visceral, gut) feeling of disempowerment arising from this threat, all of which feelings coalescing into the anxiety of this negative, future possibility.

While in the ensuing painful state of consciousness, she is then asked by the counsellor to reframe her reality in terms of the philosophical construct she embraces. For example, she then shifts her intentional object to the Sartrean concept that humans are 'the sum, organization, and aggregate of the relations that constitute such enterprises' so that, in applying for the job, she is defining herself positively, building her essence by pursuing her dreams rather than defining herself negatively as 'a broken dream, aborted hopes, and futile expectations'. Once having shifted to the philosophical state of conscious awareness, she is asked to provide a first-person report of how she is feeling.

Oftentimes counselees report having experienced an incredible sense of relief, or a sense of freedom through the shift in imagery, having been released from the bondage of a perfectionistic demand and its underlying somatosensory feelings. In some cases, the philosophy does not help to reverse the polarity of the initial negative state of consciousness or does so only slightly. This is accordingly regarded as a sign to look further for a philosophical antidote that better resonates with the counselee. Sometimes this involves taking up an entirely different philosophical construct, while other times it involves supplementing the previous philosophy. For example, not only am I the sum of my actions but also my failures serve only to make me stronger. Suffering, says Friedrich Nietzsche, ennobles (Nietzsche, 1954). Philosophical health is thereby nourished by phenomenologically building a sense of solace in the thought of failure through a philosophy or combination of philosophical ideas that resonate well with the individual counselee.

Whether it is attained through the atheistic existentialism of Sartre or Nietzsche, the fire and brimstone of Jonathan Edwards, the mysticism of Plotinus or the pragmatism of William James, the goal is to reverse the negative polarity of the counselee's irrational syllogistic constructs to the positive polarity of a philosophical construct that resonates with the counselee. As such, it does not matter if the counselee receives her uplifting philosophy through a discussion of a favourite song or literary work, or even the pondering of a quote from a complex philosophical text, or a combination of all of these. Insofar as the formal requirement discussed earlier is satisfied – no commission of cardinal fallacies, internally consistent, supporting a guiding virtue – and the philosophical construct resonates with the counselee, such that it has the power to reverse the negative polarity of the self-defeating feeling, it passes muster.

In fact, in my philosophical practice, the more a counselee practices interoceptive imagery in philosophical counselling, the more likely it is that the same intentional object (e.g. the possibility of failing at something new) that initially generated a negatively valent irrational syllogism may come to be associated with a positively valent philosophical construct (e.g. that of Sartre). In this way, the counselee may come to feel empowered by the same object rather than disempowered by it.

Developing a plan of action is essential for building and maintaining philosophical health. As mentioned previously, following the Platonic/Aristotelian model, philosophical health may be understood in terms of a set of habits or dispositions to think, feel, desire and act in ways that are rational and emotionally sound. These habits are developed and maintained through practice.

Accordingly, a plan of action involves practising the skills that are conducive to the virtues in question. Thus, a counselee who tends to demand certainty and is reticent to take reasonable risks may be asked to engage in risk-taking exercises in which she takes small insignificant risks (e.g. gambling a few dollars at the slot machines) incrementally working up to doing something important she would like to do but has been reticent to try, for example, applying for a job for which she is qualified. In so doing, the counselee works on cultivating courage, which involves the habit of rational assessment and risk-taking.

Action plans can also include cognitive exercises such as identifying irrational syllogistic constructions, refuting their irrational premises and constructing more rational ones in their stead (Cohen, 2021a). It may include engaging in mindfulness exercises, for example, practising observing one's thoughts rather than rating them in terms of language with negative illocutionary act potential ('How horrible it would be if I applied for the job and got rejected!').

Action plans could also include practising interoceptive imagery as well as dealing philosophically with threatening imagery as it arises in vivo. For example, in the process of applying for the job, you deal with threatening imagery arising from the demand for certainty by evoking Nietzschean philosophical imagery involving becoming stronger through confronting adversity or the Sartrean idea of defining oneself positively through one's actions rather than being a disappointed dream or expectation.

Conclusion

Philosophical health is an ancient concept involving a balancing of rational-emotive and behavioural tendencies through the cultivation of virtuous habits such as metaphysical security, authenticity, empathy, courage, respect, self-control, prudence, empowerment, objectivity, foresightedness and scientificity. These 'guiding virtues' may be interpreted philosophically in diverse ways. Thus, philosophical counsellors aiming at promoting the philosophical health of their counselees should avoid proselytizing for their preferred philosophies and instead help their counselees to identify and embrace philosophical perspectives that resonate *with them*. To cultivate the guiding virtues towards promoting philosophical health, counselees' philosophies need to be *applied to* their everyday lives, for example, sticking to trying to control only what is in one's power to control, namely one's own thoughts, feelings, desires, emotions and actions. In this manner, counselees can overcome common human tendencies to commit 'cardinal fallacies', chief among which are various types of demanding perfection, from which other fallacies tend to be deduced such as damnation, catastrophizing and *can't*stipation, among others.

According to LBTC, human beings bear freedom and responsibility for constructing and dismantling the latter fallacious reality constructs and building antidotal philosophical-health-promoting constructs in their stead (Cohen, 2021). Such constructs may be linguistically expressed in terms of practical syllogisms utilizing language with negative (or positive) illocutionary act potential that interactively express associated images and interoceptive feelings.

Critically assessing self-defeating, irrational constructs therefore often involves flagging and changing terms used to perform self-defeating speech acts such as awfulizing, self-damnation, and damnation of others – for example, 'awful', 'loser' and 'bastard', respectively. Interoceptive feelings such as that of necessity and feeling threatened or disempowered may be phenomenologically modulated through practising interoceptive imagery in which philosophical constructs are used to reverse the negative polarity of painful, irrational reality constructs.

Particularly, modal terms expressing possibility and necessity, which are associated with syllogistic constructions tracking anxiety, may be modulated through philosophical constructions of reality (e.g. Buddhism) that help counselees let go of their 'musts' and embrace possibility as an opportunity to find new lived meanings.

Philosophical health accordingly emerges as a fundamental goal of philosophical counselling modalities such as LBTC, among others. This chapter has provided a systematic, philosophical, constructivist approach to philosophical health which can have profound implications for managing behavioural and emotional problems of ordinary life.

References

American Psychiatric Association (2013), *Diagnostic & Statistical Manual of Mental Illness*, 5th edn. Washington DC: American Psychiatric Association.

Aristotle (2009), *The Nicomachean Ethics*, trans. W. D. Ross. New York: Oxford University Press.

Aurelius, Marcus (2017), *Meditations*, trans. M. Casaubon. Scotts Valley: CreateSpace Independent Publishing Platform.

Beck, Aaron T. (1979), *Cognitive Therapy and the Emotional Disorders*. New York: Plume.

Cohen, Elliot D. (2006), 'Critical Thinking, not "Head Shrinking"'. In P. Raabe (ed.), *Philosophical Counselling and the Unconscious*, 156–66. San Antonio: Trivium Publications.

Cohen, Elliot D. (2007), *The New Rational Therapy: Thinking Your Way to Serenity, Success, and Profound Happiness*. Lanham: Rowman & Littlefield.

Cohen, Elliot D. (2013a), *Caution: Faulty Thinking can be Harmful to Your Happiness*. Boca Raton: Trace-Wilco, Inc.

Cohen, Elliot D. (2013b), *Theory and Practice of Logic-Based Therapy: Integrating Critical Thinking and Philosophy into Psychotherapy*. New Castle upon Tyne: Cambridge Scholars.

Cohen, Elliot D. (2017), *Logic-Based Therapy and Everyday Emotions*. Blue Ridge Summit: Lexington Books.

Cohen, Elliot D. (2019a), 'Did Plato Lay the Groundwork for Freud's Psychoanalysis? Freud may not have gone far enough in Crediting Plato for His Theory'. *Psychology Today*, 12 December.

Cohen, Elliot D. (2019b), *Making Peace with Imperfection: Discover Your Perfectionism Type, end the Cycle of Criticism, and Embrace Self-acceptance*. Oakland: Impact.

Cohen, Elliot D. (2020), 'The Psychoanalysis of Perfectionism: Integrating Freud's Psychodynamic Theory into Logic-Based Therapy'. *International Journal of Philosophical Practice*, 6 (1): 15–27.

Cohen, Elliot D. (2021a), *Cognitive-Behavioural Interventions for Self-defeating Thoughts: Helping Counselees to Overcome the Tyranny of 'I Can't'*. London: Routledge.

Cohen, Elliot D. (2021b), 'What is an Emotion?' *International Journal of Applied Philosophy*, 35 (2): 171–81.

Cohen, Elliot D. (2022b), *Cognitive-Behavior Therapy for those Who Say They Can't: A Workbook for Overcoming Your Self-defeating Thoughts*. London: Routledge.

Ellis, Albert (2010), *Overcoming Destructive Beliefs, Feelings, and Behaviors: New Directions for Rational Emotive Behavior Therapy*. Amherst: Prometheus Books.

Ellis, Albert and Robert A. Harper (1990), *A Guide to Rational Living*. New York: St. Martin Press.

Freud, Sigmund (1981), 'Lecture XXXI: The Dissection of the Psychical Personality'. In J. Strachey (trans.), *The Standard Edition of The Complete Psychological Works of Sigmund Freud*, vol. 22, 57–79. London: Hogarth Press.

Freud, Sigmund (1922), *Beyond the Pleasure Principle*, trans. C. J. M. Hubback. London: The International Psycho-Analytic Press.

Kant, Immanuel (1999), *Critique of Pure Reason*, trans. P. Guyer and A. W. Wood. Cambridge: Cambridge University Press.

Nietzsche, Friedrich (1954), *Beyond Good and Evil*. In H. Zimmern (trans.), *The Philosophy of Nietzsche*. New York: Random House.

Plato (1931), *The Republic of Plato*. In B. Jowett (trans. and ed.), *The Dialogues of Plato*, vol. III, 1–338. London: Oxford University Press.

Rorty, Richard (1982), *Consequences of Pragmatism*. Minneapolis: University of Minnesota Press.

Sartre, Jean-Paul (2007), *Existentialism is a Humanism*, trans. C. Macomber. New Haven: Yale University Press.

Shantidiva (1979), *A Guide to the Bodhisattva's Way of Life*, trans. S. Batchelor. Dharamshala: Library of Tibetan Works & Archives.

Part II

The Others

6

The virtue of vulnerability

Merleau-Ponty and Minuchin on the boundaries of personal identity

Laura McMahon

This chapter offers a phenomenological account of the importance of vulnerability to our existential health as human selves, and explores the role that a lived phenomenological practice can play in our philosophical health as individuals and as groups. Part One engages with the work of Maurice Merleau-Ponty in order to argue that we are ontologically vulnerable, in the sense that our identities and perspectives on the world are not simply our own, but are always emergent from – and forever dialogically intertwined with – the behaviours and perspectives of others. Part Two argues that vulnerability is not only an ontological state but a lived activity: it is an immovable feature of our existence that we can take up and 'live' in more or less honest and healthy manners. In short, vulnerability is a virtue, in an Aristotelian sense. Part Three demonstrates the virtue of vulnerability (and its related vices) through a case study from structural family therapist Salvador Minuchin. If a central phenomenological insight is that personal identity is always already interpersonally accomplished, then psychological problems should not be sought 'in' the individual but rather in the interpersonal systems to which the individual belongs: the fundamental premise of Minuchin's family therapy. Finally, Part Four argues that in order to properly see ourselves as parts of systems rather than as ontologically distinct individuals – what happens in successful family therapy – we must adopt something like a phenomenological perspective on ourselves and the world.

Merleau-Ponty and the phenomenology of vulnerability

In what phenomenologists call 'the natural attitude', we typically think of ourselves as ontologically distinct individuals who only subsequently come into contact with other ontologically distinct individuals (Husserl, 1983: 51–62). However, a phenomenological description of the lived experience of personal identity gives us a different picture: identity is revealed as relational, dialogical and deeply vulnerable to the perspectives and behaviours of others. Merleau-Ponty's description of the experience of a good conversation can offer us a first clue into the manner in which who we are (in the process of becoming) is not simply a private matter. He writes:

> In the experience of dialogue, a common ground is constituted between me and another; my thought and his form a single fabric, my words and those of my interlocutor are called forth by the state of the discussion and are inserted into a shared operation of which neither of us is the creator . . . our perspectives slip into each other, we coexist through a single world. I am freed from myself in the present dialogue, even though the other's thoughts are certainly his own, since I do not form them, I nonetheless grasp them as soon as they are born or I even anticipate them. And even the objection raised by my interlocutor draws from me thoughts I did not know I possessed such that if I lend him my thoughts, he makes me think in return. (2012: 370–1)

This description draws our attention to the manner in which, in ordinary adult life, we are not simply the sole authors of our own thoughts. The perspectives and ideas of others 'encroach' or 'trespass' (*empiètent*) into our own (Merleau-Ponty, 1964a: 164; see also Saint-Aubert, 2004: 46–8). This adult experience of being taken up by another's thought, and of having one's own thought called forth by another, points us to a more basic phenomenon of encroachment at play in all of our lived experience: beginning in our earliest experiences as infants and young children, our most basic perceptual sense of the world, and our most basic experiences of who we are, is always already deeply informed by the perceptions and behaviours of others.

It is in this basic sense that we understand the fundamental human condition of vulnerability. Derived from the Latin *vulnus*, or wound, the term 'vulnerability' often carries with it negative connotations of weakness, powerlessness and precarious exposure to harm (Gilson, 2014: 33). While it is importantly true that the term 'vulnerability' signifies a capacity to be wounded at the hands of nature, other people and unjust social and political arrangements – and while it is important that we existentially grapple with such risk – it is also crucial to our existential health that we recognize our vulnerability as a positive capacity to be, at the hearts of our 'own' identities, open to and shaped by our intertwining with things and others in the world. In Bryan Turner's words, vulnerability is 'the capacity to be open to wounding and to be open to the world' (Turner, 2006: 28). And as Judith Butler writes on the experience of mourning and loss, 'perhaps what I have lost "in" you . . . is a relationality that is composed neither exclusively of myself nor you, but is to be conceived as *the tie* by which those terms are differentiated and related' (Butler, 2004: 22).

Merleau-Ponty offers distinct phenomenological resources for describing the nature of this fundamental 'openness' and this primary 'tie' to others. In his lecture course 'The Child's Relations with Others', Merleau-Ponty argues that before the young child has a sense of herself *as* a discrete self, she exists in a situation of 'syncretic sociability' in which the distinction between self and other, inside and outside is not clearly demarcated (Merleau-Ponty, 1964a: 119). We can glimpse the nature of syncretic sociability in adult experiences of 'emotional contagion', when we find ourselves breaking into a smile in response to the beaming face of a friend, or when we find ourselves made uneasy by an eerie landscape: our own experience is not simply our own but is pervaded by the affective sense of the situation (Whitney, 2012; Hatfield, 1993). We can also see it in the experience of emotional 'projection', when we attribute our own preoccupations, negative feelings or problematic behaviours to others (Merleau-Ponty, 1964a: 119–20, 148). For the young child, such overlay or transgression between self, other and world is the very substance of her experience; indeed, she has to learn gradually over time to *establish* boundaries between self and other, and she has to *develop* a sense of herself as a real and substantial individual with a perspective distinctive from that of others (Maclaren, 2008). This process of establishing boundaries and a sense of one's own identity is not something that is accomplished once and for all when we graduate from childhood. Rather, it is a lifelong project, precisely because the lines between self and other, inside and outside are not ontological givens that we simply discover but inherently porous and thus inherently matters of intertwining, transgression and intimate negotiation.

Indeed, how we learn to begin to establish these boundaries and experience ourselves *as* individual selves is deeply shaped by our early intimate relationships, with lifelong effects. Merleau-Ponty's conception of 'intercorporeality' helps us to see how this is so. One of the central insights of Merleau-Ponty's phenomenology is that the living body is not merely a mechanical piece of nature but an intelligent, meaningful sense of capacity, of a developed 'I can' (Merleau-Ponty, 2012: 139; see also Husserl, 1989: 269–87 and Simionescu-Panait in this volume, Chapter 10). Our bodies are 'coupled' with the world in a dialogical manner: concrete possibilities in the world 'call forth' one's specific bodily capacities – the ramp invites one to roll one's wheelchair into the lobby of the building; the crying child calls for his parents' embrace – and one's specific bodily capacities in turn help to illuminate the real 'affordances' of the world – the traversability of ramps; the burgeoning needs and possibilities of this specific child (Merleau-Ponty, 2012: 84; Gibson, 2014: 119–36). The bodily 'I can' throws us outside of ourselves, such that our bodies are not typically objects spread before our gaze but the power *behind* our gaze that allows the world to be revealed in its specific characteristics. In Merleau-Ponty's words, the lived body is 'the darkness of the theatre necessary for the clarity of the performance' (Merleau-Ponty, 2012: 103). Furthermore – and most crucially for our purposes here – this 'dark' corporeal power is not simply mine alone: my bodily powers are intimately intertwined with the bodily powers of others, before there is any relation between fully delineated, conscious subjects (Marratto, 2012: 144).

We can see such 'intercorporeality' in the bodily intertwining of infant and parent when, for example, the baby's stirring calls forth the let-down of milk in the mother (Simms, 2008: 11–12). We can also see it at play in the 'symmetrical' relationships of rivals (e.g. one child wants what his brother has *because* the latter has it) and in the 'complementary' relationships of heterogeneous pairings (e.g. the exhibitionist child needs a spectator) (Bateson, 1972: 325). Our 'own' bodily powers, desires, perceptions and behaviours are called forth and play out in intercorporeal 'dances' with others. Such dynamic intercorporeal pairings or systems can be understood in terms of the figure of a melody. A melody needs its component notes in order to be the tune that it is, but it is equally the case that each of the notes receives its proper *sense* – its meaning and direction – only within the unfolding context of the tune as a whole (Merleau-Ponty, 1963: 137). Our identities are no more simply our own than is the sound of the note in the melody is its own self-possessed reality: we cannot exist as the individuals that we are outside of the meaningful, dynamic contexts that gave rise to this identity to begin with, and that continue to give this identity a place over time.

Melodies unfold over time, with the experience of the later notes ineluctably coloured by the emotional sense of the earlier, and the earlier notes retroactively prefiguring the sense of the later. Merleau-Ponty's phenomenological interpretation of the psychoanalytic concept of *repression* speaks to the manner in which our lived experience of self, world and others is deeply shaped by certain past experiences that 'unconsciously' come to occupy a privileged place in our lives, insofar as they constitute not merely the *content* of our experience but its very habitual *form*. Merleau-Ponty writes:

> We remain the person who was once committed to this adolescent love, or the person who once lived within that parental universe. New perceptions replace previous ones, and even new emotions replace those that came before, but this renewal only has to do with the content of our experience and not with its structure. Impersonal time continues to flow, but personal time is arrested. (2012: 85)

The intercorporeal forms of which we are intimately a part – in childhood especially, but in important respects throughout our lives – come to structure our sense not only of our 'I can' but also of our 'I cannot' (Young, 1980: 146). To adapt a phrase of Merleau-Ponty's, repression is the source of both our freedom and our servitude, both our health and our illness: it is through our determinate experience with others that we become the selves that we are and enjoy the concrete possibilities that we do, but it is also on account of our determinate experiences with others that we become 'trapped' in certain outlooks and manners of behaving (Merleau-Ponty, 2012: 87; McMahon, 2021: 88–92).

Merleau-Ponty's phenomenological concepts of encroachment, syncretic sociability, intercorporeality and repression provide a vision of human vulnerability that captures the latter's inherently ambiguous and ambivalent nature. I can be hurt, or I can lose something or somebody that I love, only because I first 'have' things and others. Interpreted phenomenologically, this 'having' should be understood in the sense of our deep intertwining with things and others at the heart of our 'own' identities: we are not simply the authors or the owners of ourselves but are always already shaped elsewhere, from beyond our own purview. The determinacies of this intertwining in our early lives lay down patterns for how we will relate to things and others in our later lives, in simultaneously facilitating and debilitating manners. We cannot *not* be vulnerable in this ontological sense; however, as we shall now discuss, how we navigate this fundamental vulnerability is of great significance for our health as individuals and for the flourishing of the communities to which we belong, and which so deeply shape our identities.

The virtue of vulnerability

Vulnerability is inevitable to our ontological condition as human selves; what is at issue for our existential health is how we take up and 'live' our ontological vulnerability. In a word, I will argue that vulnerability should be understood as a virtue, in an Aristotelian sense. On its face, it might seem odd to say that something inevitable to the human condition can also be a virtue; however, a phenomenological clue that we tacitly already recognize this to be the case can be found in some commonplace ways in which we speak about people's capacities to be intimate with others. For example, a 'reality TV' show focusing on romantic relationships praises individuals' capacities to 'be vulnerable', or a university counselling website bemoans that '[s]ince childhood, many men are taught vulnerability equals weakness and therefore men are not supposed to be vulnerable' (University of Michigan CAPS, 2022). In short, vulnerability is not simply a stable state but an active condition. We can navigate the interpersonal terrain in which we are intimately shaped by others – and in which we in turn shape others in *their* most intimate identities – skilfully or clumsily, and with varying degrees of courage and cowardice, insight and obtuseness. Moreover, our capacities to be vulnerable in interpersonal situations are not ours alone but a matter of our upbringing and education – that is, a matter of the ways we are enabled to become ourselves in and through the intimate relationships of our childhood.

What does it mean to say that vulnerability is a virtue, in an Aristotelian sense? In Aristotle's philosophy, virtue (*aretē*) concerns taking up our human 'nature' or condition in an excellent way; it is to flourish as the kinds of beings that we are. Aristotle draws an analogy between virtue and physical health: if health is the flourishing of the body, then virtue is the flourishing of the character. Both health and virtue are understood as states of receptivity to what the world has to offer, and states of attuned readiness to respond to these possibilities in appropriate, and potentially self-transformative, manners. Cultivating such a state of receptivity and readiness requires that one 'hit the mark' between excesses and deficiencies of various kinds. For example, finding the 'mean' when it comes to exercise requires that, say, we lift weights in ways that are appropriate to our specific bodies and specific situations: the amount of weight that should be lifted to build strength by a football player in his prime and by an individual recovering from a traumatic injury evidently and appropriately differs, but in each case too little wastes the body's potential, while too much risks (further) injury (Aristotle, 1947: 1106a25–b7). When we insufficiently develop our particular bodily skills and strength(s), we can experience our bodies as in the way of our desired activities; to use an example from Iris Marion Young, I might experience my body as a rigid burden in the way of my traversal of a small stream on a hike (Young, 1980: 143–4). Overly enthusiastic engagement in physical activity can similarly put the injured body in the way of its desired engagements with things. When there is a reasonably good 'fit' between a ready body and a receptive world, however, our physicality does not usually announce itself in the foreground of our experience, so much as it recedes into its background: its value is felt not so much in itself as in the 'I can' and the concomitant world of self-transcending and self-transformative possibilities it opens up. As Rosemary Garland-Thomson (2011) points out – and as we shall see further below – the 'fit' between body and world is not always about the successful or failed adaption of the body to a ready-made world but also about shaping a human world that is accommodating to different kinds of bodies.

Like physical health, virtue should be understood not as a foregrounded property so much as a mean condition of readiness for action appropriate to the situation (Russon, 2013: 174). Aristotle's discussion of courage (*andreia*) makes this clear. Courage concerns having the appropriate relationship to fear. Too much fear (and too little confidence), and we habitually avoid challenging situations and shrink from conflict, perhaps at the expense of our own self-respect and values; too little fear (and too much confidence), and we risk rushing headlong into situations, without understanding their parameters or having the developed skills necessary to deal with them (Aristotle, 1947: 1115b24–35). The coward does not cultivate her personal capacities to act in skilful and principled manners as the situation demands; the reckless person risks harming or destroying sensitive situations in which he intervenes without understanding. In contrast to the cowardly and the rash, the courageous person is properly attuned to the real demands and possibilities of the situation, and is thusly prepared to skilfully and creatively intervene in this situation. One does not act courageously *in order to be* courageous but in order to rise to the demands of the situation; one forgets oneself, so to speak, in attuned action. The difference between the reckless person – whom Aristotle calls 'the pretender to courage' – and the genuinely courageous person is illuminating: while the reckless person often likes to make a display of their supposed courage, but is then not equal to the danger when it in fact arrives, the genuinely courageous person is 'keen in the moment of action, but quiet beforehand' (Aristotle, 1947: 1115b30, 1947, 1116a8–9). It is such a state of cultivated potential that constitutes not just the physical health of our bodies but the existential health of our characters.

What I would like to argue here is that our capacity to navigate the terrain of our ontological vulnerability should itself be cultivated as a central human virtue, or excellence, in its own right. If the virtue of courage concerns our relationship to fear (and confidence), then the virtue of vulnerability concerns our relationship to our own intercorporeal openness to being shaped by others in ways we cannot control and often do not readily understand. How well are we able to navigate this fraught existential terrain? And in what ways do we commonly fail to navigate it well? Merleau-Ponty's description of dialogue, with which we opened this chapter, offers a concrete route into beginning to answer these questions.

In a good conversation, we are able to strike a balance between being taken up by the thought of the other, on the one hand, and maintaining and taking responsibility for our own contributions, on the other hand. The good conversationalist, in other words, is skilled at inhabiting the thought of the other without thereby losing herself. When the good conversationalist inhabits this 'mean' condition, like the courageous person she 'disappears' as an ego: she is not self-consciously concerned with, say, displaying her own intelligence, but with collectively enabling the truths of the topic at hand to come to light. In so 'forgetting' herself she most finds or becomes herself, so to speak, *as* 'the darkness of the theatre necessary for the clarity of the performance': she is defined not so much by her own personal properties as she is enlarged by what she enables to come to life in the world.

At a more basic, affective level, the virtue of vulnerability enacts something akin to what happens in a good conversation. When I am vulnerable in a virtuous manner, I am open to being moved, shaped and transformed by my intimate relationships with another. I hold myself open to the encroachment of the other in a manner befitting my ontological condition of vulnerability: I assume in an honest way the porousness of the boundaries between self and other. At the same time, I maintain a sense of personal boundaries strong enough not simply to dissolve in the face of the influence of the other: I assume my responsibility for moving, shaping and transforming the other in turn. The virtue of vulnerability is not about being indiscriminately open but about being *both* appropriately open and appropriately closed to the influence of the other. Once again, hitting the mark here is precisely not about the promotion of the self but about making oneself the site for the appearance of larger realities; more specifically, the point is to cultivate and care for intercorporeal forms in contexts that enable the flourishing or growth of all parties involved.

There are many ways we can err in this domain, but the vices in the domain of human vulnerability fall somewhere in the direction of overly 'rigid' boundaries and a stance of defensive invulnerability, on the one side, or of overly 'diffuse' boundaries and a stance of (co-)dependency, on the other side (Minuchin, 2012: 41). Let us see some of the ways such problems can play out – and some of the ways in which they can begin to be healed – through a clinical example from family systems therapist Salvador Minuchin. We shall also see through this example the ways in which intercorporeal systems can themselves be characterized by excessive rigidity (and deficient porosity) or excessive porosity (and deficient rigidity), in manners that 'educate' the individuals involved into problematic relationships to their own vulnerability.

Minuchin and therapeutic transformation

If, in the natural attitude, we commonly think of ourselves as ontologically distinct selves, then it is also the case that in the natural attitude we tend to seek the source of emotional or behavioural problems 'in' the troubled individual. However, much as phenomenology recognizes that individual identity is in fact deeply shaped by our intimate involvement with other people, Minuchin's family systems therapy 'regards the identified patient merely as the family member who is expressing, in the most visible way, a problem affecting the entire system' (Minuchin, 2012: 100). In other words, while Minuchin is not himself a phenomenologist, family systems therapy is alive to a fundamental phenomenological insight in its search for the source of difficulties in familial relationships rather than 'in' individuals and in its use of the family system as a matrix for healing as well. One of Minchin's case studies shows us how this works.

Minuchin relays the case of a family in therapy consisting of a daughter, a son, their father and their stepmother. The children have come to live with their father and his new family after his divorce from their mother, who suffers from manic depressive episodes. The presenting problem is the daughter's 'undue sensitivity, crying spells, and feelings of being unloved' (Minuchin, 2012: 89). The stepmother is generally timid and displays a limited affective range, and the father works hard to protect his new wife from the emotional lability of his daughter (Minuchin, 2012: 89). As a result he winds up in intense and infuriating power struggles with the girl – power struggles that remind him of conflicts with his ex-wife. He thus criticizes his daughter for being too much like her mother and vocally worries that she will grow up to be 'crazy' (Minuchin, 2012: 89).

Now, if the young girl were to be referred to individual therapy (since it is she that is collectively identified as the 'problem'), the pathology might well be sought 'within' her individual experience and a solution sought through her own limited perspective on her relationship with her mother, father, stepmother and siblings (Minuchin, 2012: 2). Treating the family rather than the individual, however, allows the problem to be found in the inappropriate boundaries becoming established in this transitioning new family, rather than 'in' the scapegoated daughter. Minuchin argues that the development of appropriate and clear boundaries is crucial to healthy family functioning: they must be firm enough that members be allowed 'to carry out their functions without undue interference', but relaxed enough that they 'allow contact between the members' (Minuchin, 2012: 40). Pathology in families comes about when boundaries are overly rigid, on the one hand, or overly diffuse, on the other hand (Minuchin, 2012: 41). In Minuchin's analysis of the case in question here, father and daughter form a 'subsystem' in which he treats her more like a peer than like a child, and he projects upon her the 'ghost' of her mother in a way that does not allow her to be(come) her own person (Minuchin, 2012: 89). Meanwhile, the father and the stepmother are failing to establish an appropriate parental subsystem with one another; the father 'tries to act as a buffer to protect his wife from his daughter', and the woman is in this way excluded from the struggles at play between father and daughter (Minuchin, 2012: 89). The boundaries between father and daughter are overly diffuse – the girl is not being recognized as 'a person in her own right' – and the boundaries between father and second wife are overly rigid – the woman is kept at arm's length from her husband and is not given the opportunity to take on a parenting role with her stepdaughter.

Minuchin's work allows us to see how pathologies in the larger family system lead to pathologies on the part of individual family members (rather than the other way around). Pathology concerns not the presence of problems – all families face problems – but the way in which the family *responds* to inevitable problems. Minuchin argues that in pathological familial situations, 'demands for change have been countered by a reification of the family structure. The accustomed transactional patterns have been preserved to the point of rigidity, which blocks any possibility of alternatives' (Minuchin, 2012: 85; see also Canguilhem, 1991: 185–6 and McMahon, 2018: 613–18). Individuals become locked into overly rigid roles: the emotionally labile daughter, the aggressive but ineffectual father, the passive stepmother. Individual pathology thus cannot be separated from the pathology of the larger system; indeed, individual pathology might well constitute an intelligent response to a disturbed situation (Russon, 2003: 82). Much as 'disability' can be understood to be a problem with the 'fit' between certain bodies and an unaccommodating world, 'pathology' here should be addressed in the family system that solicits problematic behaviours, rather than 'in' the troubled individual herself. In contrast to pathology in the family system, health in the family system allows for the flourishing of the individual family members, where health is understood as the capacity for progressive transformation – rather than conservative rigidity – in the face of the challenges and demands of the situation (Minuchin, 2012: 39–40; see also Canguilhem, 1991: 197 and McMahon, 2018: 613–18). In Minuchin's words, '[s]ince the family must respond to internal and external changes, it must be able to transform itself in ways that meet new circumstances without losing the continuity that provides a frame for its members' (2012: 39–40).

According to Minuchin, therapeutic treatment aims to intervene in pathological family systems, interrupting rigid habitual patterns such that new ones can be experimented with and healthier ones ultimately established. The therapist temporarily 'joins' the family in order to act as a disrupter of habitual patterns of interaction – a disruption that can only occur when a new avenue of engagement is offered – and also as a boundary maker, 'clarifying diffuse boundaries and opening inappropriately rigid boundaries' (Minuchin, 2012: 86–7, 42). In the previous example, the therapist interrupts the rigidified family dynamic by forming a coalition with the stepmother, drawing the woman out and stressing her importance as a parental figure in this family in transition (2012: 89). He encourages her to be critical of her husband's behaviour with his daughter, and in particular to be critical of her husband's ongoing resurrection of the haunting presence of his ex-wife. This coalition in a stroke disrupts and begins to effect positive changes across the system: focus is taken off the daughter's behaviour and put onto the father's; the stepmother is afforded a new position of authority and responsibility; the daughter is allowed to be her own person – and allowed to be a child – rather than an extension of her mother (Minuchin, 2012: 90).

We can see in Minuchin's therapeutic theory and practice three things relevant to our discussion in this chapter. First, the case study illustrates our ontological vulnerability as selves whose identities are not self-sufficient but are deeply intertwined with our familial and social *milieux*, and – as we saw with Merleau-Ponty's conception of repression – carry forward the deep influence of past others into future relationships. The father's perceptions and capacities for relating to his young daughter and new wife, for example, are haunted by the 'ghost' of his first wife. Second, and relatedly, this case exemplifies common ways in which we can take up this vulnerability in problematic or 'vicious' ways. For example, while the father is *in fact* ontologically vulnerable in the manner just described, he initially does not own up to this vulnerability in an honest way but rather ignores his own way of being affected by, and his own contribution to, the family's troubles, while blaming – and affording outsized power to – his young daughter, who is in turn 'intercorporeally' solicited to behave in kind. Third, Minuchin's work shows us that, as I have been arguing in this chapter, vulnerability is not simply a state of being but an activity that we need to cultivate in our relationships with others. The healthy transformation of pathological situations requires coming to be vulnerable in the right kind of way. For example, confronted by the stepmother in coalition with the therapist, the father – initially rigid in his interpretation of the situation – must learn to be critical of himself and to be open to changing his own behaviours. In order to *be* vulnerable – rather than simply destroyed – there must be some continuity of self (as Minuchin argues there must be some continuity of family). The stepmother, then, who is problematically docile at first, must come to develop a stronger and more assertive sense of self, one that is capable of challenging her husband and taking responsibility for actively contributing to the healthy shaping of the situation. Minuchin argues that she has something to learn from her stepdaughter in this regard, while the girl, in turn, can learn from her stepmother how to retreat a bit, and be(come) herself in a different way than in acting out against her father (Minuchin, 2012: 90). If the virtue of vulnerability requires that we 'hit the mark' with respect to being appropriately open, and appropriately closed, to the influence of others, then each member of the family has distinct, and complementary, lessons to learn and behaviours to change.

Therapy as phenomenology (and phenomenology as therapy)

Minuchin's account of the techniques of the family therapist allows us to see the effectively phenomenological nature of therapeutic transformation. Merleau-Ponty's account of therapeutic transformation resonates with Minuchin's. He writes: 'Psychoanalytic treatment does not heal by provoking an insight into the past, but by first relating the subject to his doctor through new existential relations. . . .The same is true for all moments of insight: they are actual if they are sustained by a new commitment' (Merleau-Ponty, 2012: 482). The therapist's intervention into rigidified familial patterns effects a *Gestalt* shift in which patterns that were formerly invisible – that operated in the background rather than the foreground of the family members' experience – can be seen *as* problematic patterns, at the same time as new routes for engagement that make concrete sense to the individuals involved begin to come to light. Within the context of a different 'melody', the 'notes' come to sound different than they did previously, and to call forth new melodic lines. This account points us to two observations of importance to our understanding of the role of philosophy – and phenomenology in particular – in a healthy life: therapeutic insight is already a kind of proto-phenomenology, and phenomenology has distinct therapeutic value.

Luis de Miranda defines philosophical health as a situation of 'fruitful coherence between a person's way of thinking and speaking and their ways of acting, such that [. . .] the need for self- and intersubjective flourishing [is] satisfied', and he argues that this requires learning to see 'reality [. . .] as a co-creation in which we are dynamically engaged' (2022: 1, 4). Importantly, as Merleau-Ponty stresses, such insight into reality as a co-creation is a matter of lived perception rather than detached cognitive understanding. Successful therapeutic transformation occurs when individuals' 'natural attitude' views concerning their own ontological independence and the ready-made nature of reality are interrupted and when these individuals can instead come to experience themselves as parts of dynamic, intersubjective (or 'intercorporeal') systems. As John Russon writes, 'successful therapy will ultimately require that the [. . .] self become something of a phenomenologist' (2003: 136). Therapeutic transformation simultaneously requires and effects a kind of phenomenological insight into our own vulnerability and intertwining with others, and into reality not as a fixed given but as a site for transformation, and allows us to begin to live better, and more responsibly, in honour of this insight. The social and political, as well as the interpersonal, implications of such transformation could be profound.

For its part, the philosophical practice of phenomenology itself has therapeutic power. As the rigorous description of experience as it is actually lived, phenomenological description turns our attention from the *objects* of experience to the *fact of* experience itself, from the 'performance' to the 'darkness of the theatre'. How is my most personal experience and identity always already shaped by my intimate involvement with others? How is this involvement always already at work in my ways of seeing and acting? How is the world itself patterned by our collective characteristic ways of seeing and acting, and how might changes in our perception and behaviour allow the world itself to appear in a new light? To carefully attend to our own lived experience is not simply to report on a static state of being but to intervene in a dynamic activity: to attend anew to lived experience is already to begin to creatively transform it. Far from being a detached intellectual exercise, then, phenomenology properly so called is a living, transformative practice. And, much as therapeutic transformation is not carried out alone, responsible phenomenological practice requires deep and extensive engagement with the experience and thoughts of others. As we saw in our discussion of dialogue at the beginning of this chapter, in conversation with another I am given the opportunity to have my own thinking expanded, and, simultaneously, to take critical responsibility for my own contribution to the developing situation. To do this well requires, precisely, the virtue of vulnerability. We must have something to bring to the table and have the resoluteness necessary to follow our thoughts through, to defend positions we have good reason to defend and to criticize shortcomings in the thinking of others. At the same time, we must not be rigidly attached to our own habitual ways of approaching things and defensive in the face of legitimate criticism. It is only thusly that we can, to quote Aristotle, be open to the transformation of our own thought – and, indeed, of our own ways of living – in the face of 'the right things and from the right motive, in the right way and at the right time' (1947: 1115b16–18).

References

Aristotle (1947), *Nicomachean Ethics*. In Richard McKeon (ed.), *Introduction to Aristotle*, 300–543. New York: The Modern Library.

Bateson, Gregory (1972), *Steps to an Ecology of Mind*. Chicago: The University of Chicago Press.

Butler, Judith (2004), *Precarious Life: The Powers of Mourning and Violence*. New York: Verso Books.

Canguilhem, Georges (1991 [1943]), *The Normal and the Pathological*, trans. Carolyn R. Fawcett and Robert S. Cohen. New York: Zone Books.

Counseling and Psychological Services, University of Michigan (2022), 'Men and Vulnerability'. https://caps.umich.edu/article/men-and-vulnerability (accessed 1 July 2022).

Garland-Thomson, J. (2011), 'Misfits: A Feminist-Materialist Disability Concept'. *Hypatia*, 26 (3): 591–609.

Gibson, James J. (2014 [1979]), *The Ecological Approach to Visual Perception*. New York: Routledge.

Gilson, Erinn C. (2014), *The Ethics of Vulnerability: A Feminist Analysis of Social Life and Practice*. New York: Routledge.

Hatfield, Elaine et al. (1993), 'Emotional Contagion'. *Current Directions in Psychological Science*, 2 (4): 96–9.

Husserl, Edmund (1983 [1916]), *Ideas Pertaining to a Pure Phenomenology and to a Phenomenological Psychology, First Book*, trans. F. Kersten. Boston: Kluwer.

Husserl, Edmund (1989 [1952]), *Ideas Pertaining to a Pure Phenomenology and to a Phenomenological Psychology, Second Book*, trans. Richard Rojcewicz and André Schwur. Boston: Kluwer.

Maclaren, Kym (2008), 'Embodied Perceptions of Others as a Condition of Selfhood? Empirical and Phenomenological Considerations'. *Journal of Consciousness Studies*, 15: 63–93.

Marratto, Scott L. (2012), *The Intercorporeal Self: Merleau-Ponty on Subjectivity*. Albany: State University of New York Press.

McMahon, Laura (2018), '(Un)Healthy Systems: Merleau-Ponty, Dewey, and the Dynamic Equilibrium Between Self and Environment'. *The Journal of Speculative Philosophy*, 32 (4): 607–27.

McMahon, Laura (2021), 'The "Great Phantom": Merleau-Ponty on *Habitus*, Freedom, and Political Transformation'. In Jérôme Melançon (ed.), *Transforming Politics with Merleau-Ponty: Thinking Beyond the State*, 87–106. New York: Rowman & Littlefield.

Merleau-Ponty, Maurice (1963 [1942]), *The Structure of Behavior*, trans. Alden L. Fisher. Pittsburgh: Duquesne University Press.

Merleau-Ponty, Maurice (1964 [1951]), 'The Child's Relations with Others', trans. William Cobb. In James Edie (ed.), *The Primacy of Perception and Other Essays on Phenomenological Psychology, the Philosophy of Art, History and Politics*, 96–155. Evanston: Northwestern University Press.

Merleau-Ponty, Maurice (1968 [1964]), *The Visible and the Invisible*, trans. Alphonso Lingis. Evanston: Northwestern University Press.

Merleau-Ponty, Maurice (2012 [1945]), *Phenomenology of Perception*, trans. Donald A. Landes. New York: Routledge.

Minuchin, Salvador (2012 [1974]), *Families and Family Therapy*. New York: Routledge.

de Miranda, Luis (2022), 'Philosophical Health'. In Vlad Petre Glăveanu (ed.), *The Palgrave Encyclopedia of the Possible*, 1003–8. Cham: Palgrave Macmillan.

Russon, John (2003), *Human Experience: Philosophy, Neurosis, and the Elements of Everyday Life*. Albany: State University of New York Press.

Russon, John (2013), 'The Virtues of Agency: A Phenomenology of Confidence, Courage, and Creativity'. In Kevin Hermberg and Paul Gyllenhammer (eds), *Phenomenology and Virtue Ethics*, 165–79. London: Bloomsbury.

Saint-Aubert, Emmanuel de (2004), *Du Lien des être aux élements de l'être: Merleau-Ponty au tournant des années 1945–1951*. Paris: Librarie Philosophique J. Vrin.

Simms, Eva (2008), *The Child in the World: Embodiment, Time, and Language in Early Childhood*. Detroit: Wayne State University Press.

Turner, Bryan S. (2006), *Vulnerability and Human Rights*. University Park: The Pennsylvania State University Press.

Whitney, Shiloh (2012), 'Affects, Images, and Child Perception: Self-Other Difference in Merleau-Ponty's Sorbonne Lectures'. *PhaenEx*, 7(2): 185–211.

Young, Iris Marion (1980), 'Throwing Like a Girl: A Phenomenology of Feminine Body Comportment Motility and Spatiality'. *Human Studies*, 3: 137–56.

7

Philosophical health, non-violent just communication, and epistemic justice

Raja Rosenhagen

Pioneered in Germany by Gerd B. Achenbach (cf. Achenbach, 1984, forthcoming) and in North America by, for example, Pierre Grimes and Regina L. Uliana (Grimes and Uliana, 1998), Elliot D. Cohen and Lou Marinoff (cf. Cohen, 2007, 2016, 2022; Marinoff, 1999, 2002), philosophical counselling is a rapidly developing movement. Some construe it as promoting the counselee's well-being or mental health (e.g. Cohen, op. cit.; Lang, 2018). Others reject that philosophical counselling should be construed as therapeutic and take it to aim at enabling the counselee to engage in genuine thinking for themselves, at bringing out the counselee's own truth or at productively questioning their philosophical presuppositions (e.g. Achenbach, 1984; Brenifier, 2020). These conceptions, one suspects, could well be compatible. However, as per the official lore, there is considerable disagreement about the aims and the methodology, if any, that philosophical counsellors should pursue. In this situation, might we benefit from thinking of philosophical counselling as promoting *philosophical health*?

'Philosophical health' is a newcomer to the philosophical conceptual landscape (cf. de Miranda, 2021a, 2021b, 2021c), and stipulating its content is an ongoing task. Like its antonyms 'disease' or 'illness', 'health' is a contested concept (cf. Boorse, 1977; Ananth, 2008; Hamilton, 2010; Dussault and Gagné-Julien, 2015; Azevedo, 2015; Saad and Prochaska, 2020; and Svenaeus, 2022, for competing definitions). And like 'mental health' and 'mental illness', the metaphorical expression 'philosophical health' can be cashed out in various ways.

In what follows, I begin by proposing a minimal notion of philosophical health that, I think, is broadly acceptable. Turning to the question of how philosophical health may be obtained, I then introduce Luis de Miranda's list of five principles of philosophical health and sketch a proposal I have elaborated elsewhere (cf. Rosenhagen, 2023). According to it, combining elements from the works of Iris Murdoch and Marshall Rosenberg yields the notion of a practice that is a useful tool for philosophical counsellors. Next, I show that this practice promotes philosophical health in the minimal sense and suggest that we should acknowledge a specific kind of trust as a further principle of philosophical health. After arguing that promoting philosophical health helps reduce epistemic injustice and develop what Miranda Fricker has dubbed *hermeneutical virtue* and *testimonial sensibility*, I return, in closing, to our initial question: whether we can benefit from thinking of philosophical counselling as promoting *philosophical health*.

Philosophical health

What is 'philosophical health'? Since Luis de Miranda has recently proposed to take the term seriously, we can ask, more narrowly: What is philosophical health for him? One can hear this as an ontological question: What kind of item is philosophical health? If we look at de Miranda for answers, we find that he characterizes philosophical health variously as a *state* (de Miranda, 2022a), as an *idea*, as a *capacity* and as *something to be engaged in* (de Miranda, 2022a), which might perhaps be a *practice* (de Miranda, ms.; de Miranda, 2021a: 71), a *process* or an *activity* or a *programme* (de Miranda, 2020, 2022a). Presumably, de Miranda specifies philosophical health as a *process* at least partly due to his allegiance to the kind of process philosophy developed by, for example, Bergson, Whitehead and Deleuze (cf. de Miranda, 2017: 511; de Miranda, 2021a: 75). He also places 'philosophical health' in the Aristotelian tradition of *eudaimonistic* ethics. However, instead of εὐδαιμονία (*eudaimonia*), de Miranda suggests εὐδυναμία (*eudynamia*) as the τέλος (*telos*) of ethics, which he characterizes variously as 'a beneficial and generative state of ever-renewed potentiality and blissful presence in the earth, in which our intellectual capacities are not smothered' (de Miranda, 2021c: 90), as having 'a good relationship with the possible' (de Miranda, 2021b), or as having 'a healing or attuning access to the regenerative realm of multiversal possibility' (de Miranda, 2022a). However, accepting the concept of philosophical health need not commit one to process philosophy (Seibt, 2022, sec. 5, provides an overview of some challenges it faces; cf. Austin, 2020, for an argument to the effect that process ontological accounts of organisms presuppose substance ontological principles). In what follows, I side-step ontological questions and refer to philosophical health as a state (which is not meant to prejudicate matters). With de Miranda, we can assume that the idea of such a state constitutes an *asymptotic ideal* (de Miranda, 2021a: 81), something we may forever try to approach and our conception of which may continuously undergo subtle changes. We can further stipulate that subjects in the ideal state have certain characteristic capacities and engage in a practice distinctive of it, and that activities that are geared towards such an ideal state or approximate the kind of practice characteristic of it are philosophically healthy.

Generating a concise definition of 'philosophical health' is a non-trivial task, but these, I think, are two of its core aspects: *variegated coherence* and *intentional directedness at a trans-subjective good*.

Variegated coherence

According to de Miranda (2022a), the coherence characteristic of philosophical health obtains *intra-subjectively*, viz. between a philosophically healthy person's thinking, speaking, acting and feeling (cf. de Miranda, 2021a: 71, 2020, 2022a). Elsewhere (e.g. in de Miranda, ms.), it is said to obtain *inter-*, even *trans-subjectively*, that is, not just between different subjects but between beings and non-subjects, even ideas. Philosophically healthy subjects, de Miranda claims, are aware that they inhabit a shared world and that, by way of partaking in various relationships, they take up various roles as creative agents who act as part of, and jointly generate, an integrated and interdependent cohesive whole. (One is reminded here of the Buddhist notion of *pratītyasamutpāda*, often translated as 'dependent origination', which conveys the idea that all items depend (in more than one sense) on everything else.) Of course, philosophically healthy subjects need not understand *how* the cohesive whole is brought about. But they do understand *that* this whole, a specific combination of compossible states, is brought about by the joint creative activity of *all* its elements, including them. Either way, since coherence is construed as *intra-*, *inter-* and *trans-subjective* and as obtained in an integrated and interdependent coherent whole, the requisite notion of coherence is *variegated*.

Intentional directedness at a trans-subjective good

In de Miranda's work, the idea of *intentional directedness at a trans-subjective good* appears (see de Miranda, 2022a) as the stipulation that philosophically healthy subjects will act in ways that draw on their consideration of the good not just of the self, but of *all* beings on Earth, even the entire universe (e.g. de Miranda, in this volume, Chapter 17). Moreover, philosophical health is characterized as a state in which the need for self- and inter-subjective flourishing is satisfied (cf. de Miranda, 2022a). (This, I take it, is not to imply that subjects cannot be philosophically healthy unless all other beings flourish as well. Rather, it is through acting in ways that are geared at realizing the common good that philosophically healthy subjects satisfy, to the best of their ability, the need for intra- and inter-subjective flourishing.)

The idea of *intentional directedness at a trans-subjective good* is also implicated in de Miranda's notion of the holistic horizon of a harmony that extends to more than just humans, and in its correlative: the idea of collective thriving and healing growth, that is, collective flourishing (see e.g. de Miranda, ms.; de Miranda, 2020; de Miranda, 2020). *In nuce*: in pursuing the goal of harmonizing our collective capacity to feel, imagine, envision, realize and co-actualize a world, philosophically healthy subjects are intentionally directed at a trans-subjective good.

Further aspects of philosophical health

De Miranda has further aspects of philosophical health in mind, as is indicated by various characterizations of philosophical health in terms of sublimity, care, sacredness and the Creal. Some of this strikes me as optional and as inviting mystification.

Consider 'sacredness'. If contrasted with 'profane', 'sacred' carries religious connotations. Are we to consider them essential to philosophical health; is 'philosophical health' a religious notion? Or are we to assign 'sacred' a secularized interpretation, as suggested by Émile Durkheim (cf. Durkheim, 1912)? Surely, religiously inclined subjects may interpret the aspect of *intentional directedness at a trans-subjective good* in religious terms, as directedness at the divine, say, or at the implementation of a set of divine commandments. But non-religious conceptions of the trans-subjective common good are available. Accordingly, associating 'philosophical health' with a *prima facie* religious concept seems optional.

Consider, further, de Miranda's approach to philosophical health in what he calls *crealectic* terms. Like 'crealectics', 'crealectic' is a derivative of the neologism 'Creal'. Adopted from his 2008 science fiction novel *Paridaiza*, the word 'Creal' is formed by combining 'creative' and 'Real'. It serves to denote 'a creative flow of healing possibilities, of generous virtual abundance, of fecundity [. . .] [which] is constantly producing realities, and projecting the inner into the world as phenomena' (de Miranda, 2022b) or 'a creative flux of multiplicities, partial unifications and possibilities in constant metamorphosis'. Elsewhere, de Miranda maintains that '[b]y "Creal" [. . .], I mean that the Real is not only a process of infinite possibility, but that this process is pluridimensional and pluridirectional' (de Miranda, 2022a). Further, he says that '[t]he Creal may be understood as desire of Real, of Oneness, of unities, but [. . .] also [. . .] as desire of itself, and therefore plenitude without lack, rather self-love than desire' (de Miranda, 2022b). 'Crealectic', de Miranda stipulates, denotes a mode of intelligence that contrasts with analytic and dialectic modes, whereas 'crealectics' refers to 'the study and practice of co-creating diverse and harmonious realities out of a ground of absolute possibility in which human desire for sublimity is respected' (de Miranda, 2021b: 90). Finally, he wants 'Creal' to refer to a state of mind or a mode of being that is (1) positively characterized as involving a kind of self-sufficient flow experience, in which (2) the subject is characteristically sensitive to what, in and from the present moment, can be created. Through remaining in this mode, de Miranda thinks, agents can exercise something that goes beyond self-actualization: the actualization of heretofore unactualized possibilities, including 'a certain idea of paradise on earth', also dubbed *imparadising* (de Miranda, 2021b: 97).

Now, one may characterize 'philosophical health' in whatever terms one prefers. But given the various specifications of 'Creal' provided – creative flow or flux, process, state of mind, desire, plenitude – clarifying its ontological import and its content requires some work (I attempt some of this later). Also, we may simply wish to do without it. A minimal and broadly acceptable characterization of 'philosophical health', I suggest, draws on just the two core aspects already extracted. Philosophical health so construed is a subjective state characterized by *intra-*, *inter-* and perhaps *trans-subjective* coherence and a matter of being *intentionally directed at a trans-subjective good*. A philosophically healthy subject is at one with themselves in how they think, speak, act and feel, and at one with others (humans and non-humans) in being oriented in thought and action towards the actualization of the common good of all.

This minimal construal of 'philosophical health' integrates easily with various philosophical and religious frameworks. It can serve to characterize the virtuous person as imagined by Plato, the wise as described by Confucius (see Confucius, 1998: 9.28, 14.28, as referenced in Csikszentmihalyi, 2020, who points out that the wise is never confused and thus, as it were, at one with themselves), Aristotle's *phronimos*, perhaps the Boddhisattva and other religious figures. '[T]he ideal of philosophical health', de Miranda urges, 'needs to be renewed, but also democratised rather than reserved to the happy few or a sort of aristocracy of the mind', and we must avoid projecting a picture of philosophy on which it remains 'indistinguishable from a haughty training in speculative sophistry' (de Miranda, 2021a: 72). Quite so. The minimal construal, I think, accommodates de Miranda's inclination to link the concept of philosophical health to various philosophical traditions and democratizes it by removing optional and potentially mystifying elements.

Promoting philosophical health through non-violent just communication

The minimal construal of philosophical health appears broadly akin to that of *practical wisdom*, on which the wise know how to live well and succeed in doing so – which following Aristotle includes acting virtuously. Moreover, *pace* Dennis Whitcomb's unusual contention that even evil persons can be wise (cf. Whitcomb, 2010), the wise person is typically taken to be oriented towards what is good also for the sake of others; an *intentional directedness at an inter-subjective good* is a core element of the concept 'wisdom', too. The same may be said of *variegated coherence*. One can trace this feature not just in the Greek tradition, on which de Miranda mainly draws, but also in Eastern traditions. A recent example of an account of wisdom which highlights the notion of coherence is Valerie Tiberius's *Reflective Wisdom Account*. According to it, like for de Miranda, a wise person's beliefs and values are to cohere with their actions (cf. Tiberius, 2008). De Miranda's notion of philosophical health, I think, naturally connects with the wisdom tradition. This fits well with the fact that in discussing the five principles of philosophical health (see the following section), he draws on Kant's conception of how to promote wisdom.

But instead of pursuing this issue further, let us ask how philosophical health may be attained.

Five principles of philosophical health

In what follows, I sketch de Miranda's five principles that, he thinks, are characteristic of and serve to promote philosophical health.

Mental heroism

Following Pierre Hadot (cf. Hadot, 2014), de Miranda suggests that philosophical health requires a form of *courage* that, he thinks, must be had by those who dedicate themselves in thought and action to what is true and good (for all), even if they may not fully comprehend what that ultimately amounts to. Relatedly, he claims that philosophical health requires of individuals to courageously think and act as independently as possible, consistent with themselves, daily, with supernormal efforts and – drawing on Kant's conception of how to achieve wisdom (in Kant, 1786) – conceptually empathetic vis-à-vis others, that is., in a way that is attuned to what the other's understanding is like. The latter follows, de Miranda suggests, from two facts: (1) all thinking is ultimately inter-subjective, and (2) philosophically healthy subjects are 'dedicated to the service of men', which means that philosophical health goes along with an attitude of philosophical care toward the other, at least in the form of dialogue' (de Miranda, 2021a: 74). Developing such an attitude takes courage since trying to answer the hard question of what the trans-subjective good amounts to requires constant effort, trust and the courage to take risks as one engages in the kind of actions that, one hopes, are most conducive to bringing it about.

Deep orientation

Following Hadot and Kant, de Miranda thinks that philosophical health involves having a profound orientation in thinking, where 'profound' and 'deep' are to signal that such an orientation is not merely temporary, superficial, one among others, but continuously governs all aspects of the subject's thinking and acting. Such an orientation, he thinks, should be informed by the past, characterized by a focus on 'the present as a form of attentive engagement with life', and go hand in hand with a perspective on a future which is seen as containing the 'possibility of wholeness', not just for the self but for the thriving of future life on Earth. At such a possibility our 'longing for a grateful expanding, a non-fragmented nor diminished existence' may be directed, through thought and action, and not just with a merely hopeful attitude but with a combination of confidence and anticipatory trust. One is neither to pine for an ideal that is too far away nor to engage in acts of procrastination (nor, we may add, in escapism). Rather, one must actively participate in the manifestation of the ideals one admires, which include the democratic ideal of a paradise on Earth for each citizen (see de Miranda, 2021a: 75).

Critical creativity

For de Miranda, 'critical creativity' denotes a capacity to take the right decision at the right moment, based on the correct anticipation of how current crises may unfold. Through the exercise of this capacity, subjects respond to their inevitably subjective interpretation of crisis situations and in choosing a way to intervene take responsibility for how things unfold and may 'maintain, redefine, or assert [. . .] [their] orientation' (de Miranda, 2021a: 77). Exercising this capacity successfully, de Miranda stresses, does more than return philosophically healthy subjects to a pre-crisis state of equilibrium: it lifts them to an *improved* equilibrium in which they have acquired a more sophisticated capacity to respond to crises, reshaped and enhanced due to the capacity's most recent creative exercise. Through subsequent exercises, this capacity is also taken to fuel the ongoing reconceptualization of the common good.

Deep listening

Claiming that philosophically healthy subjects exhibit a continuous attentive openness towards the other, de Miranda holds that true philosophers, rather than lecturing, are capable of listening to their interlocutors and of adapting, with care and empathy, to the responses of the latter, so as to generate 'a form of dialogue that aims at becoming "consonant" with the other, with nature and with truth' (de Miranda, 2021a: 79). Successful philosophically healthy listeners pick up nuances characteristic of the individual significances that their interlocutors associate with the words they use, which in turn confronts the listeners with what for them may be new conceptual *gestalten*, idiosyncratically shaped webs of meanings, with something they may respond to with a certain curiosity for the unheard-of, with humility, and with compassion. Learning to navigate such *gestalten* enables them to connect to their interlocutors and to empathetically respond to actions that arise from worldviews that they may not share but comprehend enough to appreciate the presuppositions that shape them and the conceptions of good that orient them.

The Creal

De Miranda's fifth principle is the Creal. To extract what I think is the core of de Miranda's conception, it is useful to start from the observation that all life processes that we partake in occur against the backdrop, on the one hand, of limitations such as past impairments, social determinism or suboptimal conditions, but also in the context of freedom, subjective interpretation and individual choice (cf. de Miranda, 2021a: 82). The multiplicity of processes intersecting in the present jointly constitutes a process of continuous becoming that operates, as de Miranda says, 'within an ontological precondition of ultimate possibility' (de Miranda, 2021a: 82). Philosophically healthy subjects, he thinks, position themselves vis-à-vis this total ground of pure possibility, vis-à-vis the *creative real* (of which what turns out to be real is a mere subset), by adopting an attitude of trust and engaged faith in life, which is combined with an attitude of love and care vis-à-vis the whole. Adopting such an attitude, especially in light of the fact that there will be phenomena that 'might destabilize our well-being and deep orientation' (de Miranda, 2021a: 83), takes courage: mental heroism. Moreover, keeping one's attention focused not – in an act of Sartrean *mauvaise foi* – on the limitations of what is actual but on what is possible provides one with a perspective from which one can discharge what de Miranda thinks is our collective responsibility: 'to actualize what not only intensifies our shared potentialities in the present, but also what preserves the future as a terrain for the healthy self-actualisation and self-transcendence of newborns to come' (de Miranda, 2021a: 84). In all this, the philosophically healthy subject is oriented not just towards their own individual good but towards the common good of all, their conception of which attracts them as a possibility worth striving for. Such orientations, de Miranda claims, involve moments of felt sublimity, enable self-transcendence, and ultimately provide opportunities for the creation of new forms of life.

In nuce, then, de Miranda's five principles state that developing philosophical health takes the *courage* to stick to one's evolving conception of what is true and good (mental heroism), a stable *orientation* in thought and action towards the common good (deep orientation), the capacity to take *well-timed, and well-attuned decisions* in the face of *crises* (critical creativity), other-directed *empathy* (deep listening) and the *trust* (mental heroism, again) that through our active participation and an ongoing focus on what's possible, the *flux of constant becoming* (the Creal) will increasingly manifest the possible common good (the notion of which we may need to continually update as our understanding expands).

Non-violent just communication

Elsewhere, I proposed that we can draw on the work of Iris Murdoch and Marshall Rosenberg as resources for philosophical counselling (see Rosenhagen, 2023). After summarizing this proposal, I will relate it to de Miranda's work. The practice of *non-violent just communication* I gain through by combining Murdoch and Rosenberg's respective insights, I argue, promotes philosophical health in the minimal sense, resonates with de Miranda's list of principles, and invites us to expand it.

Philosophical counselling, on many conceptions of it, aims to promote the counselee's well-being and to improve their ability to cope with whatever brings them to the philosophical counsellor's doorstep. Many authors and practitioners take the process of counselling to primarily focus on finding hidden fallacies in the counselee's ways of reasoning about the world (see e.g. Cohen's logic-based therapy, Chapter 5 in the present volume) or on unearthing presuppositions in the counselee's conceptions of, for example, what they want, of happiness and success, and of what they can and cannot control. Doing such things is no doubt useful. But I find it striking that the aims and techniques typically proposed are predominantly geared at increasing the counselee's understanding of themselves. Comparatively little emphasis, it seems, is placed on enabling counselees to acquire another, equally important skill: to realistically appreciate their circumstances, including the reality of *other* people featuring in them. Certainly, it is important for counsell*ors* to develop their ability to look at others and truly see them. Arguably, only if they can see their counselees, circumstanced as they are, and appreciate the *gestalt* of what the latter struggle with, can counsellors hope to act towards their counselees in ways that are truly responsive to them. Likewise, only if counsel*ees* acquire a realistic understanding of others will they be able to act in ways that truly benefit themselves and others and that are likely to be most conducive to their aims.

'I can only choose within the world I can see', Iris Murdoch claims (Murdoch, 1970: 37). If we take her seriously, we must acknowledge that to understand others, which doing well by them requires, we must try to grasp what *to them*, the world within which they choose looks like. We must appreciate not just what options for action are available to others under descriptions *we* may find appropriate, but imagine what these options will look like to *them*. For how others conceptualize their options may well differ from how we do, and such differences may entail differences in evaluation and, accordingly, in what course of action will seem best.

What, then, does it take for attempts to understand others to succeed? Murdoch's answer: *love*. Since for her, vision, not movement (of, e.g., a Kantian or existentialist will), provides the most useful metaphor for moral activity, she characterizes her technical notion of love in visual terms. Following Simone Weil, she renders it as *just attention*, a way of *looking and attending* to others. To this activity – a blend of physical acts of looking and realistically imagining others in their respective circumstances – the category of justice applies. For in evaluating what one attends to, one can do or fail to do justice to others, fail or succeed in realistically imagining their needs, desires, hopes and what good they seek to achieve (even if one may disagree whether it is a good worth striving for), what options for action are available to them, and which ones to them look best.

Seeing others justly (and even more so, seeing oneself justly – see Gorlin's Chapter 1 in this volume), Murdoch insists, is difficult. Love, as she famously states, is 'the extremely difficult realisation that something other than oneself is real' (Murdoch, 1959: 51). Partly, the difficulty is that looking at others requires directing one's attention away from the self and seeing them not as the caricatures as that they appear if, looking at them through the lenses of one's egoistic desires and fears, one focuses only on how they may promote or obstruct one's own self-centred goals. However, overcoming this difficulty pays off, Murdoch thinks, for unselfish clear vision promotes virtue. We can and probably will act morally better if what we respond to are real people, not caricatures, which will strike one as especially plausible if, like Murdoch, one thinks that 'true vision occasions right conduct' (Murdoch, 1970: 66), that is, that recognizing what one takes to be the morally best option in a given situation intrinsically yields a motivation to do it.

If Murdoch is right and doing well by others requires, *inter alia*, a vision purified by love, and if coping with issues that counselees face frequently requires that they find ways of acting towards others that are based on a more realistic conception of who others are, it becomes plausible that the philosophical counsellor's toolbox should contain more than tools that help counselees engage in what one may call the philosophical analogue of psychoanalysis: logical navel-gazing. It should also contain tools that help counselees connect more realistically with their situation and with other individuals who inhabit it. Philosophical counsellors, in short, should help their counselees increase their capacity to love.

Again, achieving a clear vision of love is difficult, as is fighting what threatens to muddle it: the fat relentless ego (cf. Murdoch, 1970: 52). Which techniques can help? Citing Phil. 4.8, Murdoch recommends looking at what is true, honest, just, pure (Murdoch, 1970: 56), pondering virtue, meditating (cf. Murdoch, 1993: 337) and the daily purification of consciousness. But one wonders whether there aren't other options. This is where, I think, it is useful to draw on Marshall Rosenberg's method of *non-violent communication*. Conceptually simple, but difficult to put into practice, this method, which is employed, for example, in mediation and conflict-resolution, involves four steps: (1) observe and state what is happening in non-evaluative terms,

(2) observe and state how one feels when observing this, (3) say which of one's needs are connected to these feelings and (4) issue a request (which importantly differs from making a demand) (cf. Rosenberg, 2005: 6f.). One core assumption underlying this approach is that in conflict situations, it is not constructive to play the blame game and use evaluative terms and labels that are or can be construed as being intended to hurt the other. Communication that generates opportunities for interlocutors to connect, Rosenberg insists, must be strictly non-violent. A subject *S* who pursues the non-violent alternative Rosenberg recommends enables their interlocutors, even in situations of crisis, to see and understand *S*'s feelings and how they reflect *S*'s needs, desires, hopes and so on. More generally, *S*, instead of attacking their interlocutor, will show them how *S*, given the situation at hand, is vulnerable, perhaps in pain, and offers them ways to understand and connect with *S* by taking concrete steps to address *S*'s needs. The counterpart to this technique is empathetic listening on *S*'s part to the other party. More specifically: *S* must listen closely to determine what needs, desires and so on may underlie whatever the other says and then respond not to their (potentially violent) words but to the needs and desires underlying them. To do this, one must state what one hears, what needs and desires one thinks have been expressed, and ask the other to confirm that one's understanding is correct.

Importantly, such communication must be conducted in as evaluatively neutral a fashion as possible. According to Rosenberg, when we engage in, for example, moralizing evaluations, we are not properly taking cognisance and responsibility for what we feel, for what our needs are, and fail to realize what things the other could do for us to enable us to reconnect and heal. Evaluations, as Rosenberg has it, need not be couched in evaluative terms, but can also occur in the form of quantified expressions used in an accusatory spirit, such as in 'You *always* do x', 'You *never* help me with y', 'You are *completely* unreliable . . .' and so on (cf. Rosenberg, 2005: 30–1). Hiding our feelings and needs both from ourselves and others, he thinks, ultimately cuts off both parties from a significant part of what drives the interaction and prevents them from locating resources that could improve it. Positively put, it is through taking responsibility for and showing oneself with one's vulnerabilities (see McMahon's chapter 6 in this volume), one's feelings, and one's underlying needs, hopes and so on that others are enabled to better see and understand one. And while, as we emphatically listen to others, we may not endorse the specific needs that motivate them, we can recognize them as akin to those we harbour as well. Moreover, we can understand and connect with what it is like, for example, for one's needs to be unsatisfied or for one's hopes to be crushed; such experiences are part of the human condition. Such understanding opens up ways to respond not to what is said but to what is alive in the other. Non-violent communication, as Rosenberg puts it, employs the language of life.

Murdochian clear vision, we saw, is difficult to achieve. Rosenberg's practical method, I propose – again: simple in theory but everything but simple to stick with, especially in situations of crisis – gives us a way to help achieve it that goes beyond Murdoch's own proposals. Since Rosenberg, too, highlights the importance of empathetic listening, we may stipulate that he would be happy to take on board Murdoch's notion of *just attention*. But he adds an element that in Murdoch remains in the background: the importance for speakers to reveal themselves. Indeed, and this is the crux of the matter, he invites non-violent communicators to reveal precisely what Murdochian just attention is supposed to make visible: their being circumstanced in a context that is co-constituted by their feelings, needs, desires, aims and wishes, and as looking at others and their circumstances through the particular lens that this particular context affords. Murdoch's and Rosenberg's approaches, I think, are neatly complementary. Those who engage in both engage in what I call *non-violent just communication*.

Non-violent just communication, I argue, serves both counselees and counsellors as it helps manifest the desiderata laid out at the beginning of this section: it helps *counsellors* connect with counselees, get a better sense of the issues the latter are facing, and of what these look like to them. Simultaneously, practising *non-violent just communication* introduces *counselees* to a powerful way of communicating with others empathetically. Engaging in such communication is likely to allow counselees to elicit the kind of responses from others who coinhabit the problematic circumstances they find themselves in that enable counselees to obtain a more realistic appreciation of both these circumstances and the others featured in them. Practising *non-violent communication* makes it *easier* to engage in just attention; their combination, *non-violent just communication*, makes it easier to act well towards others, which benefits both counsellors and counselees.

Non-violent just communication and philosophical health

Non-violent just communication both promotes philosophical health and resonates with some of de Miranda's principles. Clearly, the emphasis on just attention and empathetic listening resonates with de Miranda's principle of *deep listening* and, to the extent that the requirement to listen empathetically to others is part of it, with *mental heroism*. Moreover, through engaging in *non-violent just communication*, subjects can arguably develop their *deep orientation*. Through becoming more attuned to the reality of others and to what moves them, subjects can transcend their self-centred conceptions of the good and move towards an inter-subjective one. They do this by paying attention to those that they encounter, by seeking to understand and connect with them and, subsequently, by creating habits of thinking and acting in ways that acknowledge and cohere with their thoughts, actions and, importantly, needs and desires. Acknowledging the reality of others, their feelings and underlying needs, and anticipating the legitimate requests they may issue towards us will in turn help subjects anticipate possible ways in which crisis situations will unfold and is thus likely to increase their *critical creativity*.

This leaves the aspect de Miranda calls *the Creal*, which is most straightforwardly characterized not as a principle but as an ontological conception. If there is any principle of philosophical health in the vicinity of its characterization, it is, I think, best framed as the exhortation to adopt an attitude of trust, engaged faith, love and care that is directed at the present state, at the possibilities it may afford with respect to unfolding in ways that manifest a trans-subjective good, and at other subjects (and possibly non-subjects) that feature in that present, even in the face of possible adversity.

It is the latter – trust in the face of potential adversity – that seasoned practitioners of *non-violent just communication* exhibit regularly. Even when facing interpersonal crises and emotionally fraught situations, they trustfully show themselves as potentially vulnerable, thus remaining both open and relatable. Such trust, I think, has various facets. For one, and clearly, it requires *courage* as those who show themselves may get hurt. If the other, perhaps acting from a place of pain, lashes out (which may well happen), it may take enormous courage for the *non-violent just communicator* to refrain from veering off their non-violent path. Second, Rosenberg thinks that exhibiting this kind of trust is an act of *recognizing and taking responsibility* for one's own feelings and needs. Third, showing this kind of trust may also be a conscious and studied practical acknowledgement of an oft-neglected fact (one, arguably, that philosophers find most disturbing), viz. that one is not and probably cannot ever be fully in control of how things unfold. As human beings, we are, as it were, constantly at each other's mercy. Suppose that upon realizing this condition we responded, rather than by clinging to the illusory ideal that total control is possible and worth achieving, by trusting both in the possibility of good outcomes and in those we interact with. Suppose, further, that we extended this trust even in crisis situations by way of showing others that we are as vulnerable, as endowed with feelings, needs, desires and so on, as they are. If we did this, we would create excellent opportunities for them to do well by us, viz. by responding to the requests (not demands) that we direct at them. The specific acts of trust involved in *non-violent just communication* that we engage in through showing ourselves authentically to others afford others opportunities for just attention and good actions. Both instantiate and create opportunities for virtue.

As they reveal the beliefs, feelings and underlying needs of the subject, such acts of trust also instantiate *intra-subjective coherence* in that one's revelatory actions cohere with one's overall state. Moreover, since they serve to allow interlocutors to adjust their conception of what, in the given situation, is the good thing to do, by incorporating in their evaluation of their options the recognition of the feelings and needs of others, such acts also afford opportunities to increase the *inter-subjective coherence* of the subject's thoughts, feelings and actions. If things go well, and one seizes such opportunities, one will, in doing so, exhibit an *intentional directedness at a trans-subjective good*. Such acts of trust, in other words, and the practice of non-violent just communication that make them possible promote philosophical health in accordance with the minimal construal proposed earlier. Therefore, such trust should be counted among the principles that promote philosophical health.

Non-violent just communication and epistemic justice

Here, I suggest, is a further advantage of the practice of *non-violent just communication*: it promotes epistemic justice in helping one develop what Miranda Fricker has dubbed *hermeneutical virtue* and *testimonial sensitivity* (see Fricker, 2007; also: Geuskens, 2018).

Non-violent just communication and hermeneutical virtue

Epistemic injustice, according to Fricker, comes in two flavours: *testimonial* and *hermeneutical*. In both, the injustice in question involves 'a wrong done to someone specifically in their capacity as a knower' (Fricker, 2007: 1). Hermeneutical injustice, as per Fricker's generic definition, is 'the injustice of having some significant area of one's social experience obscured from collective understanding owing to hermeneutical marginalisation' (Fricker, 2007: 158). The core idea, roughly, is that the lack of hermeneutic resources – such as having words to express how things are for one – can render both the marginalized victims and the perpetrators involved in an unjust practice unable to understand and make sense of that practice. Enriching the expressive capacities of language through the addition of terms expressive of harmful aspects of the social experience of the marginalized, Fricker argues, can thus enable the participants to verbalize the unjust aspects of the practice, raise awareness, and ultimately enable them to take steps to modify it.

Hermeneutical injustice, Fricker emphasizes, is due to systemic features of a shared communicative practice and not (or not primarily) an injustice that subjects inflict upon each other. Can the practice of *non-violent just communication* address such systemic issues? To see how, note Fricker's characterization of hermeneutical justice:

> [H]ermeneutical justice [. . .] is an alertness or sensitivity to the possibility that the difficulty one's interlocutor is having as she tries to render something communicatively intelligible is due not to its being nonsense or her being a fool, but rather to some sort of gap in collective hermeneutical resources. [. . .] The virtuous hearer, then, must be reflexively aware of how the relation between his social identity and that of the speaker is impacting on the intelligibility to him of what she is saying and how she is saying it. (Fricker, 2007: 169)

Non-violent just communication, we saw, involves showing oneself with one's feelings, needs, hopes and desires, but also attending to one's interlocutor justly, empathetically hearing past the potentially hurtful or inappropriate words they may use to connect with the interlocutor's feelings and the needs, hopes, and desires that underlie them. Non-violent just communicators, rather than focusing on what is being said, focus on what is being felt and on how this reflects what is needed, hoped and, perhaps, requested. Hermeneutical injustice is an injustice that hinges on what kind of expressive resources a given communicative practice affords to talk about the particular wrongs experienced especially by those who are marginalized – marginalized also in the sense that the way they are treated amounts to the construction and perpetuation of a social identity attributed to them that they cannot easily escape, one that keeps them in a position of little social power, and that prevents their flourishing.

Non-violent just communication, however, is a practice designed to be hermeneutically just. I already indicated that *non-violent communication* sounds simple in theory yet is difficult to put into practice, like *just attention* and, by implication, *non-violent just communication*. Partly, the difficulty is that both require that the practice participants engage in with each other be radically egalitarian and equitable. Non-violent just communication requires, *inter alia*, verbalising what one has understood and asking one's interlocutor to confirm that one's understanding is appropriate. It is thus *extraordinary* in terms of the demands it places on ensuring that all communicating parties are heard and understood. Engaging in it successfully arguably enables practitioners to avoid hermeneutical injustices that may beset their ordinary communicative practices. If things go well, it may even allow them to remedy them by finding ways to suitably enrich ordinary language with terms expressive of the particular kinds of experiences of which, through non-violent just communication, they become aware.

Non-violent just communication and testimonial sensibility

Testimonial injustice, Fricker stipulates, is sustained by a speaker just in case 'she receives a credibility deficit owing to identity prejudice in the hearer' (Fricker, 2007: 28). Testimonially unjust speakers take others to be less credible than they are by attributing a kind of social identity to them which they associate, discriminatorily, with a low degree of credibility. As Fricker sees it, the trouble with testimonial injustice is that it is frequently a matter of the hearer's theory-laden perception of the speaker. Irresponsible hearers engage in a kind of social (mis)perception, according to which, based on some acquired social stereotype or other, they perceive the speakers as being more or less credible than they are (cf. Fricker, 2007: 71). Virtuous hearers, in contrast, exhibit a partly inherited, partly acquired and trained, and ultimately uncodifiable *testimonial sensibility* that allows them to pick up on the actual credibility of the speaker by *correcting* for possible prejudicial influences.

In short, what goes for hermeneutical injustice goes for testimonial injustice: non-violent just communicators are to refrain from using societal labels. As they employ non-violent just communication, they create a communicative context that is extraordinary with respect to the demands it places on ensuring that all communicative parties are heard and understood. In other words, through exercising the kind of empathetic understanding characteristic of the extraordinary practice of non-violent just communication, practitioners are likely to avoid testimonial injustice and likely to develop their testimonial sensibility.

Philosophical health and philosophical counselling

Above, I thought it plausible that 'philosophical health' belongs in the tradition of practical wisdom, understood as involving the capacity to live a good and virtuous life that is oriented towards the common good. Does philosophical counselling aim at philosophical health; does it aim at wisdom? I find this thought attractive. But whether we accept it or not, we can, I think, construe different schools of philosophical counselling as aiming at philosophical health, or at significant aspects of it.

Consider Cohen's *Logic-Based Therapy* (see Cohen's Chapter 5 in this volume). A main aim of this rather logocentric approach is to improve the counselee's well-being by enabling them to detect fallacies in their reasoning. Practitioners of this method hope that an increase in the counselee's understanding will yield better actions and improve their well-being. In terms of our minimal account of philosophical health, this aim appears to align with that of establishing subjective coherence, not, or not primarily, with that of developing an intentional directedness at a trans-subjective good.

Consider, next, Marinoff's so-called PEACE process (cf. Marinoff, 1999: 38f.). According to it, philosophical counsellors first determine the problem (P), the counselee's emotional reactions to it (E), analyse the available options for solving the issue (A), and, through helping them contemplate and cultivate a unified philosophical view of the situation (C), they help them reach equilibrium (E), that is, a stage at which they are ready to take the necessary action. Again, the aim seems to be a certain kind of coherence, one obtaining between one's thoughts, ideas, emotions and, ultimately, actions. As Marinoff says about stage (C), '[y]ou need a conception of how everything fits together – all the elements of your situation, all the elements of your world, all the elements of your philosophy' (Marinoff, 1999: 43). Once that has been achieved, one is to act accordingly.

Marinoff's specification does not mention a trans-subjective good. Of course, contemplating it may well feature in stage (C). Similarly, Cohen might hold that contemplating such a good may be triggered by the antidotes he thinks philosophical counsellors ought to prescribe to enable counselees to replace habits of engaging in fallacious reasoning with better ones. I am not claiming that these two accounts afford no room for such considerations, only that in neither method, the contemplation of the common good seems to be foregrounded.

Contrast, third, what I dubbed the extraordinary communicative practice of *non-violent just communication*. It invites both counsellors and counselees to engage in the attempt to achieve coherence between their own beliefs, emotions, needs, desires, hopes and so on and that of others, and a better understanding of what others are like. Implicit in the imperative to empathetically acknowledge the reality of others (of the counselee and of those they interact with), we also find the recommendation to act in ways that are governed by the notion of a trans-subjective good that is responsive to and mediated by the good that we realize is pursued by those we interact with (see also de Miranda's Chapter 17 in this volume for how this attitude might include non-human beings). Notably, engaging in this practice is beneficial not just for the counsel*ee* but also for the counsel*lor*. Philosophical health, to be promoted in others, must be constantly developed further in the counsellor's practice.

Thinking about various approaches within the field of philosophical counselling in terms of the minimal notion of philosophical health, I think, is productive. Perhaps the notion could even help us resolve long-standing debates about what philosophical counselling aims at. Moreover, 'I am seeing a philosophical counsellor to improve my (philosophical) health' sounds rather innocuous, whereas 'I am seeing a philosophical counsellor to become wiser' may sound rather pretentious. In establishing a relatively jargon-free use of 'philosophical health', we thus may gain a conceptual tool to compare and contrast different approaches of philosophical counselling that also allows us to promote philosophical counselling in a way that makes neither the counselee nor the counsellor seem overly pretentious. Of course, establishing such a use is something we can only do together. Doing so, I think, might be ~~wise~~ philosophically healthy.

118 *Philosophical Health*

References

Achenbach, Gerd B. (1984), *Philosophische Praxis. Mit Beiträgen von Matthias Fischer, Thomas H. Macho, Odo Marquard, Ekkehard Martens*. Köln: Verlag für Philosophie Jürgen Dinter (=Schriftenreihe zur Philosophischen Praxis. Band I).

Achenbach, Gerd B. (forthcoming), *Philosophical Practice*, trans. from German by Michael Picard. Lanham: Lexington / Rowman & Littlefield.

Ananth, Mahesh (2008), *In Defense of an Evolutionary Concept of Health. Nature, Norms, and Human Biology*. Hampshire: Ashgate Publishing.

Austin, Christopher J. (2020), 'Organisms, Activity, and Being: On the Substance of Process Ontology'. *European Journal for Philosophy of Science*, 10 (2): 1–21.

Azevedo, Marco A. (2015), 'Health as a Clinic-Epidemiological Concept'. *Journal of Evaluation in Clinical Practice*, 21 (3): 365–73.

Boorse, Christopher (1977), 'Health as a Theoretical Concept'. *Philosophy of Science*, 44 (4): 542–73.

Brenifier, Oscar (2020), *The Art of Philosophical Practice*, trans. from French by Karl-Stephan Bouthillette. Independently Published.

Cohen, Elliot D. (2007), *The New Rational Therapy: Thinking Your Way to Serenity, Success, and Happiness*. Lanham: Rowman & Littlefield.

Cohen, Elliot D. (2016), *Logic-Based Therapy and Everyday Emotions: A Case-Based Approach*. Lanham: Lexington.

Cohen, Elliot D. (2022), *Cognitive Behavior Interventions for Self-Defeating Thoughts. Helping Clients to Overcome the Tyranny of "I Can't"*. New York: Routledge.

Confucius (1998), *The Original Analects: Sayings of Confucius and His Successors*, trans. and ed. E. B. Brooks and A. T. Brooks, Translations from the Asian Classics. New York: Columbia University Press.

Csikszentmihalyi, Mark (2020), 'Confucius'. In E. N. Zalta (ed.), *The Stanford Encyclopedia of Philosophy* (Summer 2020 Edition). https://plato.stanford.edu/archives/sum2020/entries/confucius/

Durkheim, Émile (1912), *Les formes élémentaires de la vie religieuse: le système totémique en Australia*. PUF. Paris: Alcan.

Dussault, Antoine C. and Anne-Marie Gagné-Julien (2015), 'Health, Homeostasis, and the Situation-Specificity of Normality'. *Theoretical Medicine and Bioethics*, 36 (1): 61–81.

Fricker, Miranda (2007), *Epistemic Injustice: Power and the Ethics of Knowing*. Oxford: Oxford University Press.

Geuskens, Machteld (2018), *Epistemic Justice: A Principled Approach to Knowledge Generation and Distribution*. PhD thesis. S.I.: Tilburg University.

Grimes, Pierre and L. Uliana Regina (1998), *Philosophical Midwifery: A New Paradigm for Understanding Human Problems with Its Validation*. Costa Mesa: Hyparxis Press.

Hadot, Pierre (2014), *Discours et mode de vie philosophique*. Paris: Belles Lettres.

Hamilton, Richard P. (2010), 'The Concept of Health: Beyond Normativism and Naturalism'. *Journal of Evaluation in Clinical Practice*, 16 (2): 323–9.

Kant, Immanuel (1996 [1786]), 'What Does It Mean to Orient Oneself in Thinking?' In Allen W. Wood and George Di Giovanni (ed. and trans.), *Religion and Rational Theology*, 1–18. Cambridge: Cambridge University Press.

Lang, Martha (2018), 'Philosophical Counseling and the Network Theory of Well-Being, Revamped'. *International Journal of Philosophical Practice*, 4 (4): 16–27.

Marinoff, Lou (1999), *Plato, not Prozac!* New York: HarperCollins Publishers.

Marinoff, Lou (2002), *Philosophical Practice*. Cambridge: Academic Press.

de Miranda, Luis (2017), 'On the Concept of Creal: The Politico-Ethical Horizon of a Creative Absolute'. In Paulo de Assis and Paolo Giudici (eds), *The Dark Precursor: Deleuze and Artistic Research*, 510–16. Leuven: Leuven University Press.

de Miranda, Luis (2020), 'Artificial Intelligence and Philosophical Creativity: From Analytics to Crealectics'. *Human Affairs*, 30 (4): 597–607.

de Miranda, Luis (2021a), 'Five Principles of Philosophical Health: From Hadot to Crealectics'. *Eidos. A Journal for Philosophy of Culture*, 5: 70–89.

de Miranda, Luis (2021b), 'Think into the Place of the Other: The Crealectic Approach to Philosophical Health and Care'. *International Journal of Philosophical Practice*, 7 (1): 89–103.

de Miranda, Luis (2021c), 'Crealectic Intelligence'. *In V. Glăveanu (ed.), The Palgrave Encyclopaedia of the Possible*, 250–7. Cham: Palgrave Macmillan.

de Miranda, Luis (2022a), 'Philosophical Health'. In Vlad P. Glăveanu (ed.), *The Palgrave Encyclopedia of the Possible*, 1003–8. Cham: Palgrave Macmillan.

de Miranda, Luis (2022b), 'The Crealectical Moment'. *Crealectics (blog)*. https://crealectics .com/the-crealectical-moment/ (accessed 12 April 2022).

de Miranda, Luis (2022c), 'Nothing that is Possible is Bad, because it is Only Possible, Not Yet Real'. *Crealectics* (blog). Published 22 March. https://crealectics.com/2022/03/22 /nothing-that-is-possible-is-bad-because-it-is-only-possible-not-yet-real/ (accessed 12 April 2022).

de Miranda, Luis (ms), 'Summary of "Introduction: Philosophical Health as a Practice of Care"', book proposal for this volume.

Murdoch, Iris (1959), 'The Sublime and the Good'. *The Chicago Review*, 13, no. 3 (Autumn): 42–55.

Murdoch, Iris (1970), *The Sovereignty of Good*. London: Routledge & Kegan Paul.

Murdoch, Iris (1993), *Metaphysics as a Guide to Morals*. New York: Allen Lane. The Penguin Press.

Rosenberg, Marshall (2005), *Nonviolent Communication: A Language of Life*, 2nd edn. Encinitas: Puddle Dancer Press.

Rosenhagen, Raja (2023), 'Inputs from Murdoch and Rosenberg for Philosophical Counselling'. *Philosophical Practice: Journal of the APPA*, 18 (1): 3027–38.

Saad, Julian M. and James O. Prochaska (2020), 'A Philosophy of Health: Life as Reality, Health as a Universal Value'. *Palgrave Commun*, 6: 45. https://doi.org/10.1057/s41599 -020-0420-9

Seibt, Johanna (2022), 'Process Philosophy'. In Edward N. Zalta (ed.), *The Stanford Encyclopedia of Philosophy* (Spring 2022 Edition). https://plato.stanford.edu/archives/ spr2022/entries/process-philosophy/ (accessed 15 August 2022).

Svenaeus, Fredrik (2022), 'Health and Illness as Enacted Phenomena'. *Topoi*, 41 (2): 373–82.

Tiberius, Valerie (2008), *The Reflective Life: Living Wisely With Our Limits*. Oxford: Oxford University Press.

Whitcomb, Dennis (2010), 'Wisdom'. In Sven Bernecker and Duncan Pritchard (eds), *Routledge Companion to Epistemology*, 95–105. London: Routledge.

8

Philosophical health, meaning and the role of the other

A hermeneutic approach

Dennis Schutijser

Luis de Miranda defines philosophical health as 'a state of fruitful coherence between a person's way of thinking and speaking and their ways of acting, such that the possibilities for a sublime life are increased and the need for self- and intersubjective flourishing satisfied' (de Miranda, 2022). This definition paves the way to establishing philosophical health alongside more established conceptions of health. In this chapter, I will focus on the particularity of philosophical health as distinct from spiritual health on one side and from mental health on the other. My proposal is that philosophical hermeneutics can offer valuable insights into our understanding of personhood, in the question of a meaningful life and in the role of the other person, notably a philosophical counsellor.

In the first place, I will focus on the central question of the meaning of life. What does it mean to consider that my life is meaningful? And how does that relate to philosophy? While de Miranda avoids this term in his definition and refers instead to a more aesthetically charged 'sublime' life, a 'sense that life has meaning and is worthwhile' (Levy quoted in de Miranda, 2022) is both fundamental and problematic. Fundamental because meaning incurs a more profound and conscious understanding of life. Problematic because the source or origin of such meaning is anything but clear. Philosophical health has to navigate between the traditional source of meaning proposed by religion or spirituality and the contemporary phenomenological idea of meaning creation by subjective perception.

Second, we can connect the question of meaning to the individual person. To this end, I will propose a hermeneutic understanding of personhood based mainly on Paul Ricoeur's concept of narrative identity. Insofar as philosophical health is concerned with a person's speaking and acting, but also with their reasoning, narrative identity can help clarify how these three dimensions come together. To have a meaningful life, I will propose, is to be able to answer the question 'who are you': to give an account of oneself. That narrative account has to manage an irreducible complexity of elements. I will initially focus on suffering, because the mechanisms behind that complexity and the dependency of the person on meaning are shown most clearly when the sense of meaning is compromised by suffering.

Third, flourishing is not only subjective but always also intersubjective. While the analysis of narrative identity will already make this clear, the question of meaning helps identify the specificity of philosophical health and philosophical counselling as a kind of care. That care can be distinguished from both traditional spiritual care and modern psychotherapy. It borrows its uniqueness from a reply to the second way in which we can understand the question 'who are you', directed to the other person one is encountering.

Meaning in life: Do we find it, or do we make it?

The problem of the meaning of life is a question that has occupied human thought throughout the ages. It could very well be argued that both philosophy and religion originated from this preoccupation with the meaning of our existence, linking the objective 'what is there'-question with the normative enquiry 'why are things what they are'. While it may seem impossible to answer that question, what we can do is to start by observing the importance of the issue.

To consider our lives as meaningful seems to be a fundamental and existential human need (Frankl, 2020; Baumeister, 1991; Yalom, 1980). Having a sense of meaning in our lives gives us a reason to commit to our personal and professional projects; it is what inspires us in our endeavours and what keeps us going when things are tough.

How do we go about answering the question of the meaning of life? To this, two paths readily open up. On the one hand, it has long been a subject of religious or spiritual attachment. Institutional religion has, for many generations, provided the answers to the big questions, including the meaning of individual existence in larger frameworks of belief. Through such frameworks, an individual life can be associated with a divine will, a greater plan or some other source of meaning that in a way befalls us. These larger frameworks of meaning precede individuation and may be at work in implicit ways throughout our personal lives. We can refer to this encountering of a pre-existing framework of meaning, as an experience from the outside, a cosmology. The assumption is that the meaning is already present in the world, over and beyond the living subject, who subsequently experiences some meaning (the German *Sinnerfahrung*, i.e., *experience-of-meaning*, best captures this order in the constitution of meaning from world or cosmos to the secondary subject).

This long tradition of establishing meaning through the adoption by the individual of pre-established religious frameworks has lost much of its self-evidence in the present age (Taylor, 1991). Postmodern philosopher Jean-François Lyotard perhaps best translated this loss when he described the postmodern condition as the era in which 'the grand narrative has lost its credibility' (Lyotard, 2010: 37). That is to say, the uniting frameworks or grand narratives that founded our most important values in an inclusive and all-encompassing way have been revealed to be themselves unfounded. Religious truths that gave meaning to our lives have been deconstructed and devalued.

Cosmology, or the objective *experience* of meaning from somewhere outside us, is increasingly problematic as the active self-centred individual has taken its place.

Modern and contemporary humanism has inverted this traditional outlook on the meaning of our lives. Taking precedence in Husserl's phenomenology, twentieth-century thinkers such as Sartre and Heidegger have abandoned any reference to meaning originating from a cosmological narrative or a moral framework we should adopt (Heidegger and Stambaugh, 2010; Sartre, 1996). Instead, meaning is rather something imposed by the individual themselves. Meaning is a subjective perspective, an interpretation added by the individual to an inarticulate world and a meaningless existence. In contrast with cosmology, we can call this route a *worldview*, with the emphasis on the 'view', that is, on the subjective point of view onto that world (the German concept of *Sinngebung*, or *giving-of-meaning*, employed by Husserl (1991) and others, best captures this precedence of the subject: meaning is *given* to a meaningless world by that subject, effectively making it their own world).

The aforementioned Charles Taylor observed how this turn to the individual and to subjectivism entails its own difficulties. In particular, he considers it actually implies a 'loss of meaning, the fading of moral horizons' (Taylor, 1991: 10). If meaning is a purely personal affair, he notices, we become less capable, and even less willing, to actively engage in dealing with the question of a meaningful life. If there is no objective truth on which to go, 'if there is no God, Dostoyevski wrote, then everything is permitted'.

The impoverishment that marks such a life bereft of concernment with objective meaning and worth may go unnoticed. Our everyday tasks may shield us from these questions, and today's consumer society offers us a plethora of distractions. In certain moments of crisis, the problem of meaning may flare up. Contemporary afflictions such as burnout, depression or anxiety may be direct symptoms of the repressed question of meaning. But the difficulty of meaning may also appear in other moments of our lives, moments when the self-evidence of that everyday life falls short – for example, when we suffer a grave illness, have an accident, lose a loved one or in some other way are forced to rethink our lives.

In these and other moments, the ways of both cosmology (*Sinnerfahrung*) and worldview (*Sinngebung*) can fall short. It is not always enough to simply rely on the frameworks of established belief narratives and apply them to ourselves. To reduce the meaning of an individual life to the frameworks of tradition is like reducing that individual to the Baron of Munchhausen, travelling from one place to another by jumping on cannonballs that happen to be flying by. Instead of directing our own lives, we remain dependent on external forces we neither control nor understand, and which may not bring us anywhere suitable for us. But on the other hand, thinking that the individual can simply impose their personal interpretation on the world is equally implausible and undesirable. The individual who convinces themselves the meaning of their lives is the simple result of their own personal will and an authentic act of self-creation rather resembles the same Baron of Munchhausen, elevating himself out of the swamp by pulling himself up by his own hair.

How, then, can we find a balance between the purely subjective stance of individual creation of meaning, on the one hand, and the presumably objective imposition of meaning, on the other hand? This is where the concept of philosophical health plays a central role. Philosophical health can offer an alternative third way, between objective cosmology and subjective worldview, or between structuralist subjection and existentialist individualism. And accordingly, the practice of philosophical health counselling stands between spiritual guidance on one side, and psychotherapy on the other.

Suffering as an indicator for philosophical health

The question of the meaning of life can be greatly served with a phenomenological investigation into how it appears to us. What phenomenology can reveal is that the meaning of our lives only becomes a problem when it ceases to function as it does or should. It's in moments of crisis that the question for meaning is revealed to be a problem. We can compare this with Martin Heidegger's phenomenological analysis of a carpenter's hammer (Heidegger and Stambaugh, 2010: 70). The carpenter is simply using his hammer: it is a part of his world and even of his own body. He does not wonder about what it is, nor why it is what it is. The hammer only becomes an object of investigation, begins to 'exist' as hammer, when something is wrong with it. When the hammer is lost, something is blocking it or when it is broken, only then does the carpenter look up from his work to wonder about the hammer.

In the same way, philosophical health as it is concerned with living a meaningful life becomes most apparent when there is some problem with our everyday understanding of ourselves or the world around us. When that understanding is in some way lost, impeded or broken down, then we have a chance to investigate the meaning of our lives. What such a breakdown can reveal, however, is that there was perhaps already an issue at play that could be of interest for thinking about philosophical health.

Suffering from physical or mental health can be something very visible, like from a broken leg or an acute psychosis. Other forms of physical and mental illness can be much less obvious: only doctors can 'see' certain forms of cancer, and clinical depression can go unnoticed for years. The same goes for philosophical health: its 'illnesses' can be difficult to notice. But whereas in the fields of physical and mental health the issue is primarily one of diagnosis, in the case of philosophical health the issue is slightly different. This becomes clearer when we look at what it means to suffer.

The twentieth-century hermeneutic philosopher Paul Ricoeur proposes that to suffer is to experience a number of incapacities (Ricoeur, 2013). Suffering is first of all to be incapable of expressing that suffering (the same is true, by the way, of instances such as extreme joy or ecstasy; in the present context we will focus on negative instances as a topic of interest for philosophical health, but it's worth noting that the positive dimension of our lives is equally revealing). In the case of physical suffering, we can cry or wail. In the case of philosophical suffering, we lack the words, we do not know how to formulate our philosophical beliefs or the lack thereof. This could take different forms, such as falling quiet, using platitudes or just shrugging 'I don't know' when we are asked about our understanding of the world or of ourselves. A second incapacity in suffering is the incapacity to act, or more specifically to act in a deliberate way. Someone who suffers is someone who does not act but undergoes whatever is happening to them.

They are passive. To be philosophically unhealthy is to be incapable to deliberate one's actions and accord them with one's own practical reason. Another important trait of suffering is that it tends to affect the esteem a person can have for themselves. In the case of physical or psychological suffering that Ricoeur focuses on, being reduced to a patient is very often accompanied with a loss of self-esteem, with a feeling of humiliation. In the case of philosophical health, esteem also plays an important role. To be philosophically unhealthy can include having a distorted conception of one's own worth or of the surrounding world's worth.

The last point in Ricoeur's definition of suffering most clearly introduces the dimension of meaning. Our words and our actions, as well as our moral relations, already have some sort of 'meaning', or loss thereof, in the sense that words, actions and relations already 'mean' something in a semantic or semiotic way. But it is in the form of a narrative understanding that meaning takes on an existential dimension in relation to our philosophical beliefs: words, actions and relations become telling of who we were, who we are, or who we want to be. To understand ourselves, to answer the question 'who are we?', is to give a narrative account of ourselves. Philosophical illness in that perspective means losing our bearing, losing the oversight of the story of our life, or what Ricoeur calls the experience of the 'untellable' (*l'inénarrable*) (Ricoeur, 2013; 1986). I may not know who I really am, or who I want to be. I may be at a loss to give direction to my actions, feel disconnected from the world around me, or even from myself. In short, I stumble over the question of the meaning of my life.

The dynamics of narrative identity

Trying to give a narrative account of ourselves crucially introduces both stability and dynamism into our understanding of who we are. It does so, in the first place, in relation to our own identity. We are, on the one hand, a self that remains in some important ways constant. I am partly the same person I was as a child: I have the same nationality, the same parents, the same DNA; I am the same person to the extent that childhood friends will shout out I 'haven't changed a bit!' since we last saw each other years ago. Ricoeur calls this *idem*, or the part of me that remains the same (Ricoeur, 1994: 116). But there is also an important source of change within myself. As a child I could not speak a word of French; now I raise my children speaking French. When I was young, I wanted to be a doctor and cared little about the humanities. Now I work full-time and with passion in philosophy. I was once a member of the Socialist party, but last time I voted conservative. Ricoeur refers to this part of our identity as *ipse*; it is what makes me *me* via constant flux.

The second source of tension in the narrative identity and my efforts to constitute meaning in my life is what Ricoeur calls concordance and discordance (Ricoeur, 2009). If *idem/ipse* refers to my own identity and the person I am, concordance and discordance rather relate to the world we inhabit and the events that befall us. Ricoeur borrows these terms from Aristotle's analysis of tragedy in the *Poetics*, where they form two necessary poles of the plotting of a tragedy (Aristotle, 1984). Concordance refers to the unity of an account, the way in which it consists of a coherent whole; with a beginning, a middle, and an end; with fleshed-out characters; with a storyline that gives meaning to all the parts of the whole. When I present my resume, I usually try to point out the concordance, or the way in which my past experience has logically led me to where I stand now. It's my life's story, and how everything in my past adds up to where I am today. Discordance, on the other hand, consists of all the crises, mishaps, and adventures that drive a story forward. In Aristotle's understanding of tragedy, discordance is as necessary as concordance: a good story needs its setbacks. Odysseus would be a boring feat without Neptune's wrath, the Cyclops' threat, and Circe's temptation. Similarly, the order and unity in my life is constantly interrupted by accidents, a severe illness, my partner leaving me, and all the twists and turns that undermine my understanding of myself. It's perhaps what ultimately makes life interesting. Still, while I live through them, I become acutely aware of my need for narrative understanding, and of the impossibility of achieving complete understanding or control. Ricoeur perfectly summarizes this challenge when he concludes that 'we learn to become the *narrator or our own story* without completely becoming the author of our life' (Ricoeur, 1986: 131).

With these tensions of self and life at play, and with the challenge to achieve some narrative understanding of my life, the question of the meaning of life lends itself to a hermeneutic approach. Philosophical hermeneutics comes into the picture in a number of ways. First of all, the question of the meaning of life is already a hermeneutic question because it is focused not on objective being or subjective experience but on the understanding and interpretation of that being and experience. Second, the dynamic inherent to that understanding is similar to the dynamic that propels hermeneutic investigation, oscillating between the whole and the parts of our identity and our life experiences. And in yet a third way, we can approach philosophical health with the aid of the basic tools of hermeneutic understanding. This brings us, incidentally, to the question of the other person in philosophical counselling.

Philosophical counselling: A hermeneutic proposal

Others have already pointed out the potential use of hermeneutics in philosophical counselling (Raabe, 2001; Guerra Bravo, 2007). Raabe notes, for instance, that phenomenology aims to 'describe an experience in a way that is as uncontaminated by foreknowledge, personal bias, and preconceived explanation as possible', whereas hermeneutics is rather

> the attempt to understand the client by helping her to both comprehend and articulate her problems, concerns, and issues in a spiralling dialectic, and to do so within the milieu of the political, social, relational, and personal parameters of her own life within life in general – that is, in both her particular and a universal 'con-text'. (Raabe, 2001: 19)

In distinguishing the basic steps in hermeneutic interpretation, the very particular role of the other person becomes apparent. In short, this role will prove to be walking a line between the other self as an *alter ego* and the other person as radical alterity. The other person, the second-person 'you' in a hermeneutic counselling relation, borrows from both the existentialist first-person perspective of another 'I' and from the structuralist third-person perspective of objective subjectivity.

In the earlier volumes of *Time and Narrative*, Ricoeur offers a useful distinction of the methodological steps of hermeneutical interpretation. The first step he calls 'prefiguration', which refers to 'a pre-understanding of the world of action, its meaningful structures, its symbolic resources, and its temporal character' (Ricoeur, 2009: 54). In order to even begin to understand any narrative, we should already share a common framework of signs, structures and symbols. The second step in Ricoeur's methodology is called 'configuration'. This is the effort to form a plot, which 'opens the kingdom of the *as if*' (Ricoeur, 2009: 64). It's the capability to unite a variety of events, characters or other elements into one coherent story. This requires both the capacity to recognize and manage existing story structures ('boy meets girl', or 'hero overcomes impossible odds') and innovate on those existing structures ('poor boy meets rich girl on a sinking ship', or 'hero overcomes demigod villain thanks to an iron super suit'). Third, the art of interpretation includes the stage of 're-figuration', which consolidates the essential role of the reader to bring any story alive, or 'the intersection of the world configured by the poem and the world wherein real action occurs and unfolds its specific temporality' (Ricœur, 2009: 71). The reception and interpretation of a text by a reader are an integral part of that text.

Ricoeur formulates these three methodological steps in relation to the hermeneutic interpretation of texts. Still, they readily translate to the understanding of the self as a narrative identity and clarify the role of the other person in that understanding. In the first place, hermeneutic philosophical care presumes that the counsellor as 'other person' shares a common horizon of meaning with the subject. In the most obvious and general sense, this refers to something of a shared language and some common ground of understanding of the concepts we use. Without even getting in-depth into complex philosophical concepts like 'self', 'action' or 'suffering', you and I understand each other on a superficial level when I say things like 'I'm not happy with myself', 'what I did was wrong' or 'I'm in pain'. The words, the structures of our common language and the references we use make sense to the other person. This initial commonality is what we usually refer to when we invoke the capacity of 'empathy': it's the capability to see things from someone else's point of view.

But this initial common horizon is accompanied by the other person's capability to leave that horizon and perceive it from the outside. This is especially visible (and valuable) in the moments of crisis we mentioned earlier, when a narrative identity appears to come undone. When a subject is incapable to even find the words or act in any cogent way, when in some way even that prefigurative horizon of meaning is lost, the interlocutor is capable of taking the exterior position. This allows the counsellor – as other person – to take on the Socratic role of questioning implicit interpretations and understandings, of interrogating the prejudices that the subject themselves may be unaware of at that moment.

Second, the other person can accompany the subject in their more constructive efforts of finding forms of understanding and of representation of their life and situation. From an internal point of view, this configurative accompaniment allows them to form and articulate their stories, to rebuild their narrative sense of the meaning of life. At this stage, the other person is something of an *alter ego* – another self that allows the self to see itself as another.

But in another sense, the counsellor is at the same time irreducibly other. They are capable not only of listening and questioning but also of offering up concepts, symbols, thoughts, structures and interpretations that the subject themselves might not otherwise have access to. In the case of philosophical health, this contribution can consist of a variety of conceptualizations of the experience and understanding of the subject. For this, the other person as a philosophical counsellor disposes of their array of conceptual knowledge, and it is precisely the counsellor's standing outside of the subject's own understanding that allows for such input.

Third and finally, the other person is one who can subscribe to and confirm the narrative interpretations the subject ultimately comes to. This third form of support coincides with what Rita Charon in her proposal of narrative medicine calls 'affiliation' (Charon, 2008). To Charon, affiliation refers not only to the possibility of subscribing to, and reaffirming the narrative comprehension a subject may have arrived at: it also specifically entails a certain horizontality or mutual recognition of both the subject and the other person as being 'in it together'. This horizontality is of course particularly important for Charon, looking to the context of medical care, where a tendency to hierarchize patients and doctors in care relations is still very common.

But it is also proper to the hermeneutic relation that the other person is at the same time outside that relation. This exteriority refers less to the hierarchical order of the context of medical relations, but to a philosophical exteriority that allows the other person to wonder about the understanding someone may have come to of the meaning of their life. This philosophical wonder resembles the child before the emperor parading in his new clothes in Hans Christian Andersen's story. Because he stands outside of the commonly accepted 'truth', the child is able to point and laugh, thus revealing the falsity everyone seemed to overlook. The other person is at the same time close to us, someone we affiliate with, and far away, someone capable of continued amazement at our understanding of ourselves and our situation.

In short, the philosophical counsellor as other person is at the same time on the inside and on the outside of the subject's hermeneutic exercise in constituting a meaning of life. The other person is both empathic ('putting themselves into my place') and questioning; the other person both adheres to the subject's interpretative efforts and offers new concepts and structures; the philosophical health counsellor is in a close affiliate relationship with us, while also introducing a constant interrogation and some puzzlement.

Philosophical health

We can now return to the initial question of the meaning of life. Understood in a hermeneutic sense, a person's life is meaningful when they have a clear understanding of themselves and the world around them – when they can make sense of what they are doing and what is happening to them. Philosophical health is, then, to be able to reply to the question 'who are you' with a well-considered 'this is where I stand'. This does not mean the complexity has been subdued, nor that there is no place for suffering. On the contrary, a meaningful life, as Ricoeur stated, is one of which I may be the narrator, but not the author.

In this way, philosophical health is neither exclusively cosmological nor simply a personal worldview. Philosophical health is hermeneutic because it constantly moves between one's own experiences and interpretations, objective events and elements I have to relate to, and intersubjective frameworks of understanding I have to use in my understanding. Key in hermeneutics (and in much of philosophy) is the constant interplay between the particular and the universal, between the text and the context. In a similar way, philosophical health unites personal perspectives and shared interpretations. 'This is where I stand' links me to myself, but it does so in forms and voices that are never entirely mine.

Consequently, the counsellor proves to be of crucial importance within philosophical health. The question 'who are you' doesn't only inquire into the subject's own philosophical health; it also asks 'who is this "you" that I relate to in my search for philosophical health?' This intimate relation between care for the self and care for the other dates back to Plato, who linked these two matters in his *Second Alcibiades* (Plato, 1997; Foucault, 2001). In line with the hermeneutic search for a meaning in life that leans on both subjective experience (of a worldview) and objective discovery (of a cosmology) but is irreducible to either, the counsellor holds a complex position.

On the one hand, as said, the other person is another self or an *alter ego*. That is to say, they too act and speak, relate and narrate. For philosophical health, this resemblance between the other person and me is the basis for the capability of attention, representation and affiliation – the three basic elements in narrative medicine (Charon, 2008). But this recognition of a shared human condition also crucially implies not imposing any understanding on the subject. Martin Heidegger makes a distinction between a way of caring for the other person that is improper and a way that is proper (Heidegger and Stambaugh, 2010: 122). Improper care would consist in a kind of care where the other person worries for me, takes over my problems and resolves them in my place, like a mother who keeps their child from playing risky games or getting dirty. This kind of care actually deprives me of my capacity to care for myself.

From a hermeneutic perspective it is clear that, although the other person is as much a narrative identity as I am, this similarity does not mean that the actual form that meaning takes for one person is the same as for the other. We all speak and act; we all have to find a way to understand our existence. And although there will be certain similarities, they never entirely overlap, and each person has to find their own way of dealing with the meaning of life. Heidegger's understanding of proper or authentic care consists in freeing the space for a subject for their own self-care, much as the other person has to care for themselves in return.

On the other hand, the other person is less another self, and much more a radical and irreducible other. The other person, as already said, is vital to my hermeneutic understanding of myself precisely because they are not me, irreducible to myself. The other person is what Levinas calls 'exterior' (Levinas, 2012). This is what allows the counsellor to question me, to conceptualize my account of myself in ways that I could not on my own. The other person is capable of a wonder and a derision (*deridere*, or to return something differently) that allow me to exercise the self-understanding central to philosophical health.

Conclusion

Within healthcare, phenomenology has received increasing attention (Ferrarello, 2021; Toombs, 1993). Hermeneutics in turn can shed some valuable light on the contribution of philosophy to care practices, particularly to introducing the concept of philosophical health. Insofar as philosophical health is concerned with living a life that one considers meaningful, the central reflexive question 'who are you?' is often replied to narratively, from the perspective of the first-person. This reply is thought through; it combines my acts, my words, my actions and my relations, but also the complex dynamics that mark every step on the way. Living a meaningful existence both depends on me and escapes me because meaning is both a personal perspective and an objective framework and because it is neither of those exclusively. To have a meaningful life is to be able to say 'this is where I stand': an answer that is never definitive, and that is never entirely up to me.

The other person plays a central role in such a hermeneutic search for meaning. A philosophical counsellor oscillates between being another self and being radically other; their hermeneutic contribution between attention, representation and affiliation; and questioning, conceptualization, challenge and wonder. The philosophical counsellor is different from both the psychotherapist and the spiritual guide, in that their focus is neither exclusively on the subjective perception of a patient nor on the objective frameworks of meaning that religious tradition offers its subjects. Meaning of life is neither exclusively given nor received, but must be constantly created and recreated, understood and interpreted.

References

Aristotle (1984), *The Complete Works of Aristotle*, ed. Jonathan Barnes, 2 vols. Princeton: Princeton University Press.

Baumeister, Roy F. (1991), *Meanings of Life*. New York: Guilford Press.

Charon, Rita (2008), *Narrative Medicine: Honoring the Stories of Illness*. New York: Oxford University Press.

Ferrarello, Susi (2021), *Phenomenology of Bioethics: Technoethics and the Lived-Experience*. Cham: Springer.

Foucault, Michel (2001), *L'herméneutique du sujet: Cours au Collège de France (1981–1982)*. Hautes études. Paris: Gallimard.

Frankl, Viktor E. (2020), *Man's Search for Meaning*. London: Rider Books.

Guerra Bravo, Samuel (2007), *El arte de vivir con sentido: Manual de consultoría filosófica latinoamericana*. Quito, Ecuador; PUCE: Abya-Yala.

Heidegger, Martin (2010), *Being and Time*. Albany: State University of New York Press.

Husserl, Edmund (1991), *Ideen zu einer reinen Phänomenologie und phänomenologischen Philosophie*. Dordrecht: Kluwer.

Levinas, Emmanuel (2012), *Totality and Infinity: An Essay on Exteriority*. Pittsburgh: Duquesne University Press.

Lyotard, Jean-François (2010), *The Postmodern Condition: A Report on Knowledge*. Minneapolis: University of Minnesota Press.

de Miranda, Luis (2022), 'Philosophical Health'. In *The Palgrave Encyclopedia of the Possible*, 1–6. Cham: Springer International Publishing. https://doi.org/10.1007/978-3 -319-98390-5_209-1.

Plato (1997), *Complete Works*. Indianapolis: Hacket.

Raabe, Peter B. (2001), *Philosophical Counseling: Theory and Practice*. Westport: Praeger.

Ricoeur, Paul (1986), 'Life: A Story in Search of a Narrator'. In M. C. Doeser and J. N. Kraay (eds), *Facts and Values*, 121–32. Dordrecht: Nijhoff.

Ricoeur, P. (1986), 'Life: A Story in Search of a Narrator'. In M. Doeser and J. Kray (eds), 121–32. *Facts and Values*. Dordrecht: Martinus Nijhoff.

Ricoeur, Paul (1994), *Oneself as Another*. Chicago: University of Chicago Press.

Ricoeur, Paul (2009), *Time and Narrative*, vol. 1. Chicago: University of Chicago Press.

Ricoeur, Paul (2013), 'La Souffrance n'est Pas La Douleur'. In C. Marin and N. Zaccaï-Reyners (eds), *Souffrance et Douleur. Autour de Paul Ricoeur*, 13–34. Paris: Presses Universitaires de France.

Sartre, Jean-Paul (1996), *L'existentialisme est un humanisme*. Paris: Gallimard.

Taylor, Charles (1991), *The Ethics of Authenticity*. Cambridge, MA: Harvard University Press.

Toombs, Kay S. (1993), *The Meaning of Illness: A Phenomenological Account of the Different Perspectives of Physician and Patient*. Dordrecht, Boston and London: Kluwer Akademic.

Yalom, Irvin D. (1980), *Existential Psychotherapy*. New York: Harper Collins.

9

Ubuntu

An Afro-communitarian approach to philosophical counselling and health

Richard Sivil

In this chapter, I will explore the contributions the Afro-communitarian philosophy of ubuntu could make to philosophical counselling and philosophical health. The philosophical counselling movement is a significant moment that re-orientates philosophy, typically confined to the ivory tower of academia, towards everyday life. Philosophical counselling can be broadly described as 'the practical application of philosophy directed at the beliefs, values, perspectives and/or worldviews of the individual with a view to challenging, changing, and/or improving the way she thinks about herself and the world, conducts herself and comports herself' (Sivil, 2020: 8).

Admittedly, this description fails to capture the nuances and deficits of the movement. For instance, it says nothing of the diverse ends of philosophical counselling, which include the instrumental ends of solving intra- and interpersonal problems and therapy, and the intrinsic ends of scepticism, self-knowledge, wisdom and virtue (Sivil and Clare, 2018: 135). There is internal dissent regarding the legitimacy of these ends. For example, there is disagreement among practitioners who endorse the end of philosophical counselling as therapy (Cohen, 2004). Moreover, practitioners who advocate intrinsic ends charge those who advocate instrumental ends with misconceiving the philosophical endeavour (Achenbach, 1995: 68; Lahav, 2006: 3). While philosophical dissent is in itself intellectually healthy, it can make philosophical counselling appear to be 'in a state of dynamic disarray' (Raabe, 2001: xvi). Such a perception would be, however incorrect as there is a cross-cutting agreement regarding significant aspects. First, practitioners in both instrumental and intrinsic camps agree that philosophical counselling possesses therapeutic potential, that is, that well-being is an outcome (Sivil and Clare, 2018: 133–4).

Second, most practitioners employ a Socratic approach (Sivil, 2020: 30–1; de Miranda, 2021a: 92), through which the practitioner helps the participant access and assess her worldview in an attempt to uncover and clarify concepts, beliefs and values; expose hidden assumptions; and correct contradictions and fallacious reasoning. The Socratic approach is not synonymous with the Socratic Method, which does not aim to increase the interlocutor's self-knowledge but strives instead to reveal philosophical principles (universal rational truths) through reflection and express them as general judgements (Nelsen, 1980). While a Socratic approach undoubtedly has a place in philosophical counselling, some question its capability to attain the full range of professed ends (Lahav, 2006: 4; Sivil, 2020: 32–3). Given that there is much more to philosophy than Socrates and his method, I argue that philosophy has more to offer philosophical counselling. As such, restricted use of a single approach in philosophical counselling is confounding. Since such a restriction could hinder the development and expansion of philosophical counselling, opening the domain of practice to more methods, approaches and techniques is important. Addressing this requires the identification of other relevant philosophical approaches.

Some recognize the tradition of philosophy as a way of life (PWL) as worthy of consideration (Sivil, 2020; de Miranda, 2021b; Tukiainen, no date). Unlike philosophy, which tends to be scholastic theoretical discourse concerned with the exegesis of texts that is detached from everyday life, PWL is praxis in which theory serves practical ends (Hadot, 1995: 23). In particular, it is concerned with the issue of how we should live and with achieving flourishing. Hadot (1995: 83) describes it as 'an exercise in the art of living' that teaches us a new way to live, and which 'causes us to *be* more fully, and makes us better'. I argue that PWL is a good fit for philosophical counselling. Not only is it orientated to the outcome of well-being; moreover, given that each philosophical way of life aims at transformation and advocates a set of methods, practices and techniques, incorporating any philosophical way of life into philosophical counselling will likely contribute to the existing range of ends, as well as address any methodological deficit. Finally, I will argue that there is a strong connection between PWL and philosophical health defined by de Miranda (2021a: 92) as coherence between thought, speech and action.

One concern is that widely recognized philosophical ways of life (including those advocated by Epicurus, the Stoics, Schopenhauer, Kierkegaard, Nietzsche and Spinoza) are fundamentally Western in outlook and value; that is, they focus on and advocate the transformation of the individual as an individual. An associated concern is that philosophical health, viewed through the lens of individualism, might be narrowly regarded as a form of personal flourishing. Assuming that Western outlooks and values are not universally applicable, discovering a non-Western, non-individualistic philosophical way of life would be pivotal if philosophical counselling is to be successfully applied in a non-Western cultural context, such as might be found in Southern Africa. In response, I ask if there is an Afro-communitarian philosophical way of life that might be applicable to philosophical counselling. In particular, Ubuntu is a sub-Saharan African communitarian philosophy: Does it qualify as a philosophical way of life? And if it does, what contributions might it make to philosophical counselling and philosophical health?

Ubuntu – a basic overview

'Ubuntu' is a word from the southern African Nguni language group that translates as 'humanness' (Metz, 2020: 257). The core idea of ubuntu is encapsulated in the saying:

umuntu ngumuntu ngabantu – 'I am because we are'. This simple formulation conveys the idea that community is the essence of humanity and that one develops as a person through the recognition and humanity of others. Communitarian values associated with ubuntu include mutual respect, fairness, care, solidarity, consensus, reciprocity, compassion and the common good (Dandla, 1996: 70; Mthembu, 1996: 218; Matolino and Kwindingwi, 2013: 200).

Yet, this simple formulation obscures the fact that ubuntu is many things to many people. Louw (2002: 15) defines ubuntu as 'humanity' and 'humanness'. For Ramose (2005: 35) it is the 'root of African philosophy'. It is variously described by Matolino and Kwindingwi (2013: 197) as 'the authentic African ethical concept, a way of life, an authentic mode of being African, an individual ideal, the appropriate public spirit, a definition of life itself and the preferred manner of conducting public and private business'. In the latter respect, ubuntu is adopted as 'a vision, mission and strategy' (Richardson, 2008: 82). Ubuntu is also the name of an open-source operating system on Linux and has been co-opted into the title of a variety of clinics, care facilities and development organizations. This profusion of understandings and uses could point to the richness of the concept – alternatively, it could point to its degeneration, allowing it to become anything to anyone (Matolino and Kwindingwi, 2013: 201).

Despite its social and academic popularity, some are critical of the ubuntu revival. Matolino and Kwindingwi question the political intention behind the project. They regard it as an elitist move that 'is not inclusive by nature but rather seeks to emphasise certain aspects of being African' (2013: 202). They are cognizant that there are likely multiple interpretations of life that would count as being 'authentically African', but that do not necessarily align with the tenets of ubuntu (2013: 201). In light of this, they do not think that ubuntu adequately captures the wishes or serves the needs of ordinary citizens living in a diverse and multicultural society such as contemporary South Africa (2013: 203). Accordingly, they call for an end to ubuntu revivalism. Metz (2014) disagrees, arguing that it is premature to call for an end to the ubuntu project, which is only just getting started. Contrary to the position that ubuntu is outdated, Metz maintains that 'ubuntu as an ethical theory has a lot going for it as an account of how individuals and institutions should be moral in the twenty-first century' (2014: 65).

While I am aware of the complex and contested terrain of ubuntu, trying to negotiate the divergent views would be counterproductive to this chapter. I will instead confine my account of ubuntu to a single vision advocated by the South African philosopher Mogobe Ramose, who was instrumental in creating international interest in African philosophy and ubuntu.

Is Ubuntu a philosophical way of life?

To determine whether ubuntu constitutes a philosophical way of life, I will create a general schema comprising five criteria that any philosophy would have to satisfy in order to qualify as a philosophical way of life. These include that it: entails a project of transformation, is guided by a transformative aspiration, is informed by an integrated and complex philosophical system, is holistic and personally invested, and offers spiritual exercises to effect the transformation.

First, a philosophical way of life is a transformative project. It is a praxis that embodies the Ancient Greek philosophical practice of 'care of the self'. Foucault describes this as 'technologies of the self', which permit individuals to effect by their own means or with the help of others a certain number of operations on their own bodies and souls, thoughts, conduct, and way of being, so as to transform themselves' (Martin, Gutman and Hutton, 1988: 18). Hadot (1995: 265) describes this transformation as a 'radical conversion' that causes the individual to '"be" in a different way'.

Second, the transformative project of a philosophical way of life is directed by an aspiration. Effecting a transformation requires that we 'strive after that which is highest' (Hadot, 1995: 265). While Hadot identifies wisdom as the highest good, other conceptions are available. These include happiness (Epicurus and the Stoics), knowing God (Spinoza), autonomy (Kant), having a relationship with God (Kierkegaard) and strength and health (Nietzsche).

Third, a philosophical way of life is underwritten by a coherent and self-contained philosophical system. It typically comprises a metaphysics – an understanding of reality, an epistemology – an understanding of truth that provides a means to acquire knowledge of how to live, and an ethical way of living – principles and values to live by. The philosophical system is not an intellectual backdrop to the philosophical way of life but instead forms a fundamental part of the way one lives. Hadot (1995: 267) describes PWL as a 'unitary act, which consists in living logic, physics, and ethics'.

Fourth, a philosophical way of life endorses a vision of philosophizing that is holistic and personally invested. It is holistic in that it provides an account of the whole individual, typically in terms of thought (reason) and feeling (emotion). It is personally invested as the individual philosophizes with her whole being. Hadot (1995: 265, 268) describes philosophizing as 'an exercise of thought, will, and the totality of one's being'.

Finally, a philosophical way of life provides spiritual exercises (techniques and practices) that have to be incorporated into the daily life of the individual. These spiritual exercises include: meditation (silence, listening, attention and being present in the moment), developing the intellect (memory, imagination, reading, writing, dialogue and rational argumentation), mastering emotions and contemplating one's death (Hadot, 1995: 82).

That Ramose refers to ubuntu as 'a way of life' (2005: 69) and a 'philopraxis' (2005: 114) is relevant but insufficient to establish that ubuntu is a philosophical way of life. To substantiate the claim, I will show that Ramose's (2005) account satisfies the five criteria of the general schema.

Ubuntu entails a project of transformation. Not only does ubuntu affirm one's humanity through the humanity of others but at the heart of ubuntu lies the activity of forming and maintaining relations with others. While we are born human in a biological sense, the transformative project is to actively shape oneself into an ethical human being. This entails a process of 'be-ing [*sic*] becoming' (Ramose, 2005: 37). Essentially, one has to prove that one is the embodiment of ubuntu, since 'the fundamental ethical, social and legal judgement of human worth and human conduct is based upon ubu-ntu [*sic*]' (2005: 37). The transformative aspiration of ubuntu is becoming a person. Personhood is defined in terms of wholeness – whereby ontological primacy is awarded to the community through which the individual comes to know himself and the world. The person is not thought of in terms of individual physical and/or psychological characteristics but, instead, is conceived as a socially embedded being (2005: 56).

This transformative project is part of an integrated and complex philosophical system, which contains an ontology, an epistemology and a metaphysics. Ramose (2005: 35) identifies ubuntu as the root of African ontology and epistemology, and describes these as an 'indivisible one-ness' (2005: 36). Ramose bifurcates the term 'ubuntu' into *ubu* and *ntu*. *Ubu* evokes the idea of enfolded being, filled with infinite potential, and orientated toward unfolding, that is, the concretization of being (2005: 36, 45). *Ntu* is the point at which being becomes concretized and takes on a particular form and mode of being. *Umuntu* (person) is the particular concrete manifestation of the human being: the maker of laws and religion and the seeker of knowledge and truth (2005: 36).

The person – as a wholeness – is communal. This informs a particular vision of knowledge that is not only orientated towards the community but is transmitted by and through the community. In this respect, everyone in the community is involved in the epistemic project. This ensures that knowledge has an undogmatic character and is inherently dynamic (2005: 114).

The element of ontological wholeness manifests in three levels of interrelated human existence: the living, the ancestors and the unborn. While those who have died no longer have concrete bodily existence, they are believed to continue existing in an unknown world. As such, Ramose refers to the ancestors as 'the living-dead'. The unborn are future beings which the living have a responsibility to bring into existence. The ancestors and the yet-to-be-born are 'invisible beings'.

The ontology of invisible beings forms 'the basis of ubuntu metaphysics' (2005: 46). It reveals that the nature of reality is a wholeness – involving interdependence, connectedness and indivisibility (2005: 105) – and is in permanent motion – process, flux and change. Ramose regards motion as 'the essence of life' (2005: 107), and the principle of being (2005: 114), for it is only through motion that enfolded being can unfold (2005: 106).

I argue that ubuntu presents a vision of philosophizing that is holistic and personally invested. First, ubuntu does not fragment the human being by creating divisions between thought and feelings but instead recognizes these as indivisible and mutually dependent (2005: 42). Second, as said, it does not recognize the individual as an abstract entity but awards ontological primacy to the community of which the individual is a part.

Just as the individual is embedded and conditioned by experience, so too is philosophy rooted in experience (2005: 112). In light of this I suggest that the ubuntu vision of philosophizing is one of actively participating in community life. This emphasis on activity is succinctly expressed in the Northern Sotho proverb: 'You don't listen to the music seated' (2005: 43). There are several reasons the individual would invest in this way of life: the individual is not regarded as a person unless they are part of the community (2005: 58); their health is determined by relations of harmony/

disharmony with the community; successfully navigating the uncertainties of life is contingent on being an active member of the community; and finally, the individual gains immortality by becoming an ancestor, and this can only be achieved by being part of the community (2005: 65).

Spiritual exercises are an integral part of the ubuntu way of life. These include, but are not limited to, participating in ceremonies and rituals, memory, listening and the use of aphorisms. In order to become a person, one must go through a series of stages and participate in prescribed ceremonies and rituals (2005: 58). One example is the ceremony of *Imbeleko* – a ritual carried out when a child is born. The purpose of this is to introduce the newborn to the ancestors and to thank them for protecting mother and child. If the ritual is not performed, it is believed that the child will experience difficulties and will be disobedient (Bogopa, 2010).

Since the ancestors are an integral part of the community, and are consulted for guidance, sacrifices and offerings have to be made in order to honour them (2005: 64). This also serves to keep them alive in one's memory. Remembering the ancestors can be understood as a crucial spiritual exercise, for it is by being present in the memory of the living that the ancestors are immortalized (2005: 65), thereby perpetuating the integrity of the community.

Since the ancestors are consulted for guidance, listening would be an important exercise. It is more than simply being attentive to what the other speaker is saying; Marcus Aurelius (1961: 6, 53) described listening as entering 'in[to] the mind of the speaker'. A number of philosophical practitioners advocate the exercise of listening. Lahav associates it with contemplation, an activity which requires that we open 'inside ourselves an inner space of "listening"' (Lahav, 2006: 6). De Miranda (2021a: 92–3) advocates 'deep listening' – the capacity for systematically listening to the layers of what a participant discloses – as an essential quality for philosophical practitioners to facilitate philosophical health.

That ubuntu satisfies the five criteria of the general schema allows me to assert that ubuntu constitutes a philosophical way of life. This is an important move that would legitimize using ubuntu in philosophical counselling. This would go a significant way towards addressing the methodological and cultural deficits raised earlier. Yet, problematically, the strength of the assertion can be contested on at least two counts. First, the validity of my PWL schema itself can be challenged. Second, the degree that ubuntu satisfies a particular criterion can be called into question. Since these contestations could derail my project, they are worth considering.

The existence of alternative accounts of PWL, such as offered by Ure and Sharpe (2021: 13–19), might call the validity of the general schema into question. Not only do the two accounts highlight different aspects of PWL, their application elicits a different result. Ure and Sharpe (2021: 27) regard Socrates as the founder of the PWL tradition. Contrary to this, I argue that Socrates does not offer a philosophical way of life as he does not satisfy all five criteria of the general schema. While he was committed to making others take care of the most important part of their soul, he arguably didn't advocate a particular transformative aspiration. Instead, he seemed to be interested in showing those who claimed some degree of knowledge, that they were not as knowledgeable as they thought. In addition, it is not clear that he advocated a particular metaphysic, epistemology and ethic.

There might be an issue if these accounts of PWL were created to perform the same task. But they were not. I developed the general schema to identify potential philosophical ways of life, informed by the seminal work on PWL (Hadot, 1995) and tested against other widely recognized PWL, such as those advocated by Epicurus, the Stoics, Kierkegaard and Nietzsche (Sivil, 2020), while Ure and Sharpe developed theirs as a means to compare and contrast different philosophical ways of life (2021: 13) so as to track the changes that occur between them (2021: 19). Since Ure and Sharpe's account was formulated to perform a different task, it does not constitute an opposing alternative to my general schema. And yet, even if it did, Ure and Sharpe (2021: 13) recognize that their account is not definitive and admit the possibility of alternative accounts.

A second way to challenge the claim that ubuntu constitutes a philosophical way of life is to question the degree that it satisfies a particular criterion. One could argue that since self-reflection and critical conceptual engagement are fundamental philosophical practices, they should be advocated by a philosophical way of life. Hadot (1995: 59) cites self-reflection and the application of reason as central spiritual exercises. He defines self-reflection as 'being attentive to oneself' (1995: 59), and as an activity in which 'thought [. . .] takes itself as its own subject matter and seeks to modify itself' (Hadot, 1995: 82–3). He does not describe reason in a narrowly intellectual manner; instead, he regards it as 'a purely rational, imaginative, or intuitive exercise that can take extremely varied forms' (1995: 59). In accordance with Hadot, Ure and Sharpe regard critical self-reflection, the 'focused philosophical attention on one's own beliefs, attitudes and affects' (2021: 13), to be 'minimally constitutive of any PWL approach' (2021: 16). Moreover, they recognize intellectual exercises, that is, the use of reason, rhetoric and dialectic, as a feature of philosophical activity of PWL (2021: 16). Since there is no evidence that self-reflection, the use of reason and critical engagement are advocated by Ubuntu, one could argue that it does not minimally constitute a philosophical way of life.

There are several ways to respond to this. We could agree with it and dismiss ubuntu as constituting a philosophical way of life. But this could result in a counter-charge of cultural imperialism – why should Western philosophy have the final say on what counts as doing philosophy? Conversely, we could relax the specification that self-reflection and critical engagement are essential spiritual exercises, thereby allowing us to conclude that ubuntu is a philosophical way of life. The issue with this route is that it might admit a wider range of ways of living (religious, cultural) into the realm of PWL. This is conceptually and practically problematic. What, after all, would be philosophical about a way of life in which the participant does not philosophize? In response to this, we might ask: What does it mean to philosophize? To assume that it means one thing, that is, critical self-reflection, is unnecessarily narrow. It is this line of thinking that has made a Socratic approach the predominant method in philosophical counselling. To avoid falling into this trap, we would need to reconceive the notion of 'philosophizing'. One such account is offered by de Miranda (2021b: 71–2), who defines philosophizing 'as a practice of askesis, embodied exercises oriented toward the manifested ideal of a harmonious and dignified self-continuity'. I regard Ramose's vision of ubuntu (the end of personhood and the means to attain it) as according well with this account.

Ubuntu and philosophical counselling

If PWL is applicable to philosophical counselling, and ubuntu constitutes an Afro-communitarian philosophical way of life, then it follows that ubuntu is applicable to philosophical counselling. What, if anything, might it add to philosophical counselling? The transformative project of becoming a person would be an addition to the existing range of ends. Moreover, the fact that ubuntu endorses an approach that does not emphasize critical self-reflection goes a fair way to addressing the methodological deficit. But it is the orientation to community that potentially can change the way philosophical counselling is practised.

Philosophical counselling tends to be highly individualistic, in terms of not only focus but also delivery; that is, one-on-one sessions are the norm. While philosophical cafés are a non-individualistic format of delivery, these are communal in the loosest sense, constituted by a collection of individuals who share a common intellectual interest but not necessarily views and values. In contrast, the ubuntu community is bound together in a myriad of interconnected ways that include: shared beliefs and values, and shared experiences. Moreover, given that the ancestors are an integral part of the community, community membership is historical in that it is temporally located in the present and firmly rooted in the past. It is to such a community that philosophical counselling would have to be applied.

This raises the question – who would offer philosophical counselling, and how would they apply it? Without question, the philosophical practitioner would have to be a full-fledged member of the community. This in itself is not impossible to imagine, but what role would they play in such a community? If community roles are predetermined, the practitioner might assume the position of a *sangoma* (shaman) or an *inyanga* (healer). This might make ubuntu a less attractive option to some potential philosophical practitioners, or alternatively, it might challenge the notion that this constitutes philosophical counselling at all. But there is little reason to assume that community roles are predetermined. If ubuntu values and beliefs need to be conveyed to the community, perhaps this is something the practitioner might do. In this respect, they might assume the position of custodian and conveyor of ideas.

But what if Matolino and Kwindingwi (2013) are correct that ubuntu is a relic of a by-gone age? Social disharmonies, corruption, nepotism, xenophobia and tribalism in Southern African communities are a testament to the fact that ubuntu does not exist. The defender of ubuntu may protest that as an ideal, it does not need to exist – it simply needs to inspire. Sadly, the ideal will not inspire if it does not speak to the hearts of the people.

One could suggest that Ramose's vision of ubuntu is not only contemporarily non-existent, it is also undesirable. As a result of its communitarian orientation, ubuntu places a high premium on the 'other-regarding' dimension. By extension, it disregards another equally important aspect of humanness – the 'self-regarding' dimension which includes the primacy of the individual, the value of autonomy and rational agency, self-regarding virtues and individual rights. Fortunately, ubuntu does not need to be narrowly communitarian: it might be possible to reconstruct it in a manner that includes self- and other-regarding virtues, and as such would permit the consideration and protection of the rights of both individual and community (Kayange, 2022). Exactly what this would look like remains to be seen. Viewed in this light, it could be the job of the philosophical practitioner to reconceptualize ubuntu. This might expand their role to include being a re-valuator of values, legislator or even leader.

In light of the foregoing, it is apparent that ubuntu has something unique to offer to philosophical counselling. This includes expanding the ends and means of philosophical counselling, as well as the role of the philosophical practitioner. However, given the issues and concerns previously raised, it is clear that significant work in this area remains to be done.

Ubuntu and philosophical health

If ubuntu constitutes an Afro-communitarian philosophical way of life, is philosophical health necessarily implicated in it? In this section I will characterize philosophical health, outline the relationship between philosophical health and PWL and explore the possible contribution ubuntu might make to philosophical health.

Philosophical health is defined by de Miranda (2021a: 92) as coherence between thought, speech and action. It is 'a form of attunement [. . .] between our ways of thinking and our active presence in the world' (de Miranda, in this volume, Chapter 17), which contributes to an increase in flourishing. Since philosophical health connects internal (thought/feeling) and external (behaviour) dimensions, and this improves our capacity to live, it would be fair to say it offers a holistic notion of well-being. In addition, de Miranda offers five principles to cultivate philosophical health: 'mental heroism, deep orientation, critical creativity, deep listening, and the "Creal" (the creative Real as ultimate possibility)' (2021b: 70). These possess practical value as the application of them can imparadise our existence, or at the very least permit us to 'maintain a pragmatic elevation of view and creative resilience in everyday events [. . . and] critical situations' (2021b: 70).

I contend that there is a high degree of accord between de Miranda's notion of philosophical health and Hadot's conception of PWL. This is immediately evident in the language de Miranda (2021b: 71) uses to describe philosophical health: as a 'spiritual endeavour' and 'an affirmative and creative engagement with life', which is achieved and maintained through spiritual exercises.

Whether or not PWL is specifically orientated towards philosophical health, I argue that it would be the likely outcome. A philosophical way of life offers a coherent philosophical view of the world. It is highly unlikely that one would have logical inconsistencies of thought or conflicting values if one fully adopted the particular worldview espoused by the philosophical way of life. While the degree one is able to successfully supplant an old and entrenched worldview with a new one is questionable, changing values and breaking habits of thought is possible. In addition to offering a coherent philosophical worldview, many philosophical ways of life specifically encourage the development of self-reflection and critical independent thought, and this could be used to facilitate the development of a coherent worldview. Having coherence between thought and speech requires one to be aware of what one is saying, and to monitor how one's speech tracks against one's philosophical worldview.

A critically self-reflective individual would, at the very least, be aware of inconsistencies between thought and speech. Given that a philosophical way of life endorses a transformative project, the committed individual would work to correct themselves. Coherence between thought and action is a feature of a philosophical way of life. Since a philosophical way of life is a praxis, it would endorse a range of practices and techniques for the express purpose of transforming the self. While adopting a philosophical way of life does not necessarily insulate us from the world, and as such, we are subject to life's challenges, the opinion and influence of others, and our own illogical thinking, a philosophical way of life does provide a pathway to deal with these sorts of contingencies and weaknesses, thereby increasing chances for flourishing.

If philosophical health is the likely outcome of a philosophical way of life, and ubuntu constitutes a philosophical way of life, then it follows that philosophical health could be an outcome of ubuntu. An objection to this would be, once again, that the activities of self-reflection and critical engagement are key elements in obtaining philosophical health. Given that they are not emphasized by the ubuntu way of life, it is not at all clear that an adherent of this way of life would obtain philosophical health. But, as said, I think it is a mistake to assume that acquiring philosophical health entails the mere exercise of self-reflection and critical engagement. This reflects the narrow sort of intellectualist vision of philosophical outlook I have been rallying against. Moreover, I contend that a tolerant and inclusive notion of philosophical health might recognize that critical self-reflection is not essential.

According to de Miranda (2021a: 92) one engages in philosophical health 'when one's behaviour is careful [. . .] in considering not only the physical or psychological individual balance but also a certain idea of what the collective and holistic good of humans [. . .] might be'. The balance of the individual and the community is a central component of the ubuntu notion of health. Ramose (2005: 69) recognizes that illness and disease are largely cultural phenomena. According to this worldview our conception of what it means to be human impacts not only on the diagnoses of ill-health but also on the treatment of it. Given the defining element of ubuntu – that a person is a person through other people, including the ancestors – ill-health (bodily or mental) is understood to arise as a result of a 'disturbance of harmony and balance in the relations between the living and the living dead' (2005: 69). In light of this, understanding and addressing ill-health is communal in a dual sense: it involves the community of the living, and the ancestors are consulted to discover the source of the disharmony as well as its cure.

In addition, de Miranda maintains that philosophical health is animated by a 'deep orientation'. This entails having and remaining faithful to 'an overarching existential and spiritual horizon that can guide the embodied person towards her highest destiny' (de Miranda, 2021a: 97). This view of the universe anticipates the future, is informed by the past and is 'oriented towards the present as a form of attentive engagement with life via a few overarching ideas or values' (de Miranda, 2021a: 98). The ubuntu worldview offers a deep orientation that temporally connects the individual to the community of the present, the past (ancestors) and the future (unborn). It is through being connected to the community that the individual as a person emerges. Being part of the community, becoming a person and becoming immortal (as an ancestor) can be understood as the individual's highest destiny. Becoming a person is simultaneously an ethical and an existential undertaking. It is through a deep orientation to a worldview that we engage in the truth and meaning of our lives (de Miranda, 2021b: 71). For Ramose (2005: 44) to live an ubuntu way of life is 'to live the truth'. Further to this, he offers a vision of truth as 'the contemporaneous convergence of perception and action' (2005: 44). This squares perfectly with de Miranda's (2021a: 92) vision of philosophical health as coherence between thought and action.

I argue that ubuntu expands the notion of philosophical health into the realm of the Other. Viewed through a lens of individualism, one would likely see philosophical health, much like physical and psychological health, as a quality experienced and maintained by the individual, a form of personal flourishing. Adopting an ubuntu way of life alters that. That the person is understood as socially embedded – an entanglement, necessarily interconnected with others – expands the notion of philosophical health beyond a narrow coherence of the individual's thought and action to something that arises in and through the coherence of the community. This, as said, shifts philosophical health from a notion of personal flourishing to communal flourishing. Does this accord with de Miranda's idea of philosophical health as ecological (de Miranda, in this volume, Chapter 17)? Admittedly, while ubuntu expands the notion of philosophical health and flourishing beyond the individual, it does not extend it beyond the human realm. Given that the non-human realm is vast, is in a deplorable and ever-worsening state (climate change, species extinction, etc.), and that human health is integrally implicated in the health of the environment, one could argue that ubuntu does not go far enough. While I agree with the ecological sentiment, I believe that given the contemporary prevalence of an atomistic metaphysic, the notion of philosophical health as communal coherence and collective flourishing is significant and should not be undermined by broader ecological concerns.

Conclusion

I began this chapter by identifying a methodological issue in philosophical counselling: the predominance of the Socratic approach. Such an approach places a premium on getting the participant to engage in critical self-reflection, which requires the practitioner to assume a position analogous to the Socratic midwife. While the PWL tradition presents itself as an alternative, widely recognized instantiations are Western in outlook and value.

In an effort to step out of this cultural monopoly and expand the range of methods and roles available to the philosophical practitioner, I argued that ubuntu constitutes an Afro-communitarian philosophical way of life. I identified the end of individualistic personhood and the means offered to attain it as making significant contributions to philosophical counselling. In so doing, a range of possible roles for the philosophical practitioner were identified. These included being custodian and conveyor of ideas, re-valuator of values as Nietzsche advocated, legislator or even leader. I argued that philosophical health is a necessary outcome of PWL and that the ubuntu philosophical way of life would expand the notion of philosophical health to be a quality of the community.

Several issues were, however, identified. First, the fact that ubuntu does not advocate self-reflection and critical engagement, arguably essential components of what it means to philosophize, might be contentious. The fact that alternative conceptions of philosophizing exist minimizes the degree of this concern. Second, I realized that the ubuntu communitarian commitment could be at odds with the contemporary commitment to personhood, and this could render it unusable. Re-conceiving ubuntu was suggested as a means to overcome this. This exploration has revealed that more resources are available to philosophical counselling and that incorporating them into the endeavour could significantly change what it offers and how it is practised. This is far from the final word on the matter. There is more to African philosophy than ubuntu, and, likely, alternative ways to explore their relevance to philosophical counselling and philosophical health exist beyond the notion of PWL.

References

Achenbach, Gerd (1995), 'Philosophy, Philosophical Practice, and Psychotherapy'. In R. Lahav and M. Tillmans (eds), *Essays on Philosophical Counselling*, 61–74. Lanham: University Press of America.

Aurelius, Marcus (1961), *Meditations*, trans. A. S. L. Farquharson. London: J. M. Dent & Sons Ltd.

Bogopa, David (2010), 'Health and Ancestors: The Case of South Africa and Beyond'. *Indo-Pacific Journal of Phenomenology*, 10 (1): 1–7.

Cohen, Elliot (2004), 'Philosophy with Teeth: The Be Wedding of Philosophical and Psychological Practices'. *International Journal of Philosophical Practice*, 2 (2). http://npcassoc.org/docs/ijpp/CohenTeeth.pdf (accessed 17 August 2022).

Dandala, Mvume (1996), 'Cows Never Die: Embracing African Cosmology in the Process of Economic Growth'. In R. Lessem and B. Nussbaum (eds), *Sawubona Africa: Embracing Four Worlds in South African Management*, 69–85. Sandton: Zebra Press.

Hadot, Pierre (1995), *Philosophy as a Way of Life*. Oxford: Blackwell Publishers.

Kayange, Grivas (2022), 'Critical Reconstruction of Ubuntu'. Faculty of Humanities Seminar Series, University of Malawi.

Lahav, Ran (2006), 'Philosophical Practice as Contemplative Philosophy'. *Practical Philosophy*, 8 (1): 3–7.

Louw, Dirk (2002), 'Ubuntu and the Challenges of Multiculturalism in Post-Apartheid South Africa'. In P. Hensbroek, *African Renaissance and Ubuntu*, 15–36. University of Groningen: CDS Research Reports.

Martin, Luther H., Huck Gutman and Patrick Hutton (1988), *Technologies of the Self: A seminar with Michel Foucault*. Amherst: The University of Massachusetts Press.

Matolino, Bernard and Wencelaus Kwindingwi (2013), 'The End of Ubuntu'. *South African Journal of Philosophy*, 32 (2): 197–205.

Metz, Thaddeus (2014), 'Just the Beginning for Ubuntu: Reply to Matolino and Kwindingwi'. *South African Journal of Philosophy*, 33 (1): 65–72.

Metz, Thaddeus (2020), 'Humility and the African Philosophy of Ubuntu'. In M. Alfano, M. Lynch and A. Tanesini (eds), *The Routledge Handbook of Philosophy of Humility*, 257–67. London: Routledge.

de Miranda, Luis (2021a), 'Thinking into the Place of the Other: The Crealectic Approach to Philosophical Health and Care'. *International Journal of Philosophical Practice*, 7 (1): 89–103.

de Miranda, Luis (2021b). 'Five Principles of Philosophical Health for Critical Times: From Hadot to Crealectics'. *Eidos: A Journal for Philosophy of Culture*, 5 (1): 70–89.

Mthembu, D. (1996), 'African Values: Discovering Indigenous Roots of Management'. In R. Lessem and B. Nussbaum (eds), *Sawubona Africa: Embracing Four Worlds in South African Management*, 215–26. Sandton: Zebra Press.

Nelsen, Leonard (1980), 'The Socratic Method'. *Thinking: The Journal of Philosophy for Children*, 2 (2): 34–8.

Raabe, Peter (2001), *Philosophical Counseling: Theory and Practice*. Wesport: Praeger.

Ramose, Mogobe (2005), *African Philosophy through Ubuntu*. Harare: Mond Book Publishers.

Richardson, Robert (2008), 'Reflections on Reconciliation and Ubuntu'. In R. Nicholson (ed.), *Persons in Community: African Ethics in a Global Culture*, 65–83. Pietermaritzburg: University of KwaZulu-Natal Press.

Sivil, Richard (2020), 'Philosophical Counselling Beyond the Socratic: A Preliminary Investigation into Expanding and Developing Philosophical Practice' [unpublished manuscript]. School of Religion, Philosophy and Classics. University of KwaZulu-Natal.

Sivil, Richard and Julia Clare (2018), 'Towards a Taxonomy of Philosophical Counselling'. *South African Journal of Philosophy*, 37 (2): 131–42.

Tukiainen, Arto (no date), 'Philosophical Counselling and Philosophy as a Way of Life: Wide Conception of Wisdom'. http//:artotukiainen.net/practphil.html (accessed 20 February 2022).

Ure, Michael and Matthew Sharpe (2021), *Philosophy as a Way of Life: History, Dimensions, Directions*. London: Bloomsbury.

10

What is it like to counsel like a philosopher? A phenomenological reading of philosophical health

Andrei Simionescu-Panait

Introducing the philosophical consultation

What should people do when they notice there is something wrong with their lives? Is the problem of a medical or psychological nature? If not, on what aspects should that person focus to find a solution? People having issues that are not of medical or psychological nature find themselves in the philosophical counselling room. There they find out about the ability of their consciousness to produce and foreground adequate knowledge about themselves. We could take this as a preliminary description of philosophical health: knowing oneself adequately is at stake in philosophical health, mainly because people tend to contradict or lie to themselves. They usually do so to preserve aspects they like and cover up aspects they don't like about their lives. As a consequence, a philosophically healthy individual is on a path called by de Miranda the 'eudynamic' path towards oneself, the path of actualizing one's highest virtues and one's potential for a sublime life (de Miranda, 2021c). One who avoids lying to oneself and manages to know oneself will most probably know one's aspirations, resources, strengths and difficulties.

Being philosophically healthy can be achieved more or less successfully in many ways, out of which philosophical counselling, studying philosophy and hobby-philosophizing stand out. The focus of this text is on the counselling path because its process is specifically designed to assess and engage with an individual's philosophical health. The counselling process differs from studying philosophy and hobby-philosophizing. These latter two aim at other goals such as discussing other people's ideas or obtaining a feeling of profoundness. These goals do not necessarily target philosophical health. I am here interested in finding out how counselling tools impact philosophical health.

Well-known practitioners have evaluated the relationship between counsellor and counsellee (Marinoff, 1999; 2003; Zhang, 2014; Amir, 2018). These efforts usually focus on narrated case studies or on describing the ideal counselling relationship. Their purpose is generally to underline a certain methodology to be used by both aspiring and experienced counsellors. One of the most recent efforts I encountered is de Miranda's five principles for philosophical health (2021a). These serve as a methodology for counselling. The five principles and philosophical health co-define each other. Thus, a reinterpretation of these consultation principles would involve a reinterpretation of philosophical health as well. This text provides such a reinterpretation, which is supported by my background in both Husserlian phenomenology and philosophical counselling.

Others have involved phenomenology in various forms of philosophical counselling (Lindseth and Norberg, 2003; Neves, 2014; Hansen, 2015; Zavala, 2016). However, they were not explicitly preoccupied with philosophical health. Neither was I when I researched the crossroad between phenomenology and teaching philosophy (Simionescu-Panait, 2020). And yet, teaching philosophy does impact philosophical health at least regarding the person's ability to conceptualize and question. On the other hand, it does not specifically target those acts of conceptualizing and questioning in order to know oneself, so philosophical health is not the main concern there. In order to know oneself, one should be able to know what he or she can or cannot, should or shouldn't, must or mustn't. Primarily, one asks oneself: What is my life's meaning? This question immediately relates to the phenomenological concept of the 'I can' consciousness, along with the phenomenological tools to analyse it.

The health of possibilities

Is Husserl's 'I can' the same as de Miranda's 'Creal' (on the latter, see Chapters 11 and 17 of the present volume)? I first propose that we look at some background information regarding the former. Phenomenology is a famously difficult philosophy to assess and apply, especially in its classical Husserlian version. Drawing from Descartes's and Kant's philosophies, Husserl's phenomenology inherits an overly theoretical character, visible in the preoccupation with intentionality in its broadest sense. For phenomenologists, intentionality does not only refer to intention, wanting or not wanting to do this or that. Instead, intentionality is discovered to be an essential aspect of consciousness: consciousness is always directed at something, always at work constituting objects and always creating some experience. Even experienceless sleep is considered to constitute various objects of consciousness, such as dreams, or that alarm clock sound that you are not very sure you heard in your sleep earlier on. All in all, researching the conditions of possibility for consciousness and first-hand experience focuses on the common thread in all experiences. Studying intentionality in its broadest sense fosters enhanced attention to various phenomena of consciousness. This is precisely what happens in the counselling room: both counsellor and counselee pay attention to consciousness and thinking as they are performed. Just as phenomenologists study their own experiences, the counsellor-counselee team predominantly study the counselee's experience when facing reflective challenges.

The strong compatibility between phenomenology and philosophical counselling is especially visible in the *I can* concept. It describes a person's consciousness of the possible ways to keep or modify the person's thoughts, actions or values (Husserl, 1989: 261–88). The *I can* consciousness thus mirrors de Miranda's Creal, which is defined, in his words, as a 'creative possibility in perpetual becoming' (2021a). Neglecting philosophical health and one's *creality* implies a neglect of 'the background of possibility and creativity that is implied by a processual totality of being and wholeness of becoming' (de Miranda, 2021a). A person's Creal dimension is that person's necessary condition of being potentially creative and re-evaluative in relation to his or her life, values, feelings, way of thinking and actions. One's permanent sliding into creativity is taken to be part of one's subjective reality.

However, people often make their lives miserable instead of responsibly reflecting on their problems. Their sliding into creativity often gives birth to resistance, taking the shape of sticking to one's comfort zone, complacency, reluctance to try new things or even isolation and depression. Because of this, people aspiring to philosophical health would have to responsibly assess their creality and somehow manage it. Failing to manage their condition, ambivalence and pressing life questions sometimes leads them to seek help for their declining philosophical health. This is where philosophical counselling comes into play.

All in all, the Creal is very similar to Husserl's *I can* consciousness, namely a consciousness regarding possibilities, not only in the deliberate sense, where a person actively thinks about options but also on a pre-reflective level, where a person feels or intuits that he or she can rather proceed than be stopped. This is why the *I can* consciousness is described by Husserl as a practical possibility that fuels instinctive actions, a 'resistanceless doing of things' (Husserl, 1989: 270), and by de Miranda as a letting-go of resistance also present in the drive to critical creativity (de Miranda, 2021a). Otherwise, resisting one's possibilities equates to a clash with oneself, including on a pre-reflective, instinctive level.

Let us explore one more detail regarding the *I can* consciousness before moving on to phenomenological tools and the principles behind philosophical health. The *I can* is a more fundamental type of consciousness than volition or reflection. It only refers to a person being aware of his or her abilities, without necessarily being driven to use them. For instance, an athlete's *I can* consciousness refers to his or her ability to attain a certain speed or to endure a particular duration of intense effort. The athlete does not have to think or cast that feeling of potency into a judgement. The athlete has a strong yet vague sense of being able to perform in certain ways. Another example: a phenomenologist's *I can* consciousness refers to his or her ability to observe consciousness as it is unfolding, and identify the process's essential features. This can be achieved by slowly describing the backstage of experience (Simionescu-Panait, 2021: 47–51). We see that a person's *I can* might be developed in many directions; we could even stretch out and say that a person's *I can* is the result of having learned something. This does not refer to obtaining information but to a manner of performing consciously: learning to run, to self-reflect or even to question others.

Similarly, to the previous examples, a counsellor's *I can* consciousness, which I see as a Socratic attitude, refers to the sense of being aware of dialogue, listening and thinking in a certain way. The purpose is to determine the interlocutor to think on and for oneself, as well as to overcome blind spots in thinking. The Socratic attitude includes the counsellor's intuition of how he or she can proceed regardless of the situation disclosed by the interlocutor he or she is facing. This sense of being able to perform Socratically is enriched by engaging in dialogue with various counselees and their different problems. Often, counsellors rely on their Socratic attitude to push forward or delay some questions. In other words, they have a sense of being able to deal with counselees and their reactions to sensitive topics. For instance, a person in mourning would probably not be able to immediately answer a question like 'What is bad about losing your only child?' or reflect on it during the first session. Nor will the person be able to integrate ideas from various philosophies such as Stoicism, regarding the benefits of losing important things in life. In such a situation, the counsellor's Socratic attitude offers a sense of being able to handle the delicate case. It also gives the philosopher a sense of pacing throughout the consultations. This means that the counselee's Creal is not something that can be cultivated instantly. Instead, a person's creative reality is lured out of obscurity and gradually placed in the limelight through the consultation process. Out in the open, a person's creative reality reveals itself with its underlying structure, principles and values, nurturing philosophical health. These are landmarks that facilitate the person's process of knowing oneself and actualizing one's highest virtues.

This idea opens up the next question that is related to the manner of luring the Creal out in the open over and over again in consultation. How is a counselee's sense of the possible, one's *I can* consciousness, shaped by the philosophical dialogue?

Dare to listen (bracketing oneself)

Have you ever talked to someone and had the impression that the person's attention was fading away? Did you capture that person's gaze staring into nothingness? Was that person's reaction delayed by a lack of focus? If you met this kind of person, you most probably know how a deficit of listening manifests in practice. This rather common situation where one finds out that he or she is talking to walls can be avoided in the counselling room.

Usually, the philosopher uses what de Miranda sees as 'deep listening' (2021a; 2021c), which is a kind of directing attention 'to let a singular signification manifest itself, here and now, within a context of trust for the unheard-of' (de Miranda, 2021a). A person's philosophical health can thus flourish by listening and trying to understand any ideas, potentially strange ideas or ideas that the counselee was reluctant to express. I propose the idea that deep listening is a way of practising Husserl's concept of bracketing, the *epoché*, in the counselling process.

In regular phenomenological efforts, the *epoché* is the inaugural moment. Bracketing consists in leaving the natural attitude, in suspending preconceptions and prejudice about the existence of reality and our way of knowing it (Husserl, 1960; Zahavi, 2003). The scope is to create a clear ground for any investigation, free from prejudice and immovable convictions. Similarly, the philosophical counsellor tries to create a blank space free from his or her convictions but also free from the counselee's prejudice. People often manifest in the counselling room what Husserl calls the natural attitude, which mainly consists of a lack of availability to doubt and re-evaluate one's ideas and opinions. The rigidity in knowing oneself present in the natural attitude is directly impacted by bracketing ideas, or in other words, by wilfully ignoring ideas that impede thinking. The *epoché* is a way to keep both philosopher and interlocutor in a perpetual inaugural moment of thinking. This does not mean that no knowledge is advanced and no truth is pursued. This only means that each moment of dialogue remains open to rethinking. This is counter-intuitive for someone under the natural attitude because it appears as a useless, fruitless endeavour. However, the fruits of practising the *epoché* resemble those of de Miranda's deep listening: building trust and allowing for exploration in collaborative thinking.

The deep listening deployed by bracketing what one already knows (Schuster, 1991; Marinoff, 1999) impacts philosophical health. First, the counsellor manages to create a clean space for the counselee's thinking to unfold in their collaboration. The counselee's creative reality begins to fill this space, even if it often fails in making sense by giving shape to thinking in expressing arguments, conceptualizing, questioning or evaluating ideas. If that dialogue space was filled with bits of knowledge provided by the counsellor, the counselee would trip, may fall and give up under the pressure of already existing and probably smarter ideas.

A second aspect emerges after securing a clean space: creating a habit of bracketing in dialogue progressively slows the discussion's pace down to the level where ideas can be listened to, understood and assessed without pressure. Slowing down the interlocutor's playground in thinking gives the person a chance to observe oneself and to understand what one can change, even at the level of expressing specific ideas. For instance, a counselee having the habit of beginning utterances with 'I guess' is worth being observed. Why is this person inclined to guess instead of affirming? Is it a way to avoid responsibility or a fear of being harshly judged? Or could it instead be a form of playful language to alleviate the interlocutor's general boredom? In such a situation, the counselee may be invited to investigate: the discussion may thus expand from one tiny detail – the returning 'I guess' – to an entire picture of a person's mentality regarding oneself and one's thinking. The person's causes for the repetitive usage of the 'I guess' are explored and confronted by common sense and logic. Deep listening by bracketing what one knows picks up such elements and thus invites a person to look at one's *forma mentis*.

Using the *epoché* greatly impacts the counselee's philosophical health. And yet, it does not happen by transferring philosophical knowledge but by manifesting a Socratic attitude. The counselee does not benefit from simply hearing words of wisdom backed by big names in philosophy. Instead, the dialogue pace can be slowed, containing feedback loops on the person's thought process. The main benefit from this situation arrives from one of the natural attitude's characteristics: people usually do not know themselves well, what their deeper problems are, if any, and how to adequately name them. Consequently, they often contradict themselves and change their minds while simply trying to explain their thoughts to a philosopher who requires detailed clarifications. Their effort is to become comfortable with their thinking failures and with the need to retry. Under the natural attitude, failure has a strong negative connotation, so early-stage counselees can hesitate to be honest. This state indicates poor philosophical health, and more specifically, a lack of mental heroism, according to de Miranda's five principles for philosophical health (2021a). Fortunately, the deep listening emerging from bracketing one's knowledge decisively contributes to nurturing a potential form of mental heroism by building trust in the process of showing one's flaws.

Yet, trust is not enough in the counselling process. Cultivating the Socratic attitude as well as unlocking a person's creality requires some sort of structuring throughout the process.

Lateral guidance (the phenomenological reduction)

Bracketing what one knows frees the mind to try new ideas and explore blind spots regarding one's life. The downside of a free-form exploration is that one can forget what is the main theme and where the discussion started. This is true of philosophical consultation sessions as well: some practitioners tend to let the discussion loose. In the end, it becomes very difficult to identify how the main theme changed throughout the dialogue. There is no main theme anymore. Rather, the discussion becomes a collection of random judgements about oneself. To avoid this, bracketing is complemented by another concept from phenomenology, namely phenomenological reduction. Whereas the *epoché* serves as a short-range instrument that has to be summoned time and again, the reduction serves as a long-range initiative.

What is the reduction, and what does it look like in practice? While bracketing was used to identify the most basic presuppositions (Luft, 2011) people make, like the idea that the world exists and that other people think like them, the phenomenological reduction is used to focus on a specific essential direction. After we have invited the person to bracket presuppositions with, for example, reasons for other people to think differently than him or her, this exploration may very well go sideways and roam into disparate topics. For instance, the counselee's difficulty in seeing the other's differences in thinking can occur because of a strong inclination to submerge into fantasies and run away from reality. Or, that individual can be a people pleaser, readily adopting anything others prefer and end up failing to create a border between oneself and others. The phenomenological reduction is used in consultation not only to identify the main theme but to keep the consultation on a main theme or at least pursue one topic at a time. Even if the counselee keeps bringing up new information, the counsellor can stick to what seems to be the most important topic and can even ask which topic is more important or urgent for discussion.

The purpose of the phenomenological reduction is to reduce the Socratic dialogue to the counselee's essential theme. Just like a symphony has its main theme that dictates how the rest of the musical phrases gravitate around it, so does a counselee's main theme indicate how the person thinks on various other topics. Two people involved in Socratic dialogue keep returning to one's main theme and thus enrich the sense and weight of this theme for the counselee's consciousness. Looking and expanding on the person's main theme is not so much based on the idea that the interlocutor shelters an essence, an *eidos* of one's personality. The process of philosophical counselling may alter what might have been previously considered the essence of the counselee's personality. Instead, the point of the reduction is to cooperatively produce what de Miranda calls a 'deep orientation' (2021a) for the interlocutor's reflections.

Deep orientation is essential for philosophical health because it mitigates the appearance of confusion characteristic of most novice philosophical explorations. Whenever the counselee arrives at contradictory ideas, or whenever they do not know what to do next, they can reduce the dialogue to the main theme and foster the appearance of deep orientation in their thinking. People under the natural attitude tend to jump from one idea to another because the freedom to assume virtually anything allows them to assume that things they say or think make sense to anyone. Therefore, people do not bother to check with their interlocutors if what they said makes sense to the other. For instance, a philosophy professor explains Kant to his students. Towards the end of the monologue lecture, the professor asks if everyone understood what he said about Kant's philosophy. The response is overwhelmingly positive. The professor refrains from checking if this is true and ends the lesson, only to be surprised by the very low grades coming in at the end of the semester. The professor assumed that the Kantian framework in his mind was clearly expressed and that almost anyone could understand it. He did so because nothing in his consciousness stopped him from assuming a rather wild idea: students understand Kantian philosophy in a jiffy. Such a professor may very well arrive in the counselling room with the problem of being misunderstood and misjudged by others, eventually going through a prominent feeling of loneliness and isolation. This situation calls for a methodical reorientation of the counselee. Whenever the professor, now a counselee, derails the focus from self-reflection to invoking various philosophical theories to appear knowledgeable about oneself, the counsellor can reduce the dialogue to the main problem and provide the deep orientation that the professor lacks: the orientation towards the other.

A counsellor reducing the dialogue acts like the bowling lane gutter on both sides, like lateral guidance towards oneself. Reducing the dialogue to the counselee's most intimate theme is a repetitive and sustained endeavour. The reduction often sees ideas ending up like a bowling bowl on the invalidating left or right gutter. Trying time and again to think in an organized fashion contributes to a sense of orientation and even discrimination in one's thinking. Philosophical health is improved by having the interlocutor learn that not all of his or her thoughts are important. The counselee finds deep orientation into oneself by separating and even discriminating between ideas, by becoming able to manage concepts. One finds one's way through the jungle of one's thinking by cutting down paths through abundant and disorganized vegetation. Then it becomes easier for the deeply oriented person to start identifying situations on the spot where interlocutors change or slide from topic to topic. The deep orientation enacted by practising the reduction builds the counselee's confidence in one's thinking precisely by rendering some thoughts to be unimportant. By being deeply oriented, the person obtains a solid ground for achieving an ideal frame of mind called mental heroism.

Observational empathy

'The healthy philosopher is dedicated to the service of men, which means that personal philosophical health goes along with an attitude of philosophical care towards the other, at least in the form of dialogue. Mental heroism is not only about being able to resist resiliently or inflexibly toxic influences, it is also about intersubjective attention and openness' (de Miranda, 2021a). But to be able to overcome one's difficulties, one would need clarity of thought and clarity of values. The phenomenological reduction cultivates this clarity. It improves a person's philosophical health because it helps one take distance from one's ideas to better handle thoughts, ideas and concepts.

What about the need to take distance from other persons, their emotions and their impact on oneself? In what way is it philosophically healthy to be able to think about our relationship with others without having our thinking clouded by strong emotions? The phenomenological answer in philosophical consultation proposes a certain kind of empathy, which is close to de Miranda's 'intellectual empathy' (2021a), and which I call 'observational empathy'. However, this kind of empathy is counter-intuitive to what people usually mean by empathy.

Usually, empathy is understood to be a state where the empathic person imitates and lives through a feeling similar to the other person with whom one empathizes (Husserl, 2001; Zahavi, 2015). People under the natural attitude tend to say that a person is empathic when the person is visibly emotional and is ready to adopt another person's emotions with the usual goal of comforting or cheering up the other. For most, an empathic person is someone who understands, shares and acts to emotionally support another person. But this is problematic because people do not have a good grasp of their empathic performances. Counselees arrive in the counselling room on many occasions with the problem of being caught in other people's emotions. This is usually called 'to take things personally'. Often, I hear problems such as 'my mind freezes when my boss gives me that cold look', 'I cannot help but get angry when my mother tries to shame me for something I think is alright to do', or 'I feel I am talking to a wall when my partner keeps saying the same things over and over again'. These counselees are empathic on a level of instantly responding by adopting the other person's negative emotion. Because of this wild empathic response, they fail to see the bigger picture: one is not responsible for the boss's cold look, for the mother's frustration or for the partner's desperate insistence on some ideas. In addition, one could take into account that maybe the boss's cold look is a reflection of anxiety, the mother's frustration is born out of feeling she loses relevance for the child or that the partner's desperate insistence is the consequence of not being listened to in the first place. Being immediately empathic prevents from thinking about various plausible explanations. This situation calls for a more cold-headed, even intellectual empathy, which is provided by the phenomenological tradition.

Scheler famously distinguishes between the immediate mirroring that he calls sympathy and a more fundamental sense of empathy, which is about grasping the existence of the other's feeling without living through a similar feeling (Scheler, 2008: 8–11). So described, sympathy can cause many social and self-consciousness problems, leading to the need for a sustained counselling process. Being emotionally disoriented in social contexts entails a problem in knowing oneself and one's possibilities: in short, it leads to a lack of philosophical health. Because of this, Scheler's distinction is useful to at least offer the counselee a shift in understanding what empathy is and how one's emotions can be tackled.

Edith Stein would be optimistic about any person's shift from sympathy to empathy because empathy is already built into consciousness (Stein, 1964). Phenomenology brings good news to philosophical counselling. Observational empathy, though cold-headed, focuses on understanding the other. The usual empathy, or sympathy as we called it together with Scheler, does not focus on understanding the other but on becoming emotionally similar to the other, often to the detriment of understanding the other. The good news is that observational empathy is universal in human consciousness, and therefore philosophical counselling can safely work towards cultivating a detached understanding of other people. This does not mean that there are no emotions in intellectual empathy. Being cold-headed when understanding what others feel involves a range of emotions, especially that of being calm. This emotion contributes to the deep orientation towards oneself since orienting takes place easier in calm waters.

The usually mundane character of problems invoked in the counselling room (Schuster, 1992; Amir, 2013) gives way to the appearance of sympathy in the consultation process. This might become a risky situation for some counsellors because of their tendency to adopt a comforting feel-good approach that can easily forfeit the reflection and generate no progress with the interlocutor in understanding and managing the issue. The problem with feel-good approaches is that comforting the counselee makes one complacent with one's thinking and inhibits the drive to question it. To use two of de Miranda's terms, the feel-good sympathy approach inhibits both critical creativity and mental heroism. The risk in using the natural attitude's way of empathizing in the counselling room is the stagnation of self-discovery and reflection.

This does not mean that moments of sympathy should be completely erased from the consultation. Such moments could be valuable at the right time. For instance, say that after one hour of hard work both intellectually and emotionally, the interlocutor realizes that one understands other people based on how they understand oneself. Then, the counsellor can spill a very short confession and say that discovering this idea was personally vital as well. Such discreet confirmations or validations can ease up the pressure of knowing oneself. However, sympathy should be kept at bay to let the more intellectual-friendly observational empathy occur. The consequence of this manner is the fostering of mental heroism.

De Miranda defines mental heroism as 'an individual courage to think' (2021a; 2021b), and bases his idea on the three Kantian principles for reaching wisdom in his *Anthropology*: thinking for oneself, thinking consistently with oneself and thinking into the place of the other (Kant, 2007: 307). The phenomenological empathy I described so far is a direct descendant of Kant's idea that thinking into the place of the other is necessary for becoming wise, and implicitly, for being mentally heroic, for daring to think. If one were to think by affirming emotions, one would remain intellectually immature because affirming emotions creates a narrow, self-centred picture of oneself. Within this narrow picture, intellectually immature persons believe that all other people think like them and that their emotions are appropriate and crucial. This perspective removes any chance of enhancing one's philosophical health, knowledge of oneself, potential creativity and the daring to know. In fact, such a person's philosophical health is rather poor. The person will not dare to know since the person already knows it all. Therefore, mental heroism directly relies on the ability to keep one's emotions at bay and contemplate how one relates to others cold-headedly. Mental heroism also relies on abstaining from thinking that other people inevitably think like us. The diversity of possible ways of thinking discovered through philosophical counselling allows the counselee to philosophically care for others, to be open to them, adopt deep listening and orientation and, finally, to live creatively and renewably with oneself and others.

So, is philosophical health for everyone?

This phenomenological reading of philosophical health and the principles to obtain and maintain it suggest that counselees must work on their deeply ingrained natural attitude. Otherwise, they tend to repeat what they know instead of risking new ideas. They jump from one idea to another and become confused, base their thinking on emotions and limit their creative possibilities when contemplating their lives. However, people arriving in the counselling room manifest one characteristic that already shows something beneficial regarding their philosophical health: they are conscious that something can be changed for the better and they want to do something about it. The seed of being available to think together with a professional counsellor reveals a consciousness of creative possibilities.

A counselee is minimally conscious that something can be done for the self, revealing what de Miranda calls that person's 'crealectics', or capacity to shape and orient the sense of the possible. I propose that philosophical health exists whenever this minimal consciousness appears in a person's mind: I can do something for myself, to better my life, attitude, thinking and relations. This kind of person usually ends up as a counselee or even a patient in some psychotherapeutic process. Otherwise, the lack of such a consciousness suggests the dreary idea that some people are philosophically dead, lacking or even refusing any potential for understanding others and oneself, stuck in a perpetual complacency or nihilism. Then, one may ask: Is being philosophically dead reversible? Can philosophical counselling reverse something that appears to be irreversible? Does the Creal as ultimate possible remain a necessary aspect of consciousness, or is it something a person needs to work toward by living a contemplative life?

These questions show that philosophical health points to a fundamental aspect of humanity, namely self-consciousness. It is fundamental because people can either put some effort into helping their lives flourish or let their lives dry out. There is no in-between. Being philosophically healthy is difficult. But then, again, is any health matter simple?

References

Amir, Lydia (2013), 'Three Questionable Assumptions of Philosophical Counselling'. In Elliot D. Cohen and Samuel Zinaich (eds), *Philosophy, Counselling, and Psychotherapy*, 44–60. Newcastle upon Tyne: Cambridge Scholars Publishing.

Amir, Lydia (2018), *Taking Philosophy Seriously*. Newcastle upon Tyne: Cambridge Scholars Publishing.

Hansen, Finn Thorbjon (2015), 'The Philosophical Practitioner as a Co-researcher'. In Aleksandar Fatic and Lydia Amir (eds), *Practicing Philosophy*, 22–41. Cambridge: Cambridge Scholars Publishing.

Husserl, Edmund (1960), *Cartesian Meditations*, trans. Dorion Cairns. Dordrecht: Springer.

Husserl, Edmund (1989), *Ideas Pertaining to a Pure Phenomenology and a Phenomenological Philosophy. Second Volume*, trans. Richard Rojcewicz and André Schuwer. Dordrecht: Springer.

Husserl, Edmund (2001), *Sur l'intersubjectivité I*, trans. Natalie Depraz. Paris: Presses Universitaires de France.

Kant, Immanuel (2007), *Anthropology, History, and Education*, ed. and trans. Günter Zöller and Robert B. Louden. Cambridge: Cambridge University Press.

Lindseth, Anders and Astrid Norberg (2003), 'A Phenomenological Hermeneutical Method for Researching Lived Experience'. *Scandinavian Journal for Caring Sciences*, 18: 145–53.

Luft, Sebastian (2011), 'Husserl's Method of Reduction'. Philosophy Faculty Research and Publications, 199. https://epublications.marquette.edu/phil_fac/199

Marinoff, Lou (1999), *Plato not Prozac!* New York: Harper Collins Publishers.

Marinoff, Lou (2003), *The Big Questions. Therapy for the Sane or How Philosophy can Change Your Life*. New York: Bloomsbury Publishing.

de Miranda, Luis (2021a), 'Five Principles of Philosophical Health for Critical Times: from Hadot to Crealectics'. *Eidos. A Journal for Philosophy of Culture*, 5 (1): 70–89.

de Miranda, Luis (2021b), 'Think into the Place of the Other: The Crealectic Approach to Philosophical Health and Care'. *International Journal of Philosophical Practice*, 7 (1): 89–103.

De Miranda, Luis (2021c), 'Philosophical Health'. In Vlad Glăveanu (ed.), *Palgrave Encyclopedia of the Possible*, 1003–8. London: Palgrave Macmillan.

Neves, João Maria (2014), 'Phenomenology of Dreams in Philosophical Practice'. *Philosophical Practice*, 9 (3): 1475–86.

Scheler, Max (2008), *The Nature of Sympathy*, trans. Peter Heath. London: Routledge.

Schuster, Shlomit (1991), 'Philosophical Counselling'. *Journal of Applied Philosophy*, 8 (2): 219–23.

Schuster, Shlomit (1992), 'Philosophy as if it Matters: The Practice of Philosophical Counselling'. *Critical Review: A Journal of Politics and Society*, 6 (4): 587–99.

Simionescu-Panait, Andrei (2020), 'Are Constructivism and Enactivism Two Opposite Philosophies on Learning Mathematics?' *Revista Pesquisa Qualitativa*, 8 (18): 419–30.

Simionescu-Panait, Andrei (2021), *The Reconciled Body. An Essay on the Phenomenology of Elegance*. Bucharest: Zeta Books.

Stein, Edith (1964), *On the Nature of Empathy*, trans. Waltraut Stein. Dordrecht: Springer.

Zahavi, Dan (2003), *Husserl's Phenomenology*. Cambridge, MA: MIT Press.

Zahavi, Dan (2015), *Self and Other: Exploring Subjectivity, Empathy and Shame*. Oxford: Oxford University Press.

Zavala, Carmen (2016), 'The Role of Pre-linguistic Thought in Philosophical Practice. On the Relevance of Phenomenology to Philosophical Companionships'. *Philosophical Practice*, 11 (3): 1834–44.

Zhang, Lizeng (2014), 'On the Counselor-Client Relationship in Philosophical Counselling'. *Philosophical Practice*, 9 (1): 1320–6.

11

Artificial intelligence and philosophical health

From analytics to crealectics

Luis de Miranda

Introduction: Making sense of the forest of the real

The growing entanglement of humans, digital machines and artificial intelligence (AI) generates 'anthrobotic' protocols (de Miranda, Ramamoorthy and Rovatsos, 2016) that challenge our reflection on philosophical health. Whenever we forget that AI operates under human interpretation and design, then dramatic or anxiogenic narratives become unavoidable as AI is expected to autonomously outsmart humanity in the capacity to think (Geraci, 2008). We need to differentiate what, on the one hand, machines can 'help us' make sense of and what, on the other hand, humans can think fruitfully about in a non-automated fashion. Moreover, despite the widespread use of the phrase 'artificial intelligence', there is no universal agreement on what intelligence is.

The very etymology of the word 'intelligence' is ambivalent between the two Latin roots *inter-legere* and *inter-legare*. As explained by anthropologist Marcel Jousse (2016), intelligence can be about *inter-legere*, to discriminate: 'the world is an immense chaos of interactions, but in this immense chaos of interactions comes a human being who will know how to choose from this multiplicity' (p. 29). But the root of intelligence can also be *interligare*: 'to link up in the form of interactions [. . .]. Remember the great Laplace: Discoveries consist of bringing together ideas – I would say facts – that are susceptible to join but that had not been hitherto been joined' (Jousse, 2016: 29). Whether intelligence consists in picking and distinguishing parts by a process of division and segmentation, in discovering wholes, syntheses and unities by a process of association, or in organizing actualizations of possibilities – not to speak of the various historical, cultural, emotional and disciplinary variations in defining intelligence around the globe – this polysemy points to the necessity of not speaking of intelligence as if it were one universal form of manipulating symbols. If there are several forms of intelligence which are radically heterogeneous and perhaps even antagonistic, no artificial entity can be said to synthesize them all.

What should we mean, then, when we speak of AI? In what follows, I explain why AI as we know it is for the most part a display of analytic intelligence. It is dominantly implemented in the real world as a set of algorithms facilitating predictive analytics or data analytics, defined as forecasting the statistical likelihood of future actions, trends, words or patterns [. . .] on the basis of inferred relationships between variables in recorded data (Chandler and Munday, 2016). In other words, AI is a human-designed digital technology that facilitates the identification of patterns within bodies of data through the use of computers, as well as the prediction of future patterns, in order to gain insights that facilitate an automated action, a human decision or the production of a human-like result.

The specialization of AI in analytic operations sheds a renewed light, by contradistinction, on the creative, aesthetic and cosmological aspects of philosophical intelligence. This aspect was sometimes disparaged or forgotten in the recent 'analytic moment' of the history of philosophy. This meta-analytic aspect of philosophical consciousness we call crealectic intelligence, because it is a form of hyper-dialectic (Merleau-Ponty, 1968) that relies on the axiom that the ultimate Real, the forest of all experiences, is also a 'Creal', a continuous creation and realization of multiplicity and possibility (de Miranda, 2017). In order to fully intuit what crealectic intelligence might be in the light of our anthrobotic horizon (Part 3 of this chapter), we will contrast it with analytic intelligence (Part 1) and dialectic intelligence (Part 2).

The pebbles in the forest: Analytic intelligence and AI

What does the so-called automation of intelligence mean for philosophy? To understand the relevance of crealectics or philosophical creativity, we need to contrast it with the logic of its dialectical counterpart, mechanized analytic intelligence. An enabling set of algorithms is primarily an analytic machine. Analytics is the dominant approach to intelligence in our engineer-driven societies because it is more easily decomposed and mathematized into sets of operations for the sake of productive action. Analytics needs decomposable material as the primary component for its manipulation of numerical symbols and consequently manipulation of reality. This is compatible with automation and so-called evidence-based decision-making.

Analytic forms of intelligence were certainly a major step in human evolution. Some eighteen centuries ago, in his account of Aristotle's Analytics, Alexander of Aphrodisias wrote that the one who 'uses analysis [. . .] reduces composite bodies into simple bodies' (c.200 CE, 49, §2.4), thus separating an unknown into parts that are known (Arnauld and Nicole, 1996: 200). The telos of current automated analytics was anticipated by Laplace (1814), who famously believed we ought

> to regard the present state of the universe as the effect of its anterior state and as the cause of the one which is to follow. Given for one instant an intelligence which would comprehend all the forces by which nature is animated and the respective situation of the beings who compose it – intelligence sufficiently vast to submit these data to analysis – it would embrace in the same formula the movements of

the greatest bodies of the universe and those of the lightest atom; for it, nothing would be uncertain and the future, as the past, would be present to its eyes. (Laplace, 1814: 4)

This deterministic, quantitative and homogenizing closure of the world's horizon is reactivated in the dominant AI discourse as the utopia of Artificial General Intelligence (AGI).

But some inventors of computational thinking were already aware that an essential part of intelligence, namely its relationship to creation and truth, was left behind in their analytic endeavours. When Charles Babbage and Ada Lovelace designed the first 'Analytical Engine' by associating analysis with a mechanical function of 'operation' (Menabrea, 1961: 247), Lovelace was careful to add: 'The Analytical Engine has no pretensions whatever to originate anything. It can do whatever we know how to order it to perform. It can follow analysis; but it has no power of anticipating [. . .] relations or truths' (284).

Beyond this 'Lovelace Objection' to AI (Turing, 1950), there is what we might call the Whitehead Objection to the belief that analysis and concreteness are sufficient to understand the Real: analytics, while useful for purposes of manipulation and operationality, often ends up mistaking the abstract object for the concrete in a 'fallacy of misplaced concreteness' (Whitehead, 1926: 64). Out of habit or cognitive bias, we tend to believe that the parts, units or functions that we distinguished and named are truly there in the real world, like cogs in a machine (in thus doing, scientists usually forget about themselves as subjects).

Digital worlds and AI-based 'virtual reality' seem to be for our minds more and more indistinguishable from IRL ('in real-life') experiences. But such a phenomenon happens precisely because our cognition is not only analytic but also creative, as confirmed by recent trends in neuroscience (Berthoz, 2012): our consciousness produces semblances of meaning and pattern emergence that supersede the sum of the observed parts and cannot always be explained by strict analysis (Murphy and Stoeger, 2007). In the past, analytic philosophers, tempted by materialism and the ideology of concreteness, have ironically called this surplus of meaning the 'ghost in the machine' (Ryle, 2009 [1949]: 5). But to call what we experience, but cannot fully analyse, measure, demonstrate or show, a 'ghost' or 'superstition', partakes in a reductionism that can be 'detrimental both to good science and good human living' (Thompson, 1997: 219). Philosophical health is not about extreme logical intelligence.

Analysis is certainly indispensable as a step that considers reality as readable, a corpus or text. Abandoned in the forest, Hansel and Gretel find their way home with white pebbles, even if this does not get them out of trouble in the longer run. Analysis is a moment of distinctive literacy facilitating communication and the effectual manipulation of the Real. If an intentional consciousness is unable to distinguish discrete parts in the world by reading them as potential text or even operating programme, it might remain dreamy and confused (Craig, 1984: 41). Analytic elements manifest as what Noam Chomsky called a 'surface structure' (1968: 30). At the level of a written language, the surface structure is represented by discrete symbols such as pebbles, letters, code or forms. The analytic moment is the consideration of the world as possible syntax instead of chaos, or, in the language of AI, patterns versus noise. This is useful as an effectual reading of the surface structure, but analytic intelligence becomes a reductionist worldview when it claims to describe the complete depth of the Real.

In order to avoid the illusion that AI can be generally 'intelligent' without human intervention, we need to remember that the possibility of an interpretation or semantic deciphering of an environment is a subjective component of intelligence, a perspective. Even prominent computer scientists like Stuart J. Russel claim that to gain insights that improve meaningful decision-taking, AI needs the help of an interpreter, a subject who is part of a 'web of belief' (Quine and Ullian, 1978), deciding what is pertinent and what is neglectable in correlation with a given purpose (Russell, 2019). Making sense of the random noise of data is an interpretation modelled on an observer-dependent or subject-dependent perspective (Kaan, 1999). For the psychologist Piaget, intelligent behaviour involves a process of centration, of mental focus on such or such an aspect of reality made concrete because of its relative subjective importance: one pays attention to this rather than that, in a movement of intentional discrimination (Piaget, 1952). Concreteness is a useful 'ensemblance' (de Miranda, 2020), and pure analysis cannot in itself provide meaning or creative unification: more often than not, in the human realm, semblances are subjective and ensembles arbitrary.

Searle's famous distinction between syntax and semantics (1980) aimed at explaining why computers do not have an understanding of what they do and therefore cannot be said to be intelligent: 'Computation is defined purely formally or syntactically, whereas minds have actual mental or semantic contents, and we cannot get from the syntactical to the semantic just by having the syntactical operations and nothing else' (Searle, 2010: 17). In other words, meaning is provided by a human perspective.

Whether one agrees with the syntax/semantics division or not as a good explanation, one might concede that analytic intelligence as it is practised in our anthrobotic culture implies four procedures (not always in the following order): (1) selection or distinction between useful data and neglectable noise; (2) decomposition or division of a whole into parts and operations; (3) reification, transforming continuous processes or flows into discrete articulated objects; (4) a moment of digitization, the reduction of the parts into computable symbols.

In fact, as will be argued below, these four moments often imply a discursive negotiation and a creative focus that requires the concurrent display of dialectic intelligence and crealectic intelligence.

Breadcrumbs in the forest: Dialectic intelligence

Shared intelligence needs an analytic moment, for agents to clearly communicate their reading of a given situation. Once we start disagreeing with a given analysis, devising or debating aspects of it, we are adding a dialectic dimension which functions as a bridge between analytics and crealectics.

Since Plato, dialectic intelligence designates an interpretative conversation in which there is a more-or-less rational tension between different or agonistic perspectives (from *dialegesthai*: to talk through). Dialectics is 'the progression of thought through the appearance of oppositions within one and the same unity' (Bloch, 1983: 288). This form of thinking can be performed between different subjects or within the same personal mind, as in Socrates's inner dialogue with his guardian divinity, his *daimonion* (McMahon, 2013: 40), or as in Descartes's cogito, which can be defined as the human capacity for an individual internal dialectics, a form of consciousness that is capable of self-contradiction for the sake of self-examination.

There was in Plato the idea that dialectic thinking may reveal a higher, more intelligible truth, and Hegel would remember this aspect. In Hegel's grandiose variant, dialectic intelligence described the ubiquitous and necessary unfolding of a time-dependent yet absolute process of negations and performative contradictions towards the universal realization of Spirit. Hegelians believe that the Real is *really* dialectical, and therefore that dialectic intelligence is a privileged form of realism leading to objective knowledge: 'the dialectical constitutes the moving soul of scientific progression' (Hegel, 1817: §81).

In dialectic consciousness, a proposition and its opposite can be both true, thus apparently ignoring the law of non-contradiction common in analytic logic. To remember how such ambivalence is possible, we can invoke an example that is not the usual handbook illustration of Hegelian dialectics: consider human somatization, the idea that unhealthy mental or emotional states can remain unconscious and be manifested in bodily troubles. Manifesting a mental disorder or distress via physiological ways can be said to be a dialectic process: it is in some sense healthy to be able to ascribe psychological or existential conundrums to our bodies, because the physical symptoms make it possible to read materially that there is a problem before it is too late. A somatization is a relatively transparent way of manifesting existential problems that might otherwise remain unreadable; such manifestation may reveal, paradoxically, a relatively good communication between mind and body. A very simple example of somatization is crying. When Hansel and Gretel are crying in the forest because their parents abandoned them once again, their exteriorized suffering makes them conscious that something is really wrong; they can then try to find a solution.

Individual, bilateral or collective forms of dialectic intelligence rely on polarities, tensions and potential contradictions in a process that ideally moves towards a form of reconciliation, resolution or synthesis that may or may not reflect the logic of the 'World-Soul' (Hegel, 1806: 114). When fetishized as a one-fits-all tool, as in the Marxist variant, or the Sophists' version of the Ancient Greek variant, dialectical intelligence sometimes forces syntheses via deception or coercion. In Hansel and Gretel's tale, once the white pebbles cannot be accessed to mark the path, impermanent breadcrumbs are used, which may be dialectically perceived as symbols or as food. The birds win the interpretative competition by eating the crumbs. In the agonistic world of dialectics, the illusion might be that there is not enough bread for everyone (hence the possibility of political anger). It becomes difficult to identify if a synthesis is logical and objective, or rather belongs to a subjective victory of one privileged interest over another as in the Hegelian dialectic of the master and servant. Few can avoid being emotional in an antagonistic dialogue, and even Hegel admitted the importance of passion and superficial irrationality in dialectic unfolding. Hyper-communitarian times demonstrate the pitfalls of political dialectics: any legitimate position can be considered a form of scandalous usurpation or vice versa, a phenomenon of so-called *polarization* that AI chatbots and other digital echo chambers have accelerated.

The dialectic stage of understanding may be necessary to transform a reading of signs into a deliberative interpretation that encompasses real or apparent contradictions. However, this moment of intelligence is not sufficient to act holistically upon the world because the synthesis it proposes can be contested and, by definition, negated anew. If the world is only dialectically interpreted, it becomes an interminable process in which everything becomes negative and positive alternatively, any synthesis being an ephemerous plateau collapsing into a new thesis-antithesis polarity. Moreover, dialectics tends to fall into binary dichotomies, which are themselves cognitive reductions even if they seem to introduce more complexity than analytic intelligence (Elbow, 1993). For example, the two categories of disease and normal health are oblivious of possible alternative mental or physical states that are neither normal nor unhealthy (Canguilhem, 1991: 97). The human phenomenon of psychological resilience is neither pathological nor normal: it is not a mere synthesis but a novelty, a manifestation of crealectic intelligence (de Miranda, 2019).

The cottage at the heart of the forest of the real: Crealectic intelligence

Analytic and dialectic intelligences cannot exhaust our experience of intelligent agency. The analytic strategy of the white pebbles and the dialectic strategy of the breadcrumbs fail to solve the long-term problem of Hansel and Gretel, which is that their parents are not only materially but also spiritually poor and philosophically unhealthy. What saves the brother and sister of the fairy tale is the crealectic strategy of going deep into the forest rather than trying to come back home. They confront the abyss of possibility, multiplicity and sublimity. They risk their lives by the gingerbread house of plenitude guarded by the primordial witch and its oven of abundance which may dissolve or regenerate. The following paragraphs may be difficult to understand at first glance, especially if one keeps an analytic or a dialectic mindset. We hope the reader will engage in the speculative forest armed with the mental heroism of Hansel and Gretel rather than become paralysed and cry after Father Analytics and Mother Dialectics.

Social reality is polysemantic and implies a multiplicity of decisions and acts in which the factualization of data, the attribution of syntax to a given reality, is already filtered by creative and active imagination and an embodied perspective. We call 'crealectic' the existential form of consciousness that is aware of acting as an engaged person or group upon a world of multiplicity and possibility, with the idea of *intercreation* in mind. Crealectic intelligence cannot be emulated by a non-biological AI because it is grounded in desire and felt sublimity.

Crealectics deals with processing realities and imaginaries of novelty, plurality and ambiguity, rather than mere contradiction of binary polarities or operation of known bits and sets; its ontological core is the idea of creation understood ontologically as a ubiquitous stream of infinite possibility (Bergson, 1922; Whitehead, 1929; Deleuze and Guattari, 1994; de Miranda, 2017). The neologism crealectics comes from 'Creal', a contraction of Creation and Real (de Miranda, 2008). Creal designates the capacity to envision, imagine or feel a creative and virtual cosmological source of the Real as a metaphysical 'possibility of possibility' (Slife, 1994). The Creal is the Unimpossible: a simultaneously immanent and transcendent wave function of ever-emerging potentiality.

The Creal is a *it*, not a personalized God but a subliminal or subtextual process of becoming which whispers one and only thing: *it is possible*. That's the spirit we inherit: 'There is a practical consciousness, an "I can" that underlies and precedes the reflective self-consciousness of the "I think", but the "I can" is given and coeval with an "it can"' (Sinclair, 2017: 191). As was understood by existentialist philosophers, chief among them Sartre and Heidegger, the universe is a possibilization furnace. When one embodied living being says and feels, of a projected situation or idea for instance, that *it's possible*, they are connecting with the modal creal spacetime, with the essence of all there is. The embodied formula is – at least asymptotically – performative: it begins to produce something, it is the gateway to transforming a virtuality into a reality and it possibilizes, or crealectizes, even if there is no deterministic link between the feeling or thought of possibility and the actualization or realization of that impression, although a causal explanation can in some cases be given. The felt experience of possibility creates a bridge between, on the one hand, the *apossible* of apathy (from the alpha-privative prefix) or the *hypossible* of indecision (from the Greek prefix *hypo*, meaning under or not yet), and on the other hand, actualization and realization.

If we accept that the source of reality is driven by an infra-realist flux of infinite possibility, if the core of Being/Becoming is the meta-code 'it's possible', once embodied this could be (and was, for example by Lacan) described as a cosmological dynamic of desire: Spinoza called this cosmic desire the conatus (Koistinen, 2014). The idea is also familiar in Daoism as natural intelligence: 'This desire is the source from which all things in the world arise and move toward fulfilment. [. . .] Desire, then, is what incites, animates, and furnishes the content of knowing' (Virág, 2017: 77). Our desire or lust for life can indeed feel cosmic or interstellar, although things may be possible that we do not desire. We tend to sexualize desire – but sexuality probably is but a convincing ruse of evolution in the sense that sexuality might have latched onto a prior available cosmic desire: by exaptation, part of this desiring energy, previously not sexual in the mundane sense, was diverted to favour reproduction. Animals, insects and plants are likely to have a relationship to cosmic desire which is our sense of the possible (see Chapter 17 in this volume). Thus, the crealectic moment of our human intelligence might respect other beings more than analytic or dialectic intelligences do.

The ultimate desire of crealectic embodiment could be said to be – following Lacan and Heidegger – 'without object' (de Miranda, 2009). Crealectic consciousness would be attuned to the Creal and to pure desire, pure possibility, which in the end would aim at itself rather than this or that. To desire the possible is different from desiring many possibilities (but experience shows that this is hard to understand for analytic or dialectic forms of intelligence). Remembering the Latin etymology of desire (longing for a lost star), I prefer to surmise with Plato and Plotinus that cosmic desire does have an aim that is contra-distinctively induced by the multiplicity and infinite diversity of the Creal: pure unity, or 'the One' (Wiitala, 2013: 649). We do not have the space here to enter in the details of the long philosophical relationship between the One and the Multiple, and how they might imply each other. Suffice it to say that if multiplicity and unity are the two logical sides of the same cosmological core, then the union with the One is that which all things desire, which is why Plato, Plotinus and Aristotle called this prime mover the Good. Crealectics equates the Good with the Possible, thus uniting the One and the Multiple. An absolute unifying principle is the ultimate object of desire and the supreme Good from the perspective of the disparate. And from the perspective of unity, the ultimate Other is manifested by diversity and multiplicity. In his *Birth of Tragedy*, Nietzsche translated this creative dialectic into the iconic unbalanced duality of 'Dionysus', the attraction to multiplicity, and 'Apollo', the attraction to unity (Clewis, 2019: 223).

Influenced by Kant, the Romantic poet Wordsworth defined the play between 'multitude' and 'intense unity' as the essence of the 'sublime' (Clewis, 2019: 177). Crealectic intelligence transcends the borders of the actual and of the Real and therefore is related to the experience of sublimity. Artists have known or felt for long enough that 'creativity as ultimate principle' (Whitehead, 1929: 31) is a relation to the intuitions of alterity and the sublime, 'the incommensurability of reality to concept' (Lyotard, 1984: 79). The aesthetic experience of the sublime, for example in contemplating nature or in confronting a new culture or new love, manifests itself as surreal or hyper-real awe, beyond the analytic routines: 'Sublimity lifts the Absolute above every immediate existent and therefore brings about the liberation which, though abstract at first, is at least the foundation of the spirit' (Hegel, 1835: 362).

Sublime feeling sensitizes us to an 'outside and an inside' in thought, to a creative 'hyper-dialectic' between imagination, unifying reason, flesh, plurality and ambiguity (Merleau-Ponty, 1968: 94). A healthy human life and healthy thought needs to host regular moments of felt sublimity, a necessary condition to reconnect with the possibility of possibility, of regeneration or novelty. The intuition of creal sublimity becomes 'the transport that leads all thought (critical thought included) to its limits' (Lyotard, 1994: x). This paradoxical capacity to pursue belief or knowledge about something we typically ignore, but feel or desire to be real, can be productive of new knowledge, new myths and new forms of dealing with existence: it suggests the effectual agency of what Einstein called 'creative imagination' (Holton, 1978: 96).

The experience of awe, wonder, admiration or imaginative questioning, which Aristotle and Descartes considered to be the creative source of philosophy, is often seen as superfluous in sociotechnical protocols that are attached to an automated exhaustion or exploitation of the Real. Mundane practices of engineering or mathematical ordering tend to keep the imaginative or desiring subject out of their equations in order to achieve an operational description and management of a system or problem. The admirer, the contemplator, the observer, the practitioner, the interpreter, the dweller and the co-creator are not accounting categories and can hardly be taken into account in predictive analytics.

We can exemplify in many ways the dramas that hypertrophied forms of analytic intelligence can generate: for instance, speaking of getting lost in forests, in the early 2000s, the French government introduced a computerized form of New Public Management and analytic accounting into the organization of their forests, via the Office National des Forêts. The results were negative: in 2019, a report from the Commission des Affaires Économiques of the French Parliament mentions a deep crisis in which no less than forty-eight forester employees committed suicide, out of a feeling of being deskilled, distrusted and treated like machines, while the diversity of the trees became endangered (Assemblée Nationale, 2019).

Such examples do not mean that computer intelligence will necessarily be the enemy of humanity, but that intelligent-system designers need to carefully consider the human need for a healthy cycle of analytic-dialectic-crealectic understanding.

Conclusion: From analytics to crealectics

Human affairs should learn from philosophical care and its practice of embodied knowledge (Foucault, 2005). As the embodied reminiscence of the sublime possibility of possibility, crealectics may also function as a politico-ethical global social contract (de Miranda, 2017): if we comprehend that the possibility of possibility should not be addressed only with computerized solutions, we might avoid becoming a self-domesticated (Arendt, 1958) anthrobotic species. In remaining open to the 'creative generosity' of life (Canguilhem, 1991: 188), the democratization of the crealectic aspect of intelligence may allow for a new form of non-anthropocentric global consciousness. Thankfully, we cannot delegate crealectic thinking to a machine, since AI is devoid of desire, of a sense of the possible and sublimity.

The 'man-computer symbiosis' (Licklider, 1960) is not the inevitable horizon of humanity's destiny but a sub-part of a higher form of interaction between humans and the Creal. We are not living in an artificial simulation in which the universe reads its own program as it unfolds analytically, such as in the Universal Simulation hypothesis (Bostrom, 2003). Because of the feeling of cosmic desire in our bodies and the concept of possibility in our minds, which cannot be reduced to discrete bits of information, analytics is insufficient to understand our world and induce the right decisions. The world can to a certain extent be divided into concrete analytic parts for the sake of manipulation and possession; it can partly be divided into dialectic tensions of agonistic unfolding to mediate power struggles, yet neither of these two forms of understanding exhaust the Real, because the Real as a mere set of things (*res* in Latin, and *res extensa* for Descartes) does not exhaust all there is or can be.

Our existences are certainly embedded in mega-machinic sociotechnical digital systems, so complex that they might even suggest a 'technological sublime' (Jameson, 1984: 79): systems of hyper-surveillance and control under the guise of dreamlike divertissement, education and emotional relationships via handheld devices, all the mysterious aspects of everyday life, are now touched by AI. Human nature may be partly defined as 'anthrobotic', a combination of flesh and protocols. Still, we are not merely one polarity of a machine-human dialectic, because we remain emotionally, intuitively and intellectually touched by the Creal.

Philosophy is not only about a form of logic but also about the possibility of various 'forms of life' (Wittgenstein, 1958: 11). More than an analyst or a dialectician, the crealectician is an open-hearted and open-minded creative thinker who cares to take holistic decisions towards a philosophically healthy way of life, in which all beings may feel that the possible is good.

References:

Alexander of Aphrodisias (c.200 CE /1991), *On Aristotle's Prior Analytics*, trans. J. Barnes. London: Duckworth.

Arendt, Hannah (1958), *The Human Condition*. Chicago: University of Chicago Press.

Arnauld, Antoine and Pierre Nicole (1996), *Logic or the Art of Thinking*, trans. J. V. Buroker. Cambridge: Cambridge University Press.

Assemblée Nationale Française (2019), Compte-rendu 28 [Account of debate 28], Commission des Affaires Économiques, 11 Décembre 2019.

Bergson, Henri (1922), *Creative Evolution*, trans. A. Mitchell. London: MacMillan.

Berthoz, Alain (2012), *Simplexity: Simplifying Principles for a Complex World*. New Haven: Yale University Press.

Bloch, Ernst (1983), 'The Dialectical Method', trans. J. Lamb. *Man and World*, 16 (4): 281–313.

Bostrom, Nick (2003), 'Are We Living in a Computer Simulation?' *Philosophical Quarterly*, 53 (211): 243–55.

Canguilhem, George (1991), *The Normal and the Pathological*, trans. C. R. Fawcett. New York: Zone Books.

Chandler, Daniel and Rod Munday (2016), *Dictionary of Social Media*, 3rd edn. Oxford: Oxford University Press.

Chomsky, Noam (1968), *Language and Mind*. New York: Harcourt Brace Jovanovich.

Clewis, Robert (2019), *The Sublime Reader*. London: Bloomsbury.

Craig, R. P. (1984), 'Developing a Philosophy of Reading: Piaget and Chomsky'. *Reading Horizons*, 25 (1): 38–42.

Deleuze, Gilles and Félix Guattari (1994), *What Is Philosophy?* trans. H. Tomlinson and G. Burchell. New York: Columbia University Press.

Elbow, Peter (1993), 'The Uses of Binary Thinking'. *Journal of Advanced Composition*, 13 (1): 51–78.

Foucault, Michel (2005), *The Hermeneutics of the Subject*, trans. G. Burchell. New York: Palgrave Macmillan.

Geraci, Robert (2008), 'Apocalyptic AI: Religion and the Promise of Artificial Intelligence'. *Journal of the American Academy of Religion*, 76 (1): 138–66.

Hegel (1806/1984), 'Letter to Friedrich Niethammer, 13 October 1806'. In C. Butler and C. Seiler (trans.), *The Letters*, 114–15. Bloomington: Indiana University Press.

Hegel (1817/1991), *The Encyclopaedia of Logic*, trans. T. F. Geraets, W. A. Suchting and H. S. Harris. Indianapolis: Hackett.

Hegel (1835/1975), *Aesthetics: Lectures on Fine Art*, vol. 1, trans. T. M. Knox. Oxford: Oxford University Press.

Holton, Gerald (1978), *The Scientific Imagination: Case Studies*. Cambridge: Cambridge University Press.

Jameson, Fredric (1984), 'Postmodernism, or the Cultural Logic of Late Capitalism'. *New Left Review*, 1 (146): 76–80.

Jousse, Marcel (2016), *In Search of Coherence*, trans. E. Sienaert. Eugene: Pickwick Publications.

Kaan, Edith (1999), 'Syntax and Semantics?' *Trends in Cognitive Sciences*, 3 (9): 322.

Koistinen, Olli (2014), 'Desire and Good in Spinoza'. In M. J. Kisner and A. Joupa (eds), *Essays on Spinoza's Ethical Theory*, 221–31. Oxford: Oxford University Press.

Laplace, Pierre-Simon (1814/1902), *A Philosophical Essay on Probabilities*, trans. F. W. Truscott and F. L. Emory. New York: Wiley and Sons.

Licklider (1960), 'Man-Computer Symbiosis'. *IRE Transactions on Human Factors in Electronics*, HFE-1 (1): 4–11.

Lyotard, Jean-François (1984), *The Postmodern Condition: A Report on Knowledge*, trans. G. Bennington and B. Massumi. Minneapolis: University of Minnesota Press.

Lyotard, Jean-François (1994), *Lessons on the Analytic of the Sublime*, trans. E. Rottenberg. Stanford: Stanford University Press.

McMahon, Darrin (2013), *Divine Fury: A History of Genius*. New York: Basic Books.

Menabrea, Luigi-Federico (1961), 'Sketch of the Analytical Engine Invented by Charles Babbage'. In P. Morrison and E. Morrison (eds), *Charles Babbage and His Calculating Engines*, selected writings by Charles Babbage and others, 225–97. New York: Dover.

Merleau-Ponty, Maurice (1968), *The Visible and the Invisible*, trans. A. Lingis. Evanston: Northwestern University Press.

de Miranda, Luis (2008), *Paridaiza*. Paris: Plon. Published in English by Snuggly Books, 2020.

de Miranda, Luis (2009), *Peut-on jouir du capitalisme? Lacan avec Heidegger et Marx.* Paris: Max Milo.

de Miranda, Luis (2017), 'On the Concept of Creal: The Politico-Ethical Horizon of a Creative Absolute'. In Paulo de Assis and Paolo Giudici (eds), *The Dark Precursor: Deleuze and Artistic Research*, 510–16. Louvain: Leuven University Press.

de Miranda, Luis (2019), *Being and Neonness*. Cambridge, MA: MIT Press.

de Miranda, Luis (2020), *Ensemblance: The Transnational Genealogy of Esprit de corps*. Edinburgh: Edinburgh University Press.

de Miranda, Luis and Rovatsos Ramamoorthy (2016), 'We, Anthrobot: Learning from Human Forms of Interaction and Esprit de corps to Develop more Diverse Social Robotics'. In J. Seibt, M. Nørsko and S. Schack Andersen (eds), *What Social Robots Can and Should Do*, 48–56. Amsterdam: IOS Press.

Murphy, Nancy and William Stoeger (2007), *Evolution and Emergence: Systems, Organisms, Persons*. Oxford: Oxford University Press.

Piaget, Jean (1952), *The Origins of Intelligence in Children*. New York: W. W. Norton.

Quine, Willard V. O. and Joe Ullian (1978), *The Web of Belief*. New York: McGraw-Hill Education.

Russell, Stuart (2019), *Human Compatible: Artificial Intelligence and the Problem of Control*. New York: Viking.

Ryle, Gilbert (2009), *The Concept of Mind*. London and New York: Routledge.

Searle, John (1980), 'Minds, Brains and Programs'. *Behavioral and Brain Sciences*, 3 (3): 417–57.

Searle, John (2010), 'Why Dualism (and materialism) Fail to Account for Consciousness'. In R. E. Lee (ed.), *Questioning Nineteenth Century Assumptions about Knowledge*, 5–48. New York: Suny Press.

Sinclair, Mark (2017), *The Actual and the Possible: Modality and Metaphysics in Modern Philosophy*. Oxford: Oxford University Press.

Slife, Brent (1994), 'The Possibility of Possibility'. *Journal of Theoretical and Philosophical Psychology*, 14 (1): 96–101.

Thompson, H. E. (1997), 'The Fallacy of Misplaced Concreteness: Its Importance for Critical and Creative Inquiry'. *Interchange*, 28 (2 & 3): 219–30.

Turing, Alan (1950), 'Computing Machinery and Intelligence'. *Mind*, 59: 433–60.

Virág, Curie (2017), *The Emotions in Early Chinese Philosophy*. Oxford: Oxford University Press.

Whitehead, Alfred North (1926), *Science and the Modern World*. Cambridge: Cambridge University Press.

Whitehead, Alfred North (1929), *Process and Reality*. New York: MacMillan.

Wiitala, Michael O. (2013), 'Desire and the Good in Plotinus'. *British Journal for the History of Philosophy*, 21 (4): 649–66.

Wittgenstein, Ludwig (1958), *Philosophical Investigations*, trans. G. E. M. Anscombe. Oxford: Blackwell.

Part III

The World

12

Professionalization and philosophical ill-health

Maladies and counsels

Matthew Sharpe and Eli Kramer

In several pieces, including his 'Five Principles of Philosophical Health for Critical Times: From Hadot to Crealectics', Luis de Miranda has articulated five different dimensions to philosophical health. These are 'mental heroism, deep orientation, critical creativity, deep listening and the "Creal" (the creative Real as ultimate possibility)' (de Miranda, 2021: 70). Our aim in this chapter will be to show how certain features of the current professional environment for academics in general, but especially academic philosophizing, curtail the five principles of philosophical health outlined in de Miranda. They create a culture of philosophical 'ill-health'. This culture of ill-health in turn has five counterpart 'maladies', which roughly correspond to de Miranda's principles: mental cowardice, shallowness, the cult of the commentator, dismissive listening and fatalistic dogmatism. Unifying these five maladies, we contend, is an uncritical, anti-Socratic failure to consider the social and institutional preconditions which make possible today's practices of academic philosophizing.

The opening section of the chapter presents orienting critical reflections on the tensions between the dynamics of professionalization, as a sociological reality involving a number of recognized features: for example, the establishment of a formally credentialized hierarchy that divides experts in domains of knowledge from 'mere' citizens, the closure of entry to all but those who undertake specific forms of credentialization, and the possession and disposal of institutional power. While these features are constant across professions, we contend that they necessarily sit uneasily with the critical, self-reflective exercise inaugurated by Socrates: which should, as such, constantly remain aware of, and potentially critical towards, unquestioned or non-philosophical forms of symbolic and political authority.

This basic tension leads to what we will call a culture of philosophical 'ill-heath', which atrophies the ability of professional philosophers to develop an examined and enriched life. Far from questioning the importance of schools for higher learning as such, we suggest that the global neoliberal reforms of the universities since the 1980s, which institutionalize individualized performance benchmarking and competition (over against older post-Humboldtian values of collegiality) have made this ill health far worse in the last decades than previously. This pathological way of living runs counter to the Socratic paradigm, involving what could be termed an 'atopic' health. This is a way of philosophical living that would resist predominant patterns in the cultural life of the times, associated with the pursuit of wealth, fame, rank and power, as against the care of the soul (Plato, *Apology*: 29d-30c).

We then outline five maladies we think emerge from the dynamics of professionalism under neoliberal conditions, unless these dynamics are not themselves philosophically considered and problematized, and alternatives to them developed, in ways we are doing in this collection. However, it is important that we stress from the start that, while our experiences over three decades do lead us to charge that the corporatized academy at large, and professional philosophy in particular, is today not very hospitable to philosophical health, we think there is a possibility for enclaves of reform, and for individuals who can lead such reforms to create richer and healthier kinds of philosophizing, and philosophical scholars. These enclaves can also be essential sites for the training and certification of therapeutic philosophical work in non-academic cultural life. Moving beyond critique alone (which can itself engender unhealthy cynicism), this chapter therefore concludes by both acknowledging the intransigency of the academy (and academics) and advocating for ways to improve the enclaves of it that can foster philosophical health.

In our closing section, we propose one small prescription in a much-needed broader ameliorative treatment regime. Our principal suggestion is that academic institutes, faculties, departments and programmes of philosophy interested in philosophical health, and especially offering career routes in philosophical counselling/coaching, ought to follow the practices of professional counsellors and psychologists, who are required in their professional statutes in many jurisdictions to examine their own values and prejudices in relationship with a supervisor. Just so, we propose that enclaves and leaders interested in promoting philosophical health need to consider institutionalizing courses that reflect on the potential epistemic and ethical vices promoted by today's neoliberalized academies, and foster practices of craft mentorship that are built on identifying threats to philosophical and wider health, and preventing these unexamined pressures from deleteriously reshaping what we do. To do so would require new training, and a shift in professional culture, both for mentors and mentees.

'Professional (and) philosopher': A tension in the qualification

But how did we get here? In *The Culture of Professionalism: The Middle Class and the Development of Higher Education in America*, Burton J. Bledstein noted the all-too-typical experience philosophy graduate students and young scholars (and those in other fields) had in the emerging US research university system:

> At Harvard in the 1880s, nervous breakdowns occurred frequently. Promising young men wore themselves down through worry and overwork as they exhausted themselves in the classroom, anxiously curried the favor of their mentors and patrons, neglected their health, postponed marriages, moonlighted and borrowed

money to make ends meet. The victims of such a system, their emotions paralyzed, proceed cautiously and conservatively in all their movements. In 1888, for example, Josiah Royce [one of the leading figures in Classical American Philosophy] discovered himself growing dull and indecisive, and he too now 'joined the too great army of scholarly blunderers who break down when they ought to be at their best.' (Bledstein, 1976: 103)

Over 130 years later, it is not clear if much has changed. These are the sorts of stories one hears anecdotally throughout the halls of the academy. Among academics a general sense of unhappiness, poor work/life balance, coercion and bullying by superiors, and a concoction of other issues seem endemic. From a philosophy as a way of life (PWL) perspective, this overall lack of well-being is particularly ironic in philosophy, which once focused primarily on wise, fruitful, good and happy (in the broad sense of *eudaimonia*) living. Instead, today, as Pierre Hadot noted, professional philosophy is 'made up of professors who train professors, or professionals training professionals' (Hadot, 1995: 270), and a precariat of fixed-term, contracted lecturers who often remain in the precariat for decades, if they ever escape such a condition. Thus, while we suspect these maladies are endemic to the academy, we focus on professional philosophy, a discipline that is supposed to have mastered self-criticism and which is supposed to be able to reflectively criticize other disciplines. We offer a fairly detailed and critical assessment of our experience in the United States, Australia and parts of the European, higher education context. We do so in hopes of fully recognizing the ill-health in the discipline in these powerful contexts and what small enclaves of academic philosophy might do to support philosophical health for both broader culture and higher education.

Many of our exemplars in contemporary philosophy, like Martin Heidegger, or at least leading figures, like Brian Lieter, have notorious histories of poor treatment of colleagues, reactionary politics, coercion of students and laying thick verbal abuse upon perceived enemies. In the last two decades, accounts of racism and sexual harassment have become increasingly visible, but such behaviour seems rooted in far older patterns (Yancy, 2008; Kidd, 2017). It is a striking but sad fact that literature on bullying hailing from different nations reports that instances of bullying and 'mobbing' (managerially sanctioned ostracism of 'difficult' or independent-minded, nonconformist employees) are highest in the health and education sectors, including our universities (Leymann, 1990; 2002; Westhues, 1998). These experiences we suspect are 'canaries in the coal mine' unfortunately, often-unheeded warnings of deeper problems, for what has been happening behind closed doors in the academy.

While this happens, philosophical counselling and other forms of PWL practice, like the Modern Stoicism movement, have dramatically grown, as the broader public, and some academics and psychiatrists, see the deep potential for different forms of philosophy to help us all 'to live, to live well, to live better' (Whitehead, 1958: 8). Such a situation raises the question of whether the professional philosophers advocating such work are themselves living philosophical healthy lives. Do those of us committed to the examined life in some form practice what we preach, or rather are we merely occupying what the ancients would have thought of as a sophistic stance? It is our experience that even within fields that study PWL traditions which have strong commitments to holistic philosophical health, it is all too easy to find hypocrites, more interested in the discourse on their professed values than any committed practice to enact them. While all of us have our hypocritical moments, across professional philosophy we find many all too dazzled by their own webs of thought without questioning whether they catch anything of worth within them. As Pierre Hadot writes of the ancients:

> All schools denounced the risk taken by philosophers who imagine that their philosophical discourse can be sufficient to itself without being in accord with the philosophical life. They constantly attacked those who, to use the terms of the Platonist Polemo, seek to be admired for their skill at syllogistic arguing but contradict themselves in the conduct of their lives. In the words of an Epicurean saying, they develop empty discourses. According to the Stoic Epictetus, they talk about the art of living like human beings, instead of living like human beings themselves. And as Seneca put it, they turn love of wisdom (*philosophia*) into love of words (*philologia*). Traditionally, people who developed an apparently philosophical discourse without trying to live their lives in accordance with their discourse, and without their discourse emanating from their life experience, were called 'Sophists'. (Hadot, 2000: 174)

Or, as the Latin saying goes *Barba non facit philosophum* (the beard does not make the philosopher). The question today is to what extent the organizational logics within universities *faciunt philosophum*, independently of whether the philosopher professes themselves analytic, continental or belonging to any other recognized intradisciplinary subgroup.

Since the late nineteenth century, philosophy as an academic discipline has been subject to sociological forces of professionalization, pushing it towards what Robert Frodeman and Adam Briggle in *Socrates Tenured* (2016) call 'disciplinary capture'. Historically, they place this movement as a defensive response to a series of converging factors. There was first the increasing independence of scientific and social scientific disciplines, like psychology, from their home discipline of philosophy, with a correlative loss of scope for purely 'philosophical' consideration. Second was the advent of Darwinism, and its challenge to teleological accounts of phenomena, reaching up to forms of classical philosophy and theological thinking. In response to these challenges to its older forms and leading place within the humanities, academic philosophers faced a series of choices. They could present themselves as synthesizers of (or translators between) the knowledge produced in the different specializations, or they could 'go formalist', by 'providing the logical undergirding for research and education', becoming 'disciplinary specialists who focused on recondite philosophical problems in ethics, epistemology, aesthetics and the like' (Frodeman and Briggle, 2016: 8). We may add, in a different more continental mode of specialization, they could claim epistemic access to domains of inquiry 'prior' to, or 'transcendental', with regard to 'merely ontic' or 'positive' sciences.

Frodeman and Briggle's account fits well with other research on the disciplinary capture of philosophy, struggling to justify itself as having a positive project of knowledge that could be treated as a profession (Kramer, 2021: 100–15), and as choosing narrow technical problems for political reasons, as well as to follow funding opportunities in the Cold War era (Menand, 2010: 59–92; McCumber 2001). This professionalization process was exacerbated in the late nineteenth and twentieth centuries when the promise of the universality of philosophical reason to establish the epistemic or ontological foundations for the sciences was ripped from under us by advances in non-Euclidian geometry. Felix Klein and others illuminated that entire geometries could be coherent and have veracity, and yet have a logic entirely foreign to our experience; Euclid's geometry could no long provide us with the certainty and necessity we so desperately craved about what had to be the case (Cassirer, 1950: 1–117). Coupled with growing doubts about the authority of philosophy after the Einstein-Bergson debates (Canales, 2015), it became increasingly clear that the whole edifice of philosophy as a profession was precarious. As we will see this situation has affected the philosophical health of those that participated in it since that time.

With only a few small dissenters, Frodeman and Briggle contend that professional philosophers by the start of the twentieth century chose, decisively, the path of specialization:

> or more precisely, given their limited series of options, philosophers chose to discipline themselves. Philosophers were placed in departments. They inhabited libraries and classrooms. Their writings were restricted to professional diction and concern. And they wrote for and were judged by their disciplinary peers. (Frodeman and Briggle, 2016: 14)

The result was what Frodeman and Briggle called 'disciplinary capture'. What they intend by this designation is the increasing inward focus on self-referencing knowledge production, with little thought about its relation to effective dissemination and usage outside the discipline (for more, see Frodeman and Briggle, 2016: 55–76). As historian of ideas Steven Shapin has diagnosed it in professional philosophy:

> Just so there is no mistaking my point, I offer two specific examples […] much of philosophy and much of sociology. These practices have bounded themselves so effectively, and enforced disciplinary conventions so forcefully, that they have lost a substantial sense of aboutness. 'Doing philosophy,' as it is currently practiced, is often more about dexterity in manipulating the disciplinary literature than it is about knowledge, mind, or morals. . . . You can tell a self-referential discipline by the fact that no one reads its products who doesn't have to. Disciplinary members have to, or at least they acknowledge a moral responsibility to do so. Beyond those boundaries readership drops off like a cliff face. Professional success is indexed by insularity. And a mark of a hyper-professional discipline-in-trouble is that graduate students read the stuff that their senior professors only pretend to have read. Graduate students have to; senior professors have to say they have . . . self-referentiality is one way in which hyper-professional practices produce a crisis of readership, but by no means the only way. (Shapin, 2005: 239)

Of course, if one takes a minimally Socratic view of philosophy, as concerned with the best way of life, or an Aristotelian view, that it is concerned with disclosing the first principles of all the sciences, such a self-referential, hyper-specialized insularity can appear painfully discordant. It is ironic, but true, that many professionalized philosophers would still consider their work as philosophical in one of these more traditional, Socratic or Aristotelian, senses. This, even as their work is published in a narrow range of styles and venues, credentialized as 'top journals', based on bibliometrics which respond to in-group peer citation, making professional publication a kind of popularity machine (Sharpe and Turner, 2018).

What seems decisive for us, and something of an enormous elephant in the room, is the tendential conflict created by the logics of professionalization and disciplinary capture, with philosophy as a critical and reflective discipline. We need be clear, for the elephant seems necessarily to be cloaked by our professional self-awareness: the first rule of a profession, to echo *Fight Club*, is not to call into question the socio-vocational conditions of that profession. Whether we like the recollection or not, philosophy academics are subject to the same forms of symbolic competition for credentialization characteristic of other modern professions and other intellectual disciplines within the university. Again, we should pause to consider what this means for a discipline that is supposed to have meta-critical insight.

Philosophy as a separate discipline now must compete for students and preside over erudite object domains, enucleated as it is by surrounding university disciplines like psychology, sociology, political science, jurisprudence, literature and history. The philosophy discipline is also institutionalized, like all forms of professions, in forms of status hierarchies. There are senior scholars of professors on top, down to short-term non-tenure/habilitation track instructors, within schools. In the research domain, there are celebrated 'master thinkers' within analytic and continental circles around whose work subcultures and even dedicated journals have emerged. These figures are at the top of a ladder whose steps reach down, again, to emerging scholars trying to get a foot in the publishing door, and a foot *up* in the shrinking job market.

Access to positions and elevation within the ranks in these hierarchical vocational ladders is based on the accumulation of symbolic capital. The acquisition of this capital depends first on examinations: forms of essay writing in undergraduate degrees, thesis writing and defences in graduate programmes. These forms of examination, which distinguish and rank students, also ensure forms of conformity at the level of how students write, how they argue, the authorities they refer to and conventions surrounding citation of sources. To get a position, one needs to learn what to read, how to speak, how to write and who and how to defer to figures higher in the structural hierarchy. Of course, individuals can do this in different ways, with different levels of ethical probity and independence of mind, as well as producing work of differing levels of quality, evincing different epistemic virtues.

But like all other disciplines, philosophy departments within universities have been subject to the ongoing waves of neoliberal reforms. These have introduced corporatized or 'new public management' into universities, stymying collegial governance, centralizing decision-making in the hands of line managers, individualizing forms of working (notably research) and 'performance management', quantifying each of their 'outputs' (including student satisfaction) and forcing academics into ever-more-fierce competition with each other for increasingly scarce status and financial goods. As Jeff

Schmidt comments in *The Disciplined Mind*, the operative discourse surrounding this, imported from the commercial sectors, is that of 'opportunity' or 'incentivization', over against older values of collegial decision-making and intragroup solidarity. When we observe this, we see the falsity, about forty years too late, of the perpetual conservative anxiety about 'tenured radicals'. In disciplines like philosophy, the 'radicality' has become individualized and filtered via the vocational competition system into nearly compulsory adherence to loosely 'postmodern' values of difference, singularity and becoming which are increasingly also sponsored by corporate management. These values much more closely bespeak the lived realities of professionals competing for scarce status goods (positions, grant moneys, promotions, managerial capacities). Much of postmodern ontology can be read ideological-critically as projective generalizations of these intra-class realities. Foucault, Deleuze and Nietzsche are all too often the philosophers of the new professional-managerial classes; not Marx, Wollstonecraft or T. H. Green. In fact, as Schmidt notes, while professionals report very liberal social views on issues distant from their lifeworld, their sense of belonging to an increasingly threatened elite, separated from the many by their expert knowledges (including of difference and creativity), makes them a highly 'timid', conservative cohort when it comes to issues of concrete social organization, or the governance of the workplace (Schmidt, 2000: 23).

The pressures placed on academic philosophy by the neoliberal incorporation of individualized competition into every knowledge production have had profound effects. These we argue have not broken open but rather further strengthened the forces enclosing professional philosophy as an increasingly hyperspecialized pursuit. Professional philosophers would no doubt bridle at Schmidt's suggestion that they are 'disciplined minds' (Schmidt's phrase), not 'free spirits', and the authors of this article too are such philosophers. But professionalization in any field, however, aims precisely at creating an ideologically conformist, technically competent cohort capable of reproducing the profession, and fulfilling the systems-imperatives transmitted by managers, often in languages closed to outsiders. The capacity to fill a 'blank page' and make 'professional' decisions, within the scope of established vocational norms, is what is prized here. This stands in clear tension with the critical creativity, whether Socratic or associated with other thinkers, which has always been recognized as definitive of philosophy in the West. For any such practice of philosophy is precisely requiring the liberty to call into question established practices and norms, in order to imagine new ways of thinking and being. 'The qualification system maps out a domain of allowed activity that ultimately becomes the playpen of the nonradical credentialed expert and the cage of the individual working for progress in the social structure' (Schmidt, 2000: 214). One sees here another feature of professional academic work, wherein there is an overwhelming primacy of commentary and commentary upon commentary on established positions and authorities:

> Just as professionals engage in playpen creativity, innovating within the safe confines of an assigned ideology, so too they engage in playpen critical thinking. Their work involves judging whether or not the ideas of others are in line with the favoured outlook, but does not involve developing their own, independent point

of view. Hence professionals tend to be what might be called 'book review' critical, which is intellectually and politically safe because it doesn't involve developing or taking a stand for an independent outlook. Professionals generally avoid the risk inherent in real critical thinking and cannot properly be called critical thinkers. (Schmidt, 2000: 56)

It is this culture, as we shall see, which stifles what de Miranda has called philosophical health and leads to 'ill-health' in professional philosophy, characterized by ongoing tensions between core values of philosophical inquiry, and the conditions of their institutionalization, and issuing in what, in dialogue with de Miranda's work, we identify as five 'maladies' that dominate such philosophical ill-health: mental cowardice, shallowness, the cult of the commentator, dismissive listening and fatalistic dogmatism.

The five maladies of philosophical ill-health in professional philosophy

De Miranda has defined philosophical health 'as not only about logico-argumentative coherence, but more fundamentally a process of harmonious, creative, and sustainably flourishing coherence between a person's ways of thinking and their active engagement with the Real' (de Miranda, 2021: 71). As he has noted in that very same article, this is a philosophy as a way of life oriented approach to philosophy as providing an ability to critically attend to our present perception and transform our situation, collective and individual, for the better (Hadot, 1995; 2021). We see philosophical ill-health as implicating ways of living that atrophy our ability to attend to the transformative potential within reality (our situation) for the better. For one reason or another philosophical ill-heath limits our ability to call into question our lived values and ways of being, even as we in academic philosophy develop often-highly recondite, highly specialized intellectual productions. Instead, we become 'stuck in a rut', trapped by a self-created fatalism due to psychological and cultural patterns that weaken us as persons.

Mental cowardice

To begin our diagnostics of philosophical ill-health, we start with mental cowardice. The kind of mental or Socratic 'heroism' de Miranda identifies 'is not only about being able to resist resiliently or inflexibly to toxic influences'. It is 'also about intersubjective attention and openness' (de Miranda, 2021: 74). These qualities are threatened by the career pressures which especially young scholars face, pushing them not to 'rock the boat', challenge established perspectives or devote their energies to concerns shaped by extra-academic debates. As Sharpe and Turner have contended (Sharpe and Turner, 2018), these pressures, now communicated in the global reign of bibliometrics in shaping understandings of what 'serious' research work is, shape the very subjectivity of professional philosophers. One function of these metrics, like the Scimago journal rankings, or H- and i-10 indexes, is to funnel scholars into prioritizing projects that *maybe* will lead to career success and appease those with the authority to offer positions, because they have been highly cited within existing scholarship. This focus leads to a culture of self-inauthenticity and motivation to take options that will help one survive in the academy without 'causing trouble'. It incentivizes commentaries on established masters and authorities, rather than independent, critical challenges to such figures. It fosters a kind of mental cowardice for career survival, albeit one which is deeply and institutionally incentivized.

Shallowness

In turn such a way of living leads to a surface orientation, instead of the kind of 'deep orientation' de Miranda advocates for, which 'act[s] upon' the future 'with trust', as a 'form of present exercise of confidence rather than [one of] anxiety, fear, or passive hope' (de Miranda, 2021: 75). In the culture of philosophical ill-health in the academy, the future is often experienced in anticipatory anxiety about career success, fear of failure or inadequacy ('imposter syndrome') as a scholar in a field with obscure standards, and increasingly diminished hopes that one will indeed be able to secure a full and good life if one continues to teach and research philosophy. With such feelings of anxiety prevailing, any commitment to a larger normative vision, or a vision of a philosophical, more serene, enlarged way of being in the world, is constantly under pressure from the imperatives to publish or perish, and publish in the 'right' venues, on subjects and in ways those venues are likely to accept. Thus, a certain kind of surface orientation or shallowness in scholarship develops, and one's own values for a philosophically guided life become limited: one seeks instead to tailor a persona which will enable a person to survive in the academy.

Due to the legacy of disciplinary capture we saw earlier, one is pressured against writing meaningful work which speaks from and to the concerns of broader non-academic audiences (which may not attract intramural citations), and the conditions of working life reduce one's ability to live one's values.

The cult of the commentator

In the meantime, while 'critical creativity', risk-taking and boundary-breaking are admired in thinkers senior and established enough to be 'too big to fail' (e.g. Zizek or Deleuze), and constantly advertised as being nearly universal, the rest of professional philosophy is required to play the role of respondent technicians, developing their thought and treatises in admiring or acerbic, conformist literatures. Teaching is also supposed to explicate content in a similar matter, in ways that are either historical-hermeneutic (reconstructing authorities' claims) or problem-based (focusing on established subjects and problems and examining established positions on the same). What is lost is the 'cognitive critical creativity' needed to 'address and anticipate situations of crisis with an hyperstatic attitude, one that is not obsessed by a conservative and perhaps impossible return to a past equilibrium, but capable of creating new states of consciousness and existential haleness' (de Miranda, 2021: 78). Indeed, the culture of professionalism in philosophy is quite conservative: as we have noted, it is what Schmidt calls 'play pen creativity' within which already-sanctioned boundaries predominate. While any academic discipline of course should develop its projects, and its new cohorts, through inherited norms and by recourse to standard authorities, in academic philosophy the norms are not deep or creative but push for the prosaic and conformist standards of an all-too-insular discipline. Admiring a thinker's work, and drawing insights out of it, should not lead to forms of spiritual subordination in which criticizing that thinker is effectively impossible, even when (as in the case of Heidegger's *Black Notebooks*) large bodies of new textual evidence attesting to their wider positions become available, which upsets previously accepted *endoxa*. Philosophers should be friends of the truth, more than Plato, as Aristotle proverbially commented.

Dismissive listening

One of the more tragic maladies within professional philosophy is the attitude of dismissive listening found in everything from conference paper commentaries and blind peer reviewing to seminar-based teaching and doctoral student mentorship. Such a culture – one in which there is, with the advent of the internet, an unprecedented surplus of information crowding scholars' attention – leads to an all-too-often dismissive attitude among senior philosophy scholars towards ideas or thoughts that might perceive as threatening the edifice of scholarship they have built over their career. Or else, people enjoying higher status might dismiss the work of less credentialed scholars, not on the basis of their argumentation but of their place in the professional system. This malady gnaws at something all too precious in academic philosophy: most of us find it difficult to find a guide that hears us and supports us in expressing our own insight, giving us the courage and skills to bring our angle of vision into the world in our self-development, teaching, writing and public engagement. It sickens what many of us in fact went into philosophy for in the first place, for 'a dialogue with another person', for, 'philosophical listening', as 'a practice' of 'belonging to the tradition of care for truth as "emergence" and "co-naissance", a co-creative birth and burst of signification and meaning' (de Miranda, 2021: 79). As Plutarch comments in 'On Listening' (1927), as well as especially being aware of not listening through envy or impatience for the spotlight:

> if there be need of any other instruction in regard to listening to a lecture, it is that it is necessary . . . to cultivate independent thinking along with our learning, so that we may acquire a habit of mind that is not sophistic or bent on acquiring mere information, but one that is deeply ingrained and philosophic, as we may do if we believe that right listening is the beginning of right living.

Dogmatic fatalism

Finally, this culture often gives academic philosophers the most 'fatal' of maladies, almost literally: that is, dogmatic fatalism about being unable to change themselves and the world, so at most one can get by and try to get or keep a place at the professional table. One loses the central aim of philosophy as a way of life for self and community transformation:

> We get used to biological impulses, mimetic behavior, habits, rituals, ideologies, cultural traits, object-oriented norms, and we may stop paying attention to their strangeness, to their arbitrariness, to their capacity to be otherwise, and to our capacity for self-transmutation'. (de Miranda, 2021: 81)

We lose touch with what de Miranda calls the 'creal' (the creative real): 'that the ultimate Real is an infinite and multifarious creative process, here called "Creal" to insist on the fact that this real-Real is a creating influx, an onflow of disparate becoming, an ecstasy of externalizations rather than a substance' (de Miranda, 2021: 82). The creative-transformative aim of philosophy, above all in the classroom (or other learning environment) and through teaching which can change young (and old) minds and lives, is increasingly positioned as a poor second to the forms of research which build institutional status (high citation, high prestige) and bring in grant funds. We lose the desire or vision to transform self and society because our academic careers often reinforce a postured conformism to often quite insular, irrelevant scholarship (irrelevant, at least, to most of our contemporaries).

Concluding proposals: 'Philosophers, heal thy selves'?

To cure the conditions of the present professional academic illness will take, we believe, far more than any measures any individuals or even small groups may be able to accommodate. As one profession among others, but a profession tied to forms of inquiry which do not readily translate into commodifiable or patentable research, academic philosophy sits a long way downstream from larger, wider changes which would need to occur, to reconsider higher education more widely and challenge its present economistic and managerial revaluation and devaluation – as against forms of technical-managerial expertise. National governments, across countries, will need to reconsider what their role is and what role higher education might play in this role. At issue will be nothing less than a willingness *not* to unthinkingly accept the neoliberal mantras that the necessities of the economy can educate to virtue and civility, whereas deliberative government, activating democratic citizens and social movements, and drawing on independent, non-economistic or technocratic ways of thinking, can only hinder these necessities. One of the bitter ironies of the present moment is therefore that, the running down and corporatization of the universities have made such independent sources of necessary critical and creative rethinking harder to find than ever, and more marginal than ever, outside of their professional enclaves.

Ultimately, it seems to us that only widespread sociopolitical change could reshape our universities, and only concerted collegial solidarity, of the kind that the reforms of the last decades have increasingly undermined, could reshape our discipline as philosophers. Without wanting to give into dogmatic fatalism, at this time, the prospects of such collective action seem very distant or utopian. This, however, is not to say that enclaves within current education do not enact meaningful changes in the way philosophy is presently undertaken, as a way to combat the forms of epistemic vice and philosophical ill-health we have examined here: mental cowardice, shallowness, the cult of commentary, dismissive listening and dogmatic fatalism.

In fact, we have found such places and are seeking to build others through venues such as this collection. While higher education can be toxic, it still has an abundance of resources and ability to host meaningful programming in philosophical education, including, for example, programmes that support philosophical-health-based counselling and pastoral care. Institutions such as the University for Humanistic Studies (*Universiteit voor Humanistiek*) in Utrecht, The Netherlands, with its humanistic pastoral degree programming, model how one can have an impact on the broader culture (and the academy alongside it) by offering a rigorous academic education that moves beyond the stultified career trajectories we have mentioned. We hope to continue to support such work and to leverage the enclaves where we can find them for such change.

For those aspiring to further develop enclaves towards this end, we have a critical suggestion that can support philosophical health within their communities so they 'practice what they preach'. They could (especially disciplinary programmes) consciously commit to final courses/workshops (sometimes called capstone or finishing units), offered to students at the advanced levels, which are dedicated to considerations surrounding philosophical health, and the forms of epistemic vices (Sharpe, 2022) which our present hyper-individualized, -competitivized, -corporatized and -quantified disciplinary configuration directly gives rise to. We need to stop assuming that, since philosophy students and instructors have some forms of intelligence, they must be 'too smart' to need to call into question their own ways of speaking, thinking, teaching and communicating research. All of these are contingent practices which they are educated into, as professionals, and yet which too often, precisely because of this, are left invisible in the work that academic philosophers do. Socrates's *gnôthi seauton*, or 'know yourself', should be the guiding imperative here, and the old ancient insight that wider, more humane forms of intelligence and sociopolitical engagement are always predicated on such difficult self-knowledge.

On the other hand, with one look back to the ancient notion of spiritual direction by philosophers (Hadot, 2014), and one look sideways at a fellow profession – that of psychologists and counsellors – philosophers should consider instituting forms of mentorship or supervision. This would not be professional-managerial supervision, with its metrics and quantitative 'benchmarks', and increasingly ubiquitous managerial lingo. It would be, as with psychologists, ethical or therapeutic supervision. Psychologists have difficult patients and can readily become emotionally overburdened and worn down. They can let their own prejudices, or their own fatigue, affect their performance, losing sight of their orienting therapeutic goals as counsellors or therapists. For this reason, many psychological and counselling associations globally mandate that each counsellor has their own supervising counsellor, whom they can – in conditions of confidentiality – discuss the difficulties they may be facing and undergo therapeutic critique.

In the highly individualized conditions of academic work in philosophy, where – outside of teaching, which is increasingly devalued as an activity – research is often conducted alone, there seems to us a case to be made that those forms of philosophical or wider ill-health can flourish. Philosophers can be left questioning the value of their work, and the ways that they are being asked to work, and how they relate to the values (truth-seeking, curiosity, independent mindedness, a commitment to social change) which might have attracted them into the business. Philosophical ill-health, in all of the different forms it can take, could, however, be checked if philosophers were each expected to have a supervisor, with whom they could regularly discuss their work in conditions of confidentiality. This would be especially important with younger, newer colleagues in the profession but would extend to the highest levels. Supervisors in turn could be educated, through reading relevant literature on the forms of philosophical ill-health and 'vices of learning' (Kivisto, 2014) that tend to afflict career academics, so they would be able to attentively respond to different situations, symptoms and concerns philosophers might raise with them: in other cases, philosophical counsellors could be called upon to play this role. Such supervisorial relationships might foster greater communication and mutual understanding between researchers in different philosophical areas. It would leave philosophers less prey to feeling like they are all alone, pursuing a career as an isolated one in a kind of 'genius competition', rather the member of a community and communities of inquiry and genuine dialogue. New programmes and trainings would need to be created for this role, but we think many in the enclaves committed to philosophical health will be eager for such opportunities and support.

We also think such attentive dialogical care might serve the broader aims of philosophical health. Deep relationships, built on authentic and holistic engagement, for those seeking to live PWL values in the academy, can resist the toxic and bibliometrified culture of professional philosophy. They also can be a part of the broader movement of philosophical health, to 'counterbalance the totalitarian rise of artificial, arithmetic, and deterministic intelligence'. Moreover, Socratically aware philosophers, at least in some departments and in some places, can become critical champions, nurturing (in de Miranda's formulation) a global 'culture of natural and creation-affirming intelligence, within the open limits of deep listening and respectful dialogue. A crealectic global social contract should enhance a constantly renewed opening to the concept of creation as felt possibility of possibility' (de Miranda, 2021: 86). In short, we think that even a few more academic enclaves that support philosophically healthy philosophers engaged in teaching and public life aimed at philosophical health as well can be vital to helping foster the cultural renewal needed at such a critical time in global history.

References

Bledstein, Burton J. (1976), *The Culture of Professionalism: The Middle Class and the Development of Higher Education in America*. New York: Norton.

Canales, Jimena (2015), *The Physicist and the Philosopher: Einstein, Bergson and the Debate That Changed Our Understanding of Time*. Princeton and Oxford: Princeton University Press.

Cassirer, Ernst (1950), *The Problem of Knowledge: Philosophy, Science, and History since Hegel*, vol. 4, trans. William H. Woglom and Charles W. Hendel. New Haven: Yale University Press.

Frodeman, Robert and Adam Briggle (2016), *Socrates Tenured: The Institutions of Twenty-First-Century Philosophy*. Collective Studies in Knowledge and Society. London: Rowman and Littlefield International.

Hadot, Ilsetraut (2014), *Sénèque: direction spirituelle et pratique de la philosophie*. Paris: Librairie Philosophique J. Vrin.

Hadot, Pierre (1995), *Philosophy as a Way of Life: Spiritual Exercises from Socrates to Foucault*, ed. Arnold I. Davidson, trans. Michael Chase. Malden: Blackwell.

Hadot, Pierre (1995), *Philosophy as a Way of Life: Spiritual Exercises from Socrates to Foucault*, ed. Arnold I. Davidson, trans. Michael Chase. Malden: Blackwell.

Hadot, Pierre (2002), *What is Ancient Philosophy?, trans. Michael Chase*. Cambridge, MA and London: The Belknap Press of Harvard University Press..

Kidd, Ian James (2017), 'Resisters, Diversity in Philosophy, and the Demographic Problem'. *Rivista di estetica*, 64: 118–33.

Kivistö, Sari (2014), *The Vices of Learning: Morality and Knowledge at Early Modern Universities*. Education and Society in the Middle Ages and Renaissance. Leiden and Boston: Brill Publishers.

Kramer, Eli (2021), *Intercultural Modes of Philosophy, Volume One: Principles to Guide Philosophical Community*. Leiden and Boston: Brill Publishers.

Leymann, Heinz (1990), 'Mobbing and Psychological Terror at Workplaces'. *Violence and Victims*, 5: 119–26.

Leymann, Heinz (2002), *Mobbing. La persécution au travail*, trans. Edmond Jacquemot. Paris: Seuil.

McCumber, John (2001), *Time in the Ditch: American Philosophy and the McCarthy Era*. Evanston: Northwestern University Press.

Menand, Louis (2010), 'The Humanities Revolution'. In *The Marketplace of Ideas*, 59–92. New York: W.W. Norton.

de Miranda, Luis (2021), 'Five Principles of Philosophical Health for Critical Times: From Hadot to Crealectics'. *Eidos. A Journal for Philosophy of Culture*, 5 (1): 70–89.

Plutarch (1927), *De audita [Of Listening]*, trans. Bill Thayer. As published in Vol. I of the Loeb Classical Library Edition. https://penelope.uchicago.edu/Thayer/E/Roman/Texts/Plutarch/Moralia/De_auditu*.html

Schmidt, Jeff (2000), *Disciplined Minds: A Critical Look at Salaried Professionals and the Soul-Battering System that Shapes Their Lives*. Lanham: Rowman & Littlefield.

Shapin, Steven (2005), 'Hyperprofessionalism and the Crisis of Readership in the History of Science'. *Isis*, 96 (2): 238–43.

Sharpe, Matthew (2022), 'Philosophy as a Way of Life for the 21st century Academic Philosopher'. *American Association of Philosophy Teachers Studies in Pedagogy*, 6: 9–33.

Sharpe, Matthew and Kirk Turner (2018), 'Bibliopolitics: The History of Notation and the Birth of the Citational Academic Subject'. *Foucault Studies*, 25: 146–73.

Westhues, Kenneth (1998), *Eliminating Professors, A Guide to the Dismissal Process*. Lewiston: The Edwin Mellen Press.

Whitehead, Alfred North (1958), *The Function of Reason*. Boston: Beacon Press.

Yancy, George (2008), 'Situated Black Women's Voices in/on the Profession of Philosophy'. *Hypatia*, 23 (2): 155–9.

13

Philosophical health and the transformative power of storytelling

Abdullah Başaran

Beyond guaranteeing logical consistency and forming sound arguments to abstain from defective and faulty reasoning, the various practices of philosophical health make great efforts to offer philosophy as a way of dealing with real-life situations. Paying their attention not only to the daily difficulties that we all encounter but also to the critical and precarious life issues, philosophical practitioners and counsellors aim to help people to exert themselves to manage life better by transforming how they think and act and by orienting themselves more effectively towards philosophical health.

Because this dramatic change in one's life requires a demanding, hard-to-achieve equilibrium between theory (universal) and practice (particular), philosophical counsellors and those who consult them come together in a *careful* dialogue to think about *health* more attentively. As Luis de Miranda succinctly defines, philosophical health in considering philosophy as a way of life is 'a state of fruitful coherence between a person's ways of thinking and speaking and their ways of acting, such that the possibilities for a sublime life are increased and the need for self-flourishing and intersubjective attunement satisfied' (de Miranda, 2022: 1). Thus, the issue of health is so important that its analysis cannot be consigned only to doctors, physical practitioners and psychiatrists: for the individual's alienation from her own body, from society and from the world during an illness or disease is to be healed with the *continuity of meaning*, which can be achieved only by *philosophical reflection* (Tatar, 2014: 148).

To prevent any discontinuity in the world of meaning, the practices of philosophical health have a powerful cure for patients who are existentially in a critical situation: stories that foster philosophical questioning. For a story is naturally meant both to compensate for the inconsistencies (in fictional worlds and real-life issues) by combining the parts and to turn what seems meaningless at first into a meaningful whole. This sense-making logic is of use in every matter of health: the patient visits a doctor to tell about her complaints; the doctor examines her, tries to locate the problem based on what the patient says, requests some tests and further visits; and eventually, following the symptoms, the doctor professionally tries to combine the patient's story of what she undergoes with the story that the results show. Here the patient's story functions for the doctor as a bridge between the patient's corporeal body, which is an observable and physically analysable object, and her *lived* body, that is, her experience of the illness; the doctor's story, in turn, works for the patient to give this illness a reasonable narrative, which provides a meaningful explanation for her condition (Leder, 1992: 17–35; Tatar, 2014: 140). In short, a physical (or psychological) treatment begins with the patient telling the doctor that she feels ill, continues by listening to the body and following the symptoms, and ends with the doctor's more or less holistic description of what she has been through. That being so, thanks to the stories shared between the two parties, an event of health happens.

In this chapter, I propose that the therapeutic and transformative function of storytelling is an efficient way of achieving philosophical health: literary stories and philosophical texts that include transformational narratives can be used as a practice of philosophical treatment not only for the counsellors but also for those who take care of themselves, such as the readers of such texts. Philosophical stories can be instrumental for philosophical health precisely because we tell and listen to stories to make sense of everyday events and especially of concrete, critical situations that call us to apply our knowledge on to a particular situation. If we agree, as de Miranda suggests, that *critical creativity* is one of the models to cultivate philosophical health (2021: 77–8), then storytelling is a practical candidate to help to provide creative interpretations of concrete situations by inspiring the patient or the reader to discern similar and different features between her story and others. Hence, the philosophical counsellor needs to be careful in prescribing the right story, appropriate to the present situation: otherwise, the story told or read will not make sense; as a result, the counselee may fail to create a dialogue with the other and miss the opportunity of regeneration.

Philosophical practitioners need to pay more attention to the interpretation of stories of the person who seeks health. Leaving the business of analysing the patient's story to modern medicine and psychology, and the character's transformative story to literary criticism, brings about the negligence of their philosophical implications. Yet the latter may reveal the meaning of being well (Han, 2021: 11). Unlike these modern disciplines that discriminate between the doctor/analyst and *what* is analysed – that is, the disease or the linguistic problem, which is generally understood as something *external* to the patient or the reader, thereby being something to be controlled and mastered (Gadamer, 1996: 105, 111) – philosophical practitioners treat the *lived experiences* of the person whose condition is critical in terms of continuity of inner meaning.

As de Miranda emphasizes, in reference to Pierre Hadot and Michel Foucault, 'philosophising must also be conceived as a practice of *askesis*, embodied exercises oriented toward the manifested ideal of a harmonious and dignified self-continuity' (2021: 71–2). Therefore, the endeavour of philosophical health inevitably invokes a balanced correspondence between theory and practice: an appropriation of the knowledge of things in general to serve the particular case of the person who wants to be philosophically healthy (de Miranda, 2021: 74). Due to this hard-to-achieve task, Hans-Georg Gadamer compares restoring health to an art (1996: 31–44, 103–16): for health, that is., the balance in well-being, cannot be captured nor explained once and for all; since health cannot be conveyed (neither physically nor psychologically) from one person to another, not even from one's one state to another state, one needs to *interpret* one's own hermeneutical situation. Moreover, health reveals its existence in its absence – that is, in an illness: one also needs to interpret one's own body and psychology in order to acknowledge what being well means to us. While abstract logical-philosophical argumentations fail to explain this elusive character of being well, I believe storytelling is capable of fulfilling this task of making sense of the enigma of health by making coherent what may seem incoherent and incomprehensible. In the next part, I try to demonstrate how storytelling manages to help our practices of philosophical health.

Philosophical narratives

The pedagogy of storytelling for philosophical health is that personal, biographical or fictional stories of transformation have a distinctive capacity to formulate the essential concepts that bond us. The best examples of philosophical storytelling to cultivate philosophical health are the early Socratic dialogues of Plato: reading *Euthyphro* (Plato, 1997: 1–16), for instance, from a *logical* point of view to highlight the theological dilemma is one thing; reading this magnificent dialogue from a *philosophical* point of view to ponder upon the concepts of *piety* and *justice*, to adopt these problems and make them our own, is another. Euthyphro's pious action of suing his father for leaving a servant for dead is the subject matter that Socrates investigates. We read Euthyphro's story and what he thinks about the lawsuit filed against his father. But throughout the dialogue, Socratic questioning reveals the fact that neither Euthyphro is self-assured in defining what piety means nor we the readers are confident in determining what is right and what is wrong in the case of Euthyphro. Nonetheless, the peculiar case of Euthyphro is open to possible interpretations concerning what being pious and being just mean to us. The reader of the dialogue adopts the philosophical concern suggested by the story, makes the posed questions her own and may create her own answers to these essential problems. Thus, we can argue that Euthyphro's story has the power to motivate the reader to think independently for herself and courageously act upon it. The reader has the opportunity to transform herself towards a 'heroic realisation of wisdom' in her daily efforts (de Miranda, 2022: 3; 2021: 73).

The architect of philosophy as a way of life, Pierre Hadot, uses this relationship between stories and philosophical concepts in his various writings on Socrates (Hadot, 2002), Marcus Aurelius (Hadot, 1995) and Plotinus (Hadot, 1998) to constitute a philosophy of life. In *Plotinus or The Simplicity of Vision*, Hadot raises the most important question regarding the philosophy of Plotinus – that is, 'how can we live down here in this world once we have contemplated divine Beauty and felt the love of the Good? Better yet, how can we live, while still down here below, in continuous contemplation?' (1998: 73). The following chapter of Hadot's book, titled 'Gentleness', gives a response by concentrating all the focus on Plotinus's life story, from his attachment to spiritual meditation to illnesses and his everyday practices such as dietary habits, cleanliness, sleeping less, writing routine and so on. Hadot portrays Plotinus through his work and his life (1998: 22) for the modern reader to acquire a model relating theory (i.e. philosophical concepts like *beauty* and *good*) to practice (i.e. how we maintain everyday life and prepare ourselves for death). Hadot's illustration of the application of theory to practice is consonant with de Miranda's principle of deep orientation: 'The ethos of philosophical health, whether it is or is not mediated by a philosophical counsellor, is meant to guide the person via concepts, ideas, or beliefs made explicit, so that her engagement with life is coherent with her engagement with ideas and words' (de Miranda, 2021: 74). In this manner, the work and life of Plotinus are meant to generate transformative ways for the reader's soul to be healed.

Having recourse to the transformative aspect of a story was a well-known model not only for ancient philosophy but also for Christian theologians. Augustine of Hippo, in his acclaimed autobiographical *Confessions* (2006), appeals to two stories of conversion to make a better illustration of his conversion to Christianity: that of Victorinus told by Simplicianus and that of the two young men influenced by the miraculous life of Saint Antony. In chapter six of Book Eight, Augustine confesses to us that he did not know the Egyptian monk Antony, and that someone named Ponticianus introduced him, Augustine, through a story of conversion: '[the two friends of Ponticianus] found a small book in which was written the life of Antony. One of them began to read it, marvelled at it, was inflamed by it. While he was actually reading he had begun to think how he might embrace such a life, and give up his worldly employment to serve You alone' (Augustine, 2006: 151). The stories of the priest Victorinus and the two converted men had turned Augustine back towards himself (152) and compelled him to reflect upon his life and make a critical decision for himself. Their story of conversion affects Augustine deeply because he feels an intimate relatedness to those believers. As he takes his lesson from what Simplicianus and Ponticianus told him, Augustine studies the life of the saint and acquires the knowledge that Antony became a man of God via the call of the Word (159–60). Reading this in Antony's book, Augustine follows the path the saint took and immediately reads a random passage from the Scripture, which is also a tagline for the chapter: this passage, 'Now him that is weak in faith, take unto you' (Rom. 14.1), is the final image of Augustine's narrative of his own conversion.

Not surprisingly, Augustine, especially by using the second story of faith and conversion based on a book, invites us to read his *Confessions* more carefully to reconsider how we can transform our lives for the better, that is, finding the true path of God. This multi-layered composition – that is, a story embedded in another story, a book of faith admirably mentioned in another book – is a narration of a philosophical journey constructed for the reader. In *Confessions*, Augustine narrates how he has achieved intellectual serenity and spiritual peacefulness so that the reader embraces this example for her own transformation.

Philosophers writing on literature and bibliotherapy practices are already familiar with stories whose philosophical value has therapeutic effects on the reader. The power of literature, in this regard, lies in the fact that the reader and the heroes and characters share a common fate. Mythological figures such as Ariadne, Apollo and Dionysus, Heracles and Prometheus, Marduk, Thor and Loki; the figures narrated in the Scriptures; the animal and magical heroes of fables and fairy tales; and fictional characters such as Oedipus and Antigone, Hayy Ibn Yaqzan, Dr. Faust, Dr. Frankenstein, Raskolnikov, Gregor Samsa, Ulrich, Marcel, Jean-Baptiste Clamence, Oblomov, Watt,

Orlando, Palomar and Augusto Pérez – all have in common with us real human beings: they are concrete examples of human conditions. Since our childhood, we read and listen to and now even watch the physical and spiritual journeys of these heroes, the decisions they make in difficult situations, meditations about their past and the future, their way of thinking, their delirium, faults, delusions, their relationships, anxieties, troubles, friendships and loves. Sometimes we even feel more connected to their world than to ours.

A well-known anecdote from Kafka's last days would be a perfect demonstration of this connectedness and shared reality. One day the Bohemian writer and his lover Dora go for a walk and they encounter a crying little girl. When asked why, she tells them she lost her baby doll. But the tender-hearted Kafka gives the little girl good news: the doll is not lost, and he, Kafka, has been corresponding with it. Kafka promises the girl that he is going to read her doll's letter if they see each other once again. They agree to meet up. Kafka, the writer in pain because of his catarrh condition, and the little girl, who is in pain because of yearning for the doll, form a friendship mediated through the letters written by the author. Unexpectedly, their meetings continue for a while; Kafka, by writing letters, wants to make her happy, whereas the girl wants to listen to her doll's adventures and be informed about her beloved friend. As Ahmet Sarı explicitly states,

> The writer forgets his illness by taking refuge in the truth of fiction, thereby calming his soul. The reader (i.e., the little girl), on the other hand, since she is longing for the character in the fictional letters, becomes fascinated by the reality of fiction. Hence, she forgets her pain, her sorrow. . . . Here reveals itself a dual activity of healing and therapy. Fiction remedies the writer as well as the reader. (Sarı, 2020: 9)

Here the rapport between Kafta (the writer) and the little girl (the reader) is described as an exercise, a good process for either party. Kafka aspires to tell the doll's story, and the girl to listen to it: these meetings in which pain and suffering are shared become an environment of trust provided by narration. Myths, fables, stories and narratives, to use the Swiss writer Peter Bichsel's elegant words, 'calm the world' by putting imaginal possibilities up against the cold necessities of reality (Bichsel, 2020: 25–6).

All good literature and literary works of high quality have this therapeutic effect simply because of their philosophical questioning about the concepts that continually bind us together. Kafka's existential interest in loss, friendship and being well is the reason for his concern about overcoming the interruption of health, that is, the concern about the continuity of a meaningful life. The following words of Gilles Deleuze seem to accompany Kafka's endeavour of (not only physical but also) philosophical health: 'the ultimate aim of literature is to set free, in the delirium, this creation of a health or this invention of a people, that is, a possibility of life' (Deleuze, 1997: 4).

For the prospect of philosophical health, Deleuze is a unique figure in terms of attributing vital importance to literature. In his *Critical and Clinical* (1997), a collection of essays on the affinity between literature and life, he makes a great effort to offer the therapeutic power of literature for philosophical thinking: we read a short piece on the depths and the surface in Lewis Carroll's novels and stories, a Beckettian chapter on perception and cinematic images, a condensed analysis of Kant's three critiques through Shakespeare's *Hamlet* and other poetic works, Nietzsche's condemnation of Christianity along with D. H. Lawrence's symbolism, a philosophical analysis of Melville's Bartleby's 'I would prefer not to', Heidegger's remarks on language and the overcoming of metaphysics in the company of Alfred Jarry and so on. Going back and forth between literature and philosophy, between stories and concepts, Deleuze is committed to 'an affirmative and creative engagement with life' (de Miranda, 2021: 71) by demonstrating how good stories of literature are *effective* in formulating our philosophical thinking and *inspiring* for a fundamental openness to the creative power of the possible.

How stories heal us

To epitomize their transformation, some philosophers, such as Augustine, as we have seen, or Descartes in his *Meditations*, ask the reader to engage their own life stories. Others – for example, Voltaire in *Candide*, Nietzsche in *Thus Spoke Zarathustra*, Sartre, de Beauvoir or Kristeva in their plays and novels – appeal to the analogical and figurative narrative. Philosophical stories or literary stories with philosophical value heal us in many ways, not only the authors themselves but also the readers. The very reason for their therapeutic influence is that stories help us to connect with each other and bind us together on the same subject matter of concern. We tell and listen to stories not only in our daily affairs and relationship routines but also in crises like an interruption of health, physical pain, psychological trouble, nuisance, disgust or loneliness. That being so, telling your story and listening to another's story are the natural antidote that reverberates the discontinuity in one's life. Stories *make sense* in understanding the world in which we live, and that is why their potentiality should be considered carefully for the benefit of various practices of philosophical health.

This potential, however, is not, or should not be, limited to the philosophical and literary stories that the practitioner suggests or tells during the sessions, but also includes the story of the person seeking help. More importantly, her story (of pain or trouble) is why she is in the presence of a counsellor; in fact, she comes to *tell her story*. This narrative of pain (distress, trauma, loss etc.) is the first concrete, heroic move towards philosophical health. In other words, without her story being told, any attempt by the counsellor to make sense of what she has been through will eventually fail. Thus, the first and foremost duty of the philosophical counsellor is to build an environment of trust in which the counselee articulates her own story safely. The only way the practitioner can provide such an environment is to listen to her story carefully with 'the sensitive ear which is attentive to the significance of what the patient says' (Gadamer, 1996: 99). This attentiveness – or 'a protective attitude of deep listening' (de Miranda, 2022: 4) – to what is told (i.e. to the subject matter at hand) creates 'a form of dialogue that aims at becoming "consonant" with the other' (de Miranda, 2021: 79) and restores the unequal relationship between the counsellor (i.e. the professional) and the counselee (the layman) on the grounds of a philosophical dialogue (Gadamer, 1996: 112).

In this way, storytelling becomes a two-sided performance in which the two parties philosophically reflect upon the (phenomenological) aspects of the story, react to what is critical in this case and eventually conceptualize the matter in question. Luis de Miranda endorses this democratization as opposed to the subordination of philosophy to the professional and scholarly thinkers: 'A first step to understand that the idea of philosophical health is equally as important as physical and psychological health is to recognize that any human being possesses philosophical beliefs, intellectual allegiances, and more or less rationalized concerns, often not yet fully explicit or compossible, that is theoretically and pragmatically compatible' (de Miranda, 2022: 3).

In his long essay on the short story writer Nikolai Leskov, Walter Benjamin writes: 'A man listening to a story is in the company of the storyteller; even a man reading one shares this companionship' (Benjamin, 2006: 156). Companionship, in this context, is the common platform where the interaction between the counsellor/philosopher/character and the counselee/reader takes place: the person who seeks health brings her story to the fore (i.e. action), and the perspective delivered by the philosopher becomes a part of the process of convalescence (i.e. reaction). However, the problems that philosophically concern us all, the burden (of living), are shared on this platform and transform both sides of the dialogue. This situation, which Gadamer illustrates as the *fusion of horizons*, tells that the two parties participating in dialogue do not remain the same as they interact and understand each other's positions, and this fusion alienates those who come to the dialogue with their prejudices from their selves (Gadamer, 2013: 385). This means that both the narrator and the listener, the philosophical counsellor and the counselee acquire a new perspective, a new position through a healthy dialogue in which the subject matter, namely a philosophical stance, is articulated through the transformative power of storytelling.

Whether it is for professional counselling and therapy or for self-care such as reading good literature, classics or philosophical books, storytelling provides other essential benefits to the practices of philosophical health: a search for a meaningful life, a purpose to live and gratitude towards help, a community idealized, mental and bodily relief, a joyful, creative, eudynamic relationship with what is possible and so on.

First of all, *stories make sense*, because they go beyond a mere explanation of the flow of events and facts and show, or more pedagogically allow one to realize, how these facts and events are put together meaningfully. It engages us in the logic of the experiences lived by the others, by the characters or by ourselves, to prevent any destructive discontinuity in meaning. For instance, since Kafka's stories completely make sense for the little girl who lost her doll, she keeps listening to what will happen next. Or, in another context, understanding what Descartes has been through in his meditative journey is an understanding of his orientation in philosophical worldview, thereby requiring the reader/listener to adopt the philosopher's way of thinking. In order to make sense of what is past, to be better oriented in the present and provident for the future, we need stories to be read, listened to or articulated.

The philosophical counsellor needs to be careful in selecting the most appropriate story for the person who seeks connection. Otherwise, the story told during a session or a philosophical work prescribed as a reading task will not make sense to the counselee. Likewise, the counselee's articulation of her own story is being told to make sense of her experiences; to get this right, the counsellor asks her in a phenomenological manner to bracket *what* she has been through (see Simionescu-Panait, Chapter 10 of the present volume) and to concentrate on *how* she has been affected. As a consequence, the person revisits her own story from a different perspective: 'To be in a conversation', writes Gadamer, 'means to be beyond oneself, to think with the other and to come back to oneself as if to another' (Gadamer, 1989: 110).

Because, while telling our own stories to others (a doctor, practitioner, partner or a regular audience), we are both the narrator and the main character of our story (Brewster, 2022: 2). Here de Miranda explains our retrospective and prospective reaction to the continuity of meaning as follows: 'The deep orientation of philosophical health is an active care [i.e., care for the continuity of meaning] that is anticipatory of the future as well as informed by the past. Above all, it is oriented toward the present as a form of attentive engagement with life' (de Miranda, 2021: 75).

For a better engagement with life, storytelling brings forth a relief to be free. On the one hand, as recent research on neurobiology shows, while the subjects who sit in the same room have unique patterns of brain waves, the waves of the same people begin to sync when they listen to the same story. 'This alignment, or coupling', writes Annie Brewster, 'is an important part of effective communication, which assumes mutual understanding' (2022: 55–7). This mutual understanding may be a hasty conclusion; however, what is really mutual among those who attended the storytelling session is still worthwhile: their connectedness in the matter at hand, the very bond that makes them less lonely.

On the other hand, the connection between storytelling (i.e. telling your own story) and physical health is highly important. Augustine, on the edge of conversion, was complaining about the state of indecision that had given him emotional distress and bodily suffering (Augustine, 2006: 154). When we narrate what upsets us, this sharing helps us breathe better; otherwise, what remains untold lingers like a lump in our throat. For this reason, we feel relieved and unburdened by confiding our troubles in someone else. The quality of breathing is a key element of the quality of life: it allows us to control our respiratory rhythm and to manage and find our (telling) voice. To put it another way, the person who takes risks when she exposes herself in counselling sessions or the company of a friend gains not only self-confidence but also a free and independent voice by virtue of storytelling: 'A philosophical-health mindset is an authentic and diverse way of life because it does not teach which ideal-self specifically to become; rather, it advocates a transformative freedom to create a singular biography and therefore act as personally as possible' (de Miranda, 2021: 82).

Stories give purpose. A philosophical story such as Euthyphro's invites us to think for ourselves about the matter in question (viz. piety, true justice), formulate the problem and put forward our own solutions. Thus, Euthyphro's case, for instance, can be hermeneutically understood by making the case our own. This appropriation, however, is not simply an epistemological attempt at empathy towards a character's orientation of thinking but an ontological strive for understanding the concepts we live by. Through the concepts upon which we reflect, it is also possible to help others who go through similar challenges in their lives. That a small detail in Euthyphro's case or an interpretation of Augustine's conversion is adopted and applied to the counselee's (or a friend's) condition may give a remarkable perspective on the present concern that troubles her deeply.

Powerful, therapeutic stories affect us because our lives curiously resemble one another: we are living in the same world the philosophers lived once. This is even the same world in which mythologies emerged worldwide, animals in fables chattered and fictional characters reside. This possibility of healing others also makes the storyteller feel good about the process of sharing and caring. To put it differently, she knows that she *can* change the state of affairs because she can help her companion through the other's (i.e. the philosopher's) or her own story. Briefly put, storytelling gives rise to a possibility of reciprocal remedy, a mutual affection both for the teller and the listener.

As a consequence of the last point, stories indicate a community. Needless to say, storytelling is a collective activity: one tells, and the other listens to what is told; one writes, and another reads. It inherently connects us to each other. Hearing similar challenges from other people's lives, reading a character's journey that resembles the particular situation we are in, therapeutically gives us the feeling that we are not alone. These common themes that we share bind us together in terms of our common destiny. Even when we have an emotionally or a physically different story to tell, if we strongly wish others to understand what we are undergoing, we keep seeking common ground in telling how differently we experienced the events. We search for this connection in order to restore our health by feeling supported: because we know that there are others, and they might be differently bearing a similar difficulty (Brewster, 2022: 26–7). These differences coalesce into the same concern in order to constitute the heart of a community: the unity of pain, that is, the unity in convalescence and seeking health (Han, 2021: 12–13).

In this unity, (singular) individuals join a certain community and share the feeling of togetherness by performing an action together (Zahavi, 2021), which is convalescing collectively by telling our stories to each other. To be a *we* is to experience the feeling of being connected to each other *from within* (Zahavi, 2015: 156). The wounded members of a society, in this regard, (must) get together by means of the connective power of storytelling; despite the differences, one cares to listen to the story of the other. The doctor/counsellor listens to what the patient/counselee tells. In turn, the latter opens her ears to the former; we all equally suffer from the same diseases in our world of late modernism, where we undergo massacres, military coups, terror, racism, misogyny, sexual abuses, injustice, censorship, tyranny and totalitarianism – the tragedies we live every day, every moment. Thus, the following words of Peter Bichsel seem timely: 'I don't know what a non-aggressive, non-competitive, peaceful society looks like and how to create it. But I am sure that this would be a society that narrates, not historicizes, but storifies' (Bichsel, 2020: 101).

A wounded society heals its wounds together and creates a counter-world in which we are able to look at each other's eyes (Han, 2021: 25): this can only happen by *carefully* listening to someone else, lending an ear to what someone else is saying, and by telling a story to be listened to, that is, by choosing the right words that will touch someone else's ear and heart. Thus, by fostering 'creative politics and innovative citizenship' (de Miranda, 2021: 78), the practices of storytelling for philosophical health, in a more hermeneutical manner, have the intention of achieving not only the individual's transformation but also a collective change of the society.

Conclusion

What enhances the organizational and self-practices of philosophical health and the non-institutional and academic studies on philosophical health – including this volume – is the proliferation of dealing with the *meaning* of being philosophically healthy, without excluding an understanding of the meaning of being physically and psychologically healthy. In this regard, especially since the second half of the twentieth century, many attempts have been made to describe the meaning of being philosophically healthy: Michel Foucault's medical anthropology and his writings on the care of the self, Gilles Deleuze's submission to literature as a creation of health, H.-G. Gadamer's hermeneutics of the art of healing, Pierre Hadot's programme of philosophy as a way of life, Fredrik Svenaeus and Kevin Aho's hermeneutics of medicine and the phenomenology of health, Luis de Miranda's eudynamic attempts to deepen our understanding of philosophical health, the development of philosophical counselling, bibliotherapy, the augmentation of philosophical self-care. In this chapter, to participate in this festival of interpretations concerning philosophical health, I have offered storytelling as therapeutic and transformative support for the procedures of philosophical counsellors and a strategy of self-practice.

The remedial characteristic of touching stories is effective in many ways, beyond any doubt. Here I have made the attempt to underline the fact that we use stories to make sense of ourselves and the world, to generate reasonable explanations of everyday and critical events. Storytelling is a fruitful, creative, generative, constructive and effective way of constantly reidentifying ourselves with the community of others. A story that touches my heart changes me in some way, and my own story once told redefines me and those who listen to me. By addressing the examples of philosophical stories and the counselee's own courage to tell her own story, I have shown that storytelling makes us at home in the world we create together, building an attentive society to transform individually and collectively.

I would like to thank Dr. Selami Varlik for drawing my attention to the philosophical value of Augustine's conversion.

References

Augustine (2006), *Confessions*, 2nd edn, trans. F. J. Sheed. Indianapolis and Cambridge: Hackett Publishing Company.

Benjamin, Walter (2006), 'The Storyteller: Observations on the Works of Nikolai Leskov'. In H. Eiland and M. W. Jennings (eds), *Walter Benjamin: Selected Writings. Volume 3: 1935–1938*, 143–66. Cambridge, MA and London: Harvard University Press.

Bichsel, Peter (2020), *Edebiyat Dersleri: Okur/*Anlatı [Der Leser, Das Erzählen: Frankfurter Poetik Vorlesungen], trans. (into Turkish) A. Sarı and Ş. Çoraklı. Istanbul: Ketebe Publishing.

Brewster, Annie (2022), *The Healing Power of Storytelling: Using Personal Narrative to Navigate Illness, Trauma, and Loss.* Berkeley: North Atlantic Books.

Deleuze, Gilles (1997), *Essays: Critical and Clinical*, trans. D. W. Smith and M. A. Greco. Minneapolis: University of Minnesota Press.

Gadamer, Hans-Georg (1989), 'Destruktion and Deconstruction', trans. G. Waite and R. Palmer. In D. P. Michelfelder and R. E. Palmer (eds), *Dialogue and Deconstruction: The Gadamer-Derrida Encounter*, 102–13. Albany: State University of New York Press.

Gadamer, Hans-Georg (1996), *The Enigma of Health: The Art of Healing in a Scientific Age*, trans. J. Gaiger and N. Walker. Stanford: Stanford University Press.

Gadamer, Hans-Georg (2013), *Truth and Method*, trans. J. Weinsheimer and D. G. Marshall. New York: Bloomsbury.

Hadot, Pierre (1995), *Philosophy as a Way of Life: Spiritual Exercises from Socrates to Foucault*, ed. A. I. Davidson, trans. M. Chase. Oxford and Cambridge: Blackwell Publishers.

Hadot, Pierre (1998), *Plotinus, or The Simplicity of Vision*, trans. M. Chase. Chicago and London: The University of Chicago Press.

Hadot, Pierre (2002), *What Is Ancient Philosophy?* trans. M. Chase. Cambridge, MA and London: Harvard University Press.

Han, Byung-Chul (2021), *The Palliative Society: Pain Today*, trans. D. Steuer. Cambridge: Polity Press.

Leder, Drew (1992), 'A Tale of Two Bodies: The Cartesian Corpse and the Lived Body'. In D. Leder (ed.), *The Body in Medical Thought and Practice*, 17–36. Dordrecht: Kluwer Academic Publishers.

de Miranda, Luis (2021), 'Five Principles of Philosophical Health for Critical Times: From Hadot to Crealectics'. *Eidos: A Journal for Philosophy of Culture*, 5 (1): 70–89. doi: 10.14394/eidos.jpc.2021.0005

de Miranda, Luis (2022), 'Philosophical Health'. In V. P. Glăveanu (ed.), *The Palgrave Encyclopedia of the Possible*. Cham: Palgrave Macmillan. https://doi.org/10.1007/978-3 -319-98390-5_209-1

Plato (1997), 'Euthyphro', trans. J. M. Cooper. In J. M. Cooper (ed.), *Plato: Complete Works*, 1–16. Indianapolis and Cambridge: Hackett Publishing Company.

Sarı, Ahmet (2020), *Edebiyatın İyileştirici Gücü: Edebiyat-Terapi Bağlamında Düşünceler* [The Healing Power of Literature: Thoughts on Literature-Therapy]. Istanbul: Ketebe Publishing.

Tatar, Burhanettin (2014), *Din, İlim ve Sanatta Hermenötik* [Hermeneutics: Religion, Science, and Art]. Istanbul: ISAM.

Zahavi, Dan (2015), 'Self and Other: From Pure Ego to Co-constituted We'. *Continental Philosophy Review*, 48: 143–60. https://doi.org/10.1007/s11007-015-9328-2

Zahavi, Dan (2021), 'We in Me or Me in We? Collective Intentionality and Selfhood'. *Journal of Social Ontology*, 7 (1): 1–20.

14

Decolonization as philosophical health

Brendan Moran

Introduction: Decolonization and philosophical health

Decolonization requires philosophical health. This claim is elaborated in writings by the Franco-Algerian philosopher Seloua Luste Boulbina (b. 1957). It concerns the possibility that the colonized, the formerly colonized and descendants of the colonized could experience their lives, and the lives of their ancestors, without certain questionable constraints and denigrations. A philosophically healthy condition would require institutions in which these people can address their lives and the lives of their ancestors in a less constrained way than is currently possible. Luste Boulbina does not seem to use the expression 'philosophical health'. Yet she claims that health is not possible without the philosophical. Decolonization and philosophical health are complementary: philosophical health requires the dismantling of lingering colonial attitudes; those attitudes cannot be healthily dismantled without the philosophical impetus that queries constraints. The relevant care for the self requires that individuals and societies have possibilities for beginning anew, for questioning constraints (de Miranda, 2021: 77).

Luste Boulbina cites a Socratic provenance that identifies the philosophical primarily with questioning. She also draws from Gilles Deleuze, among others, to identify health with philosophical becoming, including becoming foreign – that is, rebellious. If the philosophically healthy affirms life by questioning the circumscribed life that might otherwise be lived (de Miranda, 2021: 81), decoloniality also entails the refusal to acquiesce to imperatives that are themselves illusory in their purported infallibility.

To refer to a specifically *philosophical* health in decolonization might seem fatuous – in utter disregard of the actual lives of people who are often materially quite disadvantaged and are regularly exposed to racial discrimination by police, politicians, journalists, academicians and others. The deprivation and the racism do indeed impact health in direct physical violence and in a debilitating intertwining of mental and physical malaise. The philosophical is, however, a potentially important capacity for people to question, and thereby possibly to modify, what is happening to them and – in some sense – what has happened to their ancestors. Such philosophical revisiting of one's life, and of lives preceding and influencing one, is at least conceivably possible.

'[N]o one has a monopoly over philosophy . . .. Before the Greeks, before the Egyptians, philosophical questions haunted the human being' (Ndaw, 2016: 111).

Occasionally drawing on experiences in her own life (with an Algerian father and a French mother, and a life divided between Algeria and France), Luste Boulbina reflects on how philosophical scrutiny could alter the legacy of the colonial. Her works demonstrate and concern the possibility that the relevant people – be they in colonies, in former colonies, in France itself or elsewhere – could generate subjectivities that, precisely in being philosophical, at least open the prospect of becoming healthier by rejecting a 'fate' (*destin*) ascribed to their ancestors and to themselves (Luste Boulbina, 2019: 184/2015: 40). Philosophical health is not extraneous to physical or psychological health, no more than they are extraneous to each other; philosophical health is simply the capacity to revisit and engage life-conditions without the stultification that those conditions might otherwise entail (de Miranda, 2022).

Luste Boulbina's writings demonstrate a certain courage, for it remains the case that many French politicians, journalists, academicians (including 'philosophers') and members of the so-called general population are quite defensive of France's colonial history. Prominent French politicians and a significant number of French academicians have recently decried postcolonial studies as a foreign import that threatens education, as well as the broader society, in France. Never mind that many of the philosophical bases for such studies come from France itself (Onishi, 2021), as is noted by Luste Boulbina in her borrowings from various earlier French philosophers (Luste Boulbina, 2020: 28). Luste Boulbina's writings engage in the very postcolonial studies before which some in France (and elsewhere) are aghast. Many in France are complacent about the relative deprivation in which the colonized and descendants of the colonized often live. By opposing the glorifying and the complacency in France regarding colonial and postcolonial history, Luste Boulbina is exercising the very health philosophy that her works propose, even though she relatively rarely gives first-person accounts. This health philosophy manifests itself in her questioning of the necessity for the denigration, the racism and the exclusion that is enacted upon many colonized and their descendants.

That Luste Boulbina herself does not more often undertake first-person accounts is not a contradiction, no more than it is a contradiction for this chapter to be written largely without the first-person pronoun. At stake is simply the prospect that people who rarely have the possibility of philosophical self-articulation could generate such a possibility. In a very broad sense, everyone or almost everyone is *occupied*: without the possibility to philosophize – that is, to oppose and transform – brutalities in life. Luste Boulbina is trying, however, to focus on brutalities that are somewhat specific to the colonized and their descendants.

She diverges from some of her influences, notably Michel Foucault and Gilles Deleuze, in the extent to which she associates philosophical health with first-person accounts – sometimes as these are used in psychoanalysis. She connects philosophical health with the arts, especially literature, but without ever relinquishing her priority of first-person accounts. Roberto Esposito also adapts Foucault, Deleuze and others to give prominence to the philosophically health-inducing qualities of literature. Esposito, however, identifies well-being, including justice, with affirmation of an ineradicable anonymity for which the third person is a marker and psychoanalysis might be inadequate. This chapter will delineate Luste Boulbina's conception of first-person philosophical health as a release from inconspicuous anonymity. It will then critically consider this conception in relation to Esposito's orientation of philosophy towards the third person as marker for an anonymity that liberates from I-you parameters.

Intimacy of the 'subject' against its 'history'

Although Foucault's works loom in her conception of 'care for the self' as health of the 'subject' (Luste Boulbina, 2015: 50, 54; 2019: 193, 197;), Luste Boulbina critically cites a well-known passage from *The Archaeology of Knowledge* in which Foucault says that he writes 'in order to have no face' and suggests this will release him at least somewhat from the 'morality' of 'our civil servants and our police' (Foucault, 1972: 17/*1969*: *28* [italicized page numbers for the French pagination indicate that the mentioned English translation has been modified]). Luste Boulbina retorts that the resident of a poor country, an illegal migrant or a Black woman has no dream or ideal of having no face; they are already having this 'experience, . . . reality, . . . nightmare', and might 'express themselves, on the contrary, in order to have a face' (Luste Boulbina, 2019: 74/*2020*: *113–14*). Luste Boulbina would certainly acknowledge that a poor person, a migrant or a Black woman might sometimes want release from the identity purveyed by civil servants and by police. She argues, however, that philosophical health involves the subject that generates first-person accounts.

For Luste Boulbina, philosophical health is not possible for a third person. Adapting work by linguist Émile Benveniste, Luste Boulbina claims there 'is no third *person*' and that the 'third person is tacitly a subaltern' (Luste Boulbina, 2019: 87/*2020*: *130–1*; citing Benveniste, 1966: 225–36, 251–76; 1971: 195–204, 217–36). The third person is a construction designating 'the one spoken about, the one who is, in interlocution, absent'. The third person is frequently 'addressed' without being 'the one who speaks' (Luste Boulbina, 2019: 60n90/*2020*: *74n73*; see too 96n71 and n72/*130n64 and n65*; citing Benveniste, 1966: 225–32, 255–7; 1971: 195–200, 221–2). It might seem an unavoidable condition of societal life, of course, that others speak about me and not be concerned with a response from me. I might, furthermore, not wish to respond. This supposedly normal societal condition has, however, various permutations. The 'ex-colonized – always non-European – is still the largely excluded third of a discourse whose coloniality is unmistakable. Excluded third also means object. The third is thus subjectivity cut from its history, from its language, from its gender. Try never being able to speak about yourself and hearing yourself constantly spoken about by others' (Luste Boulbina, 2019: 284/*2015*: *140*). In other words, if you are not already among the colonized or those regarded as descendants of the colonized (or those living similar conditions of highly limited cultural value), try to imagine what it would be like to be excluded from many practical and discursive venues simply because of the way you look, the accent of your speech, the look and the sound of your proper name or perhaps the place in which you were raised (248/108). Luste Boulbina has personally undergone such exclusions (Luste Boulbina, 2020: 21).

She proposes that those suffering exclusion of this sort be given more opportunity to speak about themselves, their conditions and their sense of their lineage. This would contrast with the situation in which women wearing distinctly Muslim head attire (as well as their feminist supporters) were de-subjectified in being almost entirely excluded from discussions leading to the French law of 2004 that banned such attire from certain public institutions (Al-Saji, 2010: 881, 891–2; in a broader context, see too Luste Boulbina, 2019: 171–2, 244–5/2015: 27, 104). It would not be philosophically healthy, of course, if newly released expressions were themselves never to be revisited critically. After all, as Luste Boulbina stresses (while quoting Judith Butler): "'life might be understood as precisely that which exceeds any account we may try to give of it'" (Luste Boulbina, 2019: 257–8/2015: 119; citing Butler, 2005: 43). This condition of life-eluding accounts of it in no way diminishes, however, the notion that health includes the philosophical exercise in which people are allowed to speak who normally are not heeded. Perspectives on life conditions, discrimination, police or politics might emerge that are otherwise disqualified. The disqualified of principal interest to Luste Boulbina are some whose cultural background is usually considered irrelevant or unimportant in prevailing discourse.

It would be a further denigration of self, moreover, to have wholesale recourse to the alleged objectivity of science. In *Black Skins, White Masks*, Frantz Fanon says that it would have been "'dishonest'" for him to pretend "'to be objective'". Affectively and in tactile ways he felt the "'misery'" of being Black (Luste Boulbina, 2019: 178/2015: 35; quoting Fanon, 2008: 67/1952: 84). Fanon entered the then quite disreputable area of psychiatry and 'transformed it' not only 'from inside' but simultaneously 'from the periphery' (Luste Boulbina, 2019: 193/2015: 49–50). In altering psychiatry, Fanon 'showed that decolonization must be the work of subjects' who reject, as he puts it in *The Wretched of the Earth*, the "'world configured by the coloniser'" – the world in which "'the colonized subject is always presumed guilty'". This presumed guilt, as extrapolated by Luste Boulbina, does not result from something one has done but rather is projected as inhering in one's condition as colonized or as descendant of the colonized. The 'original sin' is even projected as a scientifically determinable ancestral, supposedly biological, malady (Luste Boulbina, 2019: 193–4/2015: 49–51; citing Fanon, 2004: 16/1991: 83; see too Luste Boulbina, 2020: 26–7). The philosophic antidote is to let people speak in a way that refuses to submit to such silencing projections. The focus on 'subject' is not capitalist individualism; the colonizers and their successors could themselves well do with philosophical therapy. Openness to the challenge of others obviates vapid self-satisfaction in one's interpretative endeavours. Luste Boulbina remarks: 'Only the subject can decolonise itself, along with other subjects' (Luste Boulbina, 2019: 300). This 'along with' is integral to the activity of becoming healthy philosophically, as is, however, 'the subject'. Regardless of what is established scientifically about life trajectories, the data might not account for an often quite personal sensation of duress in ostensible integration. '[T]he step of historical objectivation is necessary, for it allows things to be established that would otherwise remain in the limbo of imagination. But it is also insufficient, precisely to the extent that nothing but the self can ultimately take care of the self' (198–9/56). If I am to render something that has happened to me, my participation in the philosophical endeavour will be indispensable no matter how much it also requires or at least involves the participation of others. Luste Boulbina cites Paul Ricœur's account of "'philosophical reflection'" and his contention that such "'reflection constantly assures us that the object of history is the human *subject* itself'" (199/56; citing Ricœur, 1965: 40/1967: 50). In this regard, Pierre Hadot expressly emphasizes '*le moi*' rather than Foucault's "'*practiques de soi*'" (Hadot, 2001: 153).

The health will be philosophical, however, precisely in the willingness of the subject to consider anew how its readings might be forced and thus questionable. According to Luste Boulbina, this contrasts with 'the scholarly historian [*(l)'historiographe*]', who has been given, 'generally and traditionally', 'the function of witness and judge much more than that of translator and interpreter' (Luste Boulbina, 2019: 200/2015: 58). The latter *philosophical* approach, which translates in provisional interpretative modes, recognizes no knowledge-monopoly. Luste Boulbina is worried that 'historiography exercises a de facto monopoly over the colonial question and therefore treats every wandering philosopher as an intruder, a spoilsport, who prevents things from running as they should'. Luste Boulbina discusses philosophy in terms of a Socratic provenance that she characterizes as dialogical and attentive to its own ignorance. Philosophy 'founds its legitimacy (or authorises itself) on . . . ignorance' (Luste Boulbina, 2019: 75/2020: 115). This is not simply the ignorance of someone who claims to know and can be shown not to know. It is also ignorance in perpetuity; it is the unthought that cannot be extinguished entirely. Michel de Certeau says: 'All thought has its truth in a "thought of the outside"' (76/115; citing Certeau, 1986: 182/1973: *129*). This precept concerns thought in its capacity to be attentive to its beyond, something it can think only as unthought.

Intimacy never translates as entirely tangible. Luste Boulbina accordingly refers to an intimate dimension in relation to which historiography is often negligent. 'Historical facts register in the subject as an interior architecture. They do not spare the intimate sphere' (Luste Boulbina, 2019: 186/2015: 41). The unspared intimate sphere is neglected by historiography based on 'distance and nonintimacy' with whatever is studied. There is lacking the psychoanalytic awareness that subjects have affective 'phantoms', which are regularly disregarded in history and in turn by historiography (196/53). If history discounts these often barely discernible affects, there is a risk that historiography will do so too. Yet these affects not only accompany colonialism but can also resonate, with new permutations, in postcolonial contexts (Luste Boulbina, 2014: 147–8; see too 2019: 196/2015: 14).

Hence Luste Boulbina's call for 'one-on-one *intimacy* with others, with foreigners, with those who are absent'. This is intimacy 'that renders truth possible'. Such a stark claim is perhaps surprising. What constitutes this *truth*? 'This *principled* intimacy, or intimacy as/of *method*, is [. . .] opposed to every declared aristocracy of the spirit, for which there exist "small" peoples, "small" people and "great" men', or 'men' rather than 'women (who, as we know well, don't count)'. Historically, women have often *not* been treated as historical actors; historiography regularly repeats, rather than scrutinizes, this disregard. The truth of the method of intimacy is its concern with those who are anonymous by being ignored; the intimacy 'demands a break [*exige de rompre*] with *anonymity*' so that the previously silenced can be heard in some way. Any 'democratisation of political and social life' includes 'a profound change of perspectives on the events of the past'. '[A]ttention' is turned 'not just' to 'the "powerful" colonisers' but also to 'the "weak" colonised' – 'not just' to 'the "whites"' but to 'the "others"' (Luste Boulbina 2019: 71/2020: 109). The actors of history are not only the militarily, economically and sociopolitically powerful but are now also those dominated.

Decolonization changes the stories told; it changes how stories are told. That is its manifestation of philosophical health. Precisely those who formerly have been explicitly or implicitly excluded are in the foreground, even if they are deceased. The dead can be reconfigured so that history recalls rather than ignores them. This does nothing for the health of the dead, but it can do something for the health of their descendants. '[D]ecolonization implies the restoration of subjectivities negated in the colony and left on the sidelines by historiography' (Luste Boulbina, 2019: 203/2015: 61). The restoration does not make history entirely transparent (Luste Boulbina, 2020: 15) but is an opening to a temporality of the weak, a temporality that scholarly history might overlook: 'Scholarly history finds itself on the side of time and its linearity; it explains.' In contrast, psychoanalysis is 'translation' – an interactive, participatory, and 'interpretive' practice concerned with 'phantoms' that historiography overlooks (Luste Boulbina, 2019: 196–7/2015: 53–5). The phantoms of concern for Luste Boulbina belong to no victorious linear temporality. Regarding ignored affective phantoms, philosophical health is complemented by a psychoanalytically impelled study that provides attentive *translation*, cautious interpretation, of wayward, elusive and weak temporality. The latter temporality is practically lost to prevailing tendencies of history (or is only addressed with superficial comments about past or potential fundamentalism, criminality and terror).

The more translatory – philosophically healthy – approach includes literal translation, moreover, for various languages can be involved, and most problematic is the colonial language, which has meanings that might be especially inadequate for the experience of the colonized. 'Translation is doubly difficult because the colony is a multilingual space dominated by one language, a European language – it is the very language of domination' (199/57). Hence, the 'work of decolonization' includes liberation from 'European languages', either by 'abandoning' the European language or by 'reappropriating' it in the expressivity of someone who is profoundly estranged in the relevant language. Either way, there is movement, passage, 'translation', 'from one world to another' (199/57; see too Luste Boulbina, 2020: 18).

In the translatory interpretative practice more broadly conceived, the overlooked, the disregarded and the denigrated are no longer an amorphous agglomeration of those with whom any sort of close acquaintance is out of the question. The intimacy changes current conditions but also – and simultaneously – our regard on the past. Philosophical health provides a corrective to scholarly history and can involve psychoanalysis insofar as the latter is open to being revisited and discussed further.

Unhealthy silence, healthy silence and philosophy

Jacques Derrida cites Ernest Renan's observation that ancient languages designated foreign peoples with 'words that signify to "stammer", to "mumble", or words that signify "mute"'. Luste Boulbina considers this signification indicative of an imposed silence; the putatively foreign people were either not to speak or to speak only in terms circumscribed by those (or some of those) declared non-foreign. Yet she recognizes a liberatory sense of 'to stammer' or 'to stutter' (*bégayer*) (Luste Boulbina, 2019: 284/2015: 140; citing Derrida, 2016: 134/1967a: 180 citing Renan, 1958: 90). Philosophy liberates in not presuming complete adequacy to life conditions. It stutters. 'The exit from . . . imposed muteness is . . . a kind of stuttering – in other words, a way of talking, of writing, of expressing oneself but also of identifying what certain ears can hardly hear.' For some, it is unbearable to hear that a presumption to adequacy would be questioned. The latter questioning becomes, however, a kind of *expressing oneself*: 'the effective possibility of elaborating a thought for oneself, for one's own use'. Luste Boulbina does not wish to be 'normative' in relation to the subjugated (that would be 'nonsensical'); she is appealing rather to the painful need people might feel to go beyond what they are currently experiencing. 'It is not a prescription but a quest. Stuttering is thus like loving: a speech yearning to go beyond what exists.' One amplifies becoming a foreigner in the language one is using and thereby invents 'new forces' that cannot be entirely circumscribed. Elaborating decolonization as philosophy, Luste Boulbina notes, that Socrates was reproached for 'stuttering like a child'. He 'spoke not Athenian but the philosophical', for 'he questioned as much as – indeed more than – he affirmed'. Like Nietzsche, Deleuze affirms by stuttering. 'Deleuze . . . took up stuttering to make it the sign of a becoming, a becoming . . . foreigner' among other things. The stuttering is philosophical rebellion, Luste Boulbina suggests. She enlists this stuttering for decolonization. 'Today, I claim stuttering as the expression of decoloniality in action' (Luste Boulbina, 2019: 284/2015: *140*; citing Deleuze, 1997: 108, 112–13/1993: 136, 141–2).

This decoloniality enacts silence. The enactment is distinct from either imposing silence or submitting to such an imposition. Adapting Deleuze, Luste Boulbina regards the 'stuttering' as the enactment of '"a silence in words"' (Luste Boulbina, 2019: 285n3; citing Deleuze, 1997: 113/1993: 141). She suggests it is necessary to stutter silence so that the setting in which communication happens is not itself glorified. The notion of stuttering silence might, however, seem contradictory. Does silence not precede the sound of stuttering? The stuttering is simply to recall silence. The silence recalled is twofold: the silence forced upon one by the communicative setting, and yet also the silence that the setting has not captured and cannot capture. To recall both the forced silence and the ineradicable silence is a *sine qua non* of philosophical health, for to deny either silence would be to try denying the undeniable.

The inexhaustible silence is treated by Derrida as something that makes speech always derivative, impelled by something that it can never simply commandeer. In the '"speaking subject [it] is no longer ... the person alone who speaks"'. The '"speaking subject discovers"' an '"irreducible secondarity"', an '"origin that is always eluded"' (Luste Boulbina, 2019: 267n67/2015: 118; citing Derrida, 1978: 178/1967b: 265).

While acknowledging this always hidden origin, Luste Boulbina is especially interested in Derrida's suggestion that theft underlies discourse; speech is a thinly veiled theft of someone else's possibility to speak (Luste Boulbina, 2019: 256–7/2015: 118–19; citing Derrida, 1981: 175/1972: 261–2). Theft is inherent in language usage; someone is always robbed of relevance. Luste Boulbina does not deny that this theft is pervasive, and she does not deny that capitalism is a system with omnipresent robbery of relevance. Her focus is, however, on conditions that would specifically cultivate philosophical health among colonized and their descendants. She considers this a neglected focus, and accordingly cites Edward Said's remarks on the way "'universalising discourses'" in the European and Anglo-American world "'assume'" the willing or unwilling "'silence . . . of the non-European world'". There "'is only infrequently an acknowledgement that the colonised people should be heard from, their ideas known'" (Luste Boulbina, 2019: 269–70/2015: 126; citing Said, 1994: 50).

Alia Al-Saji notes that colonialism is not just economically impelled but also 'cultural and representational'. Even if economic factors are decisive, the cultural or representational aspect acquires a tenacity that makes it possible to refer to people being racist beyond economic interests (Al-Saji, 2010: *passim*, see specifically 898n53; citing Said, 1979: 156). Marxist societal analysis could explore more the tenaciously racist elements of colonialism (Fanon, 2004: 5/1991: 70; Luste Boulbina, 2020: 29). Yet economic interests can, of course, be significant. In light of French economic (and political) interests, Alexis de Tocqueville, as described by Luste Boulbina, was '[s]ensitive' to some, such as the indigenous population in the United States (a context in which French economic [and political] interests were comparatively small), but 'indifferent' to other colonized peoples, especially Arabs (Luste Boulbina, 2019: 112/2020: 160; see Tocqueville, 2003 and 2008). There is a thread from Tocqueville to Pierre Mendès France and other French politicians who, near the end of much French colonialism, enacted a common 'French wish to engage in' a so-called 'dialogue' during which the French did not have to listen (Luste Boulbina, 2019: 141/2020: 198). If more respectful dialogue is important for philosophical health (de Miranda in this volume), this history of pseudo-conversation would need to be acknowledged so that more credible conversation can begin.

In the context of philosophical health, Luste Boulbina notes that Fanon is important for 'postcolonial studies' by virtue of wishing 'not to write in place of' anyone. Fanon's texts do not presume a retrospective objectivity; they are above all addressed to the colonized and their descendants, whereby instead of trying 'to *restitute* that absent speech', Fanon 'strives to *institute* it'. This distinguishes practices of 'psychiatry, or even more markedly psychoanalysis', from 'the practices of historiography' (Luste Boulbina, 2019: 256/2015: 117–18). Discussing work by Gayatri Chakravorty Spivak, Luste Boulbina warns about the tendency of even ostensibly well-meaning people to have presumed to 'speak for' 'the subaltern' (250/110; citing Spivak, 2010: 257).

It might be thought that Luste Boulbina herself has this presumption to speak for others. One can never be sure of oneself in this regard; expressly benign attention can all too easily lapse into aggression. Without a correlative self-questioning on the part of someone offering help, the offer will not be philosophy but another manipulation. Luste Boulbina suggests that philosophical health could converge, nonetheless, with a psychoanalytic practice concerned, for instance, about women's relative speechlessness in a colonial or postcolonial context. '[T]he central question becomes one of theft – stolen history, hidden speech. Gender, one might say, happens on the quiet [*sans publicité*]' (Luste Boulbina, 2019: 256/2015: 118). Luste Boulbina shares Fanon's interest in speech or writing that can initiate expression by acknowledging the past was stolen: there was an intrusion that in many ways suppressed discontent. To counter, the silenced stutter philosophically, and thereby they convey an intimacy that diverges from 'history'. The stuttering involves imaginatively insubordinate enactments of both stolen speech and the aforementioned preponderant silence or mystery that domination, despite pretences, never eradicates.

Literature and philosophical health

Literature is an important medium in which to respond to the relevant 'mute' subaltern condition (Luste Boulbina, 2020: 250/2015: 110). Indeed, literature enacts the twofold silence: the silence of suppressed expression and the silence, the mystery, that is an ineradicable basis for questioning presumptions to all-encompassing adequacy. Even if social media make almost everyone seem potential writers about their situation, this does not assure attentive regard for anyone's life conditions. Lives and words continue to be bypassed in neglect if not contempt.

Literature is inextricable from questions of philosophical health, for literature, like psychoanalysis, can take language into the intimacy in which denigration is both acknowledged and explored. With an *intimate* intertwining of perception and word, literature can accentuate the silence, the mystery, that is robbed by imposing a submissive silence. Without denying the fundamental silence that can never be extinguished, literature traces with relative freedom ways in which someone or a people is effectively deprived of the opportunity to speak. Because care requires acknowledgement both of the latter theft and of the inextinguishable silence, philosophy without literature would care less and would be less healthy. In the liberty to provide these two acknowledgements, literature is philosophically healthy.

In this philosophical healthiness, literature converges with some notion of the psychoanalytic 'unconscious', at least insofar as both literature and the unconscious require not hypostatization but creativity and inventiveness. Precisely that need for creativity and inventiveness enables literature to contribute to philosophical health. 'The unconscious is not found among the data of scholarly history. It is an elementary given of consciousness and the core of literature. Like psychoanalysis, literature has no "proper" or "natural" place' (Luste Boulbina, 2019: 201/2015: 59). In this relative independence from propriety and presumed naturalization, literature allies with psychoanalytic health and correlatively with philosophical health. Luste Boulbina thinks psychoanalysis is healthy insofar it unites with philosophical questioning of the fates that befall people, including the colonized and their descendants. Literature can help in inventing scenarios in which philosophical questioning – philosophical rebellion – is somehow enacted.

Deleuze accordingly affirms 'literature as a kind of health'. This can be health for a people hypostatized by oppressive forces. 'Health as literature . . . consists in inventing a people that is missing. It is the task of the fabulating function to invent a people. . . . The ultimate aim of literature is to set free [*dégager*] . . . this creation of a health or this invention of a people, that is, a possibility of life.' Literature aims '[t]o write for this people that is missing', whereby '"for" means less "in place of" than "for the benefit of"' (Deleuze, 1997: 4/1993: *14–15*). Luste Boulbina shares Deleuze's notion of literature as health that draws on the fabulating function to invent a people as a possibility in life, as opposed to the annulled possibility this people might be up to now. It is not that an author is healthy and thereby cultivates health in others. The medium of literature simply opens what Deleuze calls '"a possibility of life"' (see Başaran, Chapter 13 in the present anthology), which might help a people to imagine itself otherwise, to '"invent"' itself in a way enabling it to create the aforementioned '"kind of health"' (Luste Boulbina, 2019: 226/2015: 85; citing Deleuze, 1997: 4/1993: 14–15). People can care for themselves in ways making them aware – if they were not aware already – that convalescence was unduly made to seem impossible. In interaction with literature, or indeed with other arts (Luste Boulbina, 2014: 149–50, 159), philosophy can be a forum in which insubordinate possibilities of care are articulated: 'les arts aident à penser' (Luste Boulbina, 2020: 11). With the priority of questioning constraints otherwise presented as necessary, philosophical health could find literature very important – not least in a context of decolonization.

The relevant literary inventing might induce people to think themselves at least a little beyond the pathology that is an insistent, if not belligerent, presumption about what is possible or necessary. With such pathology the colonial and the postcolonial *function*. It 'is because of his interest in mental pathology that he [Fanon] takes an interest in racism and the colony, for they are part of it' (Luste Boulbina, 2019: 171/2015: 27). In Luste Boulbina's extrapolation, 'decolonization is also a matter of public health'. This was overlooked: 'mental health was far and away what was most neglected' at the 'dawn of independence' (Luste Boulbina, 2019: 206/2015: *65*). As philosophical health, decolonization translates some alleged necessities as pathologically imposed conditions. 'For decolonisation to succeed, one must . . . explore the interior architecture of subjects who found their existence, or that of their parents and grandparents, arbitrarily suspended by a foreign power.' Life preceding colonization might not have been idyllic, although it sometimes involved now neglected democratic practices (Luste Boulbina, 2014: 154). Colonization and its postcolonial reverberations constitute, however, an invasion from which the descendants of the colonized are often still reeling. Not ultimately or solely a matter of blaming individual colonizers and their contemporary ideological advocates, Luste Boulbina's foremost concern is the philosophical capacity to question denigrations and constraints. In the descendants' 'inner architecture', '[w]e will . . . discover postcolonial pathologies just as Fanon revealed colonial pathologies' (Luste Boulbina, 2019: 206/2015: 65).

Philosophy responsive to literature can be a forum in which inventively insubordinate possibilities of care are articulated, however provisionally. In this collaboration with literature, an ensuing dynamism of philosophy prevents any one interpretation or agglomeration of interpretations from dominating. Luste Boulbina draws on Derrida's notion of *pharmakon* to discuss how interpretation can waver between remedy and poison. With this sensitivity, there emerges an interpretative caution that Luste Boulbina characterizes as philosophically healthy (Luste Boulbina, 2019: 296/2018: 23; see Derrida, 1981: 61–171/1972: 77–213).

She argues specifically for such philosophical health in a colonial and postcolonial context, something that is not always easy given the contentions among politicians and in popular 'philosophical' writings, such as those of Pascal Bruckner, that 'the French are becoming colonised in their home country' (Bruckner, 2018, 127/2017: 184). These hyperbolic polemics might indicate little interest in a central question of philosophical health: justice.

Justice, philosophical health and literary anonymity: you, I and the third person

Justice is characterized by interpretative caution, for life exceeds what any voice can credibly say about it. Life exceeds our awareness of it. Roberto Esposito cites in this regard Maurice Blanchot's remarks on the inherent cloaking of the voice 'by the anonymous murmur of events'. This anonymous murmur entails 'the relation of self-non-identification', whereby the 'task of philosophy' becomes 'not to think the neutral . . . but rather to think *in* the neutral . . . outside' any dichotomy of subject and object (Esposito, 2012: 131; see Blanchot, 1993: 384/1969: 576). Luste Boulbina would obviously agree with Esposito's expressly Deleuzian view that '"[t]he subject's always something derivative"' (Esposito 2012: 134; citing Deleuze 1995: 108/1990, 2003: 146). Specifically philosophical health requires there be justice to our derivation from that of which we can never be entirely conscious. If we denied this derivation, we would be living rabid delusion, something other than philosophical health. In this sense, Luste Boulbina says justice derives from truth that is not exclusively a victory of the conscious over the unconscious (Luste Boulbina, 2020: 24).

Luste Boulbina regards the first-person account, however, as a potential remedy to the silent subservience to which colonized and their descendants are often consigned. For her, the first-person account is at least a prospective catalyst of philosophical health. Without first-person impetus, I live the life that others – ideologically, so to speak – have determined for me.

In contrast, Esposito claims that the anonymity making the subject derivative also makes the *third-person* pronoun a significant liberation from I-you exclusivity or chauvinism. In other words, philosophical honesty – a *sine qua non* of justice and its philosophical health – entails acknowledgement that the life remaining inexpressible for all eludes first-person accounts as well as first- and second-person dialogues. The third person is eminently suitable for keeping us honest about the anonymity that no one person, and no agglomeration of persons, contains or commandeers.

Drawing on Foucault's *The Archaeology of Knowledge*, Esposito claims that any 'statement is rooted in the anonymous being of language before any I begins to speak'. As Esposito notes, Foucault is not without regard for the subject, or for 'a subjective role in each statement or series of statements' (Esposito, 134). This regard for the subject evidently contributes to Foucault's influence on Luste Boulbina's notion of self-care. Esposito focuses above all, however, on language as 'a mode that is irreducible to the first or second person and congruent only with the impersonality of the third' (Esposito, 2012: 134–5).

Esposito notes that Blanchot especially pays attention to how 'literature opens up a field of intensity in which the subject is sucked into the statement and, thus, catapulted into its own outside' (Esposito, 2012: 135). None of this seems to be rejected by Luste Boulbina, but she expressly seeks a break with anonymity so that descendants of the colonized are not just talked about but are also interpreting and translating themselves and their history in a less stymied – more first person – way than is usually possible. Luste Boulbina is obviously not invoking an illusion of self-possession through communication, and there is no indication that by giving priority to first-person accounts, she is endorsing the vapid narcissism currently flourishing (not least through digital media).

Yet it is telling that Esposito does not share Luste Boulbina's association of literature and a philosophically impelled psychoanalysis: 'In contrast to the psychoanalytic tendency of defining the indeterminate through the use of the personal or the possessive, literature runs in the opposite direction, going back to the indeterminate source.' As Esposito observes, Deleuze effects a release from psychoanalysis and its first and second-person exchanges. Quite near the very passages cited earlier by Luste Boulbina, Deleuze says: 'literature . . . exists only when it discovers beneath apparent persons the power of an impersonal'. Our most ineradicable self is participation in the impersonal, for which our pronominal self is always an inadequate abstraction. The impersonal 'is not a generality' but rather the most intimate self: 'a singularity at the highest point'. Literature brings us back to this *intimately felt* anonymous impersonal. 'It is not the first two persons that function as the condition for literary enunciation; literature begins only when a third person is born in us that strips us of the power to say "I" (Blanchot's "neuter")' (Deleuze, 1997: 3/1993: 13; cited in Esposito, 2012: 145).

This emphasis contrasts with Luste Boulbina's aforementioned invocation of linguist Benveniste to argue that 'the first person designates the one who speaks' and 'the second refers to the one being addressed', whereas '[t]he third person, in fact, is not a person' and 'designates the one spoken about, the one who is, in interlocution, absent' (Luste Boulbina, 2019: 60n90/2020: 74n73; see too 96n71 and n72/130n64 and n65; also: Benveniste, 1971: 195–204, 217–36/1966: 225–36, 251–76). Hence Luste Boulbina's conclusion noted earlier: 'The third person is tacitly a subaltern' (Luste Boulbina, 2019: 87/2020: 131). She cites Martin Buber's remark that '[t]he I-thou relationship . . . is rooted in dialogue', while 'the I-it [*je-cela*, in German *Ich-Es*] relationship is anchored in monologue' (Luste Boulbina, 2019: 60n90; see too Luste Boulbina, 2020: 212–13; also: Buber, 1970: 54/1983: 10). For Luste Boulbina, philosophically impelled I-you dialogue is integral to well-being.

Esposito obviously does not consider literature to be an I-it monologue. He simply claims part of the health borne by literature is that in it all and everything are reversed into an outside in which pronominal bearings are lost; the third-person pronoun can most effectively convey this. Esposito extrapolates: 'the countering force of literary writing lies in its reversal of a [you-I] rule – the one established by Benveniste – that applies to all other types of interlocution.' Even if 'I' and 'you' are used, literature transforms these into the unfamiliar but intimately felt experience that usage of the third person might accentuate. This makes literature philosophically healthy; we are more honest with ourselves, and thus healthier philosophically, when we acknowledge within us the non-pronominal self for which the third person can be a marker. In this exercise, moreover, literature might reach those *repelled* by the pronominal organization of reality. Literature 'speaks in the third person' and is thereby 'addressed to no one, except perhaps to those who place themselves on the outer confines of language' (Esposito, 2012: 146). If Deleuze and Esposito consider part of the healthiness of literature to be that it opens to those on the fringes of language, this actually converges with Luste Boulbina's adaptation of Deleuze's emphasis on literature as always contesting, insubordinate and intimately alien. Deleuze and Esposito, nonetheless, associate the health of literature with liberation from the I-you dynamic, whereas Luste Boulbina regards this dynamic as crucial to any philosophical health that literature might induce.

At stake are two very different notions of the relationship of philosophical health with justice. In wariness of Buber's notion of 'the relation between I and you', Esposito turns to Emmanuel Levinas's emphasis on 'asymmetry' that 'removes the *you* from the logical and syntactical rules of normal linguistic communication' (Esposito, 2012: 121). There is instead 'illeity', which is 'the non-originary origin toward which both [the I and the you] extend without ever being able to reach it' (122). The other becomes not the familiar I or you but an oblique 'third term' within each of these (121), so much so that *justice* 'is not only the precisely directed intention' binding 'the *I* to the unicity of the *you*' but 'also a broader relationship, which concerns others as well: not just the other or the Other, but the other of the other, and the other of *each* other' (122). Levinas refers to '"responsibility"' that is '"troubled and becomes a problem"' as '"a third party enters"' (122; citing Levinas, 1980: 157/2000: 245). This troubling third party is in each of us as that which suspends I-you exclusivity and predominance (see de Miranda in this volume). For Esposito, justice is enacted in the philosophical health of literature: the health of going beyond I-you exclusivity and predominance.

Moving from Levinas and more towards Deleuze, Esposito underscores that literature is philosophically healthy in turning the you or the I inside out and into an oblique third party. 'Deleuze seems to open a polemical front against the theory of Benveniste . . . on the enunciative incapacity of the third person.' Literature is 'outside of, and against, the laws of linguistics', ready to become 'asyntactic', even 'agrammatical'. In its 'countering force', literary writing overturns Benveniste's rule – the rule pertinent to other sorts of linguistic interchange. In the third person, literature 'utters . . . nothingness', the nothingness resonating with those particularly estranged in language, who are acutely (or at least extremely) out in the nothing. Literature is the balm of philosophical health for those who might otherwise simply be alone in their estrangement. 'This movement of exteriorisation, or estrangement, is the salient character of true literature' (Esposito, 2012: 146).

Esposito does come close to some of what Luste Boulbina says on behalf of translatory health in postcolonial literature. This capacity of literature to translate estrangement constitutes an important aspect of its philosophical health; it encourages people to recognize that their lot in life is no necessary fate. Esposito refers to literature that can make a language become 'foreign' to itself, including in a salutary opening by another language (Esposito, 2012: 146). Such extrapolations of Deleuze's view of literature accord with Luste Boulbina's view of decolonization as philosophically healthy in provisional and relatively unencumbered translation between experiential worlds.

Yet there remains her insistence on the importance of the first person and her devaluation of the third person. She occasionally seems to imply the oft-expressed view that white men are sometimes eager to dissolve the first person just when women and other disadvantaged are starting to use the first person in ways thus far scarcely known or largely disallowed (Luste Boulbina, 2019: 74, 71/2020: 113–14, 109). In a broader context, Bruckner bitterly refers to the white man as 'un coupable presque parfait' (Bruckner, 2020). Blaming white men is not, however, Luste Boulbina's principal preoccupation. She is writing, above all, to encourage the colonized and the descendants of the colonized to exercise philosophical health – the healthiness of not letting living conditions seem an inescapable fate.

The colonized and the descendants of the colonized are emboldened by Luste Boulbina to use the first person to present their unease, their foreignness, in a healing that searches history philosophically – in an always provisional relationship with any instantiation. Luste Boulbina highlights how health in the colonized and in descendants of the colonized requires that they are not simply talked about anonymously but can speak philosophically without the inconspicuous submissiveness often expected in settings in which their cultural background is almost automatically perceived as unwelcome if not threatening.

If the justice of this philosophical health is not, however, to convert into mere narcissistic projection through first-person accounts, it is probably convalescent that Esposito and Deleuze highlight those aspects of literature that wrench the 'I' out of complacency and self-satisfaction. Personal and societal health will depend on the philosophical health that does not deny the intimately felt anonymous, non-pronominal impersonal. The latter eludes any I-you chauvinism or exclusivity, and the narcissism in which the 'I' is a self-absorbed projection.

References

Al-Saji, Alia (2010), 'The Racialization of Muslim Veils: A Philosophical Analysis'. *Philosophy and Social Criticism*, 36 (8): 875–902.

Benveniste, Émile (1971), *Problems of General Linguistics*, trans. Mary Elizabeth Meek. Coral Gables: University of Miami Press.

Benveniste, Émile (1966), *Problèmes de linguistique générale*, vol. 1. Paris: Gallimard.

Blanchot, Maurice (1993), *The Infinite Conversation*. Minneapolis: University of Minnesota Press/1969. *L'Entretien infini*. Paris: Gallimard.

Bruckner, Pascal (2018), *An Imaginary Racism. Islamophobia and Guilt*. Cambridge: Polity/2017. *Un racisme imaginaire. Islamophobie et culpabilité*. Paris: Grasset.

Bruckner, Pascal (2020), *Un coupable presque parfait: La construction du bouc-émissaire blanc*. Paris: Grasset.

Buber, Martin (1970), *I and Thou*, trans. Walter Kaufmann. New York: Simon and Schuster/1983: *Ich und Du*. Heidelberg: Verlag Lambert Schneider.

Butler, Judith (2005), *Giving an Account of Oneself*. New York: Fordham University Press.

Certeau, Michel de (1973), *L'absent de l'histoire*. Tours: Maison Mame.

Certeau, Michel de (1986), *Heterologies. Discourse on the Other*, trans. Brian Massumi. Minneapolis: University of Minnesota Press.

Deleuze, Gilles (1997), *Essays Critical and Clinical*, trans. Daniel W. Smith and Michael A. Greco. Minneapolis: University of Minnesota Press/1993. *Critique et Clinique*. Paris: Les Éditions de Minuit.

Deleuze, Gilles (1995), *Negotiations*, trans. Martin Joughin. New York: Columbia University Press/1990, 2003. *Pourparlers: 1972–1990*. Paris: Les Éditions de Minuit.

Derrida, Jacques (1981), *Dissemination*, trans. Barbara Johnson. Chicago: University of Chicago Press/1972. *La dissémination*. Paris: Éditions du Seuil.

Derrida, Jacques (2016), *Of Grammatology*, trans. Gayatri Chakravorty Spivak. Baltimore: Johns Hopkins University Press/1967a. *De la Grammatologie*. Paris: Les Éditions de Minuit.

Derrida, Jacques (1978), *Writing and Difference*. trans. Alan Bass. Chicago: University of Chicago Press/1967b. *L'écriture et la différence*. Paris: Éditions du Seuil.

Esposito, Roberto (2012), *Third Person*. Cambridge: Polity Press.

Fanon, Frantz (2008), *Black Skins, White Masks*, trans. Richard Philcox. New York: Grove Press/1952. *Peau noire, masques blancs*. Paris: Éditions du Seuil.

Fanon, Frantz (2004), *The Wretched of the Earth*, trans. Richard Philcox. New York: Grove Press/1991. *Les damnés de la terre*. Paris: Éditions Gallimard.

Foucault, Michel (1972), *The Archaeology of Knowledge*, trans. A. M. Sheridan Smith. New York: Harper & Row, Publishers/1969. *L'Archéologie du Savoir*. Paris: Éditions Gallimard.

Hadot, Pierre (2001), *La philosophie comme manière de vivre*. Interviews with Jeannie Carlier and Arnold I. Davidson. Paris: Albin Michel.

Levinas, Emmanuel (1980), *Otherwise than Being, or Beyond Essence*, trans. Alphonso Lingis. Pittsburgh: Duquesne University Press/2000. *Autrement qu'être ou au-delà de l'essence*. Paris: Le livre de poche.

Luste Boulbina, Seloua (2015), *L'Afrique et ses fantômes. Écrire l'après*. Paris: Présence Africaine Éditions.

Luste Boulbina, Seloua (2014), 'Les Arabes peuvent-ils parler?' In Edward W. Said. *Dans l'ombre de l'Occident*, trans. Léa Gauthier, 87–203. Paris: Éditions Payot & Rivages.

Luste Boulbina, Seloua (2019), *Kafka's Monkey and Other Phantoms of Africa*, trans. Laura E. Hengehold. Foreword by Achille Mbembe. Bloomington: Indiana University Press.

Luste Boulbina, Seloua (2018), *Les miroirs vagabonds ou la décolonisation des savoirs (arts, littérature, philosophie)*. Dijon: Les presses du réel.

Luste Boulbina, Seloua (2020), *Le Singe de Kafka et autres propos sur la colonie*. With a new chapter, 2nd edn. Dijon: Les presses du réel.

de Miranda, Luis (2022), 'Philosophical Health'. In Vlad Petré Glăveanu (ed.), *The Palgrave Encyclopedia of the Possible*. Cham: Palgrave Macmillan.

de Miranda, Luis (2021), 'Five Principles of Philosophical Health for Critical Times: From Hadot to Crealectics'. *Eidos. A Journal for Philosophy of Culture*, 5 (1): 70–89.

Ndaw, Alassane with Ramatoulaye Diagne-Mbengue (2016), 'Nul n'a le monopole de la philosophie'. In Luste Boulbina (ed.), *Dix penseurs africains par eux-mêmes*, 109–11: 110.

Onishi, Norimitsu (2021), 'Will American Ideas Tear France Apart? Some of its Leaders Think So'. *New York Times*, 11 October 2021. https://www.nytimes.com/2021/02/09/world/europe/france-threat-american-universities.html

Renan, Ernest (1958), *De l'origine du langue, Œuvres complètes*, vol. VIII, ed. Henriette Psichari. Paris: Calmann-Lévy.

Ricœur, Paul (1965), *History and Truth*, trans. Charles A. Kelbley. Evanston: Northwestern University Press/1967. *Histoire et vérité*. Paris: Éditions du Seuil.

Said, Edward W. (1994), *Culture and Imperialism*. New York: Vintage.

Said, Edward W. (1979), *Orientalism*. New York: Vintage.

Spivak, Gayatri Chakravorty (2010), 'Can the Subaltern Speak?' (1997). In Rosalind C. Morris (ed.), *Can the Subaltern Speak? Reflections on the History of an Idea*, 237–91. New York: Columbia University Press.

Tocqueville, Alexis de (2003), *Sur l'Algérie*, ed. Seloua Luste Boulbina. Paris: Éditions Flammarion.

Tocqueville, Alexis de (2008), *Sur l'esclavage*, ed. Seloua Luste Boulbina. Arles: Actes Sud.

15

Philosophical health in entangled cosmopolitan posthumanism

Jacob Vangeest

Introduction: Considering an entangled cosmos

What grounds obligation towards beings (both human and more than human), which are external to the 'self'? Scholars in the field of 'critical posthumanism' have offered a theory of 'entanglement' as the basis of this obligation. Entanglement, developed in Karen Barad's *Meeting the Universe Halfway*, offers a critique of more individualistic ontologies by insisting that 'Individuals do not preexist their interactions; rather individuals emerge through and as part of their entangled intra-relating' (Barad, 2007: IX). Entanglement does not describe separate entities as intertwined but instead posits a togetherness both primordial to individuals and from which individuals emerge. This process is recursive: emerging individuals are reflexively re-integrated in the entanglement. As such, prescribing a general form of entanglement is difficult: entanglement is specific to the configurations and apparatuses that they constitute (and are, recursively, constituted by). A general category of entanglement can only be minimal and abstract; it cannot determine the content of any particular entanglement.

I take the general category of entanglement to be the basis of a 'cosmopolitan posthumanism'. This concept, developed in the work of Rosi Braidotti, suggests that contemporary cosmopolitan perspectives need to account for 'the immanence of structural relationality so as to account also for the atrocities and structural injustice, as well as for the many benefits, of pan-human perspectives today' (Braidotti, 2013a: 9). Cosmopolitan posthumanism builds from Jill Didur's (2003) 'critical posthumanism': a concept that serves to problematize assumed divisions between the human and non-human (or more than human). Entanglement, as a relational ontology that poses itself as prior to individuation, refuses these divisions. Critical posthumanism does not necessarily think what comes after the human but instead poses the re-articulation of the human as entangled being with obligations towards that which is beyond itself (inclusive of other humans and the more than human). Through the concept of cosmopolitan posthumanism, Braidotti appeals to a global *ethos* inclusive of the plurality of beings that consist in a 'pan-humanity'. To offer an initial definition on the basis of this scholarship, cosmopolitan posthumanism can be taken as extending entanglement to a planetary dimension. As some scholars have suggested, cosmopolitan posthumanism 'can radically expand cosmopolitanism to include *all life*' (Narayanan and Bindumadhay, 2019: 408). Given the realities of anthropogenic climate change, the realities of entanglement should be taken as apparent: the actions of one impact all.

This chapter explores possible coherence between this entangled cosmos and what Luis de Miranda has termed 'philosophical health'. Curiously drawing from both Aristotle and the philosophies of becoming, de Miranda has posed a notion of 'crealectic philosophical health', defined as 'a program of harmonization of our collective capacity to feel, imagine, envision, realize, and co-actualize a world emerging from the cosmological source of the real as a metaphysical and practical "possibility of possibility"' (de Miranda, 2022: 4). Philosophical health brings together *eudaimonia* (flourishing) with *dynamis* (potency) to think flourishing as recursive and dynamic. By drawing upon a notion of entanglement as the basis of a cosmopolitan posthumanism, *dynamis* is tied to all beings in the planetary dimension. The philosophical health of any individual is necessarily bound to its entanglement: 'I' am obligated towards my entanglement insofar as my flourishing is bound to it.

Bringing together these three central concepts – entanglement, cosmopolitan posthumanism and philosophical health – this chapter offers two contributions: it outlines a theory of cosmopolitan posthumanism grounded in an entangled theory of obligation, while also bringing this concept of obligation into the realm of philosophical health. The chapter is composed of three sections and a conclusion. The first two sections develop a theory of cosmopolitan posthumanism: the first by taking up Kantian cosmopolitanism from the perspective of Aristotelian wisdom, and the second providing a critique of the top-down universalism found in the Kantian project. The third chapter then moves to think through the ramifications of entangled obligations as they intersect with de Miranda's concept of philosophical health. The concluding section provides a short discussion of possible shortfalls of these conceptions and possible avenues for future scholarship.

From Aristotle to Kant: Extending *eudynamia*

Luis de Miranda defines 'Philosophical health [as] a state of fruitful coherence between a person's ways of thinking and speaking and their ways of acting, such that the possibilities for a sublime life are increased and the need for self- and intersubjective flourishing satisfied' (de Miranda, 2022: 1). He ties philosophical health to Aristotelian *eudaimonia* (flourishing) in the *Nichomachean Ethics*. In building a theory of philosophical health, de Miranda aligns *eudaimonia* with Aristotelian *dynamis* (potency) to think flourishing and possibility together as '*eudynamia*'. Flourishing depends on the possibilities for flourishing in a dynamic and recursive engagement.

To think this relation politically, one might turn to Book VI of Aristotle's text. Here, Aristotle emphasizes what he terms practical wisdom and political wisdom. The former is contrasted to scientific knowledge: where science is invested in the universal, practical wisdom is concerned with human things. Practical wisdom is a judgement concerned with what is to be done. As such, practical wisdom is dynamic where science is static: practical wisdom is concerned with lived possibility. From this, political wisdom is adopted as a special form of practical wisdom: it is the universalizing of practical wisdom in the city (see Aristotle, 2001: 1140a24–1142a30). The aim of political wisdom aims beyond the flourishing of the individual to consider the flourishing of the totality of the city state. Political wisdom recognizes that *eudaimonia* in the individual is related to the *eudaimonia* of those surrounding them. Likewise, de Miranda's *eudynamia*, insofar as it produces regenerative possibilities for philosophical health, cannot be individual but demands communal coherence.

Where Aristotle's understanding of government was confined to *eudaimonia* in the city state, the contemporary global world requires a more robust cosmopolitan formulation (such a position was already recognized among Aristotle's contemporaries, and the origins of cosmopolitanism come from the Greek Cynics and Stoics). The realities of what has been called the 'Anthropocene' or 'Capitalocene' (Malm and Hornborg, 2014; Moore, 2017) reveal that the actions of one nation state impact all others. We are global whether we like it or not. Hence, where political wisdom is understood as the universalizing of practical wisdom in the city for the benefit of all citizens, the aim of cosmopolitanism is to institute a universal political framework on the international system for the benefit of all citizens of the world (*kosmopolitēs*). One cannot, however, ignore the tensions between Aristotle's *eudaemonic* value of justice and considerations of cosmopolitanism that appeals to utilitarian rights (Riesbeck, 2016: 86). As David J. Riesbeck notes, Martha Nussbaum's critique of Cicero's separation of duties of aid from duties of justice poses similar problems for any cosmopolitanism based in Aristotle (Riesbeck, 2016; see also Nussbaum, 2000). Nevertheless, while it may be possible to defend a cosmopolitanism using Aristotle's *eudaimonia* (as, for example, in Brink, 2018), any coherence between cosmopolitanism and *eudaimonia* is superfluous to the scope of this chapter. It is enough to suggest that whereas for Aristotle flourishing could only be attained for political cooperation in the city state, the possibility of flourishing in the contemporary world requires a political wisdom extended globally.

Both Aristotle and Kant appeal to a connection between the ethical and the political. For cosmopolitanism, this connection is expressed through the logic of 'rights': within contemporary renderings of cosmopolitanism, human rights take precedence over national sovereignty (Taraborrelli, 2015: xiii). The concept of right is outlined in Immanuel Kant's foundational essay 'Perpetual Peace: A Philosophical Sketch'. Kant's second article considers three notions of right: the right of citizens within a republic, the rights of nations within a federation of free states and the notion of cosmopolitan right as a necessary condition of a universal hospitality. According to Kant, the basis for cosmopolitanism emerges from a republican, social contract (Kant, 2018 [1795]: 99). It is only from a republican constitution that a state can develop a proper 'concept of right'. Despite this origin, Kant argues that right must take precedence over politics: 'the right of man must be held sacred, however great a sacrifice the ruling power may have to make… *politics must bend the knee before right*' (Kant, 2018 [1795]: 125, emphasis mine). Within Kant's cosmopolitanism, a moralistic and universal right takes precedence over the political desires of the state. In contemporary scholarship, this moral emphasis forms the basis of what has been called 'moral cosmopolitanism' (Taraborelli, 2015). One key reading of this extension of Kant's moralism comes from Thomas Pogge, who argues 'that every human being has a global stature as the ultimate unit of moral concern' (Pogge, 2002: 169). Moral cosmopolitanism emphasizes the universal and global implications of cosmopolitanism as both individualistic and inclusive (Beitz, 2004). Otherwise said, moral cosmopolitanism holds that every human being, as a human being, has a moral standing that serves as the conditions for a universal (and thus global) concept of human rights. A forceful voice in this domain, Martha Nussbaum can be taken as a key example. Nussbaum critiques a notion of liberalism and patriotism, arguing that it is unacceptable for nationality to be a barrier to equality. For Nussbaum, any political form with a commitment to equality must necessarily adopt a notion of cosmopolitan right (Scheffler, 2001: 118). She names this a commitment to humanity: 'To count people as moral equals is to treat nationality, ethnicity, religion, class, race, and gender as "morally irrelevant" – as irrelevant to that equal standing' (Nussbaum, 2002: 133).

Nussbaum's statement attests to a universalism inherent in moral cosmopolitan inclusivity: a universalism that has been critiqued in decolonial and postcolonial literature. For instance, Walter Mignolo denounces universal cosmopolitanism as an outcrop of Western scholarship resting on Kant's colonial race distribution (Mignolo, 2011: 163). A modern project, cosmopolitanism was 'first colonial and then postcolonial' (Taraborrelli, 2015: 111), often failing to account for or ignoring the history of imperialism and colonization (see Pollock et al., 2002). The reduction to equal standing in Nussbaum's statement repeats the universalizing tendencies of capitalism and colonialism given that a universal condition is imposed top-down. In response, some have posed a 'critical and dialogic cosmopolitanism' stressing diversity itself as a universal project (Pollock et al., 2002: 13). This is framed as a counter to globalization from localities: bottom-up rather than top-down (Mignolo, 2002). These 'critical cosmopolitanisms' are an attempt to build cosmopolitanism, paradoxically, through difference, alterity and exteriority rather than adopting an imposed universal and abstracted sameness (see Bhabha, 2015: 137). Critiques of cosmopolitan universalism are integral to building a cosmopolitan posthumanism. For instance, Isabelle Stengers's *Cosmopolitics* – which is central to the following discussion of obligation – takes a healthy distance from Kant: 'we need to start not like Kant from promises the West might flatter itself in propagating, but from the price others have paid for this self-definition' (Stengers, 2010: 79). Stengers takes a distance from Kant's imposed universality, including the cosmopolitan emphasis on universally imposed human rights. Similarly, Rosi Braidotti attempts to locate a coherence between the concept of cosmopolitan posthumanism and the postcolonial racial analyses of Frantz Fanon, Aimé Cesaire and Edward Said. She uses this coherence to undermine Western universalism in favour of a ground-up model. For the purposes of this chapter, Braidotti's cosmopolitan posthumanism can be taken as 'a situated cosmopolitan posthumanism' (Braidotti, 2013b: 46): a cosmopolitan posthumanism beginning from the critique at hand. This is taken up in the following section by developing a theory of entangled obligation that pushes back against a top-down consideration of abstracted rights.

Entangled foundations of obligation

Building from this decolonial and postcolonial critique, my meagre contribution is to suggest a foundation of cosmopolitan posthumanism in a notion of 'obligation' rather than in right. This entangled obligation serves as a condition for *eudaimonia* – even *eudynamia* – in the contemporary situation. Braidotti's invitation for a cosmopolitan posthumanism uses the work of Seyla Benhabib as a possible model. Benhabib stresses the inside-out logic of liberal democracy through the case of the migrant and the refugee: any person who finds themselves within a state where they are not a citizen. To examine this, she focuses on Kant's writings on hospitality and cosmopolitan right. Hospitality regards 'the right of a stranger not to be treated hostilely when he arrives on someone else's territory' (Kant, 2018 [1795]: 105). Benhabib uses this offering of cosmopolitan right to suggest that rights should be extended beyond a state's citizenry to refugees and migrants who enter a territory (Benhabib, 2006: 46). In this work, Benhabib uncovers a tension between sovereignty and the hospitality of cosmopolitan right that must be addressed through an iterative democratic process. She argues that such a process is necessary in the case of refugees. In doing so, Benhabib stresses that 'the originality of Kant's "Perpetual Peace" essay derives not only from his doctrine of hospitality, but also from the cumulative normative import of all three definitive articles of perpetual peace read together' (Benhabib, 2006: 148). While it is the case that Benhabib calls 'for situated and context-specific practices' (Braidotti, 2013b: 53), her neo-Kantian form of cosmopolitanism remains grounded in abstract and universal categories: hospitality and cosmopolitan right. Hospitality and right are integrally bound together. As an abstracted principle, right remains the basis of obligation towards others in Benhabib's legal theory of cosmopolitanism.

I want to suggest that cosmopolitan posthumanism cannot be grounded in a theory of right but must instead find its grounding in entanglement. This thesis mandates a break from cosmopolitanism's Kantian heritage. Yet, it is possible to provide a reading of Kant that argues his notion of cosmopolitan right is first grounded in practical matters. I want to suggest that Kant operates in two steps: he works to develop a theory of right from situated, practical conditions and then he imposes that theory of right universally. Recall from the earlier discussion that Kant mandates that cosmopolitanism is only possible in a republican system. Each state within the international order has its own self-interest at heart: states want to avoid war. For Kant, it is because of this self-interest that the various states in the international system would adopt a framework of cosmopolitan right. Each state agrees to the various articles of cosmopolitan right in Kant's first section because each state seeks the securities offered for itself. Universal peace is instituted because it is good for each individual participant. The aim of each state remains grounded in self-interest (the interest of each state not to be drawn into war) while appearing altruistic. As I argued in the first section, cosmopolitanism can be understood as the extension of practical and political wisdom through the universalizing of political wisdom into the international order. In 'Perpetual Peace' cosmopolitan right is adopted for very practical concerns (in Aristotle's sense of practical). The function of the whole is not originally a movement from the universal to particular but builds from the interest of particular states to be instituted as a universal. Thus, where universal right might be maintained as the final cause, political pragmatism remains the efficient cause of the cosmopolitan order. The universal notion of right arises from the practical interests of individuals. It is only after this practical interest has been affirmed as universal that politics must bend its knee to right.

My aim in presenting this reading of Kant is not necessarily to impose a top-down, universal form of cosmopolitanism. The issues of universalism have been outlined in the work of many decolonial and postcolonial critiques of cosmopolitanism. Instead, my aim in presenting this reading of Kant is to show that even in Kant one can see right as developing out of pragmatic (or to use Braidotti's term, situated) concerns that remain prior to right (even if, for Kant, this interest is reduced to individualism and contract law). In this reading, Kant reveals that the abstracted universals of moral right – those universals that serve as the basis of a universal flourishing – are grounded in a form of obligation towards the other that is grounded in self-interest: the republican state ought to adopt the norms of cosmopolitanism for the good of its own citizens. Instead of beginning with a universal and abstracted theory of right, even Kant starts with situated interests.

Obligation has a rich history as a concept of moral theory. My use of obligation, here, sidesteps that history to instead focus on the way that obligation has been used to ground a theory of ethics in science studies. Isabelle Stengers conceives of obligation as a constraint of scientific practices and experimentation. Here, obligation both emerges from *and* within scientific practice: 'obligation refers to the fact that a practice imposes itself upon its *participants* certain risks and challenges that create the value of their activity' (Stengers, 2010: 55, emphasis in original). Contemporary practices emerge from a history of practices to the extent that the new practices would be impossible without that history. These obligations cohere with what Bruno Latour terms 'matters of care' (Latour, 2004: 114). Roughly put, Latour argues that those scientific findings that are commonly taken (specifically within a positivistic framework) as 'matters of fact' are actually dependent on the history of science that produces them: facts emerge out of histories of 'concern'. Latour's use of the word 'concern' originates in Martin Heidegger's deployment of *Sorge* (care, concern). *Sorge* designates that all experiences and practices are framed through the various entanglements that shape what one cares about or is concerned with. For Latour and Stengers, scientific 'matters of fact' are actually 'matters of concern': namely, that scientific discoveries are bound to the histories and interests of scientists and those things scientists are concerned with. On this basis, Stengers adopts Latour's term 'factish' to discuss scientific measurement: the term 'factish' designates that while facts are real, they are also fabricated and fetishized by the systems of measurement and the historical practices and norms that shape scientific study (Stengers, 2010: 19). For Latour and Stengers, Scientific findings are imbricated and *obligated* with histories and matters of concern. It is possible to locate a paradoxical reciprocity in the relation between this notion of obligation and practice: practices emerge from obligations and obligations are shaped through practices. Just as the scientist is obligated to the history of scientific practices, Stengers argues that each is obligated towards its milieu, suggesting that the individual and the milieu co-emerge from these practices. One is determined by, while simultaneously relying on, its milieu.

A concept of obligation is not determined outside of but within these relationships. For a theorist like María Puig de la Bellacasa, this notion of obligation is 'inseparable from the material continuation of life' (2017: 155). Obligations are not external nor abstracted moral conditions but are the immanent and entangled relationships of one's existence.

As such, it is worthwhile to examine the notion of 'entanglement' with more depth. Karen Barad challenges classical metaphysical concepts of individualism and autonomy by arguing that agency should be understood through the concept of entanglement: *'agencies are only distinct in relation to their mutual entanglement; they don't exist as individual elements'* (Barad, 2007: 33, emphasis in original). As noted earlier, entanglement poses a concept of entangled and relational being as the source of individuation that is ontologically prior to individuals. This relational ontology challenges common sense notions of separated entities, taking a fundamental inseparability as its ontological ground. For Barad, an individual is not given as individual but emerges through the 'intra-action' of its practices. Intra-action assumes entanglement as prior to individuation. As such, intra-action is distinct from interaction, 'which presumes the prior existence of independent entities or relata' (Barad, 2007: 139). In outlining practice through entangled intra-action, Barad extends Judith Butler's notion of performativity beyond Butler's anthropocentrism to understand a 'proto-performative account of the production of [all] bodies' (Barad, 2007: 129). The body is not determined through a universal or transcendent taxonomy but through a recursive production of practices within an entangled apparatus.

For theorists within 'critical posthumanism', the prospect of entanglement produces a shift from humanism to posthumanism. Entanglement expresses an account of performativity that 'eschews both humanist and structuralist accounts of the subject' (Barad, 2007: 136), while it 'challenges the positioning of materiality as given or a mere effect of human agency' (Barad, 2007: 183). This can be described as a posthumanism, rather than a humanism, anti-humanism or inhumanism, insofar as it follows Braidotti in thinking posthumanism as moving beyond the centrality and universality of 'Man' as a measure of all things (Braidotti, 2013b: 2). The 'human' ceases as an independent, individual observer and is instead understood to be both produced by and producing with an apparatus through Barad's notion of intra-connection: the human is a participant without being a universal. Barad describes this notion of posthumanism as a 'thoroughgoing critical naturalism, an approach that understands humans as part of nature and practices of knowing as the natural processes of engagement with and as part of the world' (Barad, 2007: 331–2).

While Barad does not adopt Stengers's language of 'obligation', it is not difficult to apply that language to Barad's own ethical commitments. For instance, Barad writes:

> I argue that ethics is not simply about responsible actions in relation to human experiences of the world; rather, it is a question of material entanglements and how each intra-action matters in the reconfiguring of these entanglements, that is, it is a matter of the ethical call that is embodied in the very worlding of the human. (Barad, 2007: 160)

According to Barad and others who offer this designation, ethics is treated as distinct from moralism. Where moralism is based in the transcendent moralism of abstracted right, this ethics of obligation is instead bound to one's entanglements (whether this distinction holds is debatable, and a thorough account of the distinction would require its own chapter). Barad's ethics is an attempt to think physics *as* ethics: obligation (Stengers) or responsibility (Barad) derive from entanglement: 'We (but not only "we humans") are always already responsible to the others with whom or which we are entangled' (Barad, 2007: 393). Using Stengers's language, this ethics grounds obligation towards one's entanglement simply because one is entangled. One's practices depend on the history that makes those practices possible. These practices have obligations to that history – both for the sake of the history and for the practice itself – given that the various aspects are entangled together. To take this further, Barad suggests that 'measurements' can be understood as 'causal intra-actions' (Barad, 2007: 337), where the measuring device is entangled and obligated to these histories. This account of measurement resonates with Stengers's development of obligation through the consideration of 'factishes'. Causal intra-action has an obligation towards the things that it measures given that its practices are already entangled with matters of concern. Just as the scientist's experiments are obligated to the history that produces its practice, so too does the entangled individual have obligations to the history of practices that have produced it as well. As such, the answer to the question of why one is obligated to its milieu would be answered: I am obligated to my milieu because I am entangled with it and cannot be separated from it. I am obligated to it because this entanglement has produced me, and all of my possibilities continue to be bound up with it.

Posthuman cosmopolitanism and possibilities in entangled philosophical health

The foregoing analysis has presented a notion of obligation and entanglement. Against individual, separate entities, entanglement conceives of relation as prior to individuation. This position is not the erasure of the human. Instead, the human is reimagined as an integral phenomenon within the intra-actions of entangled practices. It is from this position that feminist posthumanisms (in which one could include Barad and Braidotti) have drawn inspiration from Donna Haraway (despite Haraway's refusal of the term, see Haraway, 2018: 79). Haraway introduces a notion of *sympoiesis* as a 'becoming' and 'developing with' that refuses the autonomy of *autopoiesis*. *Sympoiesis is* defined as 'complex, dynamic, responsive, situated, [and] historical' (Haraway, 2016: 58). As always already entangled (and shaped by entanglement), posthumanism pushes back against notions of purity that sink into taxonomized separation in classical metaphysics. This refusal of innocence follows Haraway in 'staying with the trouble' (Haraway, 2016) and learning to live a 'life without the promise of stability' (Tsing, 2015: 2). Simultaneously, the refusal of innocence understands the inter- (or, for Barad, *intra-*) dependent messiness does not equate with a political quietism, nor an acceptance of the ways things are.

Obligations enable 'matters of fact' to be understood not only as 'matters of concern' but as 'matters of care'. Heidegger's position of *Sorge* can, after all, be translated as 'concern' or 'care'. María Puig de la Bellacasa uses Stengers's consideration of obligation to think through matters of care as a form of care ethics. Using Jane Tronto's generic definition of care, where care 'includes *everything that we do* to maintain, continue and repair "our world" so that we can live in it as well as possible. That includes our bodies, our selves, and our environment, *all of which we seek to interweave in a complex life-sustaining web*' (Tronto as quoted in Puig de la Bellacasa, 2017: 3, emphasis in original). For Puig de la Bellacasa, care is a duty that emerges from entangled obligation. She argues that through entangled practices, matters of concern should instead be taken as 'matters of care'. While matters of concern recognize facts as 'factishes' entangled with historical practices, Puig de la Bellacasa argues that care goes a step further given that '"to care" contains a notion of *doing* that concern lacks' (Puig de la Bellacasa, 2017: 221).

Caring-for within entangled interdependence serves as the condition for cosmopolitan posthumanism, insofar as this concept stresses the intersubjective dimensions of philosophical health. As discussed earlier, Luis de Miranda's concept of philosophical health links Aristotelian *eudaimonia* with *dynamis* to think *eudynamia*: a recursive relation of possibility and flourishing. In the first section of this chapter, I argued that the contemporary situation of globality mandates that a consideration of *eudaimonia* requires a cosmopolitan design. Barad's consideration of entanglement suggests that the *eudaimonia* of any individual cannot be separated from that individual's entanglement. In the movement from *eudaimonia* to *eudynamia*, philosophical health moves from an emphasis on personal health towards the attempt to 'have a good relationship with the possible' (de Miranda, 2021: 100). Entanglement, through a notion of cosmopolitan posthumanism, extends the realm of the possible from a 'fruitful coherence between a person's ways of thinking and speaking and their ways of acting' (de Miranda, 2022: 1) to think a coherence with entangled phenomena in intra-action (a move very similar to de Miranda's own use of 'intercreations' in this volume). Entangled coherence becomes the condition of a good relationship with possibility. Possibility is recursively bound to the agencies that emerge from and through their entanglement (Barad, 2007: 177). Entangled possibilities are the conditions of flourishing: that flourishing is never flourishing alone but always flourishing with(in) entangled possibilities that are consistently remade by their entanglements. Entangled with entanglement, flourishing is imbricated in obligation. As Barad states, 'Intra-acting responsibly as part of the world means taking account of the entangled phenomena that are intrinsic to the world's vitality and being responsive to the possibilities that might help us flourish' (Barad, 2007: 396).

The question of self-interest and self-flourishing is entangled with the interests and flourishing that 'self' is entangled with. If required, a definition of the individual or subject would come closer to Gilbert Simondon's concept of the 'transindividual' (Simondon, 2020): rupturing the individual-collective binary, 'Transindividuation is the process by which the individual and the collective are constituted . . . seeking instead their mutual points of intersection and transformation' (Read, 2016: 6). Even without a strong theory of the subject or individual, the entanglements of that 'individual' are bound to the well-being (or perhaps, well-*becoming*) of philosophical health. These possibilities are open through the connections and alliances of intra-action that are found through entanglements and inter-/intra-dependencies. The *hedonic* and the *eudaemonic* (de Miranda, 2022) are not separate but emerge from their entanglement together. As entangled, my flourishing is imbricated with the flourishing of the entire system and structure: personal and individual flourishing depends on the flourishing of one's entanglement. This includes the flourishing not only of other humans but of plants, animals, bacteria, technologies and machines in a cosmopolitan posthumanism. The pursuit of philosophical health in a global community is bound to this form.

Conclusion

This chapter has attempted to gesture towards something like an 'ego-altruism'. This term, borrowed from the Spinozist scholarship of Alexandre Matheron and Étienne Balibar, posits that there is no real opposition between selfishness and altruism: 'The *ego* and the *alter* being assimilated to one another, we are now beyond the ego-altruism opposition' (Matheron as cited in Balibar, 2020: 42). This position holds that entanglement grounds all possibilities and that flourishing is bound to both that entanglement and the possibilities that it holds. In denying entanglement, humans and individual actions foreclose possible future possibilities: as we continue along the path of anthropogenic climate change, the possibilities for the flourishing of all life on this planet are increasingly foreclosed. In contrast, by embracing shared possibilities of entanglement 'we' might open possibilities for flourishing together: recognizing that the flourishing of forests, critters and other people increases the possibilities of individual flourishing as well. This chapter has argued that cosmopolitan posthumanism is grounded in the entanglements that produce possibility. The aim of such a political vision is to awaken possibilities of flourishing. As such, the notions of self-flourishing (*eudaimonia*) and good possibilities (*eudynamia*) that are sought in philosophical health cannot be disentangled from posthuman entanglements in which they arise. The *hedonic* is not distinct from the *eudaemonic*; egoism is not distinct from altruism. As I seek my own flourishing I am imbricated and entangled.

What this chapter has not done is deal with two fundamental problems. These problems should serve as the basis for both further discussion and scholarship. The first is that the grounding of an ethics does not, itself, motivate the ethics: many people do not care about their self, nor do they feel an obligation for self-care. The grounding in entanglement does not necessarily produce a means for enacting the practices that would produce the possibilities of good flourishing found in *eudynamia*. As such, further research and discussion are needed on the possibilities of action and motivation: not only the grounding of an ethics but how to motivate various individuals, once individuated, to act according to the possibilities of their entanglement – to realize the mutual flourishing of well-becoming. A second issue intersects with the first: it concerns the inherent anthropocentrism of the above formulation of cosmopolitan posthumanism. Despite a rendering of the planetary as inter- (or intra-) connected in entanglement, the analysis struggles to escape what is at best a notion of stewardship and at worst a notion of paternalism. Matters of concern or care for the planet, as they are presented earlier, appear to maintain a human-centric position: it is, after all, the *Anthropos* who has realized the possibilities of anthropogenic climate change. The onus of obligation and ethics derived from entanglement maintains the centrality of the *Anthropos* as a political actor. The above analysis has not adequately dealt with the inherent anthropocentrism of this position, nor the power ramifications that are largely reminiscent of various imperialisms. These two problems pose integral sites for further interventions.

In conclusion, this chapter has drawn upon the concepts of entanglement, cosmopolitan posthumanism and philosophical health to bind a consideration of *eudaimonia, dynamis* and *eudynamia* to a theory of obligation in entanglement. It is entanglement – specifically entanglement within the planetary dimension – that grounds obligation towards being (both human and more than human) that are external to the self. Building from the lineage of both Aristotle and Kant, I suggested that cosmopolitanism adopts a notion of political wisdom that is extended across the globe. From there, I suggested an alternative to universal right through the prioritization of entangled obligation. Finally, I tied philosophical health to these entangled obligations in a way that gestures towards a cosmopolitan posthumanism. For each of us, it is the case that our philosophical health, our possibilities for flourishing, and the entirety of our being is entangled with and thus dependent on the possibilities for the flourishing of all.

References

Aristotle (2001), *Nichomachean Ethics*. In Richard McKeon (ed.), *The Basic Works of Aristotle*, trans. W. D. Ross, 935–1126. New York: The Modern Library.

Balibar, Étienne (2020), *Spinoza, the Transindividual*, trans. Mark G. E. Kelly. Edinburgh: Edinburgh University Press.

Barad, Karen (2007), *Meeting the Universe Halfway: Quantum Physics and the Entanglement of Matter and Meaning*. Durham: Duke University Press.

Beitz, Charles (2004), 'Cosmopolitanism and Global Justice'. *The Journal of Ethics* 9: 11–27.

Benhabib, Seyla (2006), *Another Cosmopolitanism*. Oxford: Oxford University Press.

Bhabha, Homi K. (2018), 'Cosmopolitanism: Reflections at the Commemoration of Ulrich Beck, 30 October 2015'. *Theory, Culture & Society*, 35 (7–8): 131–40.

Braidotti, Rosi (2013a), 'Becoming-World'. In Rosi Braidotti, Patrick Hanafit and Bolette Blaagaard (eds), *After Cosmopolitanism*, 8–27. New York: Routledge.

Braidotti, Rosi (2013b), *The Posthuman*, 1st edn. Cambridge and Malden: Polity.

Brink, David O. (2018), 'Eudaimonism and Cosmopolitan Concern'. In David O. Brink, Susan Sauvé Meyer and Christopher Shields (eds), *Virtue, Happiness, Knowledge*, 270–92. Oxford: Oxford University Press.

Didur, Jill (2003), 'Re-embodying Technoscientific Fantasies: Posthumanism, Genetically Modified Foods, and the Colonization of Life'. *Cultural Critique*, 53 (1): 98–115.

Haraway, Donna (2016), *Staying with the Trouble: Making Kin in the Chthulucene*. Durham: Duke University Press.

Haraway, Donna (2018), 'Capitalocene and Chthulucene'. In Rosi Braidotti and Maria Hlavajova (eds), *Posthuman Glossary*, 79–83. London: Bloomsbury Academic.

Kant, Immanuel (2018), 'Perpetual Peace: A Philosophical Sketch'. In H. S. Reiss (ed.), *Kant: Political Writings*, trans. H. B. Nisbet, 2nd end, 93–130. Cambridge Texts in the History of Political Thought. Cambridge: Cambridge University Press.

Latour, Bruno (2004), *Reassembling the Social: An Introduction to Actor-Network-Theory*. Oxford: Oxford University Press.

Malm, Andreas and Alf Hornborg (2014), 'The Geology of Mankind? A Critique of the Anthropocene Narrative'. *The Anthropocene Review*, 1 (1): 62–9.

Mignolo, Walter (2002), 'The Many Faces of Cosmo-polis: Border Thinking and Critical Cosmopolitanism'. In Carol A. Breckenridge, Sheldon Pollock and Homi K. Bhabha and Dipesh Chakrabarty (eds), *Cosmopolitanism*, 157–87. Durham: Duke University Press.

Mignolo, Walter (2011), *The Darker Side of Western Modernity*. Durham: Duke University Press.

de Miranda, Luis (2021), 'Think Into the Place of the Other: The Crealitic Approach to Philosophical Health and Care'. *International Journal of Philosophical Practice*, 7 (1): 89–103.

de Miranda, Luis (2022), 'Philosophical Health'. In V. P. Glăveanu (ed.), *The Palgrave Encyclopedia of the Possible*, 1003–8. Cham: Palgrave Macmillan.

Moore, Jason W. (2017), 'The Capitalocene, Part I: On the Nature and Origins of Our Ecological Crisis'. *The Journal of Peasant Studies*, 44 (3): 594–630.

Narayanan, Yamini and Sumanth Bindumadhav (2019), 'Posthuman Cosmopolitanism for the Anthropocene in India: Urbanism and Human-Snake Relations in the Kali Yuga'. *Geoforum*, 106 (November): 402–10.

Nussbaum, Martha C. (2000), 'Duties of Justice, Duties of Material Aid: Cicero's Problematic Legacy'. *Journal of Political Philosophy*, 8 (2): 176.

Nussbaum, Martha C. (2002), *For Love of Country*, ed. Joshua Cohen. Boston: Beacon Press.

Pogge, Thomas W. (2002), *World Poverty and Human Rights*. Cambridge: Polity Press.

Pollock, Sheldon, Homi K. Bhabha, Carol A. Breckenridge, and Dipesh Chakrabarty, 'Cosmopolitanisms'. In Carol A. Breckenridge, Sheldon Pollock, Homi K. Bhabha, and Dipesh Chakrabarty (eds), *Cosmopolitanism*, 1–14. Durham: Duke University Press.

Puig de la Bellacasa, María (2017), *Matters of Care: Speculative Ethics in More than Human Worlds*. Minneapolis: University of Minnesota Press.

Read, Jason (2016), *The Politics of Transindividuality*. Leiden: Brill.

Riesbeck, David J. (2016), 'Aristotle and the Scope of Justice'. *Journal of Ancient Philosophy*, 10 (1): 59.

Scheffler, S. (2001), *Boundaries and Allegiances: Problems of Justice and Responsibility in Liberal Thought*. Oxford: Oxford University Press.

Simondon, Gilbert (2020), *Individuation in Light of Notions of Form and Information*, trans. Taylor Adkins. Minneapolis: University of Minnesota Press.

Stengers, Isabelle (2010), *Cosmopolitics I*, trans. Robert Bononno. Minesota: University of Minnesota Press.

Taraborrelli, Angela (2015), *Contemporary Cosmopolitanism*. London: Bloomsbury.

Tsing, Anna Lowenhaupt (2015), *The Mushroom at the End of the World: On the Possibility of Life in Capitalist Ruins*. Princeton: Princeton University Press.

16

East Asian somatic philosophies as guides to a philosophically healthy life

Lehel Balogh

Introduction: The tradition of East Asian somatic philosophies

As comparative philosopher James F. Peterman remarked, 'Any therapeutic philosophy depends in part on a distinction between health and illness. The operative notion of philosophical health depends on a conception of the human good' (Peterman, 1992: 18). The Three Teachings of East Asia – Buddhism, Daoism and Confucianism – are known to be based on complementary worldviews that extol the virtues of the good life. Albeit they all have distinct approaches concerning how one should go about attaining a higher level of ethical consciousness that would allow one to live in accord with the laws of the cosmos as well as with one's peers in society, they all agree that realizing the promise of a good life is not only possible – it is of the highest value for a human being (Zhao, 2014). This is in resonance with the modern notion of philosophical health which has been described by Luis de Miranda as 'a state of fruitful coherence between a person's way of thinking and speaking and their ways of acting, such that the possibilities for a sublime life are increased and the need for self- and intersubjective flourishing satisfied' (de Miranda, 2021a: 92) The idea that a better life is possible in this world, and that this better life can be achieved by a rigorous and methodical training that goes on for years, is a fundamental presupposition of all the major metaphysical teachings of East Asia. In actual fact, the training of self-cultivation is virtually co-temporal with one's individual processes of socialization and maturation (Dennis and Werkhoven, 2018). Regarding the self of the individual, it can be generally said that in all of these three traditions the self is construed as inherently somatic in nature: it is the inseparable unity of mind and body. In other words, it is conceived of as *embodied* whose practices are intrinsically *embedded* in the interconnecting nexus of reality. Reality, in turn, is viewed, to a large degree, as determined by the mutual interdependence of things (Confucianism) as well as by the dependent co-arising of all the separate beings (Buddhism). In Hwa Yol Jung's words 'Sinism', which imbues not only Confucianism and Daoism but also all the forms and versions of East Asian Buddhism, sustains a 'relational ontology' or a philosophy of 'Interbeing' (Jung, 2014).

As he phrases it, while formulating a contradistinction to Western philosophy's being-centred metaphysical inclination:

> what Being is to the West from Heraclitus to Heidegger, Interbeing is to the East Asia from Confucius to Laozi to Wang Yanming, Mao Zedong, and Watsuji Tetsuro. Interbeing, I submit, is the ontological foundation of constructing (*factum*) an ethicoaesthetic paradigm in transversal geophilosophy. It points to the differential topography of thinking and doing things unique to East Asia. Its twofold principium is found in the *Yijing* (the Chinese Book of Changes): (1) everything (both human and nonhuman) is connected to everything else in the cosmos . . . and (2) everything changes except change itself. (Jung, 2014: 155)

Ki-energy, self-cultivation and a good life in Buddhism, Confucianism and Daoism

In a nutshell, the Three Teachings have raised, over the millennia of their existence, a solid metaphysical, epistemological and ethical foundation that bespeak the mutual dependence of human and other beings as well as the unique importance of the personal body in the cultivation of the individual self in order to reach a harmonious and wholesome way of life (Balogh, 2014; Gu, 2018). At the very foundation of this worldview lies the notion of the generative force or vital energy of 気(*qi/chi/ki*), which 'is the transformative stuff of all that exists in an unending process of becoming' (Heisig, Kasulis and Maraldo, 2011: 1255). Ki-energy refers to a semi-material, semi-spiritual entity that has the capacity to course through both sentient and non-sentient beings and can thus connect the realm of the living with the realm of the inorganic and seemingly inanimate. In reality, however, since this energy is conceived not only as the ultimate building material of all that there is but also as the decisive factor that animates – gives 'soul' – and energizes all beings, it is hardly accurate to state that in this understanding of reality such inorganic things as rocks or metals are inanimate. On the contrary, one of the most characteristic ideas of ki-based philosophies is that, owing to the ki-energy that builds them up, all beings are potentially animated. The reason why it can be argued that even inorganic entities have a 'soul' and are, in fact, animate is that they are capable of moving, in one way or another, perhaps not themselves but other things. A sight of a rock can inspire one for a course of specific action that would not have occurred to the person before laying eyes on the rock. The sound of a metal could, in a similar fashion, 'move' one to want to touch it, use it, own it. According to the internal logic of this metaphysical paradigm, it is the particular constellation as well as the quality of the ki-energy that moves other entities to react in certain ways with other entities. A piece of copper ore will elicit different reactions from a professional blacksmith than from a bird or a wandering dog, while a wrought iron structure will, again, draw out different responses from various other people. The point is that despite them being apparently inanimate, inorganic things do bring out reactions and thus engage in a practical exchange of energies with other parties.

In Chinese medicine, upon which Korean and Japanese traditional medical knowledge and practices, are also based, the notion that the ki-energy levels fluctuate in the human body is a central conviction that underpins the entire system of thought. As Katja Triplett noted in her recent monograph on medicine and Buddhism in ancient and medieval Japan, the depletion and repletion of the heart is a basic principle of all Chinese-style medical theories. Describing the function of ki-energy in this model, she writes:

> It energizes every process including the processes in the human body. There is no single system of Chinese-style medicine, and traditions have changed over millennia and centuries. However, all known traditions refer to the idea that depletion in the circulation of qi leads to illness and shortening of life, and repletion to health and the extension of life. (Triplett, 2019: 26)

Renowned Japanese philosopher Yasuo Yuasa also underscores the salience and special importance of ki-energy in traditional East Asian philosophical cultivation and medicine. As he explains, the Chinese system of the meridians (somatic pathways), of which there are twelve regular ones and eight irregular ones, differs entirely from the circulatory and nervous system of modern Western biomedicine. The continuous flow of the ki-energy in the human body, according to the East Asian conception, is a natural life process. Some of this vital stuff travels upwards in the body inside the dorsal and lateral meridians, whereas another part of it travels downwards in the meridians that are located in the ventral areas (Yuasa: 1993: 100 ff.). It is generally thought that when the natural energy flow of the ki is blocked, the meridians will get, at certain nodal points, congested, and the body will produce symptoms of ill health to indicate the problem. The application of acupuncture needles as well as the manual manipulation of acupuncture points by means of massage is extremely widespread in Traditional Chinese Medicine, and this is precisely so because the blockage in the various body meridians is thought to be alleviated by direct intervention into the problematic zone of the body. Once the blockage is cleared away and the ki-energy can resume its natural current in the body, body and mind will recover their normal states virtually simultaneously. The purifying of ki-energy and the ascertaining of its natural flux can be further strengthened by somatic practices, such as meditation. As Yuasa explains:

> the flow of *ki* is closely connected to meditative training, and in this respect is *psychological in nature*. But when seen in light of the therapeutic effect which acupuncture demonstrates, it has the effect of *activating physiological functions*. In other words, one's body is a psychological being when it is felt as within the skin (the sensation of one's own body), whereas the body observed from outside, wrapped in skin, is a field in which the inner physiological functions issue forth. The flow of *ki* is a passage mediating between this interior and exterior. (Yuasa, 1993: 108)

Now, if the vital energy can, indeed, serve as a mediating agent between the interior of the self – where the thoughts and feelings arise and are experienced – and the exterior of the somatic self – where the rest of the world is to be found – and, furthermore, if meditation and other forms of deliberate self-cultivation foster the healthy communication of the self with its environment, then it is understandable that the ideal of good life must be eminently approachable via the purposeful cultivation and training of the body (Nagatomo, 1992). Accordingly, the overall purpose of philosophical self-care in East Asian traditions can be summed up as follows. *One*: to experientially realize the original unity of body and mind and to accustom the self to identify with its own body to the same extent as with the cognitive and emotional contents of its mind. *Two*: to stimulate and promote a vision that declares meditation and other somatic contemplative practices to be the royal road for an existential transformation – which is called *enlightenment* in Buddhism, *sageliness* in Confucianism, *perfection* in Daoism – to a more spontaneous and genuine mode of being. *Three*: to actually attain the coveted revolution of the body-mind that would eventually result in the elimination of the first two points. In the case of the first point, the need to identify with one's mental and somatic processes could be forgotten, for what is proposed to await the self after the enlightening transformation and sagely perfection is a special sort of wakeful awareness, whereby the self ceases to separate itself from the rest of the world (Carter, 2008). After the conversion, the individual would be able to maintain an effortless practice of mindfulness, which would mean the elimination of the second point as well: one would not need to *deliberately* engage in somatic practices any longer once one's entire way of existence has transformed into that of an even-minded, tranquil sage that does not need to *know* the Way, for he or she has already *become* the Way. Thus, one could argue that the merger of the subject (the self) with the appropriate object of its consciousness is *enlightenment* as a lived practice and is the ultimate goal of all East Asian somatic philosophies (Yuasa, 1987).

Naturally, for different thinkers, enlightenment as a lived practice implies different things – there is no uniform answer to or consensus regarding this ultimate question in the East Asian traditions. In the Korean Seon (Chan/Zen) Buddhist tradition, for instance, an initial all-penetrating insight into the emptiness of the self and the interdependence of reality is absolutely necessary for the ensuing somatic cultivation to be appropriate. In other words, without having the right understanding of what one is after, of what would truly constitute the final objective of meditation and the perusal of doctrinal texts, the practitioner would inevitably misunderstand both the goal and the means of cultivation. Only after one has profoundly experienced the awareness of the awakened ones, the so-called Buddha-mind, will one be able to 'trace back the radiance' of the original emptiness of the self (Buswell, 1991). That is why twentieth-century monk Chinul advocated the tripartite cultivation structure of 'sudden enlightenment' (initial intuitive insight into the nature of the self and reality), 'gradual cultivation' (the following dedicated maintaining of quiescent, yet wakeful meditative awareness) and, finally, the 'path of direct cutting'. The last stage is similar to the first one in that it offers a true understanding of what enlightenment is, but instead of a mere 'understanding-enlightenment', it is rather a true 'realization-enlightenment' (Keel, 2012). That is, instead of simply knowing what it is, one already lives the truth of that knowledge as a practical awareness. One must, of course, keep in mind the caveat that in the Seon/Chan/Zen tradition of Mahayana Buddhism trusting words and verbal knowledge is, as a rule, frowned upon. The idea that discursive knowledge is unreliable is quite common in this Buddhist approach, so instead of endorsing much philosophical analysis (although *some* of it is not entirely against the spirit of Zen), the direct seeing through of the deceitful web of words and concepts is generally more enthusiastically embraced and encouraged as the best method of forming a healthy and sincere attitude towards life's sufferings and vicissitudes (van Schaik, 2018).

In Confucianism – or as it is preferably called by specialist scholars nowadays, *Ruism*, because Confucius (Kongzi) himself did not start a new school and the *ru* were members of China's educated elite (Kalmanson, 2021: 6). – the notions of good life and cultivation of the moral self are inseparably bound together and are of unquestionably prominent significance (Wong, 2017; Peters, Besley and Zhang, 2021). As Mengzi's (Mencius) following argumentation attests, proper philosophical self-care, which in the Chinese tradition always implies some kind of practical and ethical self-cultivation, encompasses the nurturing of the right sort of ki-energy by means of philosophical reflection on the correct comportment that the sagely person ought to adopt and embody.

> Mengzi [. . .] argues that if we monitor and assess our reactions to the things we think and do by an internal act of *si* 'reflection' or 'concentration', we will be guided toward good actions and away from bad. The contemplation of good acts produces a special feeling of joy in us which in turn reinforces the moral sense and enables us, through a process of *extension*, to do more and more difficult actions. In Mengzi's own terms, such joy nourishes the moral sprouts; it provides them with a special kind of *qi*気 'energy'. . . . [this] flood-like energy . . . is the energy of moral courage, the motivation or power that enables one to perform difficult moral tasks. Like the energy of any living thing, the moral sprouts thrive when properly nourished, and without such nourishment, they wither away. (Ivanhoe, 2000: 20)

Moral courage (see de Miranda, 2021b, on mental heroism, for an interesting comparison) is indispensable for right ethical conduct and, consequently, for attaining the ideal of the good life which culminates in the benevolent humanism of Confucianism. As Li Zehou pointed out, Confucian humanism is built upon the notion that the 'pursuit of knowledge and learning', as well as the 'control and shaping of the will', will form a character that brings into correspondence the external humanism of the person (positive actions towards others) with the internal humaneness of the self that 'promotes the initiative and independence of individual character' (Li, 2020: 16–17). In this regard, Confucianism sees the philosophically healthy person as that exemplary individual who, after much reflection, learning and bodily training, has acquired a secure knowledge concerning the proper way of seeing and doing things, and can thus help to put others on the right path, too (Rošker, 2020). In addition, being pragmatic and practical has always been valued highly in the tradition. The Confucian sage does not deal primarily with sorting out abstract ideas and doctrines that are far removed from the everyday worries of society. Focusing on the actual world with its relevant and topical problems is the foremost concern of a philosophically sound person, and since the world was made in a way that is never fully complete and perfect, it needs the tending of enlightened human agents (Yang 2016: 1). In other words, the nourishment and cultivation of both the self and the world are of equal importance and are the key responsibilities of us, humans. This idea was also underlined by Leah Kalmanson in her recent book on East Asian speculative existentialism, adding to the preceding thoughts that failing to cultivate the self will reduce the individual to a lower mode of existence which does not elevate the lives of others, nor does it aid the subsistence of the universe in any meaningful way; rather, it hinders it.

> In Ruist terms, the sage (*shengren* 聖人) is the person who has put in the time and effort toward self-cultivation that enables her influence over surrounding conditions. Self-cultivation is often described as a process of manipulating the *qi* of the heart-mind to achieve stillness (*jing* 靜), numinosity (*ling* 靈), and spiritual clarity (*shenming* 神明). In contrast, petty or 'small' people (*xiaoren* 小人) fail to attain access beyond the perspective of their own limited awareness. They barely understand themselves, let alone the outside world and other people; their *qi* remains turbid and cloudy. (Kalmanson, 2021: 11)

People as such when they enter this world are far from being complete or whole, according to Confucianism. Refining their raw and coarse personal characters, polishing off their rough edges, is imperative. The world is as incomplete as human beings are, and both need each other's mutual cultivation in order to become healthier and more complete. Maturation of the self comes from attending to nature and society, through myriads of small deeds and considerations for others as well as for the world (Ivanhoe, 2016). This way, on the whole, a good social order is being realized and enacted, while the individual will also experience a growing sense of self-accomplishment. According to Yang Guorong, this element is crucial in terms of securing the upward-moving, positive transformation of the world and, likewise, of the self. 'Philosophically speaking, the self-accomplishment human being achieves in the process of accomplishing things is the result of human being knowing and transforming the self along with the world' (Yang, 2016: 2). This is why the initiative and independence of the individual character is encouraged, as Li Zehou has remarked earlier. The philosophically healthy person must be able to carry the weight of responsible decision-making and must also be capable of actively facilitating the dissemination of knowledge regarding right action and thought among the populace. As a result, education is the focal point of the entire Confucian programme (Ivanhoe, 2016). As Chen Lai maintains,

> Confucian thought is, in a broad sense, a set of thoughts on the education of man. . . . It takes the personality of the sage as the training objective of education, stressing the educational concept of adults or holistic man, highlighting the significance of 'learning' and men's own initiative in the educational process, aiming to develop men into noble men with comprehensive development. (Chen, 2019: 157, 170)

One could argue that the ideal of the mature and noble holistic sage corresponds to the ideal of a philosophically healthy individual.

Moving on from Confucianism to Daoism, what is readily apparent is that Daoism's common view of human nature appears to be more closely aligned with that of early Buddhism than that of Confucianism. Human nature, according to both Laozi and Zhuangzi, should, indeed, be cultivated, yet the cultivation's aim is generally not that of a highly refined, sociable and 'civilized' man but more of a self-sufficient individual who prefers – although not always chooses – to live without having to rely too much on other humans, with much simplicity and in close harmony with nature (Koller, 2018: 265 ff.). This idea of self-reliance and harmony with nature is accentuated especially in the *Zhuangzi* but is by no means alien to the *Daodejing*, either. Both major figures of the tradition, Laozi and Zhuangzi, would certainly agree that the key attitude to a philosophically healthy lifestyle is what they called 'non-action'; even though they would not entirely agree on what it is meant by the term. Daoist scholar Chen Guying elucidates this point:

> Both Laozi and Zhuangzi promoted non-action (*wuwei*無爲), but it meant something different for each of them. For Laozi, *wuwei* is primarily a method of caring for the state and its people that those in power should adopt. . . . Zhuangzi adopts the maxim of non-action that Laozi recommended to the powerful, but he generalizes *wuwei* and makes it more universally applicable. For him, *wuwei* is extended from its original significance as a political principle into an expression for a more general mode of meaningful and authentic existence. (Chen, 2018: 39)

Authentic existence in this context means a purportedly originary or pure manifestation of the real self of the individual which can act spontaneously and effortlessly, yet not in an arbitrary fashion, for its actions are in smooth accordance with the laws that govern the universe. The Daoist perfected persons are portrayed to master their arts in a way that they act without an excess of thought or movement: they 'know without knowing' – that is, without reflection or mental focusing – what they do and how to achieve the results they intend to achieve (Lai and Chiu, 2019). Despite clearly being an acquired skill which must be first cultivated in order to be attained, genuineness or authentic selfhood in Daoism is celebrated for its unsullied naturalness. As Moeller and D'Ambrosio point out, the ideal of philosophical sanity is inextricably linked with the notion of genuine, effortless non-action; however, to perform this 'non-action', first, one must in fact learn how to do it. 'A paradoxical unpretentiousness of genuine pretending lies at the heart of a Daoist art of maintaining sanity and achieving efficacy. Genuine pretending allows one to operate smoothly in the midst of a social environment full of hypocrisies and, at times, perils' (Moeller and D'Ambrosio, 2017: 181). To put it differently, it is obligatory that one first *pretends* to be a perfected person before actually becoming one: the inveterate habit of pretence, in turn, can transform one into a par excellence Daoist sage, whose self is doing nothing but 'wandering carefree in Nothingness' (Chai, 2019). Conceived in this manner, philosophical sanity lies in the acquired ability to stay in constant touch with the essential nature of the universe and the self while living in society, which would help one not to get entangled too deeply in human affairs. In David Chai's words: 'Carefree wandering thus translates into an aimless spirit whose journeying knows no bounds. Adapting to each and every situation as easily as water circumvents an obstacle, the sage relies on the freedom gained by the non-mind of Dao to traverse the universe' (Chai, 2019: 167).

If philosophical health in Daoism implies being able to distance oneself emotionally from the hustle and bustle of the social realities that surround us and not to get involved in pointless mental suffering for events whose occurrences are beyond one's control (as in Stoicism), this, of course, does not, at the same time, mean that one ought to become desensitized to suffering and live without a care for other beings. It is the virtue of *equanimity* that the Daoists are in the pursuit of, not the questionable qualities of indifference and unconcern. As Culham and Lin stress it, 'Daoist virtues valorise humility, compassion, gentleness, softness, non-forcedness, nourishing and nurturing, servicing and resourcing, wisdom, and so on' (Culham and Lin, 2020: viii). They turn the attention of the self inward and advise the person to commit to self-examination, self-reflection and self-cultivation. They highlight the significance of cultivating ki-energy and of learning about the correspondences between the microcosm of the human body-mind and the macrocosm of the universe.

> In particular, for the Daoist, the self is a microcosm of the entire universe, endowed with *qi*, 'the energy and spirit that permeates all existence and interconnect all existence'. . . . [it is important for the] students of Daoism to explore the depth of this energy and spirit, and to cultivate their patterning and manifestation. Such cultivation is synonymous with Daoist virtue education. As such, it is this cultivation that can support the health and harmony-promoting relationship that we may have with every thing/being in Nature, including human beings. . . . Daoist practice is the transformation of all that might impede the interconnection and interbeing of all things. (Culham and Lin, 2020: ix)

Conclusion: The staying power of ki-based philosophies to health

The Three Teachings of Buddhism, Confucianism and Daoism have been informing the cultural landscapes of East Asian societies for millennia, and among their numerous core tenets the idea of self-cultivation and the notion of ki-energy are both common and deep-seated (Barbalet, 2017; Bowring, 2017; Cawley, 2019; Rošker and Visočnik, 2015). Indigenous contemporary psychotherapeutic approaches of the region, such as the Morita and Naikan therapies, which both spread to Korea and China as well, base their principles of traditional East Asian systems of thought that all acknowledge, in one way or another, the existence of ki-energy and its crucial significance in health maintenance and in philosophical cultivation as well (Balogh, 2020a). Part of this picture is the conviction that personal sanity is somehow in connection with keeping a distance from one's egotistical tendencies and with cultivating an awareness of selflessness, whereby one experientially realizes one's surface self as fickle and one's core self as empty (Balogh, 2020c). For this realization to take place, one is strongly recommended to engage in practical self-cultivation methods whose names often still retain the characteristics of their essential philosophical components. For example, *aikido*, a popular Japanese martial art, is founded on the idea that there exists a Way (*do*) that shows a person how to bring their personal energies (*ki*) in alignment (*ai*). Chervenkova expounds:

> While in the Western languages words such as 'way' or 'road' are used either in their literal sense or as abstract metaphors for life, in Japan they also describe circumstances where one 'must learn or polish a skill'. This practical aspect of the concept of the Way, however, by no means detracts from its philosophical implications, i.e., the Japanese understanding that it is exactly through concrete physical actions and behavioral patterns that one can attain self-transformation and develop proper attitude with regard to how one relates to others, Nature and even the Universe. (Chervenkova, 2017: 24–5)

The Way that one must follow is encoded into the fabric of the universe, yet it can be deciphered not only by turning outside but by introspection and by realizing the ideal of no-self through meditation. Twentieth-century Japanese philosophers such as Nishida Kitaro and Nishitani Keiji also shared this core belief that, in fact, the self can morph into a higher mode of existence by way of diligent training of the body-mind (Balogh, 2020b). Currently, there is in the West an increased interest in and openness to the theories and practices of Eastern self-cultivation methods. In particular, we have been witnessing in recent years a *'Confucian revival'* that has been defined as 'the search for a synthesis between Western and traditional East Asian thought and is aimed at elaborating the system of ideas and values capable of resolving the social and political problems of modern globalized societies' (Rosker, 2015: xii). Specialized scholars in comparative and intercultural philosophy, religion and medicine are present in far greater numbers today than were just a decade or two ago. These experts often possess language mastery (Chinese, Tibetan, Korean, Japanese etc.) of key texts on self-cultivation and ki-based philosophies, thus they can create reliable translations of and highly informative commentaries on East Asian philosophical, anthropological and medical manuscripts. This development is clearly conducive to the process by which East Asian categories gradually become more familiar to Western readers, and, by the same token, these categories are also increasingly engaged on their own home grounds, not merely on Western metaphysical grounds, as they had been earlier.

Furthermore, today even Western medical sciences have begun to catch up with their Eastern counterparts in conducting research on the effects of ki-energy both within and without the human body (Jia, 2005; Matos et al., 2021). The innovative research area of 'biofield science' stands at the crossroads of Eastern wisdom and modern Western medicine, and has been recently declared by experts as 'the new frontier in health care' (Streeter, 2018; Jain et al., 2015). As Rubik and his colleagues assert, 'The biofield or biological field, a complex organizing energy field engaged in the generation, maintenance, and regulation of biological homeodynamics, is a useful concept that provides the rudiments of a scientific foundation for energy medicine and thereby advances the research and practice of it' (Rubik et al., 2015: 8). Following up on the ways in which the research on energy medicine will proceed will prove beneficial in enhancing our capabilities to understand and endorse to a fuller degree how our bodies could optimally function. This, in turn, would put us into a better position to evaluate what practices are likely to be conducive to nurturing superior health and well-being, and to see more clearly how philosophical health could facilitate establishing a social order that could contribute to the improvement of general health, mental balance and an altruistic, ethical, socially responsible lifestyle that allows one to engage in peaceful cohabitation with others and with one's environment, too.

This paper was supported by the AKS-2021-R095 grant of the Academy of Korean Studies.

References

Balogh, Lehel (2014), 'The Body of the Orients—The Body That Which Orients: The Significance of the Body in Traditional East Asian Aesthetic Experiences'. *Pragmatism Today*, 5 (2): 37–44.

Balogh, Lehel (2020a), 'Zen Buddhism, Japanese Therapies, and the Self: Philosophical and Psychiatric Concepts of Madness and Mental Health in Modern Japan'. *Journal of Applied Ethics and Philosophy*, 11: 1–10.

Balogh, Lehel (2020b), 'Nothingness, the Self, and the Meaning of Life: Nishida, Nishitani, and Japanese Psychotherapeutic Approaches to the Challenge of Nihilism'. *Journal of Philosophy of Life*, 10 (1): 98–119.

Balogh, Lehel (2020c), 'The Moral Compatibility of Two Japanese Psychotherapies: An Appraisal of the Ethical Principles of Morita and Naikan Methods'. *Vienna Journal of East Asian Studies*, 12 (2020): 124–48.

Barbalet, Jack (2017), *Confucianism and the Chinese Self: Re-examining Max Weber's China*. Singapore: Palgrave Macmillan.

Bowring, Richard (2017), *In Search of the Way: Thought and Religion in Early-Modern Japan, 1582–1860*. Oxford: Oxford University Press.

Buswell, Robert E., Jr (1991), *Tracing Back the Radiance: Chinul's Korean Way of Zen*. Honolulu: University of Hawai'i Press.

Carter, Robert E. (2008), *The Japanese Arts and Self-Cultivation*. Albany: SUNY Press.

Cawley, Kevin N. (2019), *Religious and Philosophical Traditions of Korea*. London and New York: Routledge.

Chai, David (2019), *Zhuangzi and the Becoming of Nothingness*. Albany: SUNY Press.

Chen, Guying (2018), *The Humanist Spirit of Daoism*, trans. Hans-Georg Moeller. Ledien and Boston: Brill.

Chen, Lai (2019), *Confucius and the Modern World*, trans. Wang Xiaohua. Oxon and New York: Routledge.

Chervenkova, Velizara (2017), *Japanese Psychotherapies: Silence and Body-Mind Interconnectedness in Morita, Naikan and Dohsa-hou*. Singapore: Springer.

Culham, Tom and Jing Lin (2020), *Daoist Cultivation of Qi and Virtue for Life, Wisdom, and Learning*. Cham: Palgrave Macmillan.

Dennis, Matthew and Sander Werkhoven, eds (2018), *Ethics and Self-Cultivation: Historical and Contemporary Perspectives*. New York and Oxon: Routledge.

Gu, Ming Dong, ed. (2018), *Why Traditional Chinese Philosophy Still Matters: The Relevance of Ancient Wisdom for the Global Age*. London and New York: Routledge.

Heisig, James W., Thomas P. Kasulis and John C. Maraldo, eds (2011), *Japanese Philosophy: A Sourcebook*. Honolulu: University of Hawai'i Press.

Ivanhoe, Philip J. (2000), *Confucian Moral Self Cultivation*. Indianapolis and Cambridge: Hackett Publishing Company.

Ivanhoe, Philip J. (2016), *Three Streams: Confucian Reflections on Learning and the Moral Heart-Mind in China, Korea, and Japan*. New York: Oxford University Press.

Jain, Shamini, John Ives, Wayne Jonas, Richard Hammerschlag, David Muehsam, Cassandra Vieten, Daniel Vicario, Deepak Chopra, Rauni Pritten King and Guarneri E. Biofield (2015), 'Biofield Science and Healing: An Emerging Frontier in Medicine'. *Global Advances in Health and Medicine*, 4 (Supplement): 5–7.

Jia, Qian (2005), *Traditional Chinese Medicine Could Make 'Health for One' True*. Geneva: World Health Organization.

Jung, Hwa Yol (2014), *Prolegomena to a Carnal Hermeneutics*. New York and London: Lexington Books.

Kalmanson, Leah (2021), *Cross-Cultural Existentialism: On the Meaning of Life in Asian and Western Thought*. London and New York: Bloomsbury.

Keel, Hee-Sung (2012), *Chinul: The Founder of the Korean Sŏn Tradition*. Fremont: Jain Publishing Company.

Koller, John M. (2018), *Asian Philosophies*. London and New York: Routledge.

Lai, Karyn and Wai Wai Chiu, eds (2019), *Skill and Mastery: Philosophical Stories from the Zhuangzi*. Lanham: Rowman & Littlefield.

Li, Zehou (2020), *A History of Classical Chinese Thought*, trans. Andrew Lambert. New York: Routledge.

Matos, Luís Carlos, Jorge Pereira Machado; Fernando Jorge Monteiro and Henry Johannes Greten (2021), 'Perspectives, Measurability and Effects of Non-Contact Biofield-Based Practices: A Narrative Review of Quantitative Research'. *International Journal of Environmental Research and Public Health*, 18 (6397): 1–29.

de Miranda, Luis (2021a), 'Think Into the Place of the Other: The Crealectic Approach to Philosophical Health and Care'. *International Journal of Philosophical Practice*, 7 (1): 89–103.

de Miranda, Luis (2021b), 'Five Principles of Philosophical Health: From Hadot to Crealectics'. *Eidos: A Journal for Philosophy of Culture*, 5 (1): 70–89.

Moeller, Hans Georg and Paul J. D'Ambrosio (2017), *Genuine Pretending: On the Philosophy of Zhuangzi*. New York: Columbia University Press.

Nagatomo, Shigenori (1992), *Attunement Through the Body*. Albany: SUNY Press.

Peterman, James F. (1992), *Philosophy as Therapy: An Interpretation and Defense of Wittgenstein's Later Philosophical Project*. Albany: SUNY Press.

Peters, Michael A., Tina Besley and Huajun Zhang, eds (2021), *Moral Education and the Ethics of Self-Cultivation: Chinese and Western Perspectives*. Singapore: Springer.

Rošker, Jana S. (2015), 'The Confucian Revival and "Different Models of Modernity"'. In Jana S. Rošker and NatašaVisočnik (eds), *Contemporary East Asia and the Confucian Revival*, xiii–xxiv. Newcastle upon Tyne: Cambridge Scholars.

Rošker, Jana S. (2020), *Becoming Human: Li Zehou's Ethics*. Leiden and Boston: Brill.

Rošker, Jana S. and Nataša Visočnik, eds (2015), *Contemporary East Asia and the Confucian Revival*. Newcastle upon Tyne: Cambridge Scholars Publishing.

Rubik, Beverly, David Muehsam, Richard Hammerschlag and Shamini Jain (2015), 'Biofield Science and Healing: History, Terminology, and Concepts'. *Global Advances in Health and Medicine*, 4 (supplement): 8–14.

Schaik, Sam van (2018), *The Spirit of Zen*. New Haven and London: Yale University Press.

Streeter, Thornton (2018), 'The New Frontier in Health Care: Biofield Science'. TEDxTalk, 15 August 2018.

Triplett, Katja (2019), *Buddhism and Medicine in Japan: A Topical Survey (500–1600 CE) of a Complex Relationship*. Berlin and Boston: De Gruyter.

Wong, Wai-ying (2017), *Confucian Ethics in Western Discourse*. London and New York: Bloomsbury.

Yang, Guorong (2016), *The Mutual Cultivation of Self and Things: A Contemporary Chinese Philosophy of the Meaning of Being*, trans. Chad Austin Meyers. Bloomington and Indianapolis: Indiana University Press.

Yuasa, Yasuo (1987), *The Body: Toward an Eastern Mind-Body Theory*, trans. Nagatomo Shigenori and T. P. Kasulis. Albany: SUNY Press.

Yuasa, Yasuo (1993), *The Body, Self-Cultivation, and Ki-Energy*, trans. Nagatomo Shigenori and Monte S. Hull. Albany: SUNY Press.

Zhao, Baoxu (2014), *To Build a Harmonious World: Ideal of Traditional Chinese Thinking*. New York and Dordrecht: Springer.

17

Philosophical health, crealectics and the sense of the possible

Luis de Miranda

A thinking self, let's call her Sophia, is considering a text. Sophia reads these lines feeling like a well-identified subject before a fixed object. She is a critical reader: she may doubt, and she thinks it is then *she* who doubts. Sophia thinks of Descartes: his eliminatory method to discover the irrefutability of being and his anthemic *cogito ergo sum* refute the potential illusion of the world, its pool of chimaeras devoid of certainty, by placing the entire edifice of the Real upon the stilts of rationalized doubt (Descartes, 1996 [1641]). As Sophia doubts, it seems to be *her* who, via philosophizing, distances *herself* from the world to reconstruct the Real from the rational standpoint of the thinking ego, the rational *I*.

Such is the second nature, the psychological stance of the modern individual: *I am an I amid things (and an eye – an evaluating perspective)*. The dominant thinking style within this individualistic view is 'analytic intelligence', a logic that divides the world into parts filtered by the instrumentalizing – or instrumentalized – self (see Chapter 11 in this book for a distinction between analytic, dialectic and crealectic intelligence). Like Sophia, most of us believe today that we have an individual self and that this self is distinct from the material world and from other selves.

Sophia now considers the phrase *philosophical health*; she expects a more embodied take on the experience of being since the phrase implies an intellectual aspect – conveyed by the word *philosophy* – and a physical, embodied or experiential aspect carried by the word *health*. A union or reconciliation of these two aspects may suggest a form of attunement between (if not a fusion of) mind and body (Shigenori, 1992), between our ways of thinking and our active presence in the world: she now knows by heart the anthem of the present anthology, repeated over and over in many of the previous sixteen chapters: 'philosophical health is a state of fruitful coherence' and so on (de Miranda, 2022).

Still doubting, Sophia asks: Can philosophical health be more than a method of self-mastery, a mind-over-body discipline still dependent on a paradigm that considers the world as a set of things, places or ideas that may either be ignored stoically or controlled anthropocentrically?

Much has been written about the blind spot of human-centrism and self-enclosure (e.g. Plumwood, 2001). Plato, Aristotle, Descartes and Hegel, among others, have been blamed for their devaluation of non-rational beings, and they have sometimes even been considered accomplices of our control-freak technicists, no-limit engineers and other instrumentalists of being (Heidegger, 1993). 'Human-centredness promotes various damaging forms of epistemic remoteness, for by walling ourselves off from nature in order to exploit it, we also lose certain abilities to situate ourselves as part of it' (Plumwood, 2001: 98).

This chapter clarifies – for Sophia and other readers – the definition of philosophical health, such that it may be understood to be life-, earth- or Creal-centred rather than only human- or person-centred, thus distinguishing it from the individualism of self-development and from other forms of existential health defined anthropocentrically (Binder, 2022). Yet, I will also argue, supported by systematic interviews I conducted in 2022 with persons, women and men, living with spinal cord injury (tetraplegia), that philosophical health should not abandon altogether the focus on the self: it should not be compared, for example, to a disembodied or sacrificial form of spiritual health.

In fact, as I hope to show, there need be no contradiction but rather an ontological correspondence between, on the one hand becoming a eudynamic flourishing self – approaching the *inner* bliss of the ever-renewed infra-personal possible – and on the other hand facilitating or curating the imparadization of a diverse world *out there* (de Miranda, 2021b). Abandoning her systematic doubt without eschewing critical creativity, Sophia should be able to say, 'I am in ec-stasy in the things' (Merleau-Ponty, 1968: 56) and the things are in ecstasy in me, realizing that all beings are in intercreative flux, neither completely one nor completely disparate (see Vangeest, in the previous chapter, on how posthumanists and new materialists share a similar view). In order to be philosophically healthy, Sophia is not only a self-standing *cogniser*, à la Descartes, but also, in her best days, an *imparadiser*, gifted with a eudynamic sense of the possible that she shares with other beings, humans and non-humans.

Philosophical health is – as many authors in this volume have pointed – not only about individual bliss and self-coherence. It is also about diving deeper, consciously embodied, into the rich mine of the intercreative multiverse and seeing it, not as a *Real* only – a set of actualized things – but also as a *Creal*, a creative, ubiquitous and immanent flux of possibility (de Miranda, 2008; 2021a). Philosophical health is the art of composing our biographies in a spirit of unified meaning *while* letting ourselves be composed by the visible and invisible elements of the stream of Creal. By a work that is a collective oeuvre, we may *find* ourselves in the world and the world *finds* itself in us, self and world being intertwined in a sense of the possible that is conducive to meaning.

Our intercreative and moving sense of the possible

The ideal of a person-centred form of philosophical care is salutary. But it may appear to be anthropocentric, focused on self-realization, and an egotistic rather than *ecocentric* ideal (Washington, 2020). Self-development is often accused of focusing on the personal human psyche at the expense of other forms of life and to the detriment of our understanding of the common nature of beings. In healthcare contexts, taking into account the person's uniqueness of values and worldview reveals significant progress compared to mechanical and de-subjectivizing forms of handling (Owens, 2015; Loughlin in the present volume, Chapter 3). Outside of the Clinique, a growing body of philosophical counsellors – a new practising corps to which I belong – are helping individuals to thrive meaningfully and make sense of their purpose in life, based on the Ancient *Know Thyself* precept. From an ecological or holistic perspective, a self-focused approach may be criticized for being limited to a moral or even neoliberal distinction between, on the one hand, philosophically ill individuals with incoherent lives (*metaphysical losers*) and, on the other hand, philosophically healthy persons with meaningful biographies (*ontological winners*). But philosophical health is not a new norm of individual conformity to a fixed idea of truth.

Limiting the horizon of philosophical health to a distinction between eudaimonic selves and depleted egos omits that we all behave in ways that cause political, social or environmental harm whether we intend to or not (DeSombre, 2018). In a philosophically healthy global world, the care of the self would need to be coextensive with the whole of earthly life, as Nietzsche foresaw more than a hundred years ago (Ansell-Pearson, 2013). We need to provide a pluralistic vision of philosophical health that, without devaluating the singular person, is simultaneously attuned to the diverse 'flesh of the world' (Merleau-Ponty, 1968: 84). To rephrase this as a Nietzschean question: What does it mean for philosophical health to be 'faithful to the earth' (Nietzsche, 2006: 6)?

Let's imagine that Sophia leads a consistent life by founding her decisions on principles grounded on a sustained worldview, such as 'respect for Gaia, etc.' (Clark, 2012: 74). One may inquire about the general validity of such a worldview or cosmology: Can or should a philosophical stance ever be universal? We may wish to avoid a purely relativistic and atomistic position regarding personal philosophies or worldviews, to embrace a salutary planetary vision (Wass, 2015) and establish a collective *Weltanschauung* or 'shared cosmology' (Abrams and Primack, 2011; see also Sivil's chapter on ubuntu in the present anthology). But such a consensus – *I am because we believe* – could be accused of failing to be philosophically healthy if the capacity to 'think for oneself' is forgotten (Kant, 2007: 307). How can anything philosophical be a common global project if philosophizing is about intellectual freedom and independent creation? If philosophical health becomes a shared transindividual vision, does it not risk becoming a form of dogmatic groupthink?

Under the notion of crealectics, I have been arguing for an ontological middle way between methodological individualism – the focus on the self – and universal entanglement – the focus on multiplicity (de Miranda, 2017). We need to recognize – to feel – the existence of creativity not only as a human productivist feature but also as a natural, continuous, immanent and all-encompassing flux, which is what most process philosophers claimed from Heraclitus to Bergson and Whitehead. Life is a ubiquitous process of constant regeneration and novelty manifestation combined with local – and ultimately ephemeral – phenomena of unification. There are many worlds, and creation is ontologically prior to becoming because a simple instance of becoming in a given world can be an instance of creation in another world. Creativity or continuous creation is the 'the universal of universals characterising ultimate matter of fact' (Whitehead, 1978 [1929]: 31), and by definition, it resists becoming reified as a dogma as well as it resists being anthropomorphized: creation is an idea that cannot be made to pertain to a dogmatic logic since the singularity and difference it presupposes is by definition the opposite of norm or law – this is an important point in the assertion that philosophical health cannot be normative nor ideological.

Bergson (1944 [1907]) and Whitehead (1978 [1929]) suggested more or less directly that all worldviews – or myths (Eliade, 1959) – refer to creation as their original ground, in a sort of minimal First Philosophy that only presupposes, as the source of the Real, an ever-renewing flux of possibility, a Creative Real (or, as I have been calling it, *Creal*), a virtual becoming that precedes and sometimes produces realities in a pan-immanent dance of intercreations, dissolutions and quasi-unifications. This ethical cosmology of the possible is the minimal social contract we could agree upon in an otherwise pluralism-friendly society (de Miranda, 2017). The therapeutic motto of *crealectics* (etymologically from *Creal: the ultimate possible* and, alternatively, *logos*: making sense or *ektos*: outside) is not *cogito ergo sum* but simply *It is possible* (see Chapter 11 in this anthology), or, alternatively, *It is compossible*, possible together.

Crealectics can be therapeutic: if our sense of the possible is strong, we can define and hold on to a sense of purpose. Philosophically, the 'Creal', like 'philosophical health', is a relatively new signifier but not a new signified: it is, once again, a variation on the ontological stances that posit creative and ceaseless becoming or naturing as the immanent source of all phenomena: the Deleuzian plane of immanence (Deleuze, 2005), Schellingian Nature (Schelling, 2004 [1799]) or even the Spinozian Substance (Spinoza, 2005 [1677]). Now, while I believe many of us can easily agree with the view that beings, things and spaces are intertwined in an intercreative flow, it is usually more difficult to conceive that this flux is ontologically prior to the institution of any specific being, subject, object or distinct reality. And yet, even some biologists today insist:

> There is no thing in biology (or, as Bohm would have it, in the world). Things are abstractions from an ever-changing reality. Reality consists of a hierarchy of intertwined processes. [. . .] The world is full of fuzzy boundaries. Seemingly unchanging entities keep on emerging and decaying if we consider them over a long enough period. Moreover, it is impossible to say precisely when they truly become what they are and when they cease to be themselves. Or where they begin and where they end. (Jaeger in Nicholson and Dupré, 2018: xi–xii)

In order to make sense of the world, we need 'to begin with undivided wholeness' (Bohm, 1980: 223), the wholeness of the multiiversal creative onflow, the metamorphic multiple, the infinitely or virtually possible. Such is a crealectic logic, beyond or before analytic and dialectic intelligences, one that recognizes that subdivisions and distinctions in our world are the product of evolving perspectives (utilitarian, habitual, speciated, social, political, cultural, aesthetic, economic, animal, vegetal etc.) built upon the common possibilizing source of all beings. The expanding multiverse is in constant exteriorization of itself, in continual *phenomenologization*, but real phenomena never reach the ontological status of being separate from their common ground of creative immanence. The Real is the *ecstasiation* of the Creal, a stretching out (*ek-stasis*): objects and subjects are never fully one in the sense of distinct entities; they are 'ensemblances' (de Miranda, 2020b), semblances of solidity, intertwinements of solidarity.

What does this mean for the sense of self? To say that *we intercreate*, are being created or that *the Creal is crealing us*, suggests a collective process. That a subject may be said to become more coherent, and philosophically healthy, does not contradict the plural reality of ongoing creation of the possible in which the cosmos, the earth and ourselves are embedded. On a therapeutic level, creation can be experienced as a healing personal feeling, a grateful emotion, a soothing intuition: the Creal is the source of our sense of the possible. Some may call this *love* (cf. Balogh on Binswanger in this volume, Chapter 2), others *desire* or *drive* (Reich, Freud); some may call it joy (Spinoza): in all cases, the living drive, the *élan vital*, is a dynamic sense of the possible.

Here again, Merleau-Ponty, who spoke not of *crealectics* but of *hyper-dialectics* (Taminiaux, 1978), is inspiring: 'My apprehension of myself is coextensive with my life, as its own possibility by principle – or more exactly, it is this possibility that is me; I am this possibility, and, through it, all the others' (Merleau-Ponty, 1968: 56). What creates the intercreative unity of a tree, of a car or a human is the possible, superficially manifested in the possibility to do something and/or to be acted upon. In the Real, there is a continuity of the compossible (Leibniz) with increasing capacity for making sense of it, and sense-making is not a human privilege.

The cosmic dynamo of Creal-One

Sophia still doubts: Is everything really in constant flux? Do we not distinguish Maria from Theo, a car from a bird, a belly from an eye? Is there no local permanence of entities and is my watch not the same as six months ago?

Depending on the time scale we adopt, what we decide to perceive as beings do exhibit plateaus of structural integrity; some things may look unchanging relative to human time. And yet they are in metamorphic flow relative to cosmic time – a child can understand this fact by looking at time-lapse videos in which images are highly accelerated and things blossom or decay in just a few seconds, while humans in the streets of our capitals look like blood cells in constant flux and reflux. On a human scale of perception, momentary equilibria of structural integrity create psychosocial phenomena of identity even if there are no fully separate unities in the universe.

Crealectics is a minimal ontology that provides us, now global humans, with a shared cosmology linked to the ancient primordial ideas of Multiplicity and Oneness (de Miranda, 2019). We may ask with Sophia: Why is there also *some thing* instead of only everything? How and why is the cosmos producing these *ensemblances* that we call realities or objects? Why does the Creal ecstasiate quasi-objects and quasi-subjects – the aforementioned structural equilibria – instead of being indifferently with itself and in itself, in a cosmic soup of indifferentiation? This, argues the cosmology (de Miranda, 2019), is a logical effect of the Creal's constitutive dynamic: if all there is *is* ultimately an undivided wholeness – the wholeness of the Creal as pure multiplicity – then such universal variety is *one*. There are many worlds but only one Creal: there is no logical need for many different *Creals* if the Creal is pure difference, and therefore the ultimate is also one, as was often recognized by Ancient Greek philosophers, chief among them Plotinus (Hadot, 1993), but less often by contemporary philosophers.

We must admit logically that the One is present in the Many (Bracken, 2001) as the ontological shadow of the Multiple. The One can be said to be the virtuality of the possible, and vice versa. Ultimate possibility is ontologically both multiple and one. Since the Creal is immanent and teeming with potentials, the fact that Creal is also a unity (of diversity) creates an internal cosmological dynamic, an immanent tension of the multiple towards unity and of unity towards the multiple. This must be true both globally and locally: any region of the multiverse – Sophia's watch, you the reader, the kingdom of Sweden – is a creative tension between two opposites: unification and dispersion. Such is the cosmic dynamo, Creal-One, our Singular-Common Logos (Binswanger on Heraclitus, see quote below, 1975: 242). This is how there can be a crealectic philosophical counselling protocol: ultimately, the stories narrated by the counselees are various instances of disbalances in personalized dynamics of unification and difference.

Because the One is the doppelganger of the macrocosmic Creal, the fact that so many humans are in quest of their unified self, their compact individuated doppelganger, while being in fact relatively scattered in moods, thoughts and actions, is a microcosmic reflection of the macrocosmic dance between multiplicity and unification, one being the asymptotic horizon of the other. This is why we need, from the perspective of crealectic philosophical health, to accept the drive towards self-development as well as our intercreative solidarity: they are the complementary sides of the same dynamic, which can be a good dynamic, a *eudynamic* expansion or elevation of the domain of the possible (de Miranda, 2021b).

To be more precise, instead of the Multiple and the One, one should rather speak of quasi-Multiple and quasi-One. Let's imagine a volcanic magma (Castoriadis) from which certain bubbles emerge and can form a perfect sphere before they explode. Equally, in all regions of the Creal, attractions towards the One, towards unity, create ectopic zones of temporary individuation (a key idea in Simondon's philosophy of the transindividual: see Combes, 2013). Reality is a foam of forms gravitating around strange attractors of ecstatic temporary order provoked by the ontological drive towards the One present at the heart of the Creal. These ectopic structural phenomena trying to emerge into permanent identity or coherence are the signifiers we call realities: they seem like closed ensembles to other ensemblances or 'represent a subject for another signifier' (Lacan, 1977: 207). Yet, the full distinctiveness of things and beings is a fabulation (Bergson, 1977 [1932]), a mesh of perspectival confabulations (Schnider, 2018). Human subjects in particular are constantly projecting pareidolic individualities into the outside, making these projections sharable by naming them, shaping them and giving them permanence and identity in discourse and practice.

Sophia is still unconvinced. When she looks at her laptop computer, she considers that it is solid and distinct from the rest of the world from the perspective of social time. Even if from a cosmic spacetime perspective institutions are just a metamorphic flow of possibilities momentarily encapsulated into unity by particular perspectives and uses (Bergson, 1944), should not our sociopolitical reality, the pragmatic world we live in, be more solid to allow for philosophical health negotiations? Why would a volcanic cosmological perspective care about us, microscopic humans? Will the Creal pay the bill?

Focusing on our shared domestic or national realities only produces an outburst of analytic intelligence, which is the intelligence of parts and bits. This is where behaviour may get problematic: a practical obsession for unities, grounded on a locally imbalanced Creal-One dynamic, grants solidity, importance and permanent reality to an ephemeral region of the Real. Crealectics is not saying that reality is an illusion – a plastic bottle takes five hundred years to decompose and that fact is sadly real. The bottle is not only solid for human consciousness but it is also solid by its enacting the cosmic dynamo via an unhealthy engineering process. Eventually, the bottle will decompose and return fully to the body of Creal, but this does not mean we should not try to make it decompose faster, more respectfully of other forms of life, biomimetically.

Each of us is a bridge between multiplicity and unification. We may desire to be one, a unique and triumphant self, and forget that we can never fully attain complete and perfect adunation, unicity, because of our participation in the multiple becoming of Creal. However, on a human timescale, we can approximate integrity and biographical coherence. We can for the sake of philosophical health maintain an ethos of regularity via, for example, an axiomatic stance, a noetic prayer or motto, or by being faithful to a virtue or a constellation of values (say the triangle *justice-truth-possible* for instance).

A philosophically healthy form of integrity is never a dogmatism, because it remains aware that our inherent multiplicity will continuously shake the ensemblance of our stabilities, challenge our feeling of identity and ultimately dissolve our being within the phenomenon we call death before we ever become fully integrated. There is wisdom and humility in accepting that we are quasi-subjects amidst quasi-objects rather than solipsistic Cartesian egos isolated from a world of hard ensembles functioning together like the cogs in a machine. The so-called hard problem of consciousness (Chalmers) is solved when we understand that nothing is ever fully *hard*. Philosophical health cannot become dogmatic or normative without being ontologically naïve, and health in this context is not the contrary of disease or illness but rather a crealectic becoming: health is, simply put, our sense of the possible.

We constantly create and are constantly created: we are a sense of the possible in flux, with ups, downs and interruptions. Our ultimate unity is in 'being singular plural' (Nancy, 2000), a field of existence where the Multiple and the One meet and dance or sometimes fight. If we are never fully one as individuals, neither are we condemned to be completely scattered; as said, we can access, in our limited lifetime, the dignity of a philosophical stance, a relatively balanced eudynamic, a good sense of the possible generated by our faithfulness to sense-making structures that may function like strange attractors within our biography. In everyday life, we need to maintain the self-hypnosis of quasi-unity to a certain extent because society pushes us to take a more-or-less distinct position in the overall structure. Because the organized world wants us to be accountable for given works, titles or roles, or the absence of it, the self may believe it is like a neon light, rigid yet fragile, unique but mimetic, flashy against darkness (de Miranda, 2019). But the self is a noetic prayer. In our globalised world, as our social identities tend to become brittle, it is healthy to cultivate a resilient philosophical identity provided that it does not degenerate into productive rigidity or intolerance for difference.

The sense of the possible and the ecological self

The version of philosophical health I advocate is one of asymptotic harmony between our philosophical sense, our sense of purpose, our sense of the possible, our sense of belonging, our sense of self, our bodily sense and our acts. Philosophical care should not – cannot – turn us into a logical machine (for a somewhat different point of view, see Cohen in this volume, Chapter 5). The kind of self that crealectic philosophical health advocates is not a private bunker on a hyperrational island, neither an empire in an empire, to use a Spinozian metaphor. From a crealectic perspective, philosophical health cannot be merely about building a strong sense of self or private ontological security: earthlings also need a strong sense of their intercreative belonging. Care of the soul cannot be domestic only but must attune with our collective becoming, especially if, as it seems, there is only one universal soul, the One-Creal (a hypothesis that transpersonal psychology has also been championing, albeit in other terms). As Viktor Frankl once put it in a television interview (Noetic Films, 2019), an impression of self-actualization might derive incidentally from engaging meaningfully with the world, but ego-centred self-realization should not be the primary goal of personal growth (this, however, does not mean that we should throw away the baby of self with the bathwater of narcissism).

A philosophically healthy person maintains an ecstatic, rationally and emotionally conscious balance between unifying tendencies and disparate ones, mental, bodily and worldly. This is done via a non-dogmatic and non-obsessive process of sense-making. During the cycle of interviews that I conducted in 2022 with tetraplegic persons living with spinal cord injury in Sweden, I conceived and applied what I called the SMILE_PH method, an acronym for *Sense-Making Interviews Looking at the Elements of Philosophical Health*: these six elements are, as mentioned, the bodily sense, the sense of self, the sense of belonging, the sense of the possible, the sense of purpose and the philosophical sense (see my Introduction to the present volume as well as the methodological Epilogue following this chapter).

How do I feel my body; what are my sensations; is my body my friend? How do I view my self; what is my identity? What is my sense of belonging; do I feel I belong to any group or to an ideal? What is my sense of what is possible, and how has it evolved over time and in different social contexts? Do I have a sense of purpose, and how would I articulate it? How do I make sense of the meaning of life, its cosmology, and do I have a philosophical worldview? I believe we share with other living beings the first four senses: plants have a bodily sense, a cat has a sense of self, dolphins have a sense of belonging and trees some sense of the possible. The sense of purpose and the philosophical sense seem – to the best of our current knowledge – to be specifically human. And yet, ironically, most of us find it very difficult to articulate our sense of purpose or our philosophical worldview, which is why philosophical health care and counselling are helpful.

When you become tetraplegic, most of your body is paralysed for the rest of your life, but your higher cognitive functions often remain intact. The interviews I conducted showed that in order to overcome this traumatic condition you need to reinvent a coherent and strong sense of self. But you also need to nurture a strong sense of the possible and sense of purpose despite your physical inabilities (for example helping newly injured tetraplegics to transcend their condition). A sense of *well-belonging* is also fundamental (de Miranda, 2020b). In what follows I will focus on the sense of the possible, which I have suggested is what constitutes the core of health.

To access the singular truth of our shared and ever-renewing origin, one may dive deeply into the sensation of the non-individual creative energy of Creal, the essence of the possible. It is not an easy task: it may feel like diving in an ocean covered by ice, or trying to prevent a cork from floating. We are held back on the surface among the phenomena we have learned to cherish or ruminate upon. We are vulnerably attached to the real world (by what Husserl called the 'natural attitude': see in this anthology Chapter 6 by McMahon and Chapter 10 by Simionescu-Panait). In our world, we may feel, alternatively, successful or a victim, and there seems to be finitude and determinacy of our own concrete possibilities in light of our own concrete past and commitments. To reconnect with our creal sense of the possible, the needed kind of diving-in we alluded to may be familiar to those who are used to daydreaming or remembering their nightly dreams (Binswanger, 1975). While dreaming, we move closer to a creative flux of soothing or virtual possibility. In our oneiric worlds, the passionate history of mutual attraction between the Multiple and the One is often unveiled more refreshingly than in our societal masquerades or domestic routines.

To swim in the flow of Creal while remaining awake necessitates some practice and training, given that we are constantly driven away from the creative and intuitive source of becoming by the apparently rigid constructs of realism, our minds being distracted and continuously framed by habits, institutions, professional imperatives, mundane tasks, normative worries, all of which seem more important than they are because they are collectively reinforced or imposed by power structures and anxious groupthink. We may be looking for objective possibilities in the so-called real world if it seems we can grab or purchase them as available choices: ready-made possibilities out there, as in consumerism, provide for a weak sense of the possible. Philosophical health focuses rather on our holistic feeling of the possible and the universal concept of the possible, which can remain somewhat intuitive. One can become philosophically healthy without a thorough analytic knowledge of philosophy's history:

> It would be rather unfortunate if our patients had to understand Heraclitus or Hegel in order to get well; but none can attain to genuine health unless the physician succeeds in awakening in him that spark of mind that must be awake in order for the person to feel the slightest breath of that *koinos cosmos*, [. . .] the life of the universal. (Binswanger, 1975: 244)

The possible can be scary. All that is possible should not become real. The practice of philosophical health dissolves the obstacles that hinder or objectify the meaning of our sense of the possible. Still, it also helps us avoid wanting to actualize all that is virtual out of greed or ontological insecurity. Not every potential should be manifested, and not every energy exploited into reality. What is virtual can also be active without necessitating an objective production: love, kindness, desire, personality, the sublime or creativity do not need to be exhausted into objects or a status quo to be effectual. A philosophically healthy being may do less (in reality) with more (in *creality*). This attitude may become deeply ecological because, on the human level, it produces less stuff, fewer *realia*, and ideally more compossibility, an harmony of the possibles.

As Merleau-Ponty suggests, the 'Logos' (or Creal-One) is always already ecological, as a prelinguistic dimension for intertwined embodied experience (Kleinberg-Levin, 2008: 17, see also McMahon in this volume, Chapter 6). Crealecticians do not need to overproduce or accumulate simulacra of economic abundance or societal success since their felt abundance is original, constitutional and sensitive. This is of course easier said than done: remaining consciously, intuitively and emotionally within the Creal-One, that is, within crealectic philosophical health in a eudynamic equilibrium between unification and *disparation*, is an everyday challenge. To avoid the efforts of mental heroism, some may privilege mediocrity and espouse the dreams or nightmares of others. Some may believe they fear the unknown. Perhaps their difficulty in nurturing a good sense of the possible persists because they identify the Creal with Nothingness or the possible with danger. The virtual, the possible may seem to some threatening or empty, a *not-yet*, a *never* or an abyss of unfathomable dark energy. Anguish or undefined guilt may deplete our sense of the compossible: because we are an anxious species, philosophical health needs to be everyday – every second! – remembering its stance. Hence the beneficial use of a personally adjusted motto, co-created via philosophical counselling sessions, to remain attuned to a specific sense of purpose, envisioning an eudynamic common world.

From a cognitive perspective, growing a confident sense of *eudynamia* (de Miranda, 2021b: 99) can be seen as a reconciliation in the same body of self-centred caring and a self-transcendent trust in the collective Creal. In discovering the plural singularity of ultimate compossibility within oneself, beyond social and psychological normativity, we get closer to overcoming the apparent dichotomy between person and cosmos: 'The human self is then basically an ecological self' (Naess, 2005: 222), a regenerative and generative worldly self.

Philosophical health as (re)generativity

In psychological discourse, the notion of generativity (Erikson, 1968) designates 'a concern for establishing and guiding future generations' (Erikson, 1963: 267) and 'a desire to invest one's substance in forms of life and work that will outlive the self' (Kotre, 1984: 10). It is also an aspect of philosophical health to desire to pass on knowledge and experience to future generations, to actively invest oneself in a practice destined to enrich an open collective, a future and imparadizing form of life, 'a new earth and people that do not yet exist' (Deleuze and Guattari, 1994: 108), the best of all compossible worlds (Leibniz). The philosophical definition of generativity also means that we are generating, constantly intercreating the future and the present, at least locally. By acting in such and such manner, we reproduce or creatively modify patterns of behaviour; we perpetuate or disrupt institutions or routines. Our thoughts and acts are performative (Austin, 1962) with more or less leveraging strength depending on their singularity and persistence.

Philosophical health supposes the awareness of the generative aspects of our utterances and deeds, which is part of the care for consistency between our thoughts and actions. It is also a form of *regenerative* singularity: the capacity for a being to maintain a recreative state of ecstatic participation in the world, despite obstacles. Singularity designates a state of personal originality, of availability to ultimate possibility, of having a source in the *Unimpossible*. If every being is a child of the One-Creal, then every being is a dynamic polarity: on the *One* hand, beings participate in *generative regularity*, a network of (quasi-)order: repetitions, identifications, algorithms, mechanisms, reproduction, protocols, patterns, laws, predictability, robustness, tradition, logic. On the *other* hand (the Creal hand), beings participate in *regenerative singularity*, a network of (quasi-)difference: spontaneity, rulelessness, chaos, creation, emergence, possibility, unpredictability, plasticity and novelty. Joining the two hands is *compossibilizing*.

Contrary to the modern discourse of democratic self-identity, individuals are not singular by themselves, by virtue of their idiosyncratic separateness from the rest of the world, and singularity is not a specific quality of individualistic humanism. Singularity is the most common, shared and universal in us, even if hidden or forgotten: it is our infra-human being/becoming in Creal, a constantly renewed inner Big Bang or black hole in which all laws break because they do not yet exist or they no longer apply. Without intuitive access to regenerative singularity, reality may appear to be purely mechanical or mineral (hence depression). On the other hand, without generative regularity, there would be no social institutions, no shared reality or *Natura naturata* to rest and build upon (hence all forms of confusion)

A philosophically healthy society should be able to nurture and curate a good balance between regenerative singularity and generative regularity. A being cannot be said to be fully healthy if their access to regenerative singularity, that is, their sense of the possible, is hindered. One cannot be said to be fully healthy if an institution or controlling group over-regulate one's access to generative regularity, by forcing us into inaction, isolation, dogmatic norms or mimetic behaviour for instance. One should not surrender one's sense of purpose to the rulers or communities who try to monopolise the organization of space and production of reality (Lefebvre, 1991), via a form of social manipulation that is today often multiplied via *anthrobotic* devices (de Miranda, Ramamoorthy and Rovatsos, 2016; see also Chapter 11 in the present volume). The caring curation we call philosophical health is an intercreation, not a production in the neo-industrial sense, with its *arithmo-maniac* obsession with statistical metrics of self-fulfilling and self-destroying prediction.

Indeed, the most alienating ideology of our times – and one serious obstacle to the propagation of philosophical health – is the belief that change for the better can only happen if it can be measured and based on measurements. Medicine or technology can fix the mechanical parts of bodies such that it leads to a state of absence of disease, but what is measured is mere dysfunction or lack of dysfunction. Regeneration of our sense of the possible is not an analytic intervention; it cannot be attained without intuitive access to the transpersonal stream of regenerative singularity. From a crealectic perspective, creation is an emotion – it is probably the most fundamental emotion.

Governments and institutions entangled in metrics and arithmetic evidence may be reluctant to support philosophical health or may support diluted versions of it. The practice of philosophical counselling, while it is attested worldwide, is for the moment more a hobby than a fully recognized profession. Academia does not yet fully welcome philosophical practice, especially where philosophy departments are overpopulated by analytic armchairs. This is why philosophical health needs to be a transnational regenerative movement before it can (if it ever should) become an institution.

The generative-regularity aspect of the world explains why biomedical medicine or technological engineering work and are socially recognized: these activities focus on the unifying and regular tendencies of the universe and its agents, and such aspect is real – it is the Real in the making. Crealectic philosophical health considers, however, that it is unhealthy to defend, as mainstream scientism tends to do, that the universe is fully made of regularities and that what seems singular and irregular is simply noise pointing to what we do not yet understand scientifically. From a crealectic perspective, the Universe is not pure machinery but, as Bergson put it paradoxically and provocatively at the very end of *The Two Sources of Morality and Religion*, a machine for the making of Gods (Bergson, 1977).

From an ecopolitical perspective, it is essential to understand that one cannot nurture and take care of regenerative singularity in the same way that one enables generative regularity. Regenerative singularity cannot be technologically engineered. We may, however, help to awaken it anew – via training, exercises, philosophical dialogue, love, deep listening, play, humour or contemplation. As some oriental practices advise, doing *no-thing* – that is, not engaging in realistic thinking, object production or consumption – is sometimes the best way to reconnect with the multiversal creative flow: it is the *wu wei* of Daoism (Lee, 2020), an intuitive practice by which we allow regenerative singularity to circulate anew within the veins of our sense of the possible. As Spinoza indicated (2007 [1670]), this contemplative aspect of philosophical health does not mean that we should be passive or fatalistic but rather that we need to listen, make sense and understand before we act, such that our actions are more attuned to what is good for us *sub specie aeternitatis*.

The same principle applies to awake regenerative singularity in non-human beings, such as animals, plants and ecosystems. There needs to be a serious amount of letting grow, letting become and allowing to evolve naturally. Ecologically speaking, fostering regenerative singularity sometimes means disappearing as a human manipulator. When it's too late for unassisted healing, we also need to prune and nurture spaces or caring modes of generative regularity. A compossible balance between generative regularity and regenerative singularity, adapted to each situation or beings at stake, is part of the difficult yet *unimpossible* art of philosophical health.

Conclusion: Joy *in extremis*

Misuse of generative regularity is *normality*. Socially speaking, normality is a dangerous imperative if not an illusion; our global human society has probably moved to a point where the normal does not exist anymore. No matter the amount of wishful thinking produced by tired or fearful brains, *back to normal* will probably not happen in the twenty-first century. As earthlings, we are increasingly living in limit-situations and our planet seems now to be existing *in extremis*. Epidemics, disruptions, wars, climate extremes, mimetic collapses, artificial intelligences and contagious ideologies: all have an over-amplified impact today. Rather than hoping for a vain return to normal, we probably need to learn to live well *in extremis*.

The good news is that philosophers have something to teach us about such a way of life (Hadot, 1995), because the most influential among them have been embodied and active challengers of normality, since Heraclitus. What Nietzsche infamously meant by *übermensch* for instance – which I propose to translate not as *superman* nor *overman* but as *overnormal* – is an ideal of joyful existence beyond (or prior to) normality, an ecstatic life in perpetual appreciation of our experience of limits, of the sublime, of the abyss and the unknown. This form of well-becoming *in extremis* is very difficult, but it can be more intense, closer to a fully embodied form of creative gratitude and heroism than a conditioned, realistic and domesticated happiness. Philosophical health would become, from this perspective, the equilibrium state of the tightrope walker, a form of Great Health (Nietzsche, 2006),an asymptotic ideal rather than a normative reality.

Normal people, whatever this expression means, may be unhappy because they have a certain idea of the *more normal* they fail to attain and believe they lack. But our virtue, virtuosity, kindness, understanding, courage or vitality are better demonstrated in extreme situations than in autopilot behaviour, institutional sleepwalking (see Sharpe and Kramer in this volume, Chapter 12) or domestic comfort. It is worth noting here that to live *in extremis* does not mean embracing violence or a cult of pain: being for instance systematically kind is sometimes much more dangerous, complex and brave – and therefore more philosophically healthy – than being cruel (although it is easy to appear cruel to the conformist by simply thinking out loud).

A few more words are needed to conclude on the idea of equanimous, autonomous and distantiated self, which is so often associated with philosophical health (see Devarakonda, Chapter 4 in the present anthology). A certain apolitical and individualistic reading of Stoicism passes today for a fashionable form of philosophical way of life, as if it were possible to live in a fully rational and somewhat disembodied state of peaceful serenity away from the noise and fury of the world. In fact, contrary to contemporary fantasies of complete detachment and escapism, the Stoics themselves thought of our default mode, of our natural state, as being *in extremis*: 'The world is [for the Stoics] anything but a calm, tranquil, and orderly place. On the contrary, it is characterised by constant and writhing change, movement, and turmoil' (Porter, 2020: 238). For Seneca, 'life is a torment' (*QNat.* 5.18.15): irregularity and variety are a feature of Nature (*QNat.* 7.27.1–6), and 'nothing is firm' (QNat 3.27.6). Even the virtuous person 'must go up and down [. . .], tossed by the waves' of contingency (*Dial.* 1.5.9). According to Chrysippus, 'the soul of the cosmos continues to grow until it consumes its matter' (*SVF* 2.604). Marcus Aurelius confirms the idea of a constantly challenging existence as irreducible: 'In human life, the time of our existence is a point, our substance a flux, our senses dull, the fabric of our entire body subject to corruption, our soul ever restless, our destiny beyond divining, and our fame precarious [. . .] Our life is a war, a brief stay in a foreign land [. . .]' (*Med.* 2.17).

Can we then avoid the turbulences of life in some private Eldorado for the happy few, some philosophical Club Med? No; philosophical health may have grand asymptotic ideals, but it is a modest societal engagement, cultivated amidst the world, not aside of it, and not in an illusiory withdrawal from the chaosmos of Creal for the sake of false comfort:

> Moral perfection is not the final overcoming of obstacles to virtue but a constant confrontation of such obstacles and permanent testing of one's self. [. . .] *Virtue comes from a direct experience of these torments* – this is what it means 'to live in accordance with the experience (κατ' ἐμπειρίαν) of what happens by nature.' Thus, virtue is 'illuminated by the very things with which it is attacked'. (*Dial.* 7.27.2) (Porter, 2020: 239)

Sophia (if you remember our doubter) now takes a deep breath. This may all be very heroic, she ponders, but the truth is that we desire reliable institutions, trustworthy governments, peacefulness in our neighbourhood, retirement or unemployment policies and some sense of security in the company of our fellow humans. And Sophia is probably right: philosophical health need not be constant Nietzschean recklessness and it should bring about some form of slowly transformative peace of mind. Philosophical health is not just about recognising the turmoil of infinite possibilities, but about favouring peaceful compossibilities: 'only insofar as we live in awareness with this interconnection – whether we call it understanding, wisdom, or reflection – are we awake' (Binswanger, 1975: 243).

References

Abrams, Nancy E. and Joel Primack (2011), *The New Universe and the Human Future: How a Shared Cosmology Could Transform the World*. New Haven: Yale University Press.

Ansell-Pearson, Keith (2013), 'True to the Earth: Nietzsche Epicurian Care of Self and World'. In Horst Hutter and Eli Friedland (eds), *Nietzsche's Therapeutic Teaching*, 97–116. London: Bloomsbury.

Austin, John L. (1962), *How to Do Things with Words*. Oxford: Oxford University Press.

Bergson, Henri (1944), *Creative Evolution*, trans. Arthur Mitchell. New York: Random House.

Bergson, Henri (1977 [1932]), *The Two Sources of Morality and Religion*. Notre-Dame: University of Notre-Dame Press.

Binder, Per-Einar (2022), 'Suffering a Healthy Life—On the Existential Dimension of Health'. *Frontiers in Psychology*, 13. https://doi.org/10.3389/fpsyg.2022.803792

Binswanger, Ludwig (1975), 'Dream and Existence'. In *Being in the World*, trans. Jacob Needleman, 222–48. London: Souvenir Press.

Bohm, David (1980), *Wholeness and the Implicate Order*. London: Routledge.

Bracken, Joseph (2001), *The One in the Many: A Contemporary Reconstruction of the God-World Relationship*. Grand Rapids: Eerdmans Publishing.

Clark, Timothy (2012), *The Cambridge Introduction to Literature and Environment*. Cambridge: Cambridge University Press.

Combes, Muriel (2013), *Simondon and the Philosophy of the Transindividual*, trans. T. LaMarre. Cambridge, MA: MIT Press.

Deleuze, Gilles (2005), *Pure Immanence: Essays on a Life*, trans. Anne Boyman. New York: Zone Books.

Deleuze, Gilles and Félix Guattari (1994), *What Is Philosophy?* London: Verso.

Descartes, René (1996 [1641]), *Meditations on First Philosophy*, trans. and ed. John Cottingham. Cambridge: Cambridge University Press.

DeSombre, Elizabeth (2018), *Why Good People Do Bad Environmental Things*. Oxford: Oxford University Press.

Eliade, Mircea (1959), *The Sacred and the Profane*, trans. Willard Ropes Trask. Boston: Houghton Mifflin Harcourt.

Erikson, Erik (1963), *Youth, Change, and Challenge*. New York: Basic Books.

Erikson, Erik (1968), 'Generativity and Ego Integrity'. In Bernice L. Neugarten (ed.), *Middle Age and Aging*. Chicago: University of Chicago Press.

Frankl, Viktor (2019), 'Self-actualization is not the Goal'. Television interview, Youtube: https://youtu.be/OL8DyVusLeE.

Hadot, Pierre (1993), *Plotinus or The Simplicity of Vision*, trans. Michael Chase. Chicago: The University of Chicago Press.

Hadot, Pierre (1995), *Philosophy as a Way of Life*, trans. Michael Chase. Oxford and Cambridge: Blackwell.

Heidegger, Martin (1993), 'The Question Concerning Technology'. In David Farrel Krell (ed.), *Basic Writings*, 311–41. San Francisco: HarperCollins.

Jaeger, Johannes (2018), 'Foreword'. In Daniel J. Nicholson and John Dupré (eds), *Everything Flows: Towards a Processual Philosophy of Biology*, xi–xv. Oxford: Oxford University Press.

Kant, Immanuel (2007), *Anthropology, History, and Education*, ed. Günter Zöller and Robert B. Louden, trans. Mary Gregor et al. Cambridge: Cambridge University.

Kleinberg-Levin, David (2008), *Before the Voice of Reason: Echoes of Responsibility in Merleau-Ponty's Ecology and Levinas's Ethics*. Albany: SUNY Press.

Kotre, John N. (1984), *Outliving the Self*. Baltimore: Johns Hopkins University Press.

Lacan, Jacques (1977), *The Four Fundamental Concepts of Psychoanalysis*. The Seminar Book XI, trans. Alan Sheridan. London: Hogarth Press.

Lee, Marcus (2020), 'Wu-Wei, Merleau-Ponty, and Being Aware of What We Do'. *Philosophy East and West*, 70 (1): 116–35.

Lefebvre, Henri (1991), *The Production of Space*, trans. D. Nicholson-Smith. Hoboken: Wiley-Blackwell.

Merleau-Ponty, Maurice (1968), *The Visible and the Invisible*, trans. A. Lingis. Evanston: Northwestern University Press.

de Miranda, Luis (2008), *Paridaiza*. Paris: Plon. English Edition 2020, trans. Tina Kover. Sacramento: Snuggly Books.

de Miranda, Luis (2017), 'On the Concept of Creal: The Politico-Ethical Horizon of a Creative Absolute'. In Paulo de Assis and Paolo Giudici (eds), *The Dark Precursor: Deleuze and Artistic Research*, 510–16. Louvain: Leuven University Press.

de Miranda, Luis (2019), *Being and Neonness*. Cambridge, MA: MIT Press.

de Miranda, Luis (2020a), 'Artificial Intelligence and Philosophical Creativity: From Analytics to Crealectics'. *Human Affairs*, 30 (4): 597–607.

de Miranda, Luis (2020b), *Ensemblance: The Transnational Genealogy of Esprit de Corps*. Edinburgh: Edinburgh University Press.

de Miranda, Luis (2022), 'Philosophical Health'. In V. Glăveanu, *The Palgrave Encyclopaedia of the Possible*. Cham: Palgrave Macmillan.

de Miranda, Luis (2021a), 'Crealectic Intelligence'. In V. Glăveanu, *The Palgrave Encyclopaedia of the Possible*. Cham: Palgrave Macmillan.

de Miranda, Luis (2021b), 'Think into the Place of the Other: The Crealectic Approach to Philosophical Health and Care'. *International Journal of Philosophical Practice*, 7 (1): 89–103.

de Miranda, Luis, Subramanian Ramamoorthy and Michael Rovatsos (2016), 'We, Anthrobot: Learning from Human Forms of Interaction and Esprit de Corps to Develop More Diverse Social Robotics'. In Johanna Seibt et al. (eds), *What Social Robots Can and Should Do*, 48–59. Amsterdam: IOS Press.

Naess, Arne (2005), 'The Three Great Movements'. In H. Glasser and A. Drengson (eds), *The Selected Works of Arne Næss*, vol. X, 219–25. Dordrecht: Springer.

Nancy, Jean-Luc (2000), *Being Singular Plural*, trans. Robert D. Richardson and Anne E. O'Byrne. Redwood: Stanford University Press.

Nietzsche, Friedrich (2006), *Thus Spoke Zarathustra*, trans. A. Del Caro. Cambridge: Cambridge University Press. Prologue, 3, p. 6 (orig. *bleibt der Erde treu*).

Owens, John (2015), 'Creating an Impersonal NHS? Personalisation, Choice and the Erosion of Intimacy'. *Health Expectations*, 18 (1): 22–31.

Plumwood, Val (2001), *Environmental Culture: The Ecological Crisis of Reason*. London: Routledge.

Porter, James (2020), 'Living on the Edge: Self and World in Extremis'. *Classical Antiquity*, 39 (2): 225–83.

Schelling, Friedrich Wilhelm Joseph (2004), *First Outline of a System of the Philosophy of Nature*, trans. Keith R. Peterson. Albany: SUNY.

Schnider, Armin (2018), *The Confabulating Mind: How the Brain Creates Reality*. Oxford: Oxford University Press.

Shigenori, Nagatomo (1992), *Attunement Through the Body*. Albany: SUNY Press.

Spinoza, Benedict de (2005), *Ethics*, trans. Edwin Curley. London: Penguin.

Spinoza, Benedict de (2007), *Theological-Political Treatise*. Cambridge: Cambridge University Press.

Taminiaux, Jacques (1978), 'Merleau-Ponty. De la dialectique à l'hyperdialectique'. *Tijdschrift voor Filosofie*, 40 (1): 34–55.

Washington, Haydn (2020), *What Can I Do to Help Heal the Environmental Crisis?* London: Routledge.

Wass, Val (2015), 'Opening Our Eyes to Global Health; A Philosophy of Universal Values'. *Perspectives on Medical Education*, 4 (6): 331–3.

Whitehead (1978 [1929]), *Process and Reality*. New York: The Free Press.

Methodological epilogue

Sense-making interviews looking at elements of philosophical health (SMILE_PH)

Luis de Miranda

Introduction: A new method to approach personal philosophies

Between January and April 2022, with the official approval of the Swedish Ethical Review Authority (Dnr 2021-04898), I conducted two series of interviews with eight tetraplegic persons (four men and four women). They had been living with a severe spinal cord injury (SCI) and a wheelchair for several decades. They led what they and their community considered to be good lives, and while their body was severely disabled, their cognitive functions were intact. I was first and foremost interested in their personal philosophy of life and how philosophizing might have helped them to accept, overcome or transcend their condition.

In the first set of interviews (phase 1), I asked them directly what was philosophically important to them and what was their personal philosophy of life. In what follows, I call this approach *rationalist* because it presupposes that individuals can answer epistemic questions about their personal existence, a problematic assumption. In preparation for the second round of interviews (phase 2), which took place two months later, I elaborated a more progressive and structured sense-making approach based on six step-by-step elements: (1) the bodily sense, (2) the sense of self, (3) the sense of belonging, (4) the sense of the possible, (5) the sense of purpose and (6) the philosophical sense. By taking the interviewees smoothly through these six elements in that order, such that the philosophical sense was this time only addressed towards the end of the interview rather than its beginning, I observed that the interviewees were much less disoriented, more comfortable in their articulations and capable of generating sharper philosophical insights than during phase 1.

In this chapter, which is primarily meant to help practitioners willing to implement a philosophical health protocol, I will first briefly introduce the phenomenology of sense-making interviews. I will then present and evaluate the SMILE_PH approach (Sense-Making Interviews Looking at Elements of Philosophical Health) with examples from my SCI interviews (phase 2). I will then, in a third part, compare the SMILE_PH method with the more rationalist and unstructured approach that is often used in empirical philosophical dialogue, here also with examples from my SCI interviews (phase 1).

The phenomenology of sense-making interviews

I present here a semi-structured phenomenological method specifically designed to approach first-person philosophies of life. Usual psychological scales such as – among many others – the Free Will and Determinism Scale (Stillman et al., 2010) are unfit for phenomenological research: they are too normative for something as complex and delicate as our personal philosophical sense. On the other hand, there is a problem with the standard interpretative phenomenological interviews (Smith, Flowers and Larkin, 2009): being fairly unstructured, they produce richer results but lack reproducibility, in particular intercoder reliability, which is a guarantee that similar interpretations and emphases will be drawn by different analysts (Campbell et al., 2013). Of course, there will always be a creative or subjective aspect in analysing unstructured or semi-structured interviews, particularly when their interpretation refers to our philosophical sense of life. Our challenge is to allow for a dialogue protocol that is both complex enough (personalised) and yet systematic enough (reproducible and comparable).

I present here SMILE_PH (Sense-Making Interviews Looking at Elements of Philosophical Health), an approach to philosophical health dialogue which, I believe, avoids the corseting pitfalls of psychologizing questionnaires and the excessive fuzziness of in-depth unstructured interviews. This approach is qualitative. The research interview is not a questioning means by which an omniscient researcher gathers measurable data transmitted by a passive subject treated as an object. In a qualitative interview, the interviewer and the interviewee are more or less equal partners in actively co-creating meaning around the interview theme. Such an interview approach is an unfolding process towards meaning-making (Holsteim and Gubrium, 1995: 52), or better: sense-making.

Because it is a continually unfolding process, I prefer the phrase 'sense-making' rather than 'meaning-making'. Sense-making is about the ongoing search for comprehensibility (Dransart, 2013), the process of elaborating meaning, while meaning itself may be the abstract result of such a process (an ideal coherent meaning). Sometimes making sense does not provide us with a fully coherent meaning despite careful attempts. One should not fetishise meaning as a product or objective result. In the case of philosophical health, the path and process of questioning and answering as thoughtfully as possible can be awareness-raising even if a coherent philosophical worldview is not produced. When different meanings might cohabit in a person or a situation, the process of sense-making tends to resolve contrasts or contradictions (Leontʾev, 1978; Kaptelinin, 2005; Bijlsma, Schaap and de Bruijn, 2016), by synthesizing them into an ensemble that points, teleologically, to increased existential or epistemic lucidity.

The word *sense*, with its intentional ambiguity between sense as meaning and sense as perception, alludes to a unity or symbiosis between body and mind. Meaning is often implicit before it becomes explicit – its unveiling resembles Socratic midwifery (Tomin, 1987). When a person makes sense of something, this is the result of a collaboration between the person's intuition, emotion, reflection, intelligence, culture, environment, languages or any other means by which we might try to interpret signs. As the interviewee speaks in the first person, 'sense-making' conveys better than 'meaning-making' that we are not looking immediately for universal abstract meanings but rather starting with embodied views and impressions. Individuals engage in sense-making under conditions of equivocality and uncertainty: they make intuitive, not always immediately or systematically rational, judgements about their existence (Weick, 1979; 1995; Sonenshein, 2007).

The goal of sense-making dialogue is to co-create a progressive and asymptotic understanding of human situations, values and events that often go unexamined or under-examined (Seamon, 2000). Humans are, potentially at least, purpose-seeking beings. However, this teleological aspect of our minds tends to be overlooked in society, work or healthcare environments, which can be objectifying and depersonalizing in their focus on physical or psychological health seen as a set of conformities to norms in the present. Similarly, a too-rational approach to philosophical health can be depersonalizing because we are not meeting the other person on her or his home ground but rather forcing an abstract or conceptual outlook.

Phenomenologically minded researchers seek to understand lived experiences by listening deeply (de Miranda, 2021a) to evocations of worlds as subjects experience them, focusing on personal or shared meanings (Finlay, 2011). A common tool is the phenomenological qualitative interview, as developed for instance, by Giorgi, Smith and Osborn, or with some variations by Van Manen (Gallagher, 2012). There are other influential approaches to sense-making, such as Brenda Dervin's (Dervin and Foreman-Wernet, 2003). In all the above cases, subjects – who are considered able to become specialists of themselves, with emphasis on *becoming* – contribute to the knowledge generation process in reciprocal interaction with the interviewer (Høffding and Martiny, 2016). Rather than a measuring or rationalist stance, an intellectually empathic stance is needed during these first-person exchanges to facilitate reflexive sense-making (Varela and Shear, 1999: 10; Kee, 2018).

We constantly make decisions that are grounded in the way in which the world appears to us as embodied beings (Roth, 2012). Such appearances are never neutral but always perspectival, carried, for example, by a more or less singular sense of self. Our first-person experience of the world is interpretative in a more or less blurry and messy way (Lemke, Kelly and Roth, 2006), and *sense* refers to an embodied perception that attempts to evaluate its environment and transpose it into meaningful action, intuition or thinking. Persons are a continuous and transformative process of points of view on specific situations or problems to which they seek to enact meaningful and ideally coherent responses (Schmitt and Labour, 2022).

The implicit or explicit intention of sense-making may be to construct order over apparent chaos (Ybema and Willems, 2015). Such a process mobilizes intertwined corporeal, emotional and cognitive dimensions (Di Paolo, Cuffari and De Jaegher, 2018). *Sense-making* is thus a term commonly understood as the process through which people interpret and give meaning to their experiences (Lam, Urquhart and Brenda, 2016). This process is progressive and may start with somewhat confused impressions. As Chia (2000: 517) puts it, we may start with:

an undifferentiated flux of fleeting sense-impressions, and it is out of this brute aboriginal flux of lived experience that attention carves out and conception names. [Meanings or interpretations] have to be forcibly carved out of the undifferentiated flux of raw experience and conceptually fixed and labelled so that they can become the common currency for communicational exchanges. (Chia, 2000: 517)

Sense-making, and a sense-making dialogue, is about the continued drafting of an emerging narrative to become comprehensive and comprehensible and to construct an identity (Weick, Sutcliffe and Obstfeld, 2005). This process of shaping unity from an embodied source of discursive possibilities or experiences necessitates at least internal dialogue. The philosophical health approach posits that sense-making is easier in an intercreative dialogue with another human being (de Miranda, 2021b). The SMILE_PH approach offers researchers and counsellors a method to formalize this intercreative dialogue in order to progressively unveil our personal philosophies, our sense of purpose and our root concepts, virtues or values.

Sense-Making Interviews Looking at Elements of Philosophical Health (SMILE_PH)

Between January and April 2022, in partnership with the rehabilitation unit of Linköping University Hospital and the Swedish NGO RG Aktiv Rehabilitering, I conducted a study among persons living in Sweden with spinal cord injury (SCI), focusing on their philosophy of life. I interviewed twice eight persons (four male and four female) who had been living what they and the spinal cord injury community considered to be an active good life. Spinal cord injury is a severe trauma and its tetraplegic variant designates the usually irreversible inability to voluntarily move or often feel sensations in the upper and lower parts of the body; the areas of impaired mobility usually include the fingers, hands, arms, chest, legs, feet and toes. The goal of this study was to determine if there were personal philosophical reasons for explaining their positive mindset, despite their condition. During this study, I designed the SMILE_PH method, anchored in my view that the sense of the possible is highly related to health.

The SMILE_PH method of dialogue does not focus only and immediately on the higher-cognitive dimension of our philosophical sense but rather proceeds step by step from a primary dimension of embodiment and sense of self, in order to progressively awaken or unveil a more philosophical sense. It is important to note that even if subjects share the same world (for instance, everyday life with a wheelchair), they may have more or less explicitly – or aspire to – different epistemic perspectives. The SMILE_PH method helps make the implicit or latent philosophical stances explicit, thus more relevant or actionable.

As mentioned earlier, SMILE_PH has six progressive steps. First, I feel (or do not), I have impressions and perceive (*bodily sense*). Then, because I feel and perceive, I can say that I *am* (*sense of self*). Because I am not alone in the world, I sometimes wish to say *we are* (*sense of belonging*). Together or alone, I sense that this, or that, or something yet to be defined *can* be done (*sense of the possible*). Later I feel that this or that, in particular, *should* be done to make *my* world and *the* world a better place (sense of purpose). Under the sense of purpose lies a view about the meaning of life and world (philosophical sense): such is the six-step process of the SMILE_PH method, designed to be epistemically gentle because gradual, from what people are familiar with to what they reflect less often upon.

Question 1 – The bodily sense

'Tell me about your bodily sense: how you feel and perceive your body, what your relationship with your body is.' This is the first step in a SMILE-PH conversation. It is connected to our irrefutable experience of physical presence in the world (Nagatomo, 1992). It takes only a deep breath to become aware of our bodily sense. In sense-making processes, we need to be attentive to the embodied mind with first-hand experience of its own living body (Thompson, 2004: 90). This embodied aspect is particularly important for a first-person phenomenological approach, especially if we are intertwined sensing bodies with different worlds but within a common 'flesh of the world' (Merleau-Ponty, 1968: 84).

We are embodied living creatures with an inner continuous life, the variations of which we can sense (Jonas, 1966). In the case of people living with tetraplegia, my study confirmed that even after the body is paralysed to a very high degree and made insensitive by a spinal cord injury, it slowly finds new ways of sensing itself, actualises new cues out of a field of possibilities. Even chronic pain can be integrated – but only to a certain extent for most of us – as a viable element of bodily presence.

I offer hereinafter one example, a unit of dialogue related to the bodily sense and taken from the first minutes of my SCI interviews (phase 2, using SMILE_PH), in which LdM designates myself as the interviewer:

LdM: We'll be talking about your bodily sense first. How would you speak about your body, its feelings, its sensations; what does that mean for you?

Interviewee C: Well, in my case, since I have a high spinal cord injury, the physical sense, from my chest, above my chest and down, doesn't exist. I can feel a little bit in my arms and a little bit in my left hand, but with my right hand, I can't feel anything. So, in my case, I had to learn how to live without the physical sense of my body, and the small parts that I can actually feel became even more important. . . . And it's very difficult to describe how it actually feels, not being able to have the full sense in your body. But I used to be a ballet dancer, and when I was dancing, I felt every inch of my body and I had control of every inch of my body. Now being paralyzed, I don't have the same control, but somehow, I feel like I can feel my body anyway. And it's very hard to explain that feeling, but with the parts I can actually use and move physically, where my nerves are still connected, I have very good control. And I think this has a lot to do with the sense of memory, the memory of how my body felt once upon a time. I can close my eyes and still feel how it felt to dance. . .

Question 2 – The sense of self

The second element in a SMILE_PH interview is the sense of self: 'Tell me about your sense of self, how you perceive your self and feel about it.' A sense of self arises after considering our embodied connections (Finlay, 2011). For a subject to be an agent with an identity, there must be some distinction between the subject and its body (which is not necessarily a dualism). The notions of individuation and self-individuation here are crucial: humans are self-organizing, self-creating, dynamic systems, which are more or less autonomous and capable of defining their own self-boundaries (Di Paolo 2005; 2009; De Jaegher and Froese 2009; Thompson 2007). Human subjects can define themselves as distinct individuals, especially in our postmodern societies, which encourage individualism.

In the case of tetraplegic people living with SCI, it became clear that a strong sense of self and personal narrative was needed to reinvent one's life after a severe trauma. Here is a fragment taken from my SMILE_PH interviews:

> **LdM**: Let's talk about the sense of self. You already said that your self is your soul. Is it anything else?
>
> **Interviewee D**: Maybe it's too simple if I say that it's just my soul, because I see myself as a person consisting of my body, my soul and my spirit, and none of these is much more important than the other . . .

Question 3 – The sense of belonging

The third step in the SMILE_PH approach is the sense of belonging, which, as the previous sense, can be perceived as depleted, problematic or fulfilled, rich, more or less free-flowing. As I have explored in detail in the book *Ensemblance*, the epistemology of this particular sense distinguishes, historically and philosophically, on the one hand, pathological forms of belonging such as groupthink and on the other hand eudynamic forms of belonging or 'well-belonging' (de Miranda, 2020). Furthermore, a phenomenological approach would perhaps tend to place the sense of belonging before the sense of self, arguing that we are a *we* before we are a *I*. This may well be true from the perspective of social ontology but less so from the perspective of person-centred care in the twenty-first century, after two centuries of now globalized individualism: in the context of a personal interview, it is more 'natural' to start with the sense of self before the sense of belonging.

Here is an example taken from my SCI study:

> **LdM**: Let's talk about your sense of belonging. Do you feel that you belong today, compared to twenty years ago? How did this sense evolve?
>
> **Interviewee E**: I have a belonging to friends or family, but through work-life it has been difficult. I have worked for several years in different companies and so on, but it is very hard to get into a new place.
>
> **LdM**: What do you mean?
>
> **Interviewee E**: You know, the unemployment statistics for persons in my situation aren't that good . . .

Question 4 – The sense of the possible

Step 4 of the SMILE_PH dialogue process wonders about the sense of the possible of the interviewee or counselee. This is the core sense from which I have inferred the other senses while designing the method (see Chapter 17 in the present anthology, as well as the introduction). It is via a meditation on health defined as depletion or increase of the sense of the possible that I conceived the possibility of a semi-structured methodology between phase 1 and phase 2 of the SCI pilot study. I asked myself: if the sense of the possible defines health phenomenologically, with what other senses does it cohabit to form a compossible ensemble?

The possible is also the root concept of various ontologies and not only crealectics (de Miranda, 2021c): as was understood by Leibniz, by phenomenologists such as Husserl (1982) or the psychiatrist Ludwig Binswanger (1960: 255), and by Existentialist philosophers like Sartre and Heidegger, the universe is a *possibilising* furnace, an opening for the making-possible (Heidegger, 1995: 364; 1996: 244). My SCI study has shown that the sense of the possible of the interviewees who were able to intercreate a flourishing life with long-term tetraplegia is very strong: 'Everything is possible', they uttered quasi-unanimously, a formulation that takes a less cliché meaning when pronounced in the context of people whose existence is dependent on a wheelchair. The fact that they all live in Sweden, a country with relatively strong disability support or institutional solidarity explains part of this positive attitude. Still, even in Scandinavia, not all people with spinal cord injuries manage to overcome their condition in a flourishing manner.

In the months that followed their traumatic accident, my interviewees were all more or less depressive, ignoring certain kinds of possibilities in their experienced surroundings (Ratcliffe, 2020). During a depressive episode, the sense of the possible falls close to zero: 'Depression manifests itself as a crisis of [...] the almost born instinct that things are fluid, that they unfold and change, that new kinds of moments are eventually possible, that the future will arrive. [...] There is [it seems] no possibility of redemption or hope' (Lott, 1996: 246–7).

Conversely, when one embodied living being starts to say and feel, of a desired situation, idea, initiative or way of life, that *it is possible*, one is connecting with one's modal dimension in a potentially transformative way. The sense of the possible is – at least asymptotically – performative: it begins to produce something which may or may not become actualised; it is the intuited gateway to transforming virtuality into reality. The sense of the possible precedes the sense of purpose and the philosophical sense: 'There is a practical consciousness, an "I can" that underlies and precedes the reflective self-consciousness of the "I think"' (Sinclair, 2017: 191).

Here is one interview fragment regarding the sense of the possible taken from my SCI study:

> **LdM**: What can you tell me about your sense of the possible?
> **Interviewee F**: Possible, possibilities? Yes, I believe, really, that everything is possible. And when I say everything, it's not like you can do exactly the same physical movements, but mentally, you can have the same possibilities and that is what really counts. Many of the mentally strongest people I've

met are people with very high lesions actually, that cannot move anything, not a finger. I've met people with an extremely strong focus, and because they cannot focus on how to move or anything, they have to focus on how they think. They develop their thinking; they have a lot of time to think. And if you cannot do it yourself, you can always think creatively about how to solve problems for others.

Question 5 – The sense of purpose

The fifth element of the SMILE_PH method is the sense of purpose. Once we have perceived and clarified our embodiment, our self, our belonging and our sense of the possible, we may begin to wonder how our actions may be purposive for the greater good.

An agent acts and thus self-regulates to achieve something – there is something it is trying to do or a goal it is attempting to reach, and in so doing, the very attempt can either succeed or fail (Barandiaran, Di Paolo and Rhode, 2009). Actions, unlike random movements, are teleological, goal-directed and hence normative, but they can also be teleological in the more elaborate sense that they are related to a higher meaning and value-guided conduct (Barrett, 2017; Di Paolo, 2005). In some cases, the sense of purpose unveils a vocation in the Weberian sense (Tickamyer, 1981).

From the perspective of philosophical health, only a minority of us have a self-examined and ambitiously altruistic sense of life purpose today. While it is easier for most people to speak of their bodily sense, of their sense of self, of the sense of belonging and of the sense of the possible, the sense of purpose is harder to formalize or conceptualize. Yet, in my experience (since 2022, I have also applied the SMILE_PH method with my regular counselees), it becomes easier to unveil a possible sense of higher purpose when this theme comes in the dialogue after the previous senses in a progressive order that generates meaning at a slower pace.

Here is one example taken from phase 2 of my SCI study:

> **LdM**: Let's move to the sense of purpose, which [. . .] seems very important for you.
>
> **Interviewee D**: Yes, to have a purpose in life is very important. To feel that you are part of something bigger, that you have a place in creation, in this world, is important for me. And it's not about being able to do many valuable things; it's not about being a very smart person or able person. It's about finding purpose in the small things. [. . .] Because no person can do everything and carry the whole burden alone. But everyone can do some part of it . . .

Question 6 – The philosophical sense

This is the final step of the SMILE-PH method of dialogue and should arrive at the end of the process (ideally, one would like to dedicate one session to each of the senses). As the philosophical health conversation unfolds, dialogical listening and sense-making empower the interviewee intellectually by raising awareness about their understanding of life and helping them to verbalize their personal worldview (Kizel, 2017). Once the person has been able to clarify their philosophical sense, they can step by step reconsider the five previous senses in a new light.

Philosophical sense requires more than searching for particular solutions to perceived problems; it requires the ability to look beyond the immediate needs to a wholesome state of consideration based on pulsating metaphysical, social, political or economic ways of living in the world (Schultz, 2005). The philosophical impulse is the impulse not only to interrogate but also to de- and reconstruct our shared experience of the world (Lin and Sequeira, 2017).

Here is one interview sample regarding the philosophical sense taken from phase 2 of my SCI study:

> **LdM**: Tell me about your philosophical sense of life.
> **Interviewee F**: I really believe that the hard times, always, will help you to develop, even if you don't think that it will be the case just at that moment. [. . .] When bad things happen, you didn't want them to happen just because it could turn out to be good in the future; but I just realized that for me, they have provided me with good things. [. . .] I actually made a diagram of the important events in my life, and it looks just like an electrocardiogram: heart rates, you know, or brainwaves [. . .]. This was bad here, and there instead with the birth of my first daughter, etc. And when you look at it, it's like a heart rhythm. Or brainwaves. It looks like that. Then I thought: that is life; it's not a straight line.
> **LdM**: Right. A rhythm. [A frequency wave].
> **Interviewee F**: Yes. Otherwise, you cannot appreciate it either. . .

Altogether, the SMILE_PH method is an alternative to an overly rationalist or purely epistemic approach to dialogue. The latter tends to assume that everyone is a philosopher or a logician capable or answering the question of philosophical sense without the progressive mediation of more familiar and mundane steps. To better understand what this distinction means with one example, let's analyse my comparative use of the rationalist approach with the same SCI interviewees.

Limitations of a rationalist approach to interviewing

I conducted the first set of interviews within the same SCI pilot study, in 2022, without a step-by-step method, in what could be defined as a rationalist hermeneutical approach, sometimes called 'beyond method' (Ironside, 2013). This was done eight to four weeks before I designed the SMILE_PH method. I initiated these conversations by asking the eight participants: 'What is your personal philosophy of life? What is most important for you in life?'

Even though the interviewees were advised that this study was about their philosophical stance, they were taken aback by the initial magnitude of the question, often expressing some form of puzzlement or difficulty in answering. This difficulty persisted to a variable extent as the interview unfolded partly because as an interviewer, I was focused on giving sense to the unique question about their philosophy of life. This is not without analogy with the puzzlement of some of Socrates' interlocutors in Plato's dialogues, partly due to his stubborn insistence on epistemic utterances. The Socratic interlocutors that perform better, like, for example, Glaucon in the *Republic*, who was Plato's brother, have usually been previously trained by Socrates into philosophizing.

The Socratic dialogue or epistemic interview (Brinkmann, 2007) is an interview form that focuses on knowledge (*episteme*) rather than opinions (*doxa*). It could seem particularly fit for studies about philosophical stances and philosophical health. But unfortunately, it can easily turn into an abstract, rationalist approach that forgets that how the interviewer calls forth the interviewee's thoughts and impressions has a direct impact on the quality and specificity of the answers (Dinkins, 2005).

One problem with beyond-method rationalist interviews is that the path can be meandrous and chaotic. Metaphorically speaking, instead of climbing a hill, the interviewees (by asking them to formulate *ab initio* their philosophical sense of life or what is most important for them in life) are immediately transported by helicopter to the top of the philosophical mountain, where oxygen might be scarce. This often leads to a need to then climb down the mountain to access more mundane topics in order to catch some air, while attempting to go up again repetitively when teased by the rationalist interviewer.

I present here two real samples taken from the first moments of my SCI pilot study (phase 1, without using the SMILE_PH method):

> **LdM:** We are here to discuss your personal philosophy, your conception of life, whatever meaning you want to give to that. And that would actually be my first question: How would you define your thoughts about your philosophy of life?
>
> **Interviewee A:** Well, do you think you can narrow it down a bit? It's such a big question, isn't it?
>
> **LdM:** It is. Let's try this for example: do you think life, in general, has a meaning or purpose?
>
> **Interviewee A:** You mean apart from living it? Apart from . . . if it's got a higher meaning? What do you mean, is it in a religious context or? . . .
>
>   *   *   *
>
> **LdM:** Welcome, and as you know, we're here to discuss your philosophy of life. And I would like to start by asking you what this phrase suggests to you. Or what are the most important ideas or values in your life? You can start wherever you want.
>
> **Interviewee B:** Well, that's, that's, that's a small question. I mean, that's . . . where do you start? . . .

In phase 1 of the SCI pilot study, in which I used a rationalist straight-to-the point approach, the vast majority of my interviewees commented on the difficulty for them to address the triggering philosophical question of the study, considered to be intimidating and too vast. Certainly, through deep listening (de Miranda, 2021a) and because of my past counselling experience, it was possible to generate interesting answers, such that the epistemic approach did not prove to be a fiasco. But the process did not feel optimal, especially with those among the interviewees that had rarely been exposed to philosophical thinking.

For the purpose of philosophical counselling, it is worth reminding us here that when an interviewee gets overwhelmed by an epistemic question, refocus on more embodied everyday matters and active listening on the behalf of the interviewer are essential, especially in an open unstructured dialogue:

> The capacity to listen attentively while remaining appropriately silent is useful during the elicitation. This can present a challenge for many researchers. Understanding what is being said and what may be hidden, responding sensitively to the cadence of the interview, and actively acquiescing to the participants' direction is important to the process of moving the interview along with inquiring questions as the narrative text is co-created. (Vandermause and Fleming, 2011: 371)

One could concede that the interviews in phase 1 unfolded reasonably well despite an abrupt beginning, but even so, the gathered information was scattered and necessitated some effort to interpret and compare. In fact, the data gathered in phase 1 became clearer only retroactively, once the SMILE_PH method was formulated and applied.

One could argue that the problem in the unstructured phase 1 was not of the interviewer but of the interviewee, who may have lacked epistemological insights and conceptual-thinking training. As is common and ethical practice, the interviewees were informed of the main theme of the study when they gave their consent several days before the first interview. Should we blame them for coming unprepared? Then we would probably have to blame most of humanity for being still unprepared for philosophizing even though philosophy was invented several millennia ago. Svend Brinkmann, although he is a psychologist rather than a philosopher, regrets that most interviewees are consumers rather than epistemic agents (2007), hence their unpreparedness for rational rather than experiential discourse:

> What is needed, I believe, is for qualitative researchers to consider the spread of Rogers's humanistic interviews and other psychologistic or doxastic interviews as a reflection of the contemporary consumer society in which the client is always right, in which his or her experiences and narratives are always interesting because they are some individual's experiences and narratives and in which the interviewer (or therapist) merely acts as a mirror of the respondent's feelings, attitudes, and beliefs. (Brinkmann, 2007: 1122)

In contradiction with his irritated lack of faith about people's capacities in the above statement, Brinkmann does, however, believe that interviews could and perhaps should be epistemic a priori, that they can focus on what people *know*. His model is again Socrates, an interviewer who sometimes talks more than his respondents, contradicts them and more often than not exhibits their lack of rationality or conceptual power rather painfully, if politely on the surface. Some philosophical counsellors today believe they must be somewhat aggressive, annoying or hyper-logical with the counselee, rather than pedagogic. I disagree: the philosophical health approach involves being patient and showing some intellectual compassion for the philosophical cluelessness of most humans, especially in a global time of anti-intellectualism and indeed consumerism in which nation states are intentionally not investing resources in the philosophical education and the critical-conceptual thinking of the younger.

My multiple-year experience of conducting philosophical dialogues with individuals is that most people do not have an explicit epistemic take on life. This does not mean they do not possess the embryo of an implicit philosophy of life, that they cannot develop a sense of purpose or elaborate a worldview; it simply means that our philosophical sense is more often than not latent and needs some training, like a metaphysical or speculative muscle. The role of the counsellor or interviewer is to help people think deeper step by step, incrementally, and be friendly as long as the interlocutor is trying to make-sense of their life with goodwill and some effort. This is what philosophy means etymologically: the philosopher is a *friend*, not a judge. A friend does not have to be flattering nor encourage mental laziness, but a friend is never destructive or condescending.

My experience of what I have called the rationalist approach is that it does not create the best kind of explicit results. Moreover, due to the lack of method or an open dialogue, the interpretative workload of the interviewer is then higher, which contains risks of wrong interpretation or epistemic injustice, that is, of the analyst speaking and conceptualizing into the place of the interviewee (Fricker, 2007; see also Rosenhagen's Chapter 7 in the present anthology). Conducting a Socratic dialogue of the kind that constantly dismantles the epistemic ground of what is said by the interlocutor with persons that are more vulnerable than others would probably not be considered ethically safe. In fact, philosophically speaking, we are all more or less vulnerable (see McMahon's Chapter 6 in this volume), given the difficulty of producing a highly-coherent philosophical explanation of concrete situations.

After the first phase of the SCI study, I felt something suboptimal with a rationalist approach and its unstructured, overly epistemic form of interviewing. What I wanted, to once again convey an alpine metaphor, is to slowly and progressively hike into the sense-making mountain side by side with the interviewee, starting from the experiential foot of the prominence, that is our indisputable embodiment, and slowly progressing toward the epistemic peak (which is not unlike Plato's metaphor of the cave).

Conclusion: Developing the SMILE_PH methodology

The SMILE_PH approach is a method which can be used in various contexts. I believe it can encourage our democratic need for philosophical health. I would expect more interviewers or counsellors to try and perform SMILE_PH interviews and compare results – this process has started thanks to a few philosophical counselling colleagues. In various domains, such as person-centred care, for instance, one may want to know more about the personal philosophy of an interlocutor. Most persons are not philosophers, which means that if we want to unveil their worldviews and implicit or embryonic philosophical stances, we need a smooth first-person approach that can also be applied to non-specialists.

The SMILE_PH approach I presented here is a proposition to approach methodically personal philosophies via structured dialogues with non-philosophers. More collective work is, of course, needed to ground and test this methodology, with questions such as: Why this order of questioning? Why these particular six senses rather than others or more than six? Will we really be able to compare the answers systematically once the interviewers or counsellors are diverse? And to what purpose?

Last but not least, there is an extent to which the number of interviews with the same person might mean that therapy and research could partly coincide. To explain this last statement, let's imagine that instead of concentrating the six steps of the SMILE_PH approach in one interview of forty-five minutes, as I did in phase 2 of my SCI pilot, the interviewer decides to spend one full session on each sense, that is at least six sessions per interviewee. Not only would the result probably be more fine-grained but it would probably generate insights on the side of the interviewer that could be transformative. As said, I have been testing this longer approach with a few of my philosophical counselees since June 2022: I spent more than six sessions with each of them unfolding the SMILE_PH approach. This slow-paced approach seems very promising, as the counselees could articulate a sense of purpose and a philosophical sense much more clearly and distinctly than they had previously been able to in more 'beyond-method' dialogues with me (the latter can still be useful in some cases, at least as a respiration in the dialogue).

In the context of the SMILE_PH method, interviewers and interviewees, counsellors and counselees, will most probably intercreate sharper results if they extend their dialogue sessions. Such a process is not only information-producing but also awareness-raising. This is why I believe that philosophical health, when applied in the field of academic research, is a part of what has been called *action research* (Barnes et al., 2016; Carr, 2006; Reason, 2003). Philosophical health is not so much about inquiring about thoughts as objects, implementing the *right* ideas or logical correctness: philosophical health is a form of consciousness available to humanity.

References

Barandiaran, Xavier, Ezequiel A. Di Paolo and Marieke Rohde (2009), 'Defining Agency: Individuality, Normativity, Asymmetry, and Spatio-Temporality in Action'. *Adaptive Behavior*, 17 (5): 367–86.

Barnes, Sandra L., Lauren Brinkley-Rubinstein, Bernadette Doykos, Nina C. Martin and Alison McGuire, eds (2016), *Academics in Action! A Model for Community-Engaged Research, Teaching, and Service*. New York: Fordham University Press.

Barrett, Nathaniel (2017), 'The Normative Turn in Enactive Theory: An Examination of Its Roots and Implications'. *Topoi*, 36 (3): 431–43.

Bijlsma, Nienke, Harmen Schaap and Elly de Bruijn (2016), 'Students' Meaning-Making and Sense-Making of Vocational Knowledge in Dutch Senior Secondary Vocational Education'. *Journal of Vocational Education & Training*, 68 (3): 378–94.

Binswanger, Ludwig (1960), 'Daseinsanalyse und Psychotherapie II'. *Acta Psychoterapeutica et Psychosomatica*, 8 (4): 251–60.

Brinkmann, Svend (2007), 'Could Interviews be Epistemic? An Alternative to Opinion Polling'. *Qualitative Inquiry*, 13 (8): 1116–38.

Campbell, John L., Charles Quincy, Jordan Osserman and Ove K. Pedersen (2013), 'Coding In-depth Semistructured Interviews: Problems of Unitization and Intercoder Reliability and Agreement'. *Sociological Methods & Research*, 42 (3): 294–320.

Carr, Wilfred (2006), 'Philosophy, Methodology and Action Research'. *Journal of Philosophy and Education*, 40 (4): 421–35.

Chia, Robert (2000), 'Discourse Analysis as Organizational Analysis'. *Organization*, 7 (3): 513–18.

De Jaegher, Hanne and Tom Froese (2009), 'On the Role of Social Interaction in Individual Agency'. *Adaptive Behavior*, 17 (5): 444–60.

Dervin, Brenda and Lois Foreman-Wernet (2003), *Sense-Making Methodology Reader*. Cresskill: Hampton Press.

Dinkins, Christine (2005), 'Shared Inquiry: Socratic-Hermeneutic Interpre-Viewing'. In M. Ironside Pamela (ed.), *Beyond method: Philosophical Conversations in Healthcare Research and Scholarship*, 111–47. Wisconsin: University of Wisconsin Press.

Di Paolo, Ezequiel (2005), 'Autopoiesis, Adaptivity, Teleology, Agency'. *Phenomenology and the Cognitive Sciences*, 4 (4): 429–52.

Di Paolo, Ezequiel (2009), 'Extended Life'. *Topoi*, 28 (1): 9–21.

Di Paolo, Ezequiel, Elena C. Cuffari and Hanne De Jaegher (2018), *Linguistic Bodies: The Continuity between Life and Language*. Cambridge, MA: MIT Press.

Dransart, Dolores A. C. (2013), 'From Sense-Making to Meaning-Making: Understanding and Supporting Survivors of Suicide'. *The British Journal of Social Work*, 43 (2): 317–35.

Finlay, Linda (2011), *Phenomenology for Therapists: Researching the Lived World*. Hoboken: Wiley.

Fricker, Miranda (2007), *Epistemic Injustice: Power and the Ethics of Knowing*. Oxford: Oxford University Press.

Gallagher, Shaun (2012), 'Taking Stock of Phenomenology Futures'. *The Southern Journal of Philosophy*, 50 (2): 304–18.

Heidegger, Martin (1995), *The Fundamental Concepts of Metaphysics*, trans. W. McNeill and N. Walker. Bloomington and Indianapolis: Indiana University Press.

Heidegger, Martin (1996), *Being and Time*, trans. J. Stambaugh. Albany: SUNY Press.

Høffding, Simon and Kristian Martiny (2016), 'Framing a Phenomenological Interview: What, Why and How'. *Phenomenology and the Cognitive Sciences*, 15 (4): 539–64.

Holstein, James and Jaber Gubrium (1995), *The Active Interview*. London: Sage Publications.

Husserl, Edmund (1982), *General Introduction to Pure Phenomenology*, Vol. II of *Edmund Husserl: Collected Works*, trans. Fred Kersten. The Hague: Martinus Nijhoff.

Ironside, Pamela M. (2013), *Beyond Method: Philosophical Conversations in Healthcare Research and Scholarship*. Wisconsin: University of Wisconsin Press.

Jonas, Hans (1966), *The Phenomenon of Life: Towards a Philosophical Biology*. Evanston: Northwestern University Press.

Kaptelinin, V. (2005), 'The Object of Activity: Making Sense of the Sense-Maker'. *Mind, Culture, and Activity*, 12 (1): 4–18.

Kee, Hayden (2018), 'Phenomenology and Naturalism in Autopoietic and Radical Enactivism: Exploring Sense-Making and Continuity from the Top Down'. *Synthese (Dordrecht)*, 198 (9): 2323–43.

Kizel, Arie (2017), 'Philosophy with Children as Enabling Community of Multi-Narratives'. In Ching-Ching Lin and Lavina Sequeira (eds), *Inclusion, Diversity, and Intercultural Dialogue in Young People's Philosophical Inquiry*, 69–84. Rotterdam: Sense Publishers.

Lam, Mei Chun L., Christine Urquhart and Dervin L. Brenda (2016), 'Sense-Making/Sensemaking'. In P. Moy (ed.), *Oxford Bibliographies in Communication*. Oxford: Oxford University Press. https://www.oxfordbibliographies.com/display/document/obo-9780199756841/obo-9780199756841-0112.xml.

Lemke, Jay, Gregory Kelly and Wolff-Michael Roth (2006), 'FORUM: Toward a Phenomenology of Interviews: Lessons from the Phenomenology of Interviews'. *Cultural Studies of Science Education*, 1 (1): 83–106.

Leont'ev, A. N. (1978), *Activity, Consciousness, and Personality*. Englewood Cliffs: Prentice Hall.

Lin, Ching-Ching and Lavina Sequeira (2017), *Inclusion, Diversity, and Intercultural Dialogue in Young People's Philosophical Inquiry*. Rotterdam: Sense Publishers.

Lott, Tim (1996), *The Scent of Dried Roses*. London: Viking.

Merleau-Ponty, M. (1968), *The Visible and the Invisible*, trans. A. Lingis. Evanston: Northwestern University Press.

de Miranda, Luis (2020), *Ensemblance: The Transnational Genealogy of esprit de corps*. Edinburgh: Edinburgh University Press.

de Miranda, Luis (2021a), 'Five Principles of Philosophical Health: From Hadot to Crealectics'. *Eidos: A Journal for Philosophy of Culture*, 5 (1): 70–89.

de Miranda, Luis (2021b), 'Think into the Place of the Other: The Crealectic Approach to Philosophical Health and Care'. *International Journal of Philosophical Practice*, 7 (1): 89–103.

De Miranda, Luis (2021c), 'Crealectic Intelligence'. In Vlad Glăveanu (ed.), *The Palgrave Encyclopaedia of the Possible*, 250–7. Cham: Palgrave Macmillan.

Nagatomo, Shigenori (1992), *Attunement through the Body*. Albany: SUNY Press.

Ratcliffe, Matthew (2020), 'Psychiatric Euthanasia, Mental Capacity, and a Sense of the Possible'. *Philosophy, Psychiatry, & Psychology*, 27 (3): E-1-E–15.

Reason, Peter (2003), 'Pragmatist Philosophy and Action Research: Readings and Conversation with Richard Rorty'. *Action Research*, 1 (1): 103–23.

Roth, Wolff-Michael (2012), *First-Person Methods: Toward an Empirical Phenomenology of Experience*. Rotterdam: Sense Publishers.

Schmitt, Daniel and Michel Labour (2022), 'Making Sense of Visitors' Sense-Making Experiences: The REMIND Method'. *Museum Management and Curatorship*, 37 (3): 218–34.

Schultz, Robert (2005), 'Philosophical Sense: An Ampliative Twist in Gifted Education'. *Roeper Review*, 27 (3): 152–7.

Seamon, David (2000), 'A Way of Seeing People and Place: Phenomenology in Environment-Behavior Research'. In Seymour Wapner, et al. (eds), *Theoretical Perspectives in Environment-Behavior Research: Underlying Assumptions, Research Problems, and Methodologies*, 157–78. Alphen aan den Rijn: Kluwer Academic Publishers.

Sinclair, Mark (2017), *The Actual and the Possible: Modality and Metaphysics in Modern Philosophy*. Oxford: Oxford University Press.

Smith, Jonathan, Paul Flowers and Michael Larkin (2009), *Interpretative Phenomenological Analysis: Theory, Method and Research*. Thousand Oaks: Sage.

Sonenshein, Scott (2007), 'The Role of Construction, Intuition, and Justification in Responding to Ethical Issues at Work: The Sensemaking-Intuition Model'. *The Academy of Management Review*, 32 (4): 1022–40.

Stillman, Tyler F., Roy F. Baumeister, Kathleen D. Vohs, Nathaniel M. Lambert, Frank D. Fincham and Lauren E. Brewer (2010), 'Personal Philosophy and Personnel Achievement: Belief in Free Will Predicts Better Job Performance'. *Social Psychological and Personality Science*, 1 (1): 43–50.

Thompson, Evan (2004), 'Life and Mind: From Autopoiesis to Neurophenomenology. A Tribute to Francisco Varela'. *Phenomenology and the Cognitive Sciences*, 3: 381–98.

Thompson, Evan (2007), *Mind in Life: Biology, Phenomenology, and the Sciences of Mind*. Cambridge, MA: Harvard University Press.

Tickamyer, Ann R. (1981), 'Politics as a Vocation'. *The Pacific Sociological Review*, 24 (1): 17–44.

Tomin, Julius (1987), 'Socratic Midwifery'. *The Classical Quarterly*, 37 (1): 97–102.

Vandermause, Roxanne K. and Susan E. Fleming (2011), 'Philosophical Hermeneutic Interviewing'. *International Journal of Qualitative Methods*, 10 (4): 367–77.

Varela, Francisco and Jonathan Shear (1999), 'First-Person Methodologies: What, Why, How?' *Journal of Consciousness Studies*, 6 (2–3): 1–14.

Weick, Karl E. (1979), *The Social Psychology of Organizing*. New York: McGraw-Hill.

Weick, Karl E. (1995), *Sensemaking in organizations*. London: Sage.

Weick, Karl E., M. Sutcliffe Kathleen and David Obstfeld (2005), 'Organizing and the Process of Sensemaking'. *Organization Science*, 16 (4): 409–21.

Ybema, Sierk and Thijs Willems (2015), 'Making Sense of Sense-Breaking'. *Academy of Management Proceedings*, 2015 (1): 14563.

Index